MODELLING
URBAN HOUSING
MARKET DYNAMICS

Studies in Regional Science and Urban Economics

Series Editors

ÅKE E. ANDERSSON
WALTER ISARD
PETER NIJKAMP

Volume 18

NORTH-HOLLAND – AMSTERDAM • NEW YORK • OXFORD • TOKYO

Modelling Urban Housing Market Dynamics

Evolutionary Patterns of Households and Housing in Amsterdam

LEO VAN WISSEN
Department of Spatial Economics
Free University
Amsterdam, The Netherlands

and

ANNEMARIE RIMA
Department of Spatial Economics
Tinbergen Institute
Rotterdam/Amsterdam, The Netherlands

1988

NORTH-HOLLAND – AMSTERDAM • NEW YORK • OXFORD • TOKYO

ISBN: 0 444 70441 8

Publisher:

ELSEVIER SCIENCE PUBLISHERS B.V.
P.O. Box 1991
1000 BZ Amsterdam
The Netherlands

Sole distributors for the U.S.A. and Canada:

ELSEVIER SCIENCE PUBLISHING COMPANY, INC.
52 Vanderbilt Avenue
New York, N.Y. 10017
U.S.A.

PRINTED IN THE NETHERLANDS

INTRODUCTION TO THE SERIES

Regional Science and Urban Economics are two interrelated fields of research that have developed very rapidly in the last three decades. The main theoretical foundation of these fields comes from economics but in recent years the interdisciplinary character has become more pronounced. The editors desire to have the interdisciplinary character of regional sciences as well as the development of spatial aspects of theoretical economics fully reflected in this book series. Material presented in this book series will fall in three different groups:

- interdisciplinary textbooks at the advanced level,
- monographs reflecting theoretical or applied work in spatial analysis,
- proceedings reflecting advancement of the frontiers of regional science and urban economics.

In order to ensure homogeneity in this interdisciplinary field, books published in this series will:

- be theoretically oriented, i.e. analyse problems with a large degree of generality,
- employ formal methods from mathematics, econometrics, operations research and related fields, and
- focus on immediate or potential uses for regional and urban forecasting, planning and policy.

Åke E. Andersson
Walter Isard
Peter Nijkamp

To our parents

Preface

This book emerged out of four years of joint work at the Department of Spatial Economics at the Free University of Amsterdam. We started with the notion that existing urban models were unable to cope with the complex dynamic population and housing market processes in modern urban agglomerations. At the same time we felt that new developed methods in various disciplines such as economics, geography and demography, could contribute substantially to the field of applied urban modelling. Coming from different backgrounds (econometrics and geography) we hoped that the combined research effort in this interdisciplinary project would be a stimulating experience and have synergetic effects on the output of the project. After four years we have indeed experienced the benefits of the joint work but whether the synergetic effects mentioned really have occured can only be judged by the reader.

The book should be of interest for analysts and planners in the field of urban population, residential mobility and the urban housing market. The central idea developed here is that life-cycle adjustments related to the housing situation are the key elements in explaining and predicting household relocation in an urban housing market. This is empirically verified in the Amsterdam metropolitan area. Additionally a number of scenarios for the housing market are developed based on this notion.

We have relied on a large number of people whose assistance was invaluable in establishing our research goals in various stages of the project. First of all, we want to thank Professor Peter Nijkamp who has been a very stimulating supervisor. His continual enthousiasm has always been an example for us. Valuable comments and criticisms were also made by other people in the academic field. Dr. Michael Wegener from the University of Dortmund has always followed our work with great interest. Without the outstanding example of his model for the Dortmund Region we would never have succeeded. We also thank Professor J.M.M. Ritzen and Professor G.A. van der Knaap from the Erasmus University of Rotterdam, Professor H.J.P. Timmermans from the Technical University of Eindhoven, Professor F.J. Willekens from the University of Utrecht and Professor A.A.I. Holtgrefe from the Free University for their comments and criticism.

Building a model based on concrete data for the Amsterdam Region would have been impossible without the help of people from the Municipality of Amsterdam, especially Frank le Clerq, Michiel Weijs, Daan Smit and Marcel Janssen. Their ideas and suggestions were very valuable for us at various points in the project. Moreover, they were very kind to provide us with the necessary data to run our model.

Additionally, a number of people helped us reading and correcting the manuscript. Tom and Jackie Golob read the first draft and Winnie Browne carefully checked the final draft. Of course we are responsible for all remaining errors.

Special words of thanks, gratitude and admiration go to our friends Marie-Therésè and Jeroen. They supported us in good and bad times. Life was certainly not always easy with us, especially in the last phase of the project. We are also grateful and glad that our parents live to see the result of a period in which they sympathized so much with our work.

Table of Contents

Part II: Design and Parameter Estimation

Part III: Simulation

CHAPTER 10. MODELLING RESULTS FOR THE PERIOD 1971 - 1984

CHAPTER 11. HOUSING MARKET SCENARIOS FOR THE PERIOD 1985 - 2000

CHAPTER 12. RETROSPECT AND PROSPECT

CHAPTER 1. THE AIM AND SCOPE OF THE BOOK

1.0 Introduction

Housing has been the dominant function of the cities for many centuries. Even in the first half of the twentieth century an increasing number of people were attracted to the cities, hoping to find a job, better housing and living conditions. But many parts of the urban housing environment have deteriorated heavily. This was by no means a new phenomenon in the city but the scale of the process was much larger than experienced in the past. Moreover, increased income and mobility levels enabled many people to choose alternative living environments in the suburbs or in rural places. Consequently, population levels of the urban centres decreased dramatically in the last decades. A parallel development could be observed in economic sectors. Old industries and traditional economic activities, which were mainly located in the cities have disappeared, resulting in relatively high unemployment figures. Although there are large differences between countries and regions in timing and scale of this proces of suburbanization, the similarities in form of urbanization and suburbanization are striking (van den Berg et al., 1982).

But at the same time a whole spectrum of new lifestyles has emerged since the sixties. An increasing number of people choose to live in small household units. These households can be found especially in the urban areas that offer many opportunities for specific lifestyles or jobs. At the same time new technologies and economic activities develop and they tend to be concentrated in a number of national or international 'growth poles'. More and more the national economy is being replaced by a system of internationally oriented metropolitan areas with thriving economies and cosmopolitan cultures. It seems that a new urban culture is emerging after a period of suburbanism and anti-urbanism. This trend is reflected in urban policies aimed at revitalization of the cities.

The question of the future of the city is urgent. On the one hand one may argue that the massive suburbanization which is so typical for the developed world since many decades will result in the death of the city. On the other hand it is possible that the emergence of new lifestyles will result in a revitalization of urban society. The authors of this book believe that the understanding and modelling of household development processes in an urban context can give important answers to the question of the future of the city. This book attempts to make a contribution in that field.

Structural changes are taking place in the composition of households that have major impacts on the housing market, especially in urban regions. Processes of new household formation and dissolution have a direct impact on housing demand and supply. But ageing and changes in the life cycle of existing households have a clear impact on housing demand too. Housing consumption levels change in the course of a lifetime. For policy makers it is highly relevant to understand the dynamics of these household development processes and the impacts on the housing market. Housing construction programmes have to anticipate the composition of households in the future. If housing demand and supply do not match locally then household redistribution processes will occur that affect the composition of households in urban areas even more. These developments may be the desired policy goal, but this is not always the case. Suburbanization was stimulated for a long time in spatial policies but now much effort is needed to redirect the negative consequences of it. Usually the second and higher order effects of policy measures are unforeseen or underestimated. In terms of population and housing it is possible to predict the direct consequences of a local housing construction programme on the composition of the population in that area, but through migration and vacancy chains there will be side effects in other areas. A housing construction programme developed to fulfil the local current housing needs may lead to vacancies in the future if no account is taken of future household developments and housing demand. The construction of large residential areas with a limited range of dwelling types will result in a highly uniform local household composition in the short run. Consequently life cycle adjustments and changing housing consumption levels will be uniform to a large degree resulting in high mobility rates and high levels of housing demand in other areas in the future. So, in the long run the structure of the total housing market is affected by local developments and a policy aimed at solving local imperfections may be inadequate for attaining global urban or regional population or housing policies in the long run. In order to estimate both short and long run effects of policy measures on the housing market a <u>dynamic</u> perspective on households and housing market processes is needed. Modelling of household dynamics in relation to the housing market and household relocation is one way of attaining this.

In this book a model of household dynamics within the context of housing demand and the urban housing market is developed and applied in the Amsterdam region. The model combines both elements of household demography and housing market modelling in one integrated framework. Although in the development of the model a number of decisions were taken that are specific to the Dutch situation the structure and the results of the model are relevant to other situations as well.

In the course of the project a number of important theoretical and methodological issues emerged that were relevant to the design and development of the model. These will be discussed briefly in the following two sections and more thoroughly in the subsequent chapters.

1.1 Issues in the Dynamic Modelling of Housing Market Behaviour

Life Cycle Changes and Housing Market Behaviour

The concept of life cycle is useful in analysing and modelling housing market behaviour. Rossi (1955) showed that residential mobility could be interpreted as a process of adjusting housing consumption to the housing needs that are generated by changes in the household composition that accompany life cycle changes. Not only the mobility process itself, but also housing preferences are directly related to the stage reached in the life cycle. As a household moves through various stages in the life cycle it adjusts its housing consumption in various incremental steps (Michelson, 1977, 1980), until a satisfactory level of housing has been achieved. The path that a household takes in the housing market is often called a housing career (in the same way a working career might be defined). Brown and Longbrake (1970), Gleave and Cordey-Hayes (1977), Clark (1982), and Clark and Van Lierop (1986) point out that changes in life cycle and housing unit characteristics are by far the predominant explanatory factors for residential mobility within the same housing market area. Changes in location of the workplace and other factors become increasingly important in explaining moving residence over a distance of more than 40 kilometres (see also Relou and Heida, 1986). This phenomenon is depicted in figure 1.1.

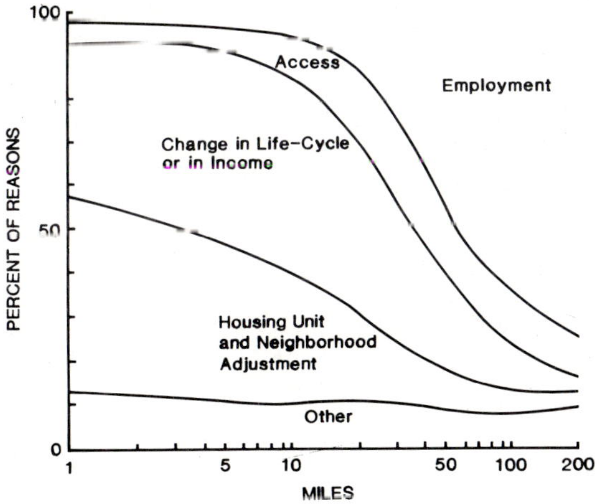

Figure 1.1. Distribution of reasons for moving by distance (adapted from Gleave and Cordey-Hayes (1977))

Although there is no clear break in the reasons for mobility, a distinction between work motivations for longer distances and life cycle and housing market motivations for short distances can be made. For the Netherlands there is some empirical evidence to support this point of view. Clark et al. (1984), in a study on the relations between housing consumption and residential mobility, found that the birth of a child was a significant trigger in the mobility process, especially in the private and public sector rental submarket. The birth effect was much less pronounced in the more spacious homeownership sector. This result also implies that there is an interaction between life cycle changes and the housing market situation of the household. Klijzing (1986) found a significant positive influence of the birth of a child on the mobility behaviour of households.

However, changes in life cycle are not the only reason for household relocation. Verster (1986) has most recently shown that commuting costs also play a role in the decision to migrate even at distances under 40 kilometres. This particular explanatory factor has not been taken into account in the present version of the household relocation model. It is recognized that while life cycle changes are related to mobility decisions it does not necessarily mean that they are the main cause of those decisions. However, many economic and other events are closely associated with changes in life cycle. Good examples of this are changes from one income households to a double income household which may occur when two employees join or marry and the change from active work status to retirement. This would imply that a model based on life cycle changes has good prediction capabilities, since it implicitly captures the impact of a number of other related events. Finally, life cycle changes and housing market behaviour in an intra-regional context have to be considered in their relationship to the market constraints; i.e. the availability of houses, housing regulations and the institutions which govern this process (Kendig, 1984). The model which has been developed attempts to capture these elements.

Household Formation and Economic Variables

Of special relevance in studying the relationship between life cycle events and housing market behaviour is the event of household formation. This is especially true in an urban area such as Amsterdam with a large percentage of students and young employees. As will be described in Chapter 2 the impact of institutional elements is also important in this respect.

Whether housing market conditions or life cycle changes are predominant in the process of starting a new household is difficult to answer. Hickman (1974) in the USA, Ermisch (1981) in Britain and Van Fulpen (1985) in the Netherlands found economic influences on household formation processes. However, a major explanatory variable in their model specifications is the autonomous demographic development. A log-

log-linear relation between housing needs and income was found in the Netherlands (Roest, 1973). Van Fulpen (1985, p.102) states that housing needs, housing consumption and household formation are closely related synchronical decisions. He estimated models for each of these variables based on time series for the Netherlands in the period 1960 - 1983. His results indicate that economic factors are more important in the long run than in the short run for household formation, and that the impact of economic factors is larger on the housing stock than on the number of households. So it seems plausible to assume that in the short run demographic events related to household formation are relatively autonomous, but that longer term developments in household formation processes have to be explained also by economic factors.

Housing Preferences

The household decision process leading to a demand for a new dwelling is often seen in terms of dissatisfaction generated by distinct events (Brown and Moore, 1970; Speare et al., 1975) and these notions were formalized in stress inertia models by geographers (Huff and Clark, 1978) or in disequilibrium models by economists (Hanushek and Quigley, 1978). A central concept in these theories is the "propensity to move" or "willingness to move". Although the term "intention to move" would be a more appropriate definition for the behavioural process, the first two terms will be used because they are common use in housing market literature. The willingness to move can be seen as a notional demand that can be effectuated depending on the market conditions. Housing market behaviour includes the choice of a new dwelling. Here also a distinction can be made in notional demand (housing preferences) and effective, or realized demand (allocation). For intra-urban housing relocation decisions this distinction seems crucial, since actual behaviour is highly dependent on the housing supply, institutional arrangements and other market constraints (Brown and Longbrake, 1970). Therefore a two-stage process in the analysis of housing market behaviour is needed.

First, the preferred actions on the housing market should be analysed. This stage is often subdivided into two parts, viz. the analysis of the propensity to move (mobility processes) and the analysis of the preferred new dwelling (housing submarket choice). Second, housing demand and supply have to be matched in order to generate actual housing market transactions. Van Lierop (1986) showed in an ex ante and ex post study of residential relocation that almost all households that had actually moved in a two year period were indeed willing to move at the beginning of that period. However, a significant part of those who preferred to move had not changed residence in that period. This implies that a necessary but not sufficient condition for household relocation is the willingness to move. This statement does not apply to forced migrations due to developments on the supply side (e.g. housing demolitions).

Housing Market Behaviour

The matching process of housing demand and supply is dependent on the organization of the market. In a free market system, the housing price is the equilibrating mechanism. This is the case in most American housing markets, but not in many European housing markets, at least not in the short run. There exists a number of models developed for a free housing market system. As yet, for a regulated market system the situation is quite different. For instance, Anas recently developed a model for a 'prototype' regulated market, the Stockholm housing market, but the empirical verification so far has been very limited. An overview of various relevant housing market models is given in Chapter 4.

The Dutch housing market is highly regulated, including complicated pricing and subsidy mechanisms. The Amsterdam housing market is even more complicated since a large number of local rationing measures exist. Supply is totally controlled by the central government. A full model would include prices and subsidies, swapping, grey and black market behaviour, rent-control, rationing mechanisms and queuing. However, this goal would be far too complicated to achieve at the present moment.

Micro and Macro events

The first stage in the household relocation process involves the generation of housing preferences. This is essentially a micro level process. The second stage, the realization of aggregate demand with aggregate supply is a macro level process. The simultaneous treatment of these processes not only involves aggregation of individual demand (bottom up) and supply, but also feedbacks from aggregate market conditions to individual preferences (top down). Households adjust their preferences for dwellings in various submarkets on the basis of some form of information about their chances of realizing a call in that submarket. Thus, a housing market model cannot be based on micro-level market behaviour alone but should also contain macro-level elements and cross-level relations.

Housing Policy and Household Relocation

In the Dutch political situation, housing is viewed as a merit good (Memorandum on Rent- and Subsidy-policy, 1974). This means that higher levels of housing consumption should be stimulated by the central government. One way of achieving this is to stimulate household relocation behaviour in order to adjust housing consumption to meet household aspiration levels. From a social housing policy point of view, housing preferences and household relocation are key variables for the evaluation of those policies. These variables will be the central variables of the model to be developed.

<u>Housing Market Dynamics</u>

The concept of static equilibrium has to be abandoned in situations where structural changes are taking place, both in exogenous variables and in structural relationships. It can be assumed that the direction of the system change is governed by a path leading towards a (changing) equilibrium position. However, since there are so many institutional and regulatory constraints in the Dutch housing market, adjustments take place over a longer time period than would be the case if the market were unregulated. If prices are fixed in the short run, and subsidies are available related to the rent-income ratio, the housing price distribution is relatively flat within submarkets and does not have a strong impact on demand in the short run. Rather, dynamic factors other than price are dominant in the generation of intra-regional demand, i.e. life cycle and housing stock dynamics (housing demolitions and renovations). In a supplier's market, it is also likely that potential movers have a notion about the chances of realizing a call for a dwelling in different submarkets, and adjust their preferences for different dwelling types accordingly. Thus, micro-level evaluation of housing choice is influenced by macro level housing market conditions. This top-down influence on housing preferences will be analysed in detail in Chapter 8, in the consideration of housing demand functions.

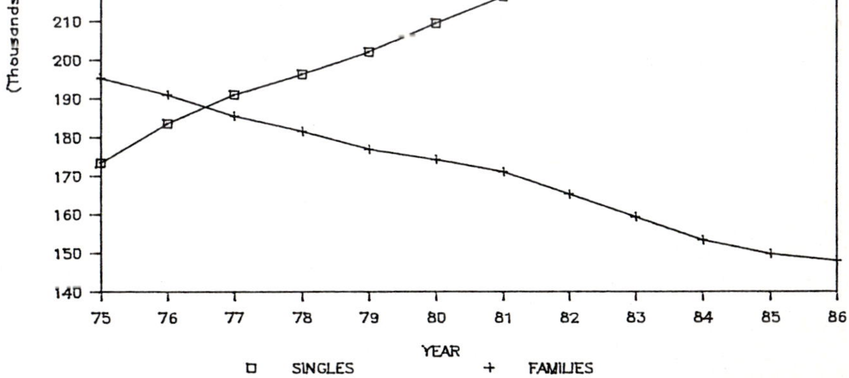

Figure 1.2. Development of singles and families (census definition) in Amsterdam, 1975 - 1986 (source: Yearbooks Amsterdam)

Heterogeneity of Households

Since the sixties a multitude of new household forms has developed. The family-concept is no longer appropriate in analysing household dynamics. Especially the urban centres have been the foci of new life-style experiments and forms of cohabitation. Figure 1.2 depicts the development in the number of families and singles in Amsterdam since 1975. Most of the new ways of cohabitation are hidden in the category singles, for example two or more unmarried persons living together. These households are usually found in the younger age categories, and they have a significant influence on the household dynamics and household relocation in Amsterdam. The household model to be developed in Chapter 7 is not based on the traditional census definitions but classifies households on the basis of household size and age of the head.

The various household categories also have varying housing preferences in terms of housing type and housing location (see also Deurloo, 1987). This calls for a substantial disaggregation, both at the household level and at the dwelling level.

Spatial Dimension

Urban and regional models can be classified in two categories: continuous and discrete space representations. While theoretically a continuous space representation is more appropriate (Golob, 1982) there are strong practical arguments for adopting a discrete space representation. Firstly, the mathematical structure of discrete space models is usually less complicated (Wilson, 1981). Secondly, data availability is usually restricted to zonal aggregates (city district, municipality). It is likely that in the future geographical information systems will allow the collection of continuous space variables, thus allowing continuous space models to be tested more rigorously. At present for dynamic model building a discrete space representation seems to be the most feasible solution to the spatial dimension problem. This issue is closely related to the data problem for dynamic modelling in general.

Data Requirements

The combination of spatial and temporal dimensions in urban modelling, together with a high level of disaggregation of household and housing types is only possible in situations with a high level of information collection and processing. The development of large-scale computerised data bases for regional research started in the sixties. In the Netherlands since 1972 many basic regional population and housing data are stored in binary form and can be used for planning and research purposes. In addition to the national data more local and regional information is collected by the city of Amsterdam. For both population and housing detailed annual information is collected. However, the level of disaggregation is usually not as high as is needed for disaggregated model development. Some methods exist that can cope with these problems by estimating the micro-level information from known meso or macro level data. For simulation purposes this usually leads to satisfactory results. Not all problems are solved by using this technique. A common problem in household modelling is the lack of data on households. Population statistics are based on the individual level. Moreover, the data describe an anachronism. As pointed out in the previous subsection, family composition, marital status and marriage and divorce figures describe only part of the household structure, and even less of the dynamics in household composition. A dynamic urban model of household relocation should somehow cope with these data problems.

Parameter Estimation and Simulation

Usually there is not enough information to simultaneously estimate all coefficients of a dynamic model that includes more than one submodel. Moreover, analysis of time-series of basic micro relationships is often impossible, due to the lack of longitudinal data. In the absence of such possibilities, reliance is often placed on some form of simulation, where basic intensities are set and varied exogenously. Examples of this approach are numerous. The development of dynamic urban models in the last ten years has mainly been speculative (cf. Allen et al, 1984; Wilson, 1970, 1983), due to the large problems of parameter estimation. For example, the Dortmund Model (Wegener, 1982, 1983, 1986), uses 'guestimates' in a micro-simulation context. Mixed forms are also possible. The PRIMOS-household model (Cordijn and Heida, 1985) is a mixed estimation and simulation model in a macro-simulation context. By using plausible assumptions a realistic time path of the system can be generated. So far, dynamic urban models have only been estimated successfully by paying the price of a high level of aggregation and a simplified specification of the underlying theory (cf. Haag and Weidlich, 1984; Weidlich and Haag, 1983).

Summary

The above statements are summarized in this subsection. This list can be viewed as the point of departure for the design and implementation of the dynamic household relocation model for the Amsterdam Region.

1. The household relocation process in an intra-urban environment can be explained as a household response to dissatisfaction with the housing situation caused mainly by life-cycle changes and related housing unit factors

2. A clear distinction has to be made between household preferences (notional demand) and actual allocation (effective demand) in order to explain the household relocation process. Household preferences can be analysed on a micro level, while the allocation is essentially a macro level process

3. Housing market regulations and institutional setting are important for understanding the behaviour of individuals and households on the housing market, and they have to be taken into account in modelling efforts

4. Given the housing market restrictions in the Dutch situation, a classical economic equilibrium model cannot be applied. Price is fixed and supply is almost totally controlled by the Government

5. Housing preferences and relocation behaviour of households are the focus of the model since in the Dutch situation they reflect the household's optimization process of housing consumption and thus the extent of attainment of one of the major social housing policy goals, i.e. a high level of housing consumption for all households

6. A multitude of household categories and life styles have evolved since the sixties, especially in the cities, with varying types of preferences on the housing market. This heterogeneity of households calls for a high level of disaggregation, of both household and dwelling types

7. The city limits are no longer appropriate for delineating the urban area. Instead a regional perspective is needed, that includes the functionally related suburban residential areas

8. Data requirements for a zonal, dynamic disaggregated urban model are extremely high, both at the micro level (detailed surveys) and at the macro level (census information for population, housing and allocation figures). For simulation purposes sophisticated estimation methods can be used for missing data

9. Application of a dynamic model not only involves the estimation of basic parameters, but usually also the simulation of the system behaviour over time through suitable parameter adjustments

1.2 Objectives and Basic Hypotheses

The purpose of this study is to develop an empirical, policy oriented, integrated dynamic model of household relocation in the housing market of the Amsterdam housing market. Therefore, its main characteristics are:

Empirical: the model should be based on existing data and real world phenomena

Policy oriented: key variables for household and housing policy should be included so that **ex post** and **ex ante** policy evaluations are possible

Integrated: housing market behaviour in an intraregional context cannot be studied in isolation from population and household processes. Thus, the model should have a modular structure with linked submodels of household and housing market processes

Dynamic: the housing market is treated as a dynamic system where the underlying-system path is governed by a move towards equilibrium that is usually not attained in the short run, since there is no short-run clearing mechanism, such as the housing price. Annual changes take place in key parameters and exogenous factors of the market that move the system towards another equilibrium point

Regional: the Amsterdam housing market region, including the major suburban areas, is taken as the study area, subdivided in a number of distinct zones

There are two central hypotheses that underly the development of the model:

1. Life cycle dynamics related to the housing situation are the major factors that motivate a household to relocate within the same housing market area.

2. Household preferences and actual housing choice are two highly related but distinguished phenomena. Preferences are influenced by the expectation of realizing a demand for a particular dwelling so the availability of dwellings is an important element in the preference functions of households for dwelling submarkets.

Further, there are two basic assumptions underlying the development of the model:

1. The allocation of households to dwellings is the result of matching aggregate household preferences (demand) with housing supply

2. There is no short run equilibrium in the Amsterdam region housing market. Market behaviour is determined by a slow movement directed towards equilibrium points, which change rapidly, due to structural changes in exogenous factors and relationships

The hypotheses will be tested statistically in the phase of specification of the housing demand model. The two basic assumptions can be shown to be valid in the model simulations.

Goal of the model

The goal of the model is the simultaneous calculation of household and population dynamics, housing demand and allocation and migration flows between housing submarkets within an urban region.

The model to be developed combines both household dynamics and housing market behaviour in an urban context in a consistent framework. First, it calculates the total number of life cycle transitions in the region relevant for housing market behaviour. Second, it relates these life cycle transitions to the generation of individual housing demand. Third, by aggregating individual (household) housing demand into homogeneous household and matching total demand with supply actual housing market transactions are modelled and household flows between submarkets predicted. The model is applied in the Amsterdam Region.

1.3 Outline of the Study

This book is divided into three sections as follows: in Part I some necessary preliminaries are presented. The next two parts describe in various steps the development and results of the Amsterdam model: part II contains the general design of the model and the estimation of the parameters of the submodels, while in Part III the simulation results are presented and some general conclusions are drawn. The last page of the book can be folded out for reference and includes a map of the study area and two tables with a list of categorizations used in the study for households and dwelling types.

Part I: Preliminaries

First, in Chapter 2, the housing market of Amsterdam is described in more detail. After a historical note of the development of the Amsterdam region and the housing market, the structure and the institutional setting of the market is described. The next two chapters give a survey of the types of models used in the two subsystems that are distinguished in the Amsterdam model: Chapter 3 gives an overview of household models currently used in dynamic household modelling. In Chapter 4 a number of representative housing market models is presented that integrate residential mobility and housing market behaviour (choice of submarket).

Part II: Design and Parameter Estimation

Chapter 5 gives a description of the assumptions and decisions underlying the model, and a general overview of the complete model. This is in fact the introduction to the Amsterdam model. Next, in Chapter 6 attention is focussed on one important aspect, viz. a technique for estimating missing data. This technique is used in various places in the model simulation part to generate the most probable multivariate frequency distribution of a set of variables, given marginal and other types of information for that distribution. Chapter 7 describes the design and empirical estimation of a dynamic household model, using longitudinal data collected in the region for the period 1975-1980. This model is the heart of the household submodel, and generates the input for the housing market model described in the next chapters. This last submodel consists of two parts: the housing demand model and the allocation model. The estimation of the housing demand model involves first the estimation of a binary choice function of the propensity to move and second, a nested multinomial logit formulation of housing preferences in Chapter 8. Next, the structure of the demand- and allocation model is described in Chapter 9.

Part III: Simulation

Household relocation in the Amsterdam housing market is simulated by confronting housing demand with (exogenous) supply. First, in Chapter 10 the period 1971-1984 is simulated *ex post* in order to validate the model and to derive a plausible time-path for a number of key parameters in the model. In the next chapter a number of demographic and housing policy scenarios are evaluated for the period 1985-2000 starting from the optimal model found for the '71 -'85 period in chapter 10. In Chapter 12 the model is evaluated and some general conclusions are drawn with respect to housing policy in the Amsterdam region.

Part I
Prerequisites

CHAPTER 2. THE HOUSING MARKET OF AMSTERDAM: A HISTORICAL OVERVIEW

2.0 Introduction

The purpose of this chapter is twofold. First, a brief sketch of the Amsterdam housing market is needed, as the model design and outcomes presented in the following chapters cannot properly be interpreted without knowing the historical development of the housing market of Amsterdam and its surroundings. Second, the institutional-economic framework plays a role in the allocation model (see Chapter 9), so that a sketch of this framework is necessary as well. A number of policy instruments and institutional rules apply also on the national scale, but we will position them also in the specific context of Amsterdam.

In section 2.1 the history of the housing system is given with special emphasis on the city of Amsterdam. The influence of the planning system on the housing market developments is briefly described in section 2.2. Pricing and financing aspects are the subject of section 2.3, while the allocation rules and the phenomenon of the black market are discussed in section 2.4. Some facts and figures with respect to the housing market and the population development in the city and the agglomeration of Amsterdam are given in section 2.5. The chapter ends with some concluding remarks in section 2.6.

2.1 The Development of the Housing System

The evolution of the housing stock in Amsterdam can be subdivided into a number of distinct development periods, which will be described in short below. The characteristics of these development periods can only be understood in the light of the economic, social and institutional setting of each individual time period. This historical overview provides a background for the understanding of the household relocation model, presented in the subsequent chapters.

Before 1900

Amsterdam was a thriving city in the "Golden Age" of the 17th century when it dominated the international trade and financial world. Prosperity led to a new ring of expensive housing and other new activities emerging around the medieval city, and resulted in a planned development of canals and radial streets that gave the city its characteristic concentric form (see map 2.1). However, in the 18th century economic decline set in, and this resulted in an almost complete cessation of building activities for more than a century. Although the government had previously followed a policy of strict non-intervention in the housing market, after 1870 it was increasingly felt among the ruling class that poor housing conditions could have negative external effects on other aspects of society. Consequently, some form of government intervention was proposed by the more radical liberals at the end of the 19th century.

The year 1870 represented a turning point in the economic position of Amsterdam. Growth took place in various parts of the country, but mainly in the cities, and the resulting population flow from rural to urban areas also had an impact on Amsterdam. Between 1870 and 1910 ten thousands of new houses were built in Amsterdam, many of them of low quality. The largely unplanned growth of the city constitutes what is now called the 19th century ring (see map 2.1) which is the core of present-day urban renewal problems.

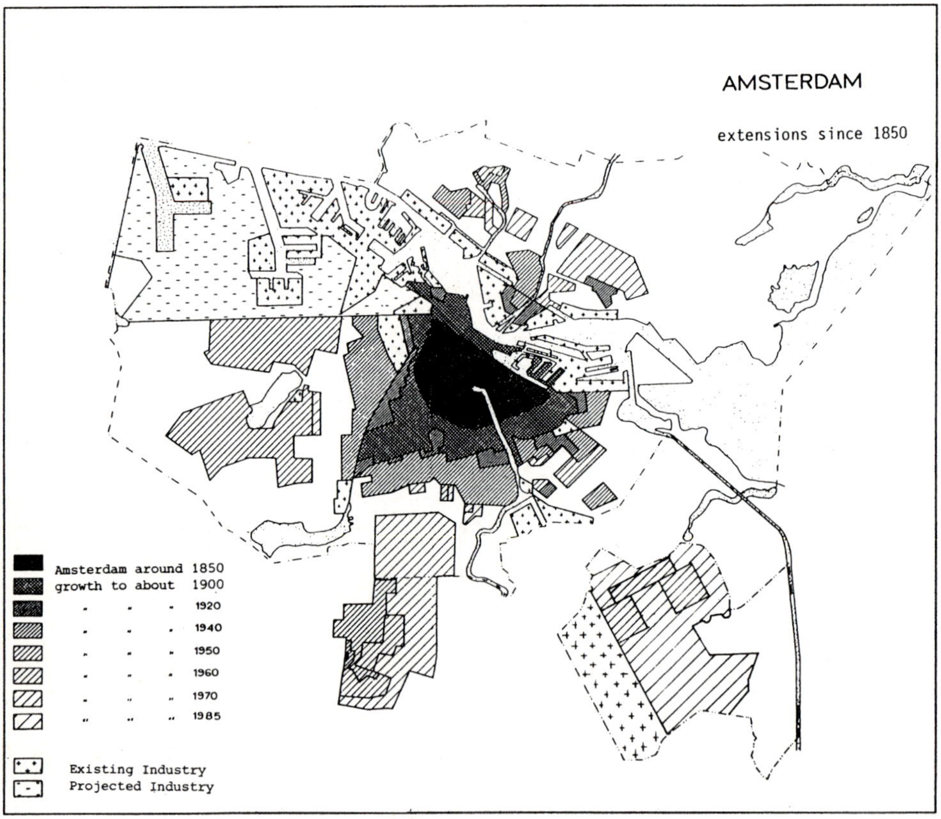

Map 2.1. The city of Amsterdam

The Period 1900-1945

The arguments in favour of government intervention resulted in the National Housing Act of 1901. This Act enabled local and central governments to intervene in the housing market. Its intention was not only to end the existing miserable housing conditions (through slum clearance, directives to landlords to improve and maintain their property, expropriation and clearance orders), but also to prevent future inferior housing (through building codes, building inspectors, and town plans).

A very important element of this Act was the possibility of intervention on the supply side of the housing market. Local governments, non-profit housing corporations and building societies could qualify for low interest rate loans to buy land or build houses for the working class (Van Weesep, 1982). In principle, houses had to be rented at the market price, but in special circumstances some subsidies could temporarily be given to renters.

Amsterdam played an important role in the implementation of the Act. The building-by-laws set up in Amsterdam were very strict, and many municipalities followed this example.

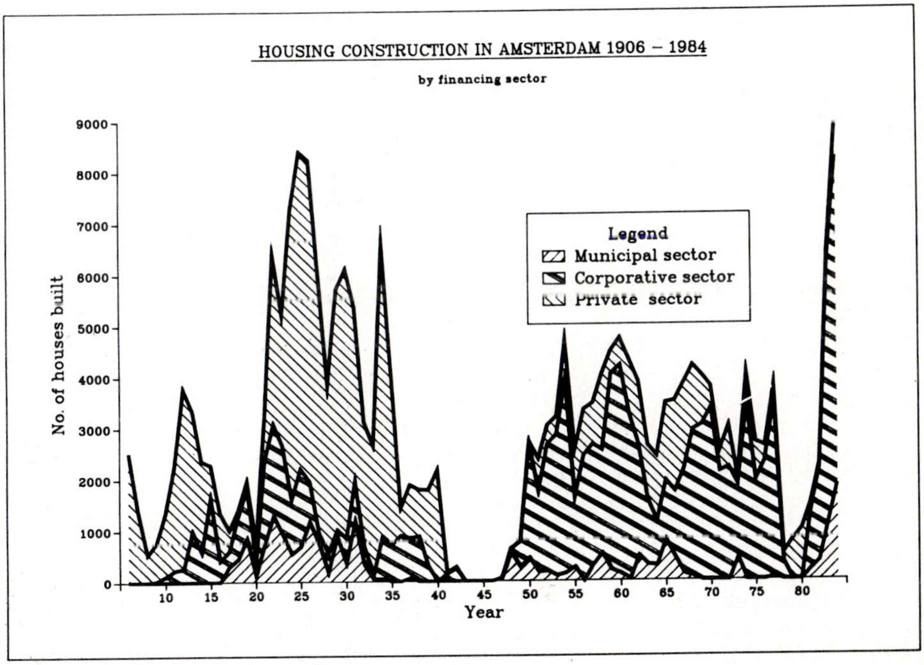

Figure 2.1. Housing construction in Amsterdam by financing sector, 1906-1984

Active intervention on the supply side did not start before 1910. Then the first World War caused an almost complete collapse of private construction (see figure 2.1), and the central government was forced to play an active role on the supply side. Non-profit houses were built, mostly by the housing corporations.

After 1920 the building industry profited from a general increase in economic activity, and this marked a return to a free market, in which the non-profit sector played a marginal role. It provided housing only for the lower income segment of the housing market that was unprofitable for private investment.

The housing stock built in this period is clearly of a higher quality than that from the 19th century construction period. Many houses were built during the period 1900-1945 in Amsterdam (118,668 in total), of which 71.9% belonged to the private sector; 18.8% were provided by housing societies and corporations, and 9.3% were municipally funded.

The Period 1945-1965

The stagnation in the housing construction sector after 1935 and the subsequent World War resulted in an enormous housing shortage after 1945.

The national housing shortage was estimated to be 300,000 units, with Amsterdam accounting for 31,000 dwellings. The national government adopted a policy focusing on limited growth of personal incomes and consumption.

Correspondingly, rents had to be kept at a low level (see figure 2.2). To achieve this objective, various housing market laws were adopted:

- the Housing Allocation Act, an instrument for establishing a fair housing distribution, i.e. a housing permit system and the possibility to require vacancies for residential purposes,
- the Rent Act, fixing the rents of all dwellings at their 1940 level; renters were given extensive tenure protection,
- the Reconstruction Act, providing the central government with instruments for a national construction program, and regional construction quotas.

A number of problems arose in this period. First, due to rent control, virtually no investment funds could be attracted to the housing sector. The pre-war situation of limited intervention changed into a situation of full public control over the housing market. A second problem was the dramatic increase of construction costs of housing. New techniques were sought and they were particularly suited for the construction of multi-storey apartments. This became the dominant housing type in the new urban districts. The so-called "garden cities", in the western part of Amsterdam, built in the fifties and the sixties, were predominantly multi-storey apartments. These new areas had a highly uniform character which was not always preferred by consumers.

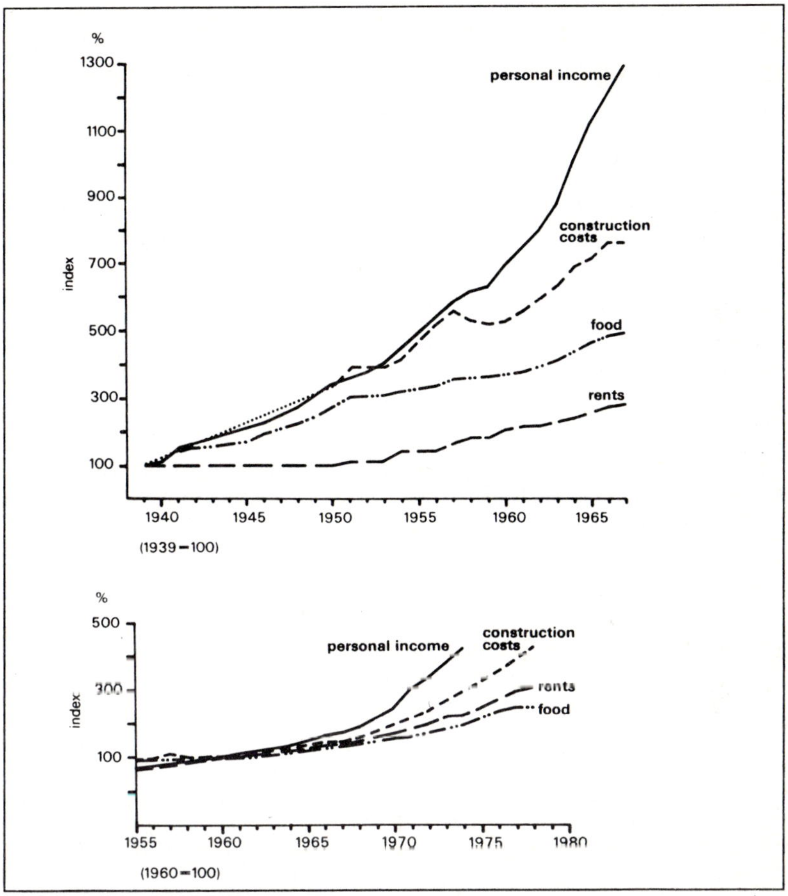

Figure 2.2. Development of selected indices, 1940-1980 (source: Central Bureau of Statistics)

At the same time, deterioration became a major problem, especially in the 19th century housing stock of Amsterdam. A number of policy documents on urban renewal and slum clearance were produced, but for a number of reasons hardly any action was taken in the sixties. First, the local planning and housing departments had to adjust themselves to reconstruction and maintenance of existing neighbourhoods. Secondly, the city policy was to construct high quality housing in the lower density areas, while the residents demanded simpler and cheaper houses in higher density areas. In the city's view, building high quality houses would guarantee a general improvement in housing conditions through the adjustment process of upward filtering. However, this filtering process did not work, due to the large gap in price between the old and the new dwelling stock. A third problem in the urban renewal process was caused by the conflicting views of the various local departments involved in the housing planning process, and the organizational aspects of their cooperation. Finally, the lack of legal instruments and financial resources provided by the central government prohibited any efficient renewal activities.

After 1965

In the second half of the sixties a national policy of liberalization and harmonization was adopted in order to return to a free housing market situation, and to obtain a more rational rent structure. The Housing Allocation Act was suspended in 1969 in those parts of the country where the quantitative housing shortage was solved, but this was not the case in Amsterdam.

Housing shortage increased in the sixties in the city despite the decrease in total population since 1957 and the huge housing construction programme. This increase was mainly due to the overall reduction in family size (figure 2.3) and to urban renewal (figure 2.4).

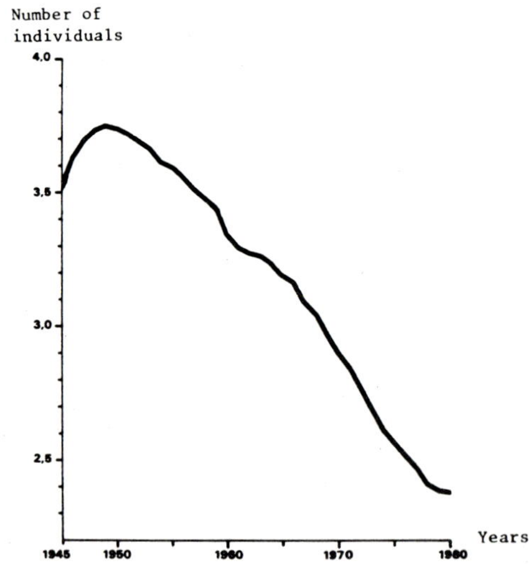

Figure 2.3. Average gross family size in Amsterdam, 1945-1980 (source: Yearbooks Amsterdam)

The clearance of inferior houses in a tight market is problematic, and in order to produce more housing units a solution was found in extended suburbanization. A number of municipalities within commuting distance of Amsterdam (e.g. Amstelveen, Purmerend, Zaandam) were able to build houses for the Amsterdam population. These units were charged to the Amsterdam construction quota (see table 2.3 in section 2.5). Thus, the housing market was extended towards the regional level.

Urban renewal and planned suburbanization were viewed as complementary processes. From 1965 onwards a growing number of people left the city; this outflow reached a peak in 1973. These migrants were mainly young and relatively affluent families with children, whose relocation contributed to a growing imbalance in age structure between the central city and the surrounding suburban communities.

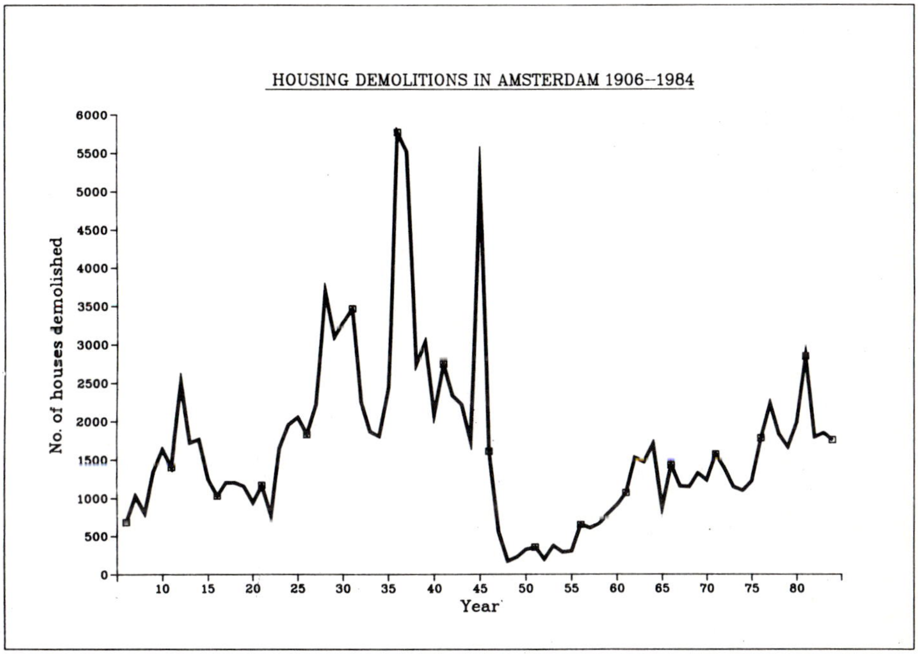

Figure 2.4. Housing demolitions in Amsterdam, 1906-1984

The consequences of this suburbanization process are well known: a reduction of the threshold level for public and private services, an insufficient local tax base in the central city to cope with the negative spill-over effects of suburban municipalities (i.e. traffic, central facilities). This suburbanization process was also encouraged by the central government. In the <u>Tweede Nota Ruimtelijke Ordening</u> (Second Memorandum on Physical Planning, 1966) the principle of 'bundled deconcentration' was introduced: a controlled outflow of population from the central cities to a limited number of growth centres. In the Derde Nota Ruimtelijke Ordening (Third Memorandum on Physical Growth, 1973) the negative consequences of suburbanization for both the central cities and the rural areas were stressed.

Amsterdam enlarged its city area through the incorporation of former rural land in the south-east. Here the city built a large scale new high rise housing district. Amsterdam South-East (the so-called Bijlmermeer, zone 11) contains more than 90 percent multi-storey apartments. It was planned as a high quality residential zone for approximately 100,000 people, with much open space and high quality (split-level) traffic and transportation services. However, the houses were too expensive, and despite the housing shortage a large number of apartments were left vacant. In order to avoid exploitation problems, the housing corporations that owned these apartments allowed non-members (of housing corporations) and non-citizens to rent an apartment in this area, and thus a large group of residents entered the housing market, who would otherwise never have obtained a dwelling unit in Amsterdam.

In the seventies, the negative effects of the suburbanization were felt, and by the end of the decade the need for revitalization of the city was manifested at the local level in the concept of the "compact city", the use of open spaces within the city boundaries for residential and economic purposes. After 1973, migration rates dropped and by the end of the seventies the overall economic recession had a severe impact on the housing market. Housing prices began to drop and many homeowners were unable to sell their houses. However, the economic recession seemed to work in favour of the compact city policy. In 1985, the population of Amsterdam increased for the first time since 1957. Whether this represents a structural change in the urban development of Amsterdam or a temporary shift is unclear at the moment. This depends on the success of future housing politics in Amsterdam (Chapter 11).

2.2 The Planning System

There are three spatial planning levels in the Netherlands: state, province and municipality. The physical planning process, as described in the Physical Planning Act, and the programming of housing construction are important elements in the housing sector, especially for a large city like Amsterdam. In this section both these planning processes will be described briefly.

The Physical Planning Process

The main elements of Dutch national policies and plans are executed through the instrument of the Planologische Kernbeslissing (The Key Decision on Physical Planning). In addition, each province has its own planning policies; these are described in the regional plan. However, the "master plan" is the key instrument in the physical planning process, and it can be established at the local level only. Every municipality is obliged to prepare a master plan for areas outside the built environment. Depending on the circumstances, the local government may also develop a master plan for parts of the built-up area as well. Anyone whose interests are negatively affected by a proposed plan can object to the plan. Due to the extensive protection of individual interests of citizens, the approval procedure may take many years, and in general this system is quite inflexible. Therefore some simplified procedures have been adopted in recent years.

Besides the master plan, the municipality can also prepare a more general town plan, a so-called structure plan. In a structure plan the long-term development of the municipality (or even a group of municipalities), is described.

In order to overcome some of the problems in the master plan in planning urban renewal areas, the Urban Renewal Act was adopted in 1984. The Act offers the legal basis to reconstruct or improve urban areas without a master plan. An urban area can be given the status of a Renewal Area, a principal decision that needs approval on national level, and guarantees financing by the national government.

Programming of Housing Construction

The planning of housing construction and rehabilitation and the allocation of production quotas to municipalities is an ad hoc procedure that is nevertheless very important for local housing markets. Every year housing quotas for new construction, reconstruction and improvements by the central government are allocated to each region.

In order to determine the quotas, local governments must first determine their housing needs for the next five years, usually on the basis of a housing plan. These local housing needs are reported to a state committee, and an overall plan is prepared for every province. Taking into account budgetary constraints and policy issues, the quotas are allocated over the provinces and the four major cities (including Amsterdam). The large cities usually benefit from this allocation procedure, since a relatively large share of the quota is first allocated to them before the remainder is allocated to the provinces and smaller municipalities.

2.3 Pricing and Financing

In this section two submarkets of the housing market are discussed separately, i.e. the rental sector and the owner occupied-sector, since there are large differences with respect to the pricing and financing mechanisms between these two sectors.

The Rental Sector

In 1979 the Huurprijzenwet Woonruimte (Housing Rent and Allocation Act) was introduced. The Act prescribes the annual changes of rents in the rental housing stock in the private as well as the subsidized sector.

In the subsidized sector initial rental prices and the annual rent increase are determined by the so-called "housing quality rating system": the number of scores a dwelling rates determines its allowable rent and rent increase. In this rating system points are given for instance for the presence of a central heating system, a bath, but environmental elements are also valued, such as presence of schools, parks, shops, public transport. These environmental points are set by the municipality for every city-quarter and this is often used by the local authorities to influence rent levels in certain areas.

In the private housing sector landlords and renters are in principle free to negotiate about the initial rent level. However, the common rule is that the norms set by the rating system are followed. When tenants vacate the dwelling the number of points determined by the rating system are recalculated and according to these the new rent is set. In practice, the landlord seldom increases the rent above the annual trend determined by the national government. Thus, on the regulated market it is difficult for landlords to collect excess rents. It is argued that this system of housing quality rating will lead to a "harmonic" rent level in the housing stock: equal quality, equal price, and also the rents in the reconstruction sector and the newly built rental stock are determined by the rating system.

Due to the increased financial burden for renters, a system of object and subject subsidies, with special subsidies for dwellings in urban renewal areas was introduced. Since investors were dependent on the government for the annual rent increases, more profitable alternatives for large pension funds and insurance companies were available outside the public housing sector. The relative share of housing in the real estate market of pension funds and insurance companies has been reduced by 25% between 1961 and 1981 (Blankenstein-Bouwmeesters and Lukkes, 1984).

The Owner Occupied-Sector

The government also plays an important price-regulation role in owner occupied housing. Three types of subsidies can be distinguished which depend on housing prices, premiums-A, -B and -C. The premium-A category is the least expensive housing category (maximum allowable price of these houses is Dfl. 142,000 in 1985), followed by the premium-B category (maximum price Dfl. 162,000), and the premium-C category (maximum price Dfl. 180,000). The subsidies given in the three categories are dependent on the housing price and income of the household willing to buy a subsidized dwelling. The subsidy is considered as income, and is therefore taxable, while interest on mortgages is tax-deductible.

2.4 The Allocation of Households to Dwellings

The allocation of households to dwellings in Amsterdam is highly regulated by the various Acts mentioned in section 2.1 and 2.2. Until 1975 a housing permit was necessary for every new dwelling occupation. After 1975 some parts of the market were freed from the obligation (the expensive rental sector and the expensive owner-occupied sector).

The main conditions for obtaining a housing permit are:

- household size appropriate to the size of the available dwelling. In 1985 the standards were described by the following scheme:

household size	maximum number of rooms
one or two persons, no child	three
household, one or two children	four
household, three, four or five children	five
household, six or more children	six or more,

- minimum age of 18 years,
- minimum length of stay in Amsterdam of two years, for residence, work or study.

In addition to the housing permits a system of urgency certificates is applied. Persons and households having an urgency certificate are actively mediated by the Gemeentelijke Dienst Herhuisvesting (GDH). They enter a waiting queue where the position in the queue is determined by the degree of urgency. Important factors affecting the household's urgency status are:

- age
- income
- current housing conditions
- social and medical circumstances
- length of stay in Amsterdam and in the queue
- place of work

The rental housing market of Amsterdam is divided into two sectors, i.e. the distribution sector and the free market sector. All rental dwellings above a certain minimum rent level and below an upper level are included in the distribution sector. In 1985 the limits were Dfl. 150 and Dfl. 450 per month respectively. In the eighties some specific submarkets were excluded from the distribution sector in order to make them more attractive, namely dwellings located in the

Bijlmermeer, and one room dwellings. A dwelling in the distribution sector can be owned by one of the following three parties:

- private landlords
- housing corporations
- the municipality

Houses owned by the municipality are under GDH-control, i.e. every vacancy is allocated to a household in the waiting queue of holders of urgency certificates. Private landlords and corporations have to report vacancies in the distribution sector to the GDH, which can be "claimed" by the GDH, i.e. the GDH allocates a urgent household to the vacant dwelling. This is done on a 50/50 percent basis. Alternately a landlord (or housing corporation) and the GDH can allocate the dwelling to a household. For every landlord and corporation a record is kept by the GDH to preserve the 50/50 percent allocation.
Due to insufficient supply the households in the waiting queue for urgencies have little chance of being allocated by the GDH, unless they need a dwelling immediately (e.g. urban renewal, calamities). Both urgent and non-urgent households can act on the housing market themselves, but must take into account the criteria that apply for obtaining a housing permit, for both the rental and owner-occupied submarkets.

A recapitulation of the institutional rules and regulations with respect to the urgency certificates and housing permits can be found in figure 2.5 below.

housing submarkets:	housing permit	urgency certificate
<u>rental market</u>:		
distribution sector: (rent: dfl.150-450)		
- allocated by the GDH	+	+
- allocated by private landlords and corporations	+	-
free market sector:		
- rent < Dfl.150 and 450-600	+	-
- rent > Dfl. 600	-	-
<u>owner occupied market</u>:		
- price < Dfl.180,000	+	-
- price > Dfl.180,000	-	-

Figure 2.5. The rules of housing permits and urgency certificates in Amsterdam in 1985.

With regulated prices, there exists a huge gap between demand and supply which is a heavy burden for the functioning of the GDH. Many people do not accept the strict regulations and enter the black market. Different forms of "illegal" behaviour can be distinguished. The supplier of housing can accept a tenant without a housing permit, or he/she can withdraw the dwelling from the distribution market. The landlord can also inflate rents, require key money. Additionally, the tenant, with or without permission of the landlord, can occupy a dwelling without a housing permit. Although the municipality can evict households which illegally occupy a dwelling, actions outside the distribution rules are still worth trying for both the tenant and the landlord.

Occupancy of a dwelling without permission of the landlord is called squatting ("kraken"). Figures with respect to squatting are very difficult to obtain, but in 1981 it was estimated that approximately 1,500 dwellings in Amsterdam were squatted. Since then this number has certainly increased. Initially, the Amsterdam municipality was very sceptical about squatting, but now it is legalized if a house is left vacant for more than six months (Hanemaayer, 1983).

As can be concluded from the previous sections the housing market of Amsterdam is highly regulated and institutionalized. On both the demand side and the supply side of the housing market, regulations and rules apply with respect to pricing, subsidies. It is very difficult to incorporate all these mechanisms in the design of the housing simulation model. However, some of these elements will be taken up in the next chapters. The housing construction quota will be taken into account in the scenario-building in Chapter 11.

In the last section of this chapter some facts and figures with respect to housing and population of both the city and agglomeration of Amsterdam (for precise definitions, see Chapter 5), will be presented.

2.5 Facts and Figures of the Housing Market and Population of Amsterdam

In this section data will be given on the past and current population and housing situation in Amsterdam and its surroundings (see map 2.2). However, first some information is given with respect to the geographical location of Amsterdam in the Netherlands.

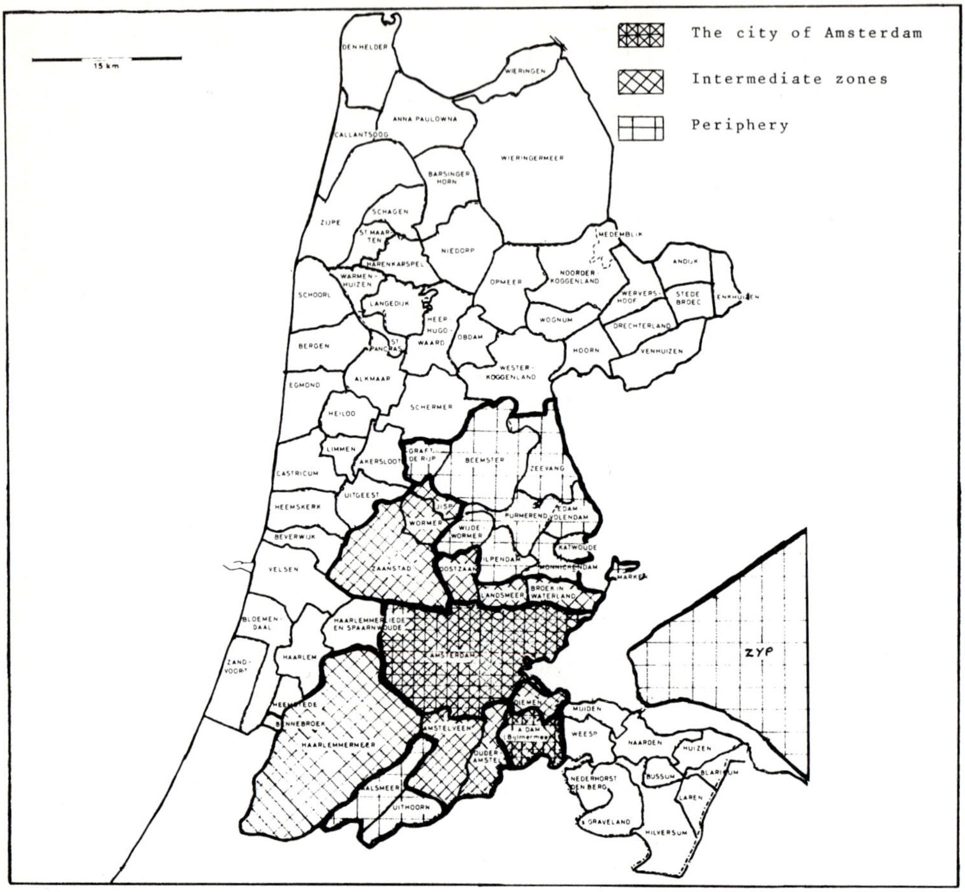

Map 2.2. Amsterdam and surroundings

Geographical Location

Amsterdam, the capital of the Netherlands, has nowadays a population of 676 thousand (1985) or about 4.8% of the Dutch population. The area occupied by the city is 20,760 hectares (85 square miles). The municipality of Amsterdam is part of the province of North Holland (see map 2.3). At the east side, it is bordered by the interior lake, the IJsselmeer; at the west side, the North Sea Canal connects the city with the North Sea. Ships of up to 100,000 ton can reach the ports of the city.

Historically, overseas trade has been the main stimulus for the development of Amsterdam, but since the end of the 19th century Rotterdam, the second large city of the Netherlands has taken over the position as main port of the Netherlands. Nowadays, Amsterdam is an important service centre noted particularly for commercial trade, banking and financing. It is also the main cultural centre of the Netherlands.

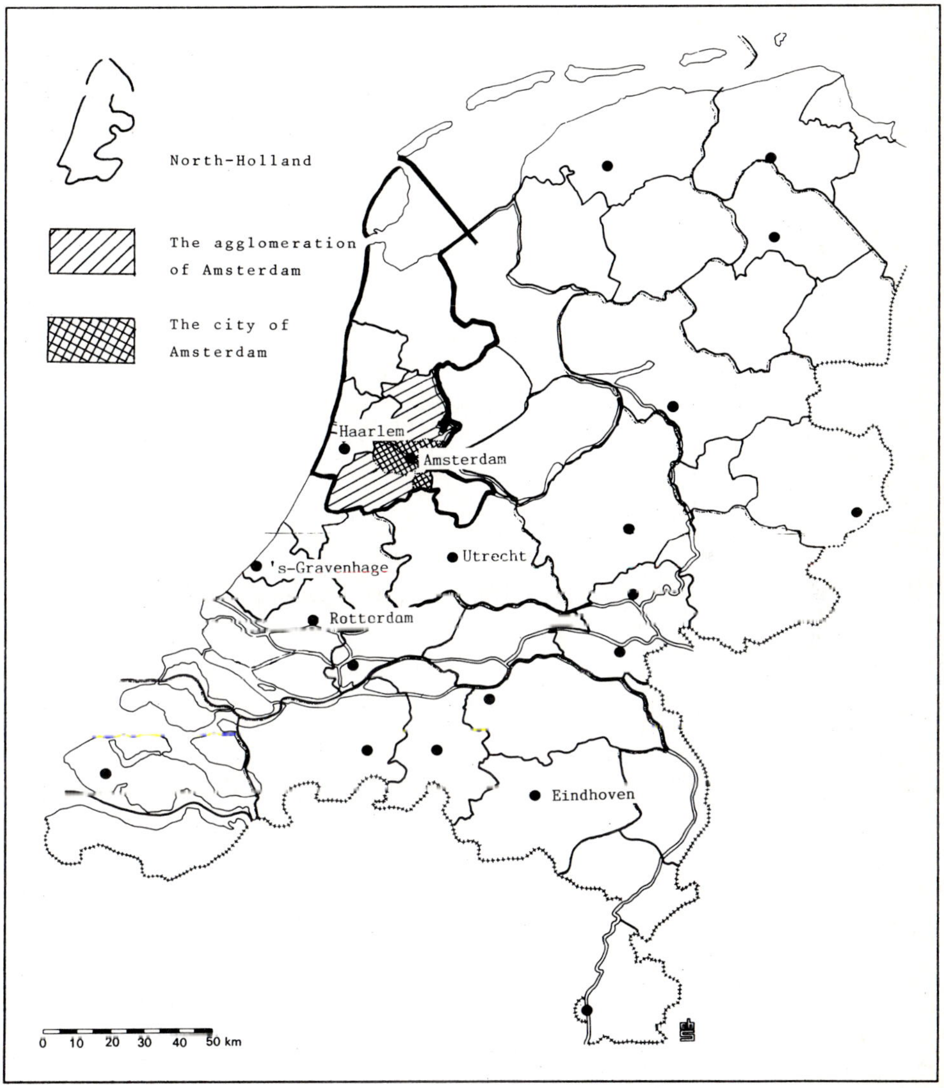

Map 2.3. The geographical location of Amsterdam in the Netherlands

Amsterdam is also part of the Rim-city, a large conurbation that includes Rotterdam, The Hague and Utrecht, with a total population of approximately 6 million people. The city is the centre of gravity of the northern wing of the Rim-city, and includes also the industrialized area around the North Sea Canal (IJmuiden, Velzen), and more major urban centres (Haarlem, Zaanstad). In addition, a number of suburbs have developed since the fifties. Amstelveen and Uithoorn to the South, Purmerend to the North, and Lelystad and Almere to the East. The major foci of economic development are the south-east (Bijlmermeer) and the area around Schiphol airport and the connecting railway south of the city. New population development also takes place in the Southeast. In the near future new developments will take place in the west.

Population

In figure 2.6 the basic components of population development in Amsterdam since 1945 are depicted. Despite the decrease of population in the city of Amsterdam, the population of the total agglomeration has been continually growing in size (see table 2.1).

Area*	1960 abs.	%	1971 abs.	%	1976 abs.	%	1981 abs.	%	1985 abs.	%
Amsterdam	864747	75	807100	66	751156	61	711982	56	675570	53
Intermediate zones	218159	19	294200	24	322370	26	335268	27	339801	26
Periphery	71161	6	128896	10	166199	13	214383	17	271013	21
Total agglomeration	1154067		1230196		1239725		1261633		1286384	

Table 2.1. Total population in the Amsterdam agglomeration, 1960-1985 (source: Yearbooks Amsterdam), for definitions: see map 2.2

Population growth since 1960 is 11%, which is relatively low when compared with the national rate of 27%. Due to the aforementioned migration to the suburbs, Amsterdam's population share has dropped.

Closer examination of the demographic statistics reveals some remarkable differences in age structure between Amsterdam and the Region (defined as the agglomeration of Amsterdam minus the city itself; figure 2.7). Elderly people and adults under 30 years are overrepresented, and children and middle aged households are underrepresented in Amsterdam. This is a direct result of the outmigration of young families to the suburban rings.

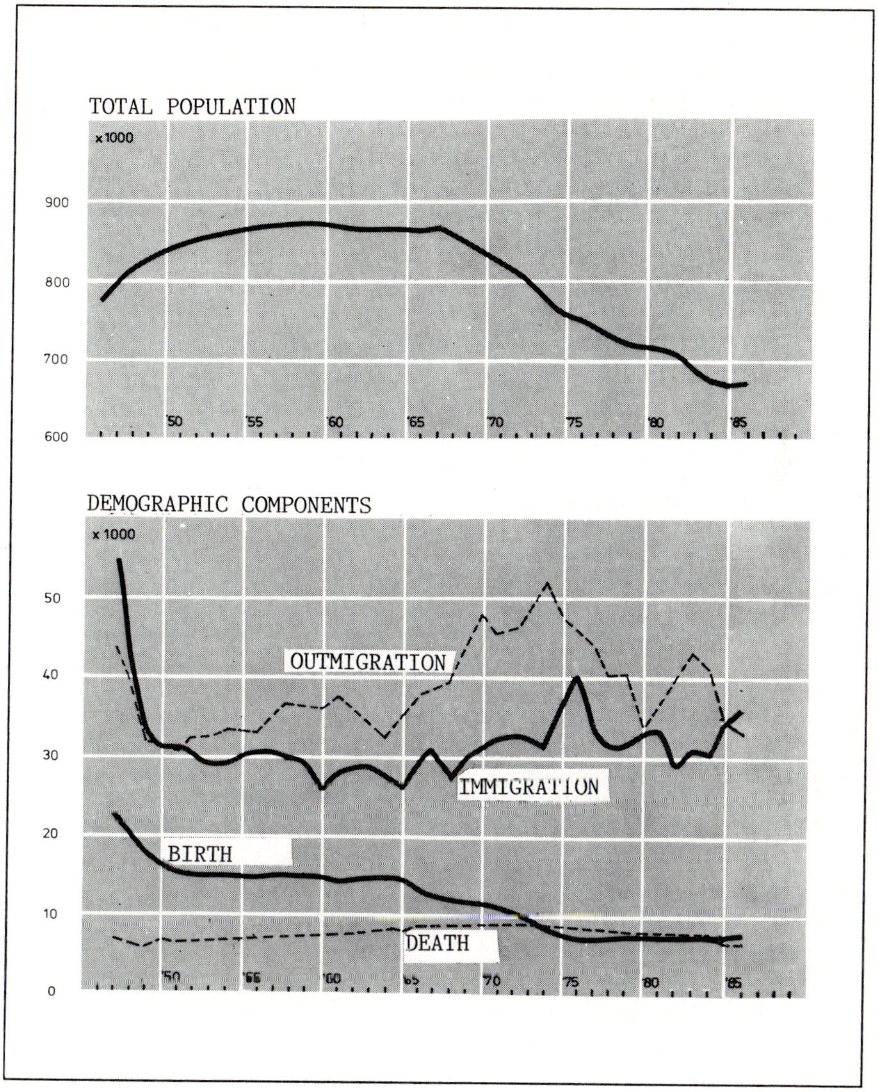

Figure 2.6. Total Amsterdam population and components of demographic change, 1945-1984 (source: yearbook Amsterdam 1985)

Differences in age structure are reflected in the various household types, but here differences are even more dramatic (table 2.2). In 1981 almost 40% of Amsterdam households were single, compared to only 20% in the rest of the agglomeration (Region). Approximately 30% of Amsterdam households contain three or more persons, compared with more than 50% in the Region.

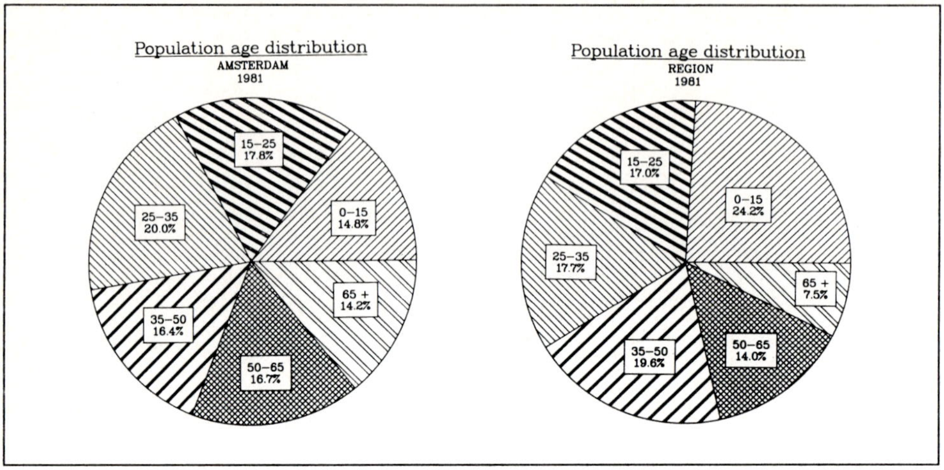

Figure 2.7. Age structure of Amsterdam and the Region, 1981

household category	Amsterdam abs.	%	Region abs.	%
one person < 35 year	51346	15	7325	4
one person 35-64 year	38243	11	11162	6
one person 65+ year	39556	12	11940	7
two persons < 35 year	35173	11	18100	10
two persons 35-64 year	33894	10	19286	11
two persons 65+ year	29340	9	12414	7
three persons, one child < 18 year	25372	8	18303	10
three persons, one child 18+ year	16452	5	10294	6
four+ persons, all children < 18 y.	31470	9	49819	27
four+ persons, one child < 18 year	20061	6	21544	12
other	13648	4	4153	2
Total	334555	100	184340	100

Table 2.2. Household structure in Amsterdam and the Region, 1982 (source: WBO)

The Housing Stock

In 1985 there were approximately 320,000 dwellings in Amsterdam, this is about 60% of the stock of the total agglomeration. If we look at the housing production in Amsterdam and the Region, it can be seen that the Amsterdam share has increased sharply since 1982, while its population has decreased (figure 2.8). More details concerning the housing stock can be found in figures 2.9 and 2.10).

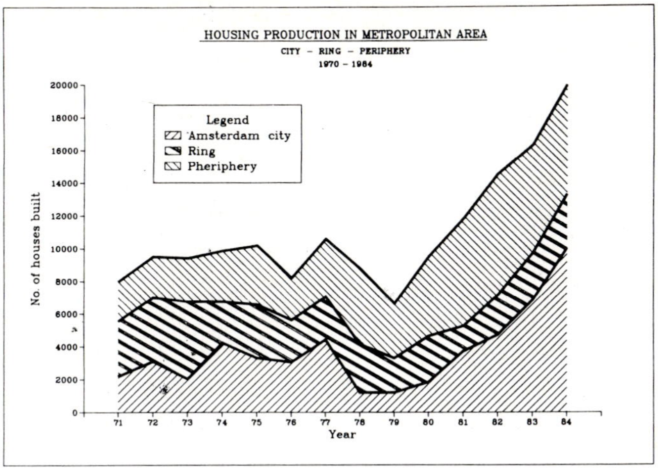

Figure 2.8. Housing production in the Amsterdam agglomeration, 1971-1984

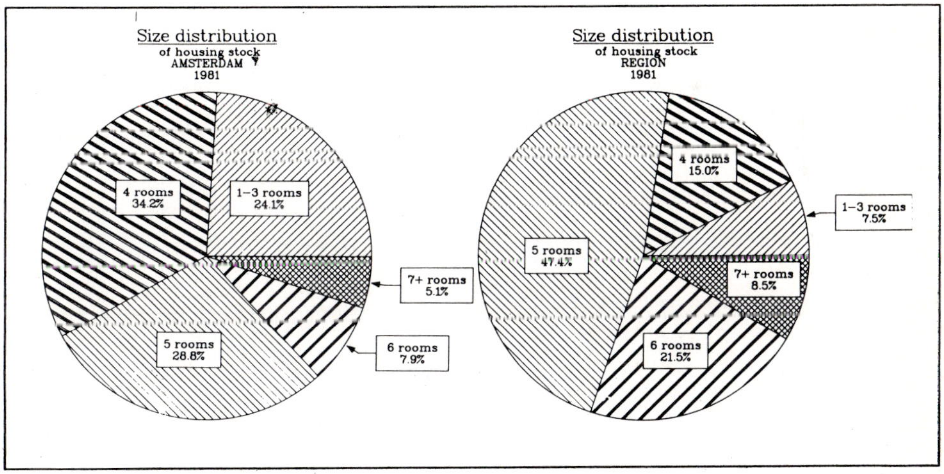

Figure 2.9. Size distribution of dwellings in Amsterdam and the Region, 1982 (source: WBO)

Figure 2.9 presents the size distribution of dwellings in Amsterdam and the Region in 1981. Almost 60% of all dwellings in Amsterdam have four or fewer rooms (kitchen included), against 25% in the Region. Another difference between Amsterdam and its surroundings is the age of the housing stock, denoted in figure 2.10.

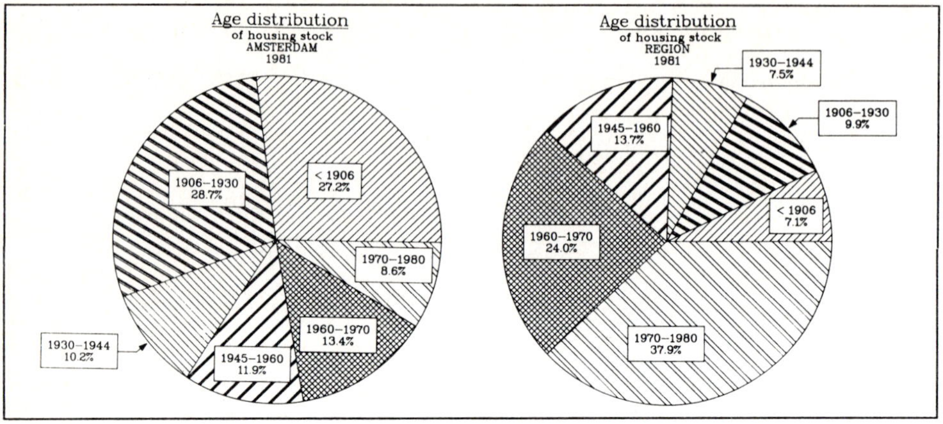

Figure 2.10. Year of construction of dwellings in Amsterdam and the Region, 1982 (source: WBO)

More than half of the houses were built before 1930, and new construction (since 1970) amounts only to 15% of the total number of dwellings. In the Region the reverse pattern is true; more than half of the total housing stock was built after 1970. Parts of the new construction in the Region -in the so-called growth-centers- is specially built for people living in Amsterdam (table 2.3).

municipality	1980	1981	1982	1983	1984	for Amsterdam
Alkmaar	1130	2370	1740	1340	1000	15 %
Hoorn	915	1330	1470	1670	1070	60 %
Purmerend	365	570	2000	1960	1460	70 %
Lelystad	2050	2370	2025	1775	1500	70 %
Almere	1850	2730	2760	2280	2700	64 %
Total	6310	9370	9995	9025	7730	
for Amsterdam	3600	5000	5730	5280	4590	
in %	57 %	53 %	57 %	59 %	59 %	

Table 2.3. Housing construction in the growth-centers and percentages built for Amsterdam, 1980-1984 (source: VH-plan, 1983)

Dwelling Occupancy

Table 2.4 and figure 2.11 provide some information about the occupancy of dwellings by household types in Amsterdam. From figure 2.12 it is clear that more than 90% of the one and two-room dwellings are occupied by one or two persons. It is also apparent, however, that about 40% of large houses (five or more rooms) are occupied by one or two persons.

household category	number of rooms (in %) 1+2	3	4	5+	total
family, 0 children	21	44	2	9	54320
family, 1 or more children	7	32	44	17	57896
single parent family	10	37	38	15	20457
single	45	29	13	5	97561
other	27	35	22	15	53285
total	26	34	25	11	283519

Table 2.4. Occupancy of dwellings by household types in Amsterdam, 1983 (source: Werkgroep Koppeling Vastgoed-Bevolking)

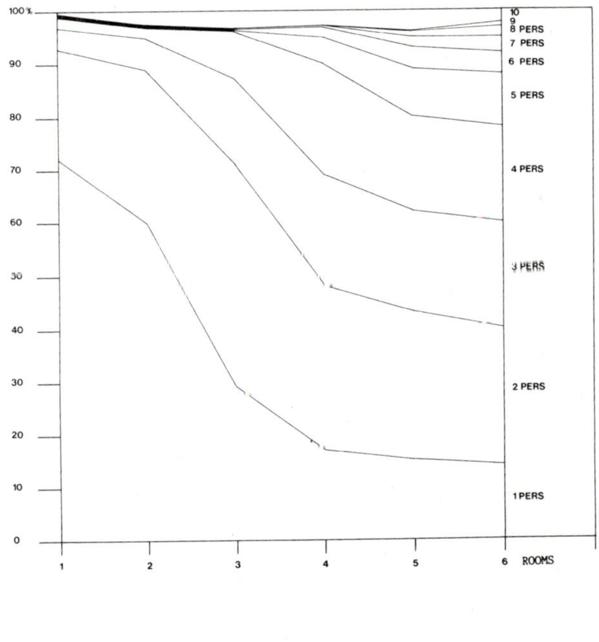

Figure 2.11. Dwelling size by number of persons per dwelling in Amsterdam, 1983 (source: Werkgroep koppeling Vastgoed-Bevolking)

Mobility

In 1973 the outmigration from Amsterdam reached a peak of more than 50,000 persons, but since then the figures have dropped considerably. In 1984 in- and outmigration nearly balanced. Compared to intra-urban moves, the magnitude of interurban migration is much smaller. This can be seen in figure 2.12, where both intra- and inter-urban migration since 1970 are displayed. Also included is the number of persons in households that were allocated to a new dwelling in Amsterdam, receiving a housing permit.

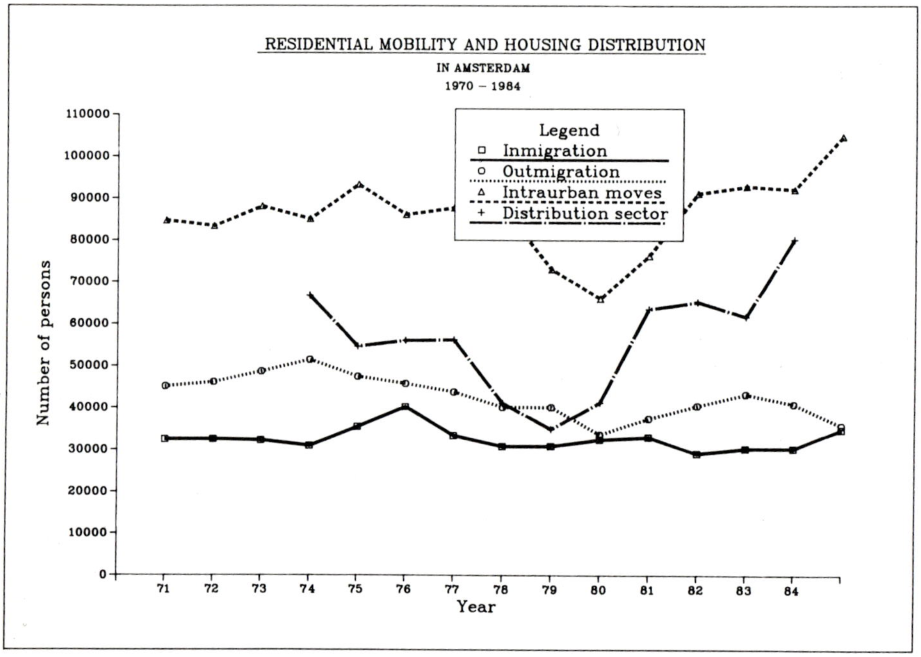

Figure 2.12. Intra- and inter-urban mobility for Amsterdam, 1971-1984

The age composition of movers is quite different from that of the overall population (see table 2.5). In general, movers are relatively young, especially the immigrants: almost three-quarters of immigrants are under 30 years of age (probably due to the large supply of higher education in Amsterdam).

age	intra-urban movers abs.	%	inter-urban immigration abs.	%	outmigration abs.	%	Amsterdam population abs.	%
0-19	22988	22	8559	25	7704	22	134774	20
20-29	42835	41	16430	47	11207	31	142587	21
30-39	18288	17	5419	16	7595	21	115706	17
40-49	7305	7	2094	6	2856	8	71453	11
50-64	6731	6	1481	4	3529	10	103573	15
65+	6674	6	852	2	2929	8	107477	16
total	104821	100	34835	100	35820	100	675570	100

Table 2.5. Age composition of intra- and inter-urban migrants compared with the Amsterdam population, 1984 (source: Yearbook Amsterdam, 1984)

2.6 Conclusion

As can be seen in this chapter Amsterdam has experienced a large number of changes with respect to the housing market and population in the last decades. The description of these developments and prediction of future developments on the basis of the past by means of a combined household and housing market model are the major aims of the subsequent chapters.

CHAPTER 3. DYNAMIC HOUSEHOLD MODELS

3.0 Introduction

The modelling of household dynamics has for long been a neglected subject among demographers and other scientists who have an interest in the study of population dynamics. A possible explanation for this neglect is the inadequacy of conventional Markov models for dealing with such a complex phenomenon. In this chapter an overview of a number of models and methods used in the demography of the household will be given. The problems appear to be manifold. First, there is a definition problem: what is a household and is it different from a family, etc.? A second problem lies in the great variety of household types. Before discussing various models and methods for studying households we will first discuss the definition of a household used in this study, and then consider the variety of household types.

The Definition of Households

The exact definition of a household depends on the subject under study. The United Nations definition (U.N., 1973) defines the household as an arrangement made by persons to provide themselves food and other essentials for living. They usually occupy a housing unit, but this is not a necessary condition. In many Third-World countries it is not uncommon for a household to have no housing unit. The United Nations Multilingual Demographic Dictionary defines the household as a socio-economic unit, consisting of individuals who live together. A family, is defined as a relationship which pertains to or arises from reproductive processes and which is regulated by law or custom.

In the Dutch context, the Dutch Central Bureau of Statistics (CBS) defines a household as a group of two or more persons who live together in a domestic relationship and share living essentials such as living quarters, cooking equipment, food etc. Thus according to that definition a single person is not a household. For a study of household behaviour on the housing market, a definition is required which captures the residential situation. But even here the concept is ambiguous. In general a household is a group of persons sharing the same housing unit. But the types of groups that can be found under one roof are numerous. A basic distinction is that between the 'ordinary' household and 'collectivities' (Schmid, 1984). Collectivities are people living in boarding schools, religious or military institutions, student dormitories, houses for the elderly, etc.

From an economic perspective a household may be defined as a consumption unit where consumption is shared among the members. Given the above mentioned common components of the 'ordinary household' this pertains, among other things, to housing consumption. In practice however it could be argued that a household is 'anything what a census is able or willing to record' (Schmid, 1984). This is indeed plausible but can lead to problems when various data sources are compared.

In this study a household is defined as one or more persons who live together in a domestic relationship. This includes the CBS household definition plus singles. Households may be main-tenants or sub-tenants but a necessary condition is that they have separate living quarters. The 'collectivities' will be referred to as non-households.

Household Types

A second problem is the variety and changing nature of household types. Since the sixties many new forms of households have emerged, and these alternative forms were not always recognized by the standard demographic accounts of marriage and divorce. The development of non-conformist households is particularly associated with urban areas. In the Netherlands, Amsterdam can be seen as a 'trend setter' in this respect for the rest of the country. Examples are non-married couples (of different sexes or the same sex), one parent households, married couples without children, multi-couple households etc. As an illustration the following table gives an impression of the trend towards alternative forms of cohabitation in Amsterdam.

Persons living at address	Year 1979	1983	Difference	%
one single	84870	103134	18264	+ 21.5
two singles	25678	31204	5526	+ 21.5
three singles	3997	4640	643	+ 16.1
four+ singles	1034	1182	148	+ 14.3
families	152025	137666	-14386	- 9.5
total	267604	277826	10222	+ 3.8

Table 3.1. Forms of cohabitation at addresses in Amsterdam in 1979 and 1983 (source : Werkgroep Koppeling Vastgoed-Bevolking, 1981)

From this table we can observe some drastic changes in the development of the household structure in Amsterdam. Singles, and unmarried couples of two and more persons increasingly dominate the composition of households in the city while families show a drastic decrease in number. The time span observed here is only four years, so these trends imply really dramatic shifts in household structure in the city.

Hence it is clear that any household model used in this context should explicitly recognize these developments and should not be based purely on the basic demographic facts of marriage and divorce.

This chapter is organized as follows. In section 3.1 a framework is presented that could be used to classify various models. The subsequent sections (3.2 to 3.7) are then devoted to the presentation of a number of models developed since the seventies in demography that are relevant for household modelling. The choice of models presented here is not exhaustive and reflects to some extent the bias of the present authors towards micro-oriented dynamic approaches. In the last section (section 3.8) we evaluate the various contributions to household modelling while some conclusions are drawn regarding the design of an empirical household model for the housing market study in Amsterdam. The model actually developed is described in Chapter 7.

3.1 A Modelling Framework

The models presented in this chapter can be classified according to a number of characteristics. They all share the common feature that they are dynamic in nature, although many differences in scope and objectives exist. General distinctions which are typical in many disciplines and which will also be made here are the following dimensions:

(1) a micro versus a macro approach,
(2) process oriented versus structure oriented models,
(3) analytical versus simulation models.

Bongaarts (1983a), in an overview of household demography, distinguishes between: (a) analytical models, (b) microsimulation and (c) macrosimulation approaches, thus focusing on dimensions (1) and (3). Keilman (1984), discussing dynamic macro oriented models, classifies household models according to static versus dynamic methods, while a further distinction is between econometric, micro and macro models. So we can conclude that more than one classification scheme is possible, depending on the relevance of the classifying criteria.

For the housing market study, the first two dimensions seem particularly relevant. Because the household model is embedded in a broader structure than household modelling alone the level of analysis should be consistent, or at least transferable from one model to another. Since in our case the household model is connected to the (micro) housing demand model this restricts the types of models to be used for the household dynamics. Another prerequisite is the emphasis on a dynamic transition approach. In process oriented models the transitions from time t to time t+1 are modelled explicitly, so that the time path of (groups of) households can be followed. Structure oriented models, on the other hand, focus on household projections in the future time periods t+1, t+2, t+3 without consideration of actual transitions between states. Since household transitions are an important input for the housing demand model, the model to be used in the housing market project should thus be process oriented.

In the following sections an overview is given of a number of household models currently in use in household demography. The main properties are briefly described and evaluated in terms of usefulness in a dynamic housing market context. The last section of the chapter includes a classification scheme of these models along the most important dimensions.

3.2 Traditional Household Projection Models

In this section the main traditional methods for household projections are briefly described. First two simple methods are presented, viz. (1) the simple households-to-population ratio method, and (2) the vital statistics method. Next the headship rate method is described. This is nowadays by far the most frequently used method for household projections. Finally, some attention is devoted to the ordinary life table method. In section 3.7 the discussion of life table methods is continued in the context of multistate demography.

The Simple Households-to-Population Ratio Method

This method is based on a constant ratio between total population and number of households, i.e.:

$$H = \alpha P \tag{3.1}$$

or:

$$\delta H = \alpha \; \delta P, \tag{3.2}$$

where H is the number of households, and P is the total population. δ the change within one time period and α is the head ratio in the population . A variant of this function is to take only the population into account in the relevant age category , i.e. P^{adult} instead of P. However, the assumption of a constant ratio is not very realistic in our study area since Amsterdam has lost much of its population since 1958, but the number of households has increased considerably.

Vital Statistics Method

A second method takes account of the reported demographic figures on marriage and divorce, deaths and net immigration (see also CBS, 1959).

The total number of projected households for a given year t is calculated as :

$$F_t = F_0 + \sum_j (M_j - D_j + N_j - S_j), \quad (3.3)$$

where F_0 is the number of families in the base year, F_t is the number of projected families, M_j and S_j are the number of marriages and divorces per year j respectively (j=1,..,t), N_j is the number of net immigrant families and D_j is the total number of deaths of married people. The total number of families is converted into the total number of households by applying a correction formula :

$$H_t = h_t F_t \,/\, (1 - n_t) , \quad (3.4)$$

where h_t is the ratio of family households to families and n_t is the ratio of non-family households to total households.

While this could be considered as a stock-flow model of families, it is inappropriate in situations where the number of non-family households is relatively large and evolves in a direction different from the number of families. The model hinges on the assumption that the trend in family households completely reflects the trend in the non-family households. It could however even be argued that these groups are more or less competitive, i.e. that the decrease in the family households is due to the growth in the non-family households. See table 3.1 for an illustration.

The Headship Rate Method

The headship rate method (HRM) has as its starting point the population projections by age and sex, and sometimes by more detailed classifications of marital status. The HRM was recommended by the United Nations as the most appropriate method for detailed projections of future household composition (U.N.,1973). The headship rate is defined as :

$$h(i,j,t) = H(i,j,t) \,/\, P(i,j,t) \quad (3.5)$$

where H(i,j,t) is the number of heads of households with sex i, age j at time t, and P(i,j,t) is the population with sex i, age j at time t. Household projection then follows the population projection but in the more sophisticated HRM's assumptions concerning the prospective changes in headship rates are made. A number of variants can be mentioned here. First a simple extrapolation of past trends in rates can be made. Second, and this is the most common situation, a regression approach is followed where the rate is dependent upon a set of relevant predictors, for example income, degree of urbanization, social class. Finally, a normative approach is sometimes taken, relating the headship rates to explicit housing or welfare policies. The HRM is very useful in projecting future household numbers and can be applied at both the national and the regional or local level. However, it is essentially a static method. The dynamic aspects of the household life cycle are not taken into account and it is unclear how transitions in household structure take place.

The Ordinary Life Table Method

The life table method is sometimes referred to as the decrement life table method. We will discuss its properties in more detail, because it led in the seventies to an important generalization: the multistate life table. This important development offers a fruitful approach for household modelling and in section 3.7 we elaborate on it. The decrement life table has also been used for household projections and is worth discussing in its own right.

The life table is a basic concept in demography and in its original form it is a scheme for expressing the facts of mortality in terms of probabilities (Keyfitz, 1975, p.5). The life table gives the probability of dying during age interval $(x, x + \delta x)$. A function can be derived that relates the 'force of mortality' μ to the age x :

$$\mu(x) = \lim_{\delta x \to 0} \frac{l(x) - l(x + \delta x)}{l(x)\delta x} = \frac{-d \log l(x)}{d(x)} , \qquad (3.6)$$

where $l(x)$ is defined as the stationary population. It is a theoretical distribution of population by age x that would develop out of an initial cohort $l(0)$ with a mortality regime defined by $\mu(x)$. The probability of surviving h years later for a person of age x can be calculated using (3.6). Integrating and solving for $l(x)$ we get :

$$l(x) = l(0) \exp \left[\int_0^x \mu(t)\, dt \right] = \Omega(x) l(0) , \qquad (3.7)$$

which implicitly defines Ω. The probability of surviving h years after age x is therefore :

$$p(x) = \Omega(x+h) \ / \ \Omega(x) \qquad (3.8)$$

The number of people dying between x and x + 1 is :

$$\int_0^1 l(x+t)\mu(x+t)dt \qquad (3.9)$$

and this is known as the decrement.

The concept of the life table can be applied not only to mortality, but also to other demographic events, such as fertility or marital status. It has also been applied in other fields such as working force participation (see, among others, Wolfbein, 1949).

In these applications the single decrement table has been extended to allow for multiple decrements, i.e. the turnovers to more than one other state.

The marital status life table has been used to estimate the number of households. Glass and Davidson (1951) divided the population by age, sex and marital status (single, married and divorced), and they derived transition probabilities for children to married state and to single state, from married to divorce. The life table only allows for decrements from one state to another; so the resulting figures for singles and families without assumptions concerning doubling-up in households (i.e. two singles joining) had to be interpreted as the upper limit of household formation (U.N., 1973, p.25). By assuming a considerable amount of doubling-up in households a more realistic picture emerged.

The major drawback of applying the decrement life table to household modelling is the non-recursive nature of the process. Once a transition has taken place, the individual cannot re-enter the same state. Moreover, assumptions have to be made concerning inflow to and outflow from the states. For instance, no person changes from the married state to widowhood before the age of maximum share (i.e. before the top of the unimodal distribution) of married persons, and no persons enter the state of marriage after the age of maximum share of married persons (i.e. after the top of the unimodal distribution). Similar assumptions apply to the other transition rates. Another disadvantage of the method is that it has no direct correspondence with population projections. This can be a major problem in cases where both household and population forecasts have to be made.

3.3 The Akkerman Model

Akkerman (1980, 1982, 1985) has developed the idea of the household composition matrix in the field of regional planning and of a simultaneous population and household projection. The model is relatively straightforward and can easily be applied.

The basic model starts with the concept of the household composition matrix, **A**, of dimension n x n (n being the number of age categories) and with elements $\{a(i,j)+d(i,j)\}$. The element a denotes the average number of household members in age category i who live in a household with the householder in the age category j, and d(i,j) is 1 for i = j and 0 otherwise. Thus $\{a(i,j) + d(i,j)\}$ gives the average number of persons (members and heads) of age i who live in a household with age of head in category j. The matrix has the following properties :

1. The sum of the elements in each column j of **A** equals the average number of persons per household: s_j.
   Thus, $s_j = 1 + \sum_i a(i,j)$,

2. The elements of row i of $\mathbf{A}$, appropriately weighted with the total number of households type j, g_j, equals the average number of persons per household in age category i: r_i. So,

$$r_i = \frac{g_i + \sum_j a(i,j)\, g_j}{\sum_j g_j} \qquad (3.10)$$

where g_i is the number of heads in age category i.

3. The matrix is decomposable into $\mathbf{A}_m + \mathbf{I}$, and is therefore non-singular, where $\mathbf{A}_m$ is a matrix of average number of non-heads.

The following relations hold :

$$\underline{k} = \mathbf{A}\, \underline{g} \;, \text{ or } \quad \underline{g} = \mathbf{A}^{-1}\, \underline{k} \qquad (3.11)$$

where $\underline{k}$ is a n x 1 vector of population distributed by age, and $\underline{g}$ is a n x 1 vector of households distributed by age of the head. So, $\mathbf{A}$ is the mapping of households on population. Since $\mathbf{A}$ is non-singular the mapping of population back onto households ($\mathbf{A}^{-1}$) holds too.

The dynamic element in the Akkerman model is introduced through the Leslie matrix $\mathbf{P}$. In discrete demographic models the Leslie-matrix is a basic concept for population projection (Keyfitz, 1977). The Leslie matrix contains birth and survivorship rates per age category and enables population projections by age as a set of linear first order homogeneous difference equations with constant coefficients. The matrix has the following form :

$$\begin{bmatrix}
0 & 0 & 0 & \alpha_1 & \alpha_2 & \alpha_3 & \alpha_4 & \alpha_5 & \alpha_6 & \alpha_7 & 0 & 0 & 0 & 0 \\
\beta_1 & 0 & 0 & 0 & 0 & 0 & 0 & 0 & 0 & 0 & 0 & 0 & 0 & 0 \\
0 & \beta_2 & 0 & 0 & 0 & 0 & 0 & 0 & 0 & 0 & 0 & 0 & 0 & 0 \\
\cdot & \cdot & \beta_3 & \cdot & \cdot & \cdot & \cdot & \cdot & \cdot & \cdot & \cdot & \cdot & \cdot & \cdot \\
\cdot & \cdot & \cdot & \beta_4 & \cdot & \cdot & \cdot & \cdot & \cdot & \cdot & \cdot & \cdot & \cdot & \cdot \\
\cdot & \cdot & \cdot & \cdot & \beta_5 & \cdot & \cdot & \cdot & \cdot & \cdot & \cdot & \cdot & \cdot & \cdot \\
\cdot & \cdot & \cdot & \cdot & \cdot & \beta_6 & \cdot & \cdot & \cdot & \cdot & \cdot & \cdot & \cdot & \cdot \\
\cdot & \cdot & \cdot & \cdot & \cdot & \cdot & \beta_7 & \cdot & \cdot & \cdot & \cdot & \cdot & \cdot & \cdot \\
\cdot & \cdot & \cdot & \cdot & \cdot & \cdot & \cdot & \beta_8 & \cdot & \cdot & \cdot & \cdot & \cdot & \cdot \\
\cdot & \cdot & \cdot & \cdot & \cdot & \cdot & \cdot & \cdot & \beta_9 & \cdot & \cdot & \cdot & \cdot & \cdot \\
\cdot & \cdot & \cdot & \cdot & \cdot & \cdot & \cdot & \cdot & \cdot & \beta_{10} & \cdot & \cdot & \cdot & \cdot \\
\cdot & \cdot & \cdot & \cdot & \cdot & \cdot & \cdot & \cdot & \cdot & \cdot & \beta_{11} & \cdot & \cdot & \cdot \\
\cdot & \cdot & \cdot & \cdot & \cdot & \cdot & \cdot & \cdot & \cdot & \cdot & \cdot & \beta_{12} & \cdot & \cdot \\
\cdot & \cdot & \cdot & \cdot & \cdot & \cdot & \cdot & \cdot & \cdot & \cdot & \cdot & \cdot & \beta_{13} & \beta_{14}
\end{bmatrix}$$

The α's denote the age specific fertility probabilities and the β's denote the age specific survival probabilities. The remaining cells contain zeros. The standard form of the Leslie projection matrix assumes that projection period and age interval are of equal length.

The population projection model can be written as :

$$\underline{k}(t+1) = \mathbf{P}\ \underline{k}(t) \qquad (3.12)$$

Substituting (3.12) into (3.11) gives :

$$\underline{g}(t+1) = \mathbf{A}^{-1}\ \mathbf{P}\ \underline{g}(t) \qquad (3.13)$$

and this relates population in time t to households in time t+1. The household vector $\underline{g}(t+1)$ can also be related to the household vector at time t by substitution of (3.11) into (3.13) :

$$\underline{g}(t+1) = \mathbf{A}^{-1}\ \mathbf{P}\ \mathbf{A}\ \underline{g}(t) \qquad (3.14)$$

Various extensions of this simple model have been worked out by Akkerman. The first row of the household composition matrix, the elements a(1,j), can be interpreted as household fertility and the household composition matrix can be used to establish a relationship between household composition, age distribution and fertility (Akkerman, 1980). Another development has been to allow the household composition matrix to be rectangular and to use matrix updating techniques to estimate regional net household migration. Given a base year matrix $\mathbf{A}^{\circ}$ of households by age of the head and by region this matrix $\mathbf{A}^{\circ}$ is updated to be consistent with regional population projections. The updating algorithm is not mechanical, as qualitative restrictions are set on the growth and decline of each household category. The final result of the model is a projection of the total number of households per region and the net migration per region (see Akkerman, 1985).

Some comments regarding the application of the model can be made. First, the model is essentially a linear projection model and could be viewed as an extension of the HRM model (see previous section). Dynamic household processes leading to a new household vector are not taken into account. Moreover, the assumption of linearity may not be valid in periods of rapid change in household structures, as in the Amsterdam case. An improvement of the model would be to make the matrix time dependent. Nevertheless, the household composition matrix is a very useful instrument for the transition of population into households.

3.4 The Swedish Household Model

The model described here was developed in the seventies by Holmberg, Hårsman, Marksjo and Snickars, and is described in various publications (Hårsman and Marksjo, 1977; Hårsman and Snickars, 1983; Hårsman, 1985). Its main aim is to give a detailed treatment of demographic factors and to predict simultaneously the total number of households and households by categories.

The model is essentially an entropy maximizing model (or, equivalently an information gain minimizing model, see also Chapter 6) and results in a detailed household breakdown by type and by transitions between two periods in time. So, the transitions between t and t+1 are modelled explicitly.

The central equation of the model is given by the information gain statistic :

$$I = \Sigma_i \Sigma_j P_{ij} \log (P_{ij} / P^o_{ij}) \qquad (3.15)$$

where P^o_{ij} is the observed transition matrix of households being in household category i in time t and in household category j in time t+1. The model outcome P_{ij} should be as close as possible to the observed flows P^o and be consistent with a number of constraints. These constraints reflect the amount of information available concerning the number of households by category at the beginning and at the end of the projection period. The following set of constraints is reported in Hårsman (1985). For convenience the notation has been simplified if necessary :

1. The population distribution of persons over the household categories at the beginning of the period should be equal to the distribution at the end of the previous period a_i:

$$\Sigma_j P_{ij} = a_i \qquad (3.16)$$

2. The projected number of persons per age class should be consistent with population forecasts b_k :

$$\Sigma_i \Sigma_{j \in (\text{age group } k)} P_{ij} = b_k \qquad (3.17)$$

3. The projected number of immigrants plus births should be equal to the population forecasts c_k :

$$\Sigma_{i \in (\text{inflow group } k)} \Sigma_j P_{ij} = c_k \qquad (3.18)$$

while a similar constraint can be formulated for j with respect to outflows.

4. For consistency, a number of accounting relationships must be established between the estimated flows. They pertain to the ratio of householders to non-householders in households of various sizes. Hence, if k^* is the average household size for household class k, then the following constraint is necessary:

$$\Sigma_i \Sigma_{j \in (\text{heads of } k^*\text{-size hh})} P_{ij} =$$

$$(k^* - 1)\ \Sigma_i \Sigma_{j \in (\text{non-heads of } k^*\text{-size hh})} P_{ij} \qquad (3.19)$$

Similar relations hold between the number of children and householders in single-parent households and the number of children and householders in three or more person households.

New pieces of information can be incorporated without many problems. For instance, the total number of projected households of a certain type can be fixed in advance, introducing a new constraint. A variant of this approach is to project the total number of households using the HRM and regressing the headship rates on exogenous variables such as income and other economic indicators and next introducing these aggregate forecasts as constraints in the model (Hårsman, 1985).

The best way to characterize the method is to state that it is a consistent way of putting different pieces of information together (Hårsman, 1985). The model is not behavioural in nature, but gives highly disaggregate information on household transitions. In order for the process to attain reliable transition rate forecasts, a basic table of observed transitions P° is necessary. In terms of information gain this basic set of values usually contains the highest amount of information relative to the constraints added. If no observed set of transitions is available a uniform distribution can be used, but then the optimal values will in general be unsatisfactory. For more details concerning entropy maximization and information gain minimization methods the reader is referred to Chapter 6.

3.5 The PRIMOS Model

The PRIMOS model was developed at PSC-TNO (at present INRO-TNO) in Delft (The Netherlands) by Gordijn and Heida for the Dutch Ministry of Housing (Gordijn and Heida, 1985). It is essentially a macro-demographic simulation model for the national level. Local forecasts are derived from this model through the application of a detailed HRM approach. The aim of the project was to estimate a household transition matrix the form of which is given in table 3.2. The square 5 x 5 matrix in the inner part of the table denotes the transition events in the existing population categories. In this submatrix the process of leaving the parental home is identified by the events (1) to (3). Event (6) relates to the marriage plus cohabitation transitions and (8) pertains to the process of splitting up or divorce, while (10) is remarriage or cohabitation for the second (third) time. In the lower rectangle we find the inflow into the system, i.e. births and immigration, while the right rectangle represents the outflows through deaths and outmigration.

Not all transitions are available and in order to fill the whole matrix a series of continuous functions was estimated using household information from the 1981 one percent sample on housing needs (WBO, 1981). In addition, a number of assumptions was necessary to fill in remaining data gaps. Next, the model was run and the national household development in the period 1971 - 1981 was simulated, starting with the 1971 national census. There again, a number of plausible assumptions had to be made concerning the development of the transition probabilities in time. The simulation resulted in a good fit with the observed 1981 household structure. Finally, some projections were made for the period 1982 - 2000. This model demonstrates the intrinsic problems associated with testing and calibrating dynamic empirical household models. The lack of data has to be balanced by plausible assumptions concerning key parameters in the model. Although the data used is a large sample containing a large amount of information on household structure there is still a lack of flow data, viz. the number of people that start a single person household, the number of people moving to and from institutions.

HOUSEHOLD STATUS time = 2	time = 1 dependent child	single	married/ cohabiting	ever married/ cohabited	institution	deaths	out-migration
dependent child	-	**	*	*	**	12	13
single	1	-	*	*	**	12	13
married/ cohabiting	2	6	-	10	**	12	13
ever married/ cohabited	*	*	8	-	**	12	13
institution	3	7	9	11	-	12	13
births	4	**	**	**	**		
immigration	5	5	5	5	5		

- : no transition
* : transition impossible
**: number of transitions negligible

Table 3.2. The transition matrix of the PRIMOS model

If this kind of information is available from panel or retrospective data the modelling orientation has to shift from the macro to the micro level. In the next sections two forms of micro oriented models will be presented.

3.6 Microsimulation Models

Microsimulation models were popularized in the seventies in various fields through the work of Orcutt et al. (1961). If processes are too complex to model analytically, microsimulation, often in conjunction with Monte Carlo techniques offers a way out. The complexity usually entails the interdependencies between events and decisions. In microsimulation there is virtually no limitation to the complexity that can be incorporated. Simple conditional probabilities and a random number generator are the main ingredients of the model. Formally it can be written as (see Wilson, 1983) :

$$x_i^r = x_i^r \, [\, P_i(x/\ldots), \, R_i^r \, , \, \Gamma \,] \tag{3.20}$$

where x_i^r is the random variable r for an observation i. The probability that this variable takes on the value x is conditional on whatever follows the slash, the outcome of the random number generator R for this observation, and a set of constraints that restrict the outcome of the process. Further, a distinction can be made concerning the organization of the system at hand. In a contingency form the observations are organized in aggregate form in a multiway table. But if the number of variables is very large the number of cells in the contingency table becomes intractable. For instance, a table with 5 variables each having 4 categories contains 1024 cells. Moreover, continuous variables cannot be handled in a contingency table without the loss of much information. So a complete list of all elements in the system, or alternatively a representative sample with weights attached to every observation can be more efficient in many situations. The model reads the list element by element and calculates the outcomes x based on a set of exogenous probabilities. The following example, taken from Galler (1984), provides some insight into the usefulness of the method for household modelling.

The example presented below has been developed in Frankfurt in the seventies and the eighties by Galler and his colleagues. It simulates household formation and dissolution in a listwise approach. Figure 3.1 gives the overall structure of the model. In block I, transition probabilities are assigned to all individuals in the system. The following processes are taken into account : (1) ageing, (2) mortality, (3) transitions to and from institutions, (4) divorces, (5) selection of marriage candidates, and (6) children leaving home. All events are stochastic except the ageing process. The probabilities are conditional on person characteristics, for example age, sex, marital status and other relevant variables. No actual changes take place. A flag is set for every individual who will make a transition.

In the second block the households are reorganized. The households are split up according to the process outcomes in the first block and new households are being formed. However, for a two person household, the combined decision of two persons is necessary for the event to take place, and therefore the candidates for a couple enter the so-called marriage market in block III.

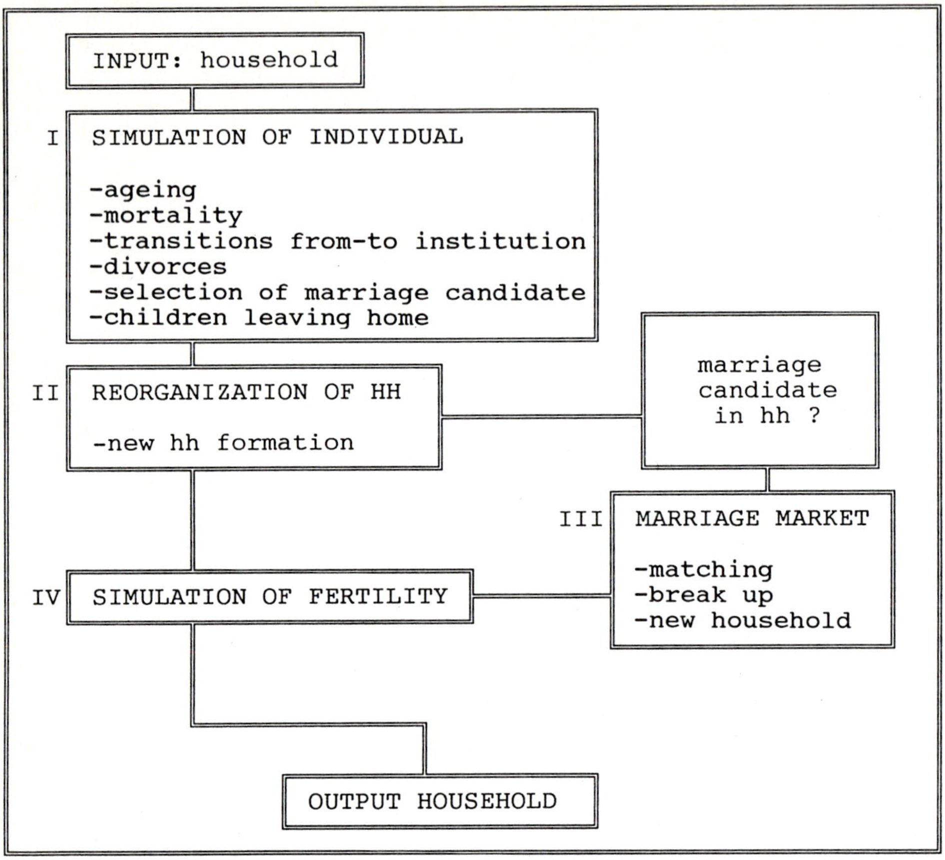

Figure 3.1. Basic structure of Galler's microsimulation model

The event of forming a two-person household starts with the woman searching for a male partner. The outcome of this process is conditional upon age, occupational status and marital status (no unmarried couples can be formed in the present formulation of the model but this can easily be incorporated).

After the new households and singles have been formed, all households enter block IV where the fertility is modelled for every household. This is the final step of the simulation and the list of transformed individuals in the new household situation is written out.

While there are virtually no modelling constraints on the inclusion of more and complex causal relationships, the bottleneck associated with this approach is the data itself. The intensities of the various transition processes have to be set in advance and, as is the case with the macro-simulation PRIMOS model, good judgement and plausible assumptions have to fill the gap in data resources. Here too, a longitudinal survey can provide much of the missing information. These types of surveys have recently become available. Examples are the ORIN-project in the Netherlands (Klijzing, 1984), the Bielefeld project in Germany (Kaufmann et al., 1982) and the OPCS longitudinal study in England (Brown and Fox, 1984). Another possibility is the estimation of missing data. This approach is followed by Wegener (1983) in his urban model of Dortmund, that includes a microsimulation model for household development (see also Chapter 6).

3.7 Multistate Demography

The exposition of the ordinary life table approach in section 3.2 makes it clear that the nature of the household formation process is more complicated than can be handled by this decremental method. People can enter and leave various stages in the life cycle in the course of their life and this is accompanied by various household situations. Typical of these processes is that they are two-way: a single may become part of a couple, but may -after splitting up- re-enter the single state again. Next, he or she can rejoin.

In the seventies new methods were developed in order to cope with the multidimensionality of many demographic processes. Rogers (1973a, 1973b, 1975) generalized the single decrement life table to the multiregional case, using matrix algebra. At the same time new methods were developed by Schoen and Nelson (1974), and Schoen (1975) in the same direction, but with a different methodology. Schoen showed how explicit analytical solutions could be derived in increment-decrement life tables where the number of tables is two or three. However, Rogers and Ledent (1975, 1976) showed that this approach, although different in some respects, was highly similar to their lucid matrix method. Ledent (1980) showed that the matrix notation leads to equivalent formulae as in the single decrement case, using vectors and matrices rather than scalars. Recent contributions on estimation of these tables come from Willekens and Drewe (1984) and Gill and Keilman (1987).

Multistate life tables have been applied in various fields of demography and in related fields like labour force participation (Willekens, 1980). In demography the applications include the analysis of marital status tables (Willekens, 1980, Espenshade, 1983, for instance), interregional migration (Rogers, 1973, 1975), and the analysis of the family life cycle and household modelling. Contributions in this field come from Glick (1977), Ryder (1977), Bongaarts (1983a, 1983b) and Brass (1983). Kuysten (1984) has applied this method in the Dutch context.

In this subsection an introduction to multistate demography is presented. Since the multistate demographic model will be applied in the Amsterdam context, the detailed treatment of the methodology is deferred until Chapter 7.

In multistate demography, or increment-decrement life table analysis, a cohort is followed as it moves from the initial state through a number of intermediate and intercommunicating states towards the absorbing state of death. The initial state is single, and from there a transition is possible to either the married state or death. In the married state a transition is possible to either single or death. This example is a simplified marital status life table. Espenshade (1983) and Willekens (1980) define four states before death, i.e. never married, presently married, divorced and widowed (figure 3.2).

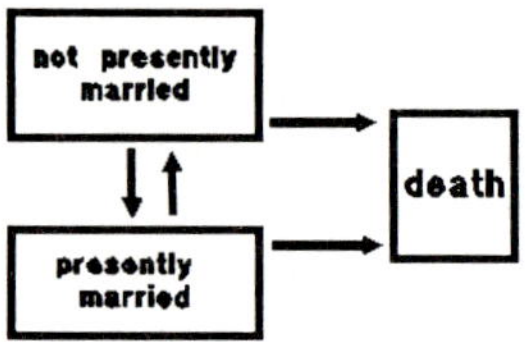

Figure 3.2. A simplified marital status table

Although the process is multidimensional, there exist many similarities with the single decrement life table, as shown by Ledent (1980). First, for every transition, a rate can be defined, equivalent to the 'force of mortality' in the ordinary case. So we can define $\mu_{ij}(x)$ as the instantaneous rate of transition from state i to state j, for a person of age x. These rates are the 'force of mobility' between states. For every state a transition is possible to the state of death, denoted as $\mu_{id}(x)$. Note that state-specific death rates are possible. The set of rates $\{\mu_{ij}\}$ can be organized in matrix notation as follows :

$$\mu(x) = \begin{bmatrix} \mu^*_{11}(x) & \mu_{12}(x) & .. & .. & .. & \mu_{1I}(x) \\ \mu_{21}(x) & \mu^*_{22}(x) & .. & .. & .. & .. \\ .. & .. & .. & .. & .. & .. \\ .. & .. & .. & \mu^*_{ii}(x) & .. & .. \\ .. & .. & .. & .. & .. & .. \\ .. & .. & .. & .. & .. & .. \\ .. & .. & .. & .. & .. & .. \\ \mu_{I1}(x) & .. & .. & .. & .. & \mu^*_{II}(x) \end{bmatrix} \qquad (3.21)$$

The diagonal elements $\mu^*_{ii}(x)$ denote the total force of mobility out of state i, whereas the off-diagonal elements contain the force of mobility from state i to j $\mu_{ij}(x)$ multiplied by -1. The diagonal elements are defined as:

$$\mu^*_{ii}(x) = \Sigma_{k \neq i}\ \mu_{ik}(x) + \mu_{id}(x) \qquad (3.22)$$

The matrix of rates can be used to estimate the matrix of transition probabilities between the states **P**(x). Similar to the single case, but with matrices replacing scalars **P** can be defined as the set of probabilities that a person alive in state i at age x will be in state j h years later, i.e. at age x+h. Once the transition probabilities have been derived, a number of useful descriptive statistics can be derived related to duration in states and future life expectancy of cohorts.

The input for the model is a matrix of transition rates per age cohort x: $\mu(x)$. With respect to these rates a movement and a transition approach can be followed, depending on the data availability (Ledent, 1980). In the transition approach, the state of an individual is known at consecutive points in time. In a movement approach, the actual events of transition are reported. The choice of method depends on the data at hand. The transition approach is less prone to implementation problems. A basic requisite for the transition approach is that the time span between two points in time is not too long to allow recurrent moves between states. According to Ledent, even a 5-year period is short enough for the transition approach for many demographic events.

3.8 Evaluation

Table 3.3 gives the most relevant characteristics in the present context of the methods discussed in this chapter. The methods are variously characterized by their name or, in the absence of a name, by the place of origin. For some models the range of applications is so wide that no reference is made. These are indicated by an asterisk. For other methods, only a few relevant references are given. The text usually gives more. The distinction between Demography and Housing is sometimes somewhat arbitrary. Some methods, currently in use for purely demographic purposes could be adjusted to give relevant information on housing categories. This is especially true for multistate demographic models. The range of applications is in principle unlimited and depends on the system state definition. If rates are available, a multistate demographic household model can be used in a housing market context.

The multistate life table is in principle a very useful device for studying the household development process. Developed only 10 years ago it is the most elegant and sophisticated technique that can be used at the micro scale. Applications have been mainly in the field of the family life cycle, where one can rely on vital statistical data on fertility, mortality, and marriage. In previous subsections it was concluded that this approach is not fruitful in modelling households in Amsterdam. The family approach offers only a partial picture of the total 'household life cycle'. Therefore the applicability of multistate demography in household dynamics hinges on the availability of data. Like other micro oriented models these data requirements are large, and in the absence of census information various complementary assumptions and data estimation techniques have to be used. However, a longitudinal survey can provide rates that cannot be observed in a cross-sectional survey. If such a data source is available, the choice of a multistate model is no doubt a good strategy for household modelling on a micro scale.

The level of analysis in all the models presented has been the individual. In general, this seems to be a good research strategy (Willekens, 1984; see however Webber, 1983, for a counter-example and the discussion in Chapter 7). The transition probabilities can be derived from the individual basis, and the consequences for the household level can be derived through an aggregation scheme, such as the household composition matrix. This seems a fruitful modelling strategy for the present study and the consequences of this strategy will be worked out in Chapter 7. All problems concerning the individual-household dichotomy are not solved however. It can be argued that the household is the decision unit in many instances, and the household decision process is something other then just the sum of the individual decisions. This will probably be one of the future major research topics in household demography in years to come.

This concludes the survey of demographic household models. The emphasis so far has only been on the demographic aspects of the modelling approaches. In order to incorporate a dynamic household model in a housing market framework we have to look at the impact of these processes on the housing market. The next chapter provides this link between demography and housing market behaviour of households.

Method	Applications	Scale	Structure/ Process	Analytical/ Simulation	Demographic/ Housing
1.Ratio	*	macro	structure	analytical	demographic
2.Vital Statistics	*	macro	process	analytical	demographic
3.Headship Rates	*	macro	structure	analytical	both
4.Ordinary Life Table	*	macro	process	analytical	demographic
5.Household Composition Matrix	Akkerman (1980,1982, 1985)	macro	structure	analytical	demographic
6.Swedish Model	Hårsman & Marksjo(1977) Hårsman & Snickars(1983)	macro	process	analytical	housing
7.PRIMOS	Gordijn & Heida (1985)	macro	process	simulation	housing
8.Micro-Simulation	Galler (1987)	micro	process	simulation	demographic
9.Multistate Demography	Willekens (1980,1982); Espenshade (1983); Kuysten(1987); van Dam & Keilman(1987)	micro	process	analytical	demographic

Table 3.3. An overview of household models and their characteristics

CHAPTER 4. HOUSING MARKET MODELS

4.0 Introduction

Analysing and modelling the housing market have become very popular in the past decades. Starting with the seminal work of Alonso (1964), Muth (1969) and Wilson (1970), a large variety of models related to the activities and choices on the housing market has been developed. These models can be distinguished into three main research areas (see also table 4.1):

(1) models concentrating on the study of residential mobility
(2) models concentrating on housing location
(3) models trying to link the first two research fields (relocation models)

Several modelling strategies have been used such as LP-models (Herbert and Stevens, 1960), gravity and entropy models (see for instance Wilson, 1970), log-linear models (Willekens, 1983, Scholten, 1984, and Veldhuisen, 1985), and discrete choice or random utility models (see inter alia, McFadden, 1978; Quigley, 1978; van Lierop, 1985; Fischer and Nijkamp, 1987). These models have different viewpoints and characteristics in terms of level of sophistication, policy-orientation, micro- or macro-based level of aggregation, dynamic or static character, etc.

	Level of household aggregation					
	Macro (Aggregate)				Micro (Disaggregate)	
	Statistical	Heuristic/ entropy-gravity	Economic equilibrium	Disaggregate behavioral input	Statistical	Behavioral
Mobility	Moore, 1969 Simmons, 1974				Huff & Clark, 1978 Clark, Huff & Burt, 1978 Dieleman, 1983	Wolpert, 1965 Brown & Moore, 1970 Goodman, 1976 Hanushek & Quigley, 1978a Weibull, 1978
Location		Wilson 1970	Herbert & Stevens, 1960	Porell, 1982	Segal, 1979	Alonso, 1964 McFadden, 1978 Kain et al., 1976 Muth, 1969 Pollakowski, 1982
Sequential/ simultaneous mobility and location			Anas, 1982 Porell, 1982 Ingram et al., 1972	Wegener, 1980		Porell, 1982 Van Lierop & Rima, 1982 Smith & Clark, 1982 De Palma & Ben-Akiva, 1981 Onaka & Clark, 1983

Table 4.1. A classification of methods for analysing the housing market (source: Clark and Van Lierop, 1986)

No attempt is made here to provide an exhaustive enumeration of residential mobility and location models (overviews can be found in Clark, 1982, and Clark and Van Lierop, 1986). For a number of reasons residential mobility and (re)location cannot be studied separately. First, it can be argued that the reasons for a move are given not only in terms of push, but also in terms of pull factors, being a function of the attractiveness of the possible destinations. Second, whether a move actually takes place depends on the market stress in the possible destination market segments. Finally, a move out of a dwelling usually creates a vacancy, thus influencing the market supply of a specific submarket in a specific zone; as a consequence, the probability of a move taking place to that specific zone and submarket will increase. So, out- and immigrations are linked through a so-called vacancy chain. At a macro level this is reflected in a high correlation between zonal out- and immigration (see e.g. Simmons, 1968).

From these motivations, it is also clear that the distinction between housing market preferences and actual behaviour is relevant, especially in supply-oriented markets, such as the Dutch housing market. Therefore both the willingness to move and the actual move towards a specific zone (spatial allocation) and housing type (dwelling choice) will be modelled in our housing market model (see Chapter 8). So the description of models in this chapter is restricted to subclass (3) of housing market models i.e., having both a mobility and a (re)location component.

The present chapter is organised as follows. In section 4.1 a number of model characteristics is discussed, which will be used in the actual description of the models in section 4.2. In section 4.3 two planning models are described briefly that were developed in the Netherlands and have contributed to the growing interest in housing market modelling in the Netherlands. These models will be evaluated in section 4.4 in relation to the housing market model developed in chapters 7-9.

4.1 Characteristics of Housing Market Models

In this section a number of characteristics of housing market models is presented, with special emphasis on those characteristics which are relevant for the development of the housing market model (see Chapter 1).

As mentioned before we will restrict our analysis of housing market models to those models which deal with both household mobility and household location. Furthermore, attention is restricted to zonal housing market models, i.e., models taking into account migration between a certain number of zones. As can be seen in figure 4.1 a link can be established at different aggregation levels.

For the description of models in section 4.2 we will distinguish between the following three levels:

- macro level with macro input
- macro level with micro (behavioural) input
- micro level

Housing market models can be dynamic or static. Here dynamic models have a general formulation: they can occur either through differential or difference equations or through the use of different time periods and time series.

Another distinction can be made between theoretically- and empirically-oriented models. A theoretical model is defined as a model that mainly concentrates on theories, while its empirical use is mainly restricted to a simplified application for the purpose of understanding the model features. A model which is built mainly for its use in describing and simulating real world phenomena, both in scientific and in policy analysis, is called an empirically oriented model.

The models of section 4.2 all incorporate behavioural elements in estimating the demand for housing, and they will be distinguished by the model approach used (adopted from Clark and Van Lierop, 1986):

- linear programming
- gravity and entropy
- discrete choice and random utility models (logit and probit)
- micro-simulation

In section 4.2. a short description is given of the third subclass of models mentioned in table 4.1.

4.2 Description of Existing Housing Market Models

In this section a (non-exhaustive) number of housing market models which incorporate household mobility as well as household location, will be described with respect to the characteristics mentioned in section 4.1.

Ingram, et al.

The Urban Simulation Model of Ingram et al. (1972) is the first comprehensive model which incorporates mobility and location. In the movers submodel a movers pool of households is generated. This movers pool consists of intrametropolitan movers, new households, and migrants from other regions. The movers pool is allocated to dwelling types in the demand allocation submodel. Finally, in the market clearing submodel the movers pool (and their dwelling types) are assigned to the supply per dwelling type, using a linear programming model with minimising transportation costs. Although the model is a long-run equilibrium model, it is considered to be a dynamic model, since household and housing market characteristics are modified each time period, and discrepancies between supply and demand can be visualized. Movers are generated on the basis of historical mobility rates by household types and are not based on changing household characteristics (it is a macro model with macro input). The model is clearly empirically-oriented, with a large variety of dwelling and household types, and it has been applied to various study areas, such as St. Louis, San Francisco, and Pittsburgh (for an overview see Kain and Quigley, 1975).

Although the model has some serious limitations (such as the independence between the movers submodel and the allocation submodel), it has been of vital importance to the development of integrated housing market models and an example for many of the models described below.

Porell

The model developed by Porell (1982) is called "a short-run model of intra-urban residential relocation". "The model is founded on the rational behaviour of households seeking to maximize utility in their choice of housing consumption" (Porell, 1982, pp. 59-60) (so it is clearly a macro level model with micro input). It is called a short-run model because it is based upon the concept of short-run static equilibrium. "The short run is defined as a period of time that is sufficiently long for price shifts to act as an balancing mechanism, yet sufficiently short so that housing suppliers may not adjust housing services to long-run equilibrium levels. The housing stock is assumed fixed throughout the time period under consideration" (Porell, 1982, p. 64). The housing market is divided into M submarkets (depending on dwelling type and geographical characteristics), and households are stratified into K homogeneous classes. Using the multinomial logit model, demand functions for the M submarkets are estimated.

The advantage of the model compared with the previous developed models of long-run equilibrium (of inter alia Ingram et al., 1972; Kain and Quigley, 1975) is that in the short-run the assumption of complete adjustment of the housing stock can be dropped and that relocation costs can be incorporated. A disadvantage, however, is that the system of residential submarkets is treated as a stable and closed system. Dynamics of households such as household formations, household dissolutions, immigration, outmigration, and dynamics on the housing market such as building and withdrawal of dwellings, are not considered: both the stock of housing and households is kept constant.

The empirical part of the model is devoted to Wichita, Kansas, divided into 13 spatial units. Although policy implications can be drawn from the empirical results, we prefer to call the model theoretical since the application faces some major problems which will influence the outcomes (for instance, by not taking into account owners of dwellings).

Anas

The model of Anas (CATLAS) is one of the earliest examples of a macro model with micro input. The strength of the model is its completeness in modelling the urban economy, and the sophisticated way of model building. "CATLAS is an economic urban simulation model primarily intended for testing the effects of transportation policies on housing and land values, on residential land development and on mode choice patterns" (Anas and Duann, 1983). Although the original model (Anas, 1982) is static, afterwards some attempts have been made to incorporate dynamics (Anas and Duann, 1983). The housing demand is estimated by means of a nested multinomial logit model. However, the estimation of the parameters is not based on individual or household interviews, but on aggregated data. Prices play an important role in the market clearing submodel. This price concept cannot be used in a restricted housing market, like that in Amsterdam, since rents are determined exogenously and not as the result of a free market mechanism (see also Chapter 2).

The impact of demographic changes of households on the housing market is underestimated in the model. Due to its thorough theoretical underpinning and extensive use of its applications in policy and planning, it is difficult to judge this model to be either theoretically- or empirically-oriented. The model has been applied to the Chicago SMSA, divided in almost 5,000 zones, but also recently for the Stockholm area. This model for the Stockholm area is described separately in the next subsection.

Anas and Cho

Models of housing market behaviour in regulated markets are scarce. Recently, Anas and Cho (1986) have worked out a micro-economic dynamic model for the Swedish housing market (i.e. a macro model with micro input), combining previous work of Weibull (1983) with the mathematical framework of the Chicago-model. The model, which is empirically oriented, distinguishes between three submarkets, viz. a free submarket, a 'semi-regulated' submarket and a 'fully regulated' submarket. Free buying and selling by homeowners, black markets, rationing, queues and swaps are also included in the model. In a number of annual runs short term equilibria are attained by equating effective demands with effective supplies.

The demand and supply functions are, as in the Chicago model, specified in the form of random utility maximizing behaviour (using a multinomial logit model). Free market prices, side payments, black money premiums and shadow prices in the regulated market are the endogenous determined variables in the model. A preliminary version of the model was calibrated using partial real, partial 'guestimated' data collected for the Stockholm region.

There is no doubt that this is the most rich and advanced model for dynamic analysis of the housing market nowadays. A number of important phenomena typical for regulated markets are comprehensively formalized together into one model structure for the first time. It is to be expected that this model will be applied in other contexts as well. However, the model is still in an experimental phase, due to severe data requirements. A spatial element is not included, but this would make the data-problems probably prohibitive. Although the Swedish market is in many respects similar to the Dutch, the model should be adjusted to fit in the Amsterdam situation.

<u>Wegener</u>

Originally the model of Wegener is based on Monte Carlo Simulation (see for instance, Wegener, 1983), but the micro simulation is driven by logit choice functions. Thus, although the probabilities are not derived from observed choice frequencies, we classify the model as a <u>logit model</u>. The model has been applied to the Dortmund region (30 zones) for a large variety of policy questions, and is one of the few urban housing market models which is both theoretically well developed and has been applied in real world situations. The migration model is household based, since it is taken for granted that migration decisions are not made by individual household members but usually by the household as a whole. Household dynamics are modelled by a Markov type of transition model driven by household-based transition rates. These rates are aggregated from person-based events (such as marriage, birth, etc.) occurring to individual household members. <u>Dynamic</u> patterns are incorporated through an updating of all variables in the Aging Submodel. Both the supply and demand side of the housing market are modelled at a <u>macro level with micro input</u>.

The housing market model developed in our chapters 7-9 can to some extent be seen as an extension of the Dortmund model (see also section 4.3), in which both the household model and the housing demand model are expanded to deal with more realistic assumptions regarding demographic changes and household behaviour. The model concept developed by Wegener has become very popular nowadays in <u>empirical</u> urban housing market modelling, and 'improved' versions of the model are now also being applied to Vienna (Fischer and Aufhauser, 1986) and to the Netherlands (Dekker et al., 1985).

<u>De Palma and Ben-Akiva, Clark and Onaka, Van Lierop</u>

We will discuss De Palma and Ben-Akiva's (1984) model, also Clark and Onaka's (1985) and Van Lierop's (1986) in one subsection because they show much resemblance. All three models use a nested logit approach (see Chapter 8 for a detailed description of the nested logit model) in a dynamic framework for the estimation of housing demand.

In the nested structure the decision to move, the zonal decision and the dwelling type decision are taken into account (see figure 4.1).

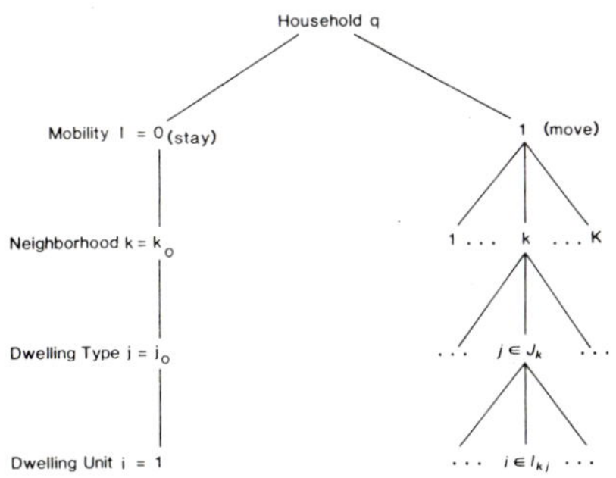

Figure 4.1. The decision structure in the nested logit approach for housing demand (adopted from Clark and Onaka, 1985)

All three models are mainly theoretically-oriented and have been applied only at a limited scale (the model of Onaka and Clark has been applied for St. Joseph County, using the HASE data). A major drawback of these models is that they remain at the micro level, which implies that for instance more general conclusions with respect to the relation between supply and demand cannot be drawn. However, for the description of the demand side of the housing market these models are very promising.

An alternative for the nested logit approach is given by Van Lierop (1986) by means of the multinomial probit model, applied to the housing market in the Netherlands. Although the probit model has some theoretical advantages (see Chapter 8), the computational problems are not solved yet and the costs are so far too high to use the model for disaggregate model building with many different household types, dwelling types and zones.

4.3 Applied Residential Location Models in the Netherlands

Two Dutch examples of housing market models will be discussed in this section since they have played and still play an important role in the development of housing market policy in the Netherlands. The first model to be discussed was developed by Veldhuisen and Kapoen (1977) for the Region Eindhoven and the second is the model developed by Floor and De Jong (1981) for the Amersfoort Region. Both models are planning models, with an emphasis on application of existing theories and methods.

Veldhuisen and Kapoen

The aim of this model is to formulate a planning model for residential location and the testing of the underlying theory by applying it in a real world situation. The model developed is comprehensive. It includes a demographic submodel that predicts total population and external migration using a cohort-survival method, and various subsystems, including households, jobs, transportation and housing. A distinction is also made between housing preferences and allocation. Housing preferences of households are determined by the journey to work and by the attractiveness of the residential zone and the dwelling. The total mover pool of relocating households consists of new households who enter the market and potential mobile households who want to move to another dwelling. New households are calculated from the change in population in the total region in the prediction interval using suitable ratios collected from census data. Potential mobile households are generated from the total household stock by applying sample percentages per household group and zone previously observed in the area. Housing opportunities are generated through new housing construction and household relocation. The total number of household dissolutions and housing demolitions are also taken into account. In a series of rounds demand and supply are matched, until all demand is allocated. The highest income group is allocated first, the lowest income group last. A number of additional allocation rules are specified to guarantee that demand and supply match in all submarkets.

Despite the comprehensiveness of the model the methodologies used in the various submodels are fairly simple and sometimes have an ad hoc character. Demand and allocation are totally deterministic and lack an explicit utility framework. Due to this partially ad hoc character and data availability problems it remains unclear whether the model could be transferred successfully to other housing markets.

Floor and De Jong

Although this model does not include a residential mobility component it is included in this chapter because the model has become popular in the Netherlands for modelling household allocation. The model is less comprehensive than Veldhuisen and Kapoen's model. It does not include demography nor distinguish between housing preferences and allocation. The aim of the development of this model was the application of geographical theories and methods in regional planning. The model developed is an extended version of Wilson's (1970) 'family of spatial interaction models'. It also incorporates some elements of economic housing market models. The introduction of changes in job and dwelling makes the model 'quasi dynamic'. Following Wilson's argument, four types of households are distinguished:

- households seeking both a job and a dwelling
- households seeking a job
- households seeking a dwelling
- households seeking neither a job or a dwelling

As in Veldhuisen and Kapoen's model, allocation of households is determined by the distribution of workplaces over the zones. Other key factors influencing the allocation of the population are the mean family size and the activity ratio (the share of workers in the total population). Since these variables are not homogeneous over the population a disaggregation is necessary by household type. This results in group specific models, with common constraints on the total number of dwellings and workplaces, since they compete on the same housing and job market.

The total number of dwellings available for each group is determined somewhat similar to the Veldhuisen and Kapoen model. New housing construction is divided in free market, subsidized owner-occupier market and council housing. Households are allocated to the available supply using a number of deterministic rules that gives the highest socio-economic group the first choice over the expensive dwellings, next the second socio-economic group over the remaining dwellings. The model was applied to the Amersfoort Region and to Leeds.
A basic drawback of this type of model is that the distinction of the total population in the four types of households on the basis of work- and housing changes is exogenous to the model. Furthermore, two or more income households do not fit satisfactory in this framework. Residential mobility is not included, nor workplace mobility. The model only predicts transitions from one zone to another for those who change house or job. This limits the usefulness of this model for prediction purposes.

4.4 Evaluation

In table 4.2 an overview of the characteristics mentioned in section 4.1 for the different models described in section 4.2 and section 4.3 together with those of the housing market model for the Amsterdam Region is given.

The table provides a summary overview of the models presented. The Amsterdam model make use of various elements of existing models. This will be elaborated in more detail in Chapter 5. A model-concept based on price-mechanism (as most models developed in the USA) cannot be used for our purpose. In highly institutionalized housing markets the concept of a mover pool of potential demand based on preferences and allocation through a market clearing process is more suitable.

In view of the goals defined in Chapter 1 the characteristics of existing relocation models have been analysed, and the most appealing features of the models have been used for our housing market model. In this respect, use has been made, for instance, of the accounting framework of submodels developed by Ingram, et al., and of the behavioural underpinning of household decisions and the division of the households and dwellings into classes used by Porell. From Anas the concept of linking micro behaviour and macro implications is borrowed. As mentioned before, a number of model elements has been adopted from the model of Wegener, such as the concept of the occupancy matrix of households to dwellings. Following De Palma and Ben-Akiva, Onaka and Clark and Van Lierop, a nested logit model has been chosen for the estimation of the willingness to move of households and the demand per dwelling type and zone.

In combining the advantages of existing models and in avoiding their disadvantages by finding new solutions, a new housing market model has been built which has a consistent theoretical framework and can be used for empirical application as will become clear in the following chapters. A more detailed description of the characteristics of the housing market model developed can be found in Chapter 5.

autor(s)	model	aggregation level	dynamic/ static	theoretical/ empirical	model approach	applied to
Ingram, Kain and Ginn (1972)	the NBER Urban Simulation Model	macro level with macro input	dynamic	empirical	linear programming	St. Louis Pittsburgh
Porell (1982)	a short-run Model of Intraurban Residential Relocation	macro level with micro input	static	theoretical	multinomial logit	Wichita
Anas (1983)	CATLAS	macro level with micro input	dynamic	theoretical and empirical	nested logit	Chicago
Anas and Cho (1986)	a micro-economic dynamic model for the Swedish housing market	macro level with micro input	dynamic	empirical	multinomial	Stockholm
Wegener (1983)	the Dortmund-Model	macro level with micro input	dynamic	theoretical and empirical	logit	Dortmund
De Palma and Ben-Akiva (1984)	a dynamic Residential Location Choice Model with Transaction Costs	micro level	dynamic	theoretical	nested logit	-
Onaka and Clark (1985)	a joint Model of Residential Mobility and Housing Choice	micro level	dynamic	theoretical	nested logit	-
Van Lierop (1986)	a new Model to analyse Residential Choice	micro level	dynamic (static)	theoretical	nested logit (probit)	- (The Netherlands)
Floor and De Jong (1981)	a Residental Allocation Model	macro level	'quasi-dynamic'	empirical	entropy-maximization	Amersfoort, Leeds
Veldhuizen and Kapoen (1977)	a Regional Location Model	macro level with micro input	static	empirical	gravity model; other	Eindhoven
Van Wissen and Rima (1987)	a Household and Housing Market Model for the Amsterdam Region	macro level with micro input	dynamic	empirical	nested logit	Amsterdam region

Table 4.2. A overview of housing market models (including the model for Amsterdam) and their characteristics

Part II
Design and Parameter Estimation

CHAPTER 5. THE HOUSING MARKET MODEL: DESIGN

5.0 Introduction

The main goal of the study is to develop an empirical policy oriented integrated model of household and housing market dynamics in an urban region. Further, it was stressed that the life cycle is the main cause of housing market adjustments within an arban area. The model to be developed in Part II integrates these aspects. The model aims at the simultaneous treatment of household and population dynamics, housing demand behaviour, residential mobility, housing supply and vacancy chains and household relocation within a metropolitan area.

In general two main approaches can be followed for modelling a spatial interaction system such as the housing market, i.e.:

> 'One approach opts for relatively simple models, easy to program and easy to use (for instance, micro-simulation). Their purpose is to obtain a fast overview of entire systems (often including insight into their dynamics). The other approach searches continuously for more adequate models able to take into account as many details of reality as are considered necessary (for instance, by means of disaggregate models of choice). With these models careful attention can be devoted to one subsystem (or even one aspect) of the relevant spatial interaction system, rather than to the overall structure. Both lines of research are useful, the first in assisting policy-making directly, and the second in developing instruments (often in an academic environment) to aid future policy-making. Where ease of use can be provided that last group can also be used more often in direct decision-making'.
> (van Lierop, 1985, p. 61).

This paragraph is quoted because it represents precisely the aim of this project: to combine the advantages of a relatively simple model with those of a complex disaggregate model of choice to establish a model which can directly be used for planning and policy-making.

On the basis of the arguments discussed in Part I, choices were made with respect to the estimation procedure, zonal classifications, definition of households and dwellings. Before turning to the model structure in section 5.2 and 5.3, section 5.1 describes these choices more precisely in view of the main characteristics of the model to be developed, viz.:

- it is <u>dynamic:</u> it serves both to describe and analyse the development of the housing market of Amsterdam from 1971 onwards and to forecast future developments on the housing market

- it is zonal: therefore the existing 11 districts within Amsterdam are chosen and 9 zones in the surroundings of Amsterdam (see figure 5.1);
- it is micro-based: it starts at a disaggregated level in order to incorporate explicit assumptions concerning household behaviour;
- it is operational: given the data available, a combination of estimation and simulation techniques based upon empirical data will be used to explain and forecast the housing market developments.

The operational potential of the model is especially important as it is our aim to construct a realistic housing market model for Amsterdam which can be used for planning and policy strategies. In our view, the current urban housing market models are theoretically well developed, but they exhibit many limitations, causing them to fail in detailed empirical application. The cause is frequently the result of unrealistic assumptions used in the empirical analysis of a city or agglomeration (see Chapter 4). In section 5.2 the global structure of the model is presented. Here, all the submodels are introduced and their relative position and linkages explained. The detailed treatment of the complete accounting framework is given in the next section.

5.1 Definitions Used and Selection of the Study Area

Choice of study area

In addition to the arguments already mentioned in Chapter 1, the decision to build a dynamic model of household relocation for Amsterdam was fortunate for two reasons. Firstly, the municipality of Amsterdam has concentrated more effort in transportation modelling than in housing market models. Although research was undertaken with respect to population forecasts and dwellings needed (see for instance, Projektgroep bevolkingsprojekties, 1984; Werkgroep Koppeling Vastgoed-Bevolking, 1985), an integrated model which predicts in detail the housing needs for various household types per zone and dwelling type does not yet exist. Secondly, a large amount of data is available at the city level. The Amsterdam Bureau of Statistics yearly collects a large number of data concerning the population and housing market. We expected that the data needed to build a dynamic housing market model were available.

Since the housing market of Amsterdam cannot be studied in isolation from the surrounding region (because of both functional and institutional relationships), the housing markets of the other municipalities were also taken into account. Towns were selected because of their relationship with Amsterdam's housing market i.e. large migration flows, satellite towns. On the basis of their geographical location and mutual dependency the municipalities in the region of Amsterdam have been clustered into 9 zones (see figure 5.1).

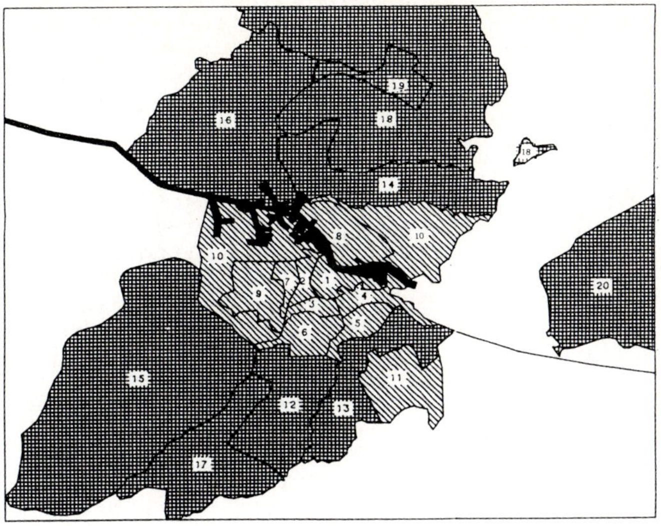

Figure 5.1. The study area divided into 20 zones

Furthermore, for the sake of comparability with other housing market research in the Netherlands one should note that the study area consists of the housing market areas of Amsterdam and the <u>Zuidelijke IJsselmeerpolders</u>, defined by the Ministry of Housing (<u>Ministerie van Volkshuisvesting</u>, 1982). The area under study consists of 20 zones, 11 within Amsterdam and 9 outside Amsterdam (already known as the Region).

Choice of Time Period

The base year 1971 was chosen for the following reasons. In that year a census was held; so a large number of data related to households and dwellings were available. Furthermore, as mentioned in Chapter 2, the seventies experienced a peak in suburbanization (1973), while a reversal of population trends occurred in the eighties resulting in an increase of the population after 1985. This was accompanied by new concepts in migration policy of the municipality of Amsterdam (see also Chapter 2). A period of 14 years (1971-1984) was considered by us to be sufficient to verify our model for the prediction phase for the year 1985 and further.

Choice of Household and Dwelling Types

Demographic developments and migrations are distinct, but interrelated phenomena. The relation between demographic changes of an individual and the behaviour of that individual with regard to the housing market has been the subject matter of much research (see Chapters 3 and 4). However, the decision of this individual cannot be seen independently from the decisions of other individuals with regard to the housing market. In the last decades it was recognized that the basic decision unit in the housing market model is the household (Wegener, 1983; Fisher and Aufhauser, 1986; Clarke et al., 1985). For our purpose, the household is defined as a group of individuals who live together in a dwelling and make a decision to move together. The composition of the household can change at every time period due to, for instance, birth of a child, divorce, marriage. There may be one or two households in a dwelling. In the case of the last situation one household is called the main-tenant of the dwelling, the other the sub-tenant. Also households can be formed and disappear (see Chapter 7 for a more detailed description of definitions related to household dynamics).

The households in the study area are aggregated basically into 24 household types (see table 5.1). This aggregation is based on two major considerations. Firstly, the wish to construct a model which can be updated every year using data from the Bureau of Statistics in Amsterdam. Therefore the aggregation has been established using variables which are regularly available from that source. From the viewpoint of planning and policy-making it is not useful to build a complicated model which uses data such as income of households, rent and (purchase) prices of dwellings, when data on these variables are not collected systematically and regularly. Secondly, using known household characteristics, the households are clustered into classes with significant large numbers and show different behaviour on the housing market (see Chapters 2 and 8).

hh. size / age class	1	2	3	4+
1) <25	1	2	3	4
2) 25-34	5	6	7	8
3) 35-44	9	10	11	12
4) 45-54	13	14	15	16
5) 55-64	17	18	19	20
6) 65+	21	22	23	24

Table 5.1. The definition of the 24 household types

The considerations mentioned above for the aggregation of households are also valid for the classification of the dwellings into 11 dwelling types (table 5.2). In addition a classification is chosen for which the outcomes can be aggregated into policy-relevant classes, such as rented versus owner-occupied dwellings, small apartment buildings versus or large single-family units, etc. Table 5.1 and 5.2 are reproduced on the last page of the book for reference.

The Definition of Demand

In the household relocation model the estimation of the demand per dwelling type and zone plays a major role, while the supply of houses is mainly exogenously determined (see section 5.2). Starting point for the calculation of housing demand is the household's willingness-to-move and its preference for a specific zone and dwelling type. So instead of actual migrations, the intentions of households to migrate are used. The disadvantage of this choice is that the definition of willingness-to-move is ambiguous. Therefore the outcomes of the model must be analysed properly with respect to the definition used. However, an important advantage of using the willingness-to-move is that the potential demand is calculated and therefore the discrepancy between demand and supply can be analysed, while the actual migrations are already the result of the adaption of demand to supply. In case of housing shortage and structural changes during the time period under investigation the calculation of the notional demand is vitally important (see also Turner, 1980). The concept of housing preferences was used for the estimation of notional housing demand.

number of rooms / dwelling characteristics	1 or 2	3	4	5+
rented flats	1	5	6	9
owner occupied flats	2	2	2	2
rented single family units	3	3	7	10
owner occupied single family units	4	4	8	11

Table 5.2. The definition of the 11 dwelling types

Choice of the Estimation Model

As explained in the previous subsection, the willingness-to-move and the household preferences of dwelling types and zones are needed to model housing demand. As will become clear in section 8.1, for various reasons we preferred to estimate the willingness-to-move and household preferences using a member of the class of disaggregated choice models. This family of models consists of the random utility and discrete choice models like the various logit and probit models (McFadden, 1978; Timmermans, 1984; Fisher and Nijkamp, 1986).

Although it can be concluded from the large number of publications in the field of discrete choice models that the multinomial probit model is the most general and therefore the most preferable model from a theoretical point of view (see among others Hensher and Johnson, 1981, p. 182; van Lierop, 1985, p. 94), we will not use the probit model because of the excessively high computer time involved in using this model. Instead we use the multinomial logit model.
One of the properties of the logit model is the so-called independence from irrelevant alternatives choice axiom or IIa-property (see Hensher and Johnson, 1981, p. 135 and further). The meaning of this property is that the probabilities of choice of two alternatives depends only on their measured attractiveness or utility. The independence from irrelevant alternatives is both a weakness and a strength of the logit models. A weakness because the introduction of a new alternative affects the probabilities of the other alternatives proportionally. If the unobserved characteristics of the alternatives are interrelated one would expect that 'similar' alternatives would be affected more than 'nonsimilar' alternatives (in the literature this phenomenon is often referred to as the 'red bus-blue bus' problem). On the other hand it is a strength because the IIa-property implies that the probabilities of selecting a specific alternative is proportional to the utility of that alternative, and thus the decision process can be decomposed into a series of related choices. A justification for choosing the nested logit model from the class of multinomial logit models is given in section 8.1.

As mentioned before, the coefficients estimated with the help of the logit model will be used in the housing demand model. The data samples used in the logit model are too small to estimate coefficients for all 20 zones in the study area. Therefore the coefficients from the Amsterdam model are used for all zones within Amsterdam, and the coefficients from the Region are used for all zones within the Region. This brings us to the issue of transferability of model parameters. The main reason for transferring model parameters from one location to another location (spatial transferability) or from one time period to another time period (temporal transferability) are mainly saving resources like data and computer time. Hensher and Johnson (1981, pp. 214-215) propose a number of procedures to diminish the errors in transferring the parameters. Unfortunately, these procedures cannot be applied in our case, since they require samples of at least 200 observations for every zone and for different periods in time and these samples are not available for Amsterdam and the Region. Studies in transportation (cf. Silman, 1979; Hensher and Johnson, 1981) using the logit model give strong evidence to support the transferability power over short-range planning periods.

Concluding Remarks

Many of the decisions taken with regard to the framework of the housing market model were made on grounds of practicality and based upon the analysis of the history of the Amsterdam housing market and existing household and relocation models. Where possible already developed models and estimation techniques were used. Our practical orientation led us to concentrate our efforts in the collection, transformation and estimation of the data needed (see Chapter 6). We recognize that with respect to zonal choices, dwelling types and other categorizations more or less arbitrary (though justifiable) decisions have been made, which can cause specification errors and biases of the estimated coefficients (see Anas, 1982, p. 121). Deurloo (1987) gives a detailed treatment of the choice of categories in this kind of analyses using the concept of entropy. The analysis of these and other theoretical problems goes beyond the scope of our empirically oriented research.

Although economic data such as income and rent -variables which are not collected on a regular basis- are not incorporated we consider the model to have a social-economic basis. One of the main economic elements in the model is the way in which individual household behaviour is dealt with, i.e. the assumption that households choose the alternative with the maximum utility or attractiveness. Furthermore, social and economic household characteristics are the underpinning of the decisions of households, for instance in a specific age-class.

5.2 The Structure of the Housing Market Model

The general structure of the dynamic household relocation model is depicted in figure 5.2 by means of an accounting framework. An accounting system is a classification of elements in organized series (vectors, matrices). It is sometimes argued that an accounting system is nothing more or less than double-entry book-keeping (see Stone, 1971). Input-output analysis is one of the earliest examples of such a system. The main advantage of an accounting framework is its coherent and consistent representation. The double-line rectangles represent the state matrices at time t; the single-line rectangles represent the models in which the transition matrices are calibrated.

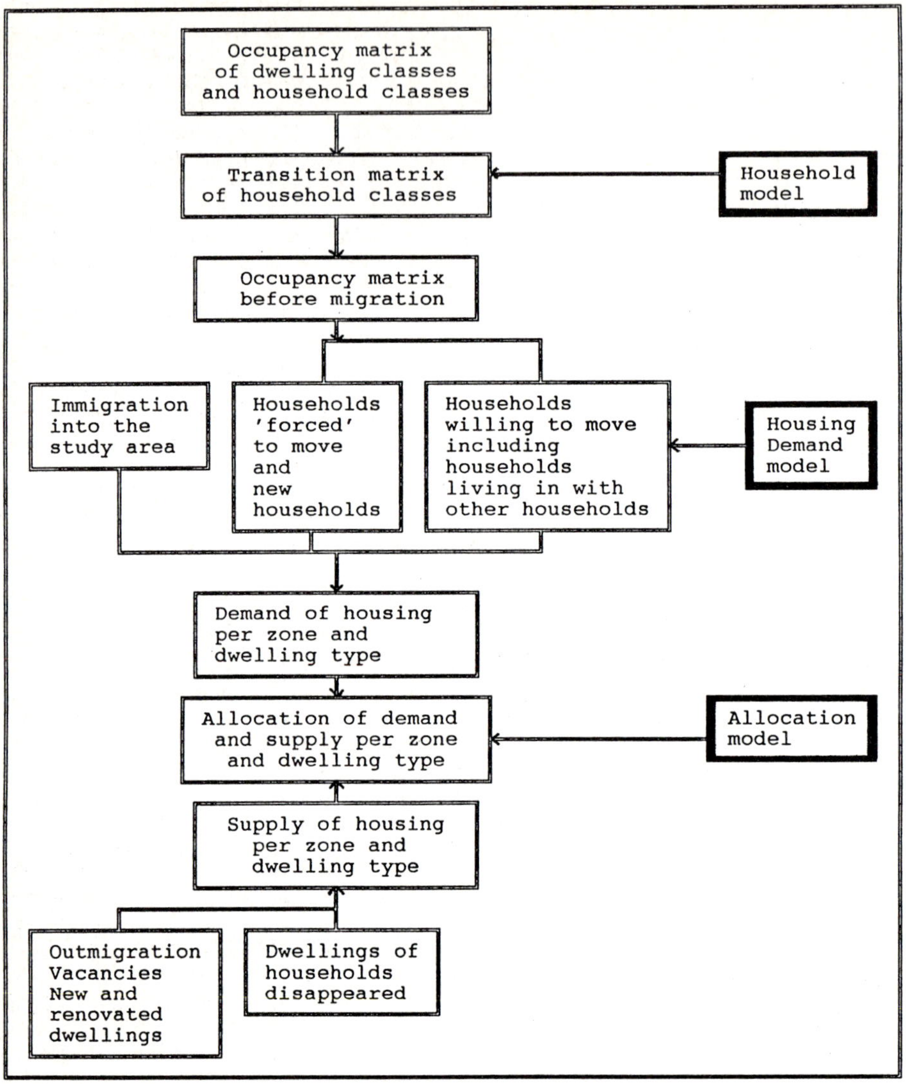

Figure 5.2. Accounting framework for the housing market model

The accounting framework is used for every time period (year) and all 20 zones in the study area. In the final section the detailed structure is presented and every submodel described.

The starting point in every time period t is the occupancy matrix: the number of households per household type and dwelling type. Next, in the household model (see Chapter 7) the transition matrix of household types is modelled. The result is a matrix with cell entries the number of households moving from one household type to another. Multiplication of these two matrices gives the occupancy matrix before migration. This matrix is the major input in the housing demand model (see Chapter 8), in which the potential demand per dwelling type and household type for every zone in the study area is calculated. Finally, in the allocation model (see Chapter 9), housing demand is allocated to the housing supply. The resulting occupancy matrix forms the input for the next time period t+1.

Having described the overall design of the housing market model, we turn to a more detailed treatment of the accounting structure in the next section. Here, the general accounting principles are discussed and the relations between the submodels shown.

5.3 The Detailed Accounting Framework of the Model

Following the scheme set out in the previous section we distinguish between the following phases in the model:

1. The starting configuration of the model in every year at primo year t (the **Occupancy matrix** of households by dwelling type)
2. Demographic changes in population and households that take place between primo and ultimo year t (the **Household model**)
3. The estimation of housing demand related to life cycle, life cycle dynamics and housing situation (the **Housing demand model**)
4. Generation of **Housing Supply**
5. Allocation of housing demand to supply and the estimation of vacancy chains that generate new supply (the **Allocation model**)
6. Updating the changes in households and population in year t to arrive at the situation ultimo year t. This is the starting configuration of the model in year t+1 (the **Accounting rules**)

At the start some indices and symbols have to be introduced. Due to the high level of disaggregation some notational conventions are used throughout this section. They will be introduced below.

Indices

Variables denote either the situation before or after a transition. In the household model the household composition

is adjusted. In the allocation model the dwelling status and place of residence is changed. This is reflected in the notation of the indices. An index without a prime indicates the situation primo year t. A prime over an index indicates the state after transition which equals the situation ultimo year t. A complete list of the categories used in the model can be found in Chapter 5 and in the back of the book.
The following indices are used:

- x is an index of 5-year age categories of persons (x=1,..,14; x=14 denotes persons over 65 of age)
- y is an index of age categories of heads of households (y=1,..,6; with class boundaries 25, 35, 45, 55 and 65)
- s is an index of household size where the highest size class denotes four or more persons in the household (s=1,..,4). Depending on usage, category s=5 denotes household formation (transition from s=5 to s') or dissolution (transition from s to s'=5)
- i is the combined index of s and y (i=1,..,24) denoting household types
- j is an index of dwelling classes. In fact, this is the combined cross-classification of dwelling size g, dwelling type m and tenure category h into 11 dwelling types and a 12th class for the category subtenant. For the present purpose it is sufficient to put these three dimensions into one index j (j=1,..,12)
- z is the zone index (z=1,..,20) with z=1,..,11 denoting zones within Amsterdam and z=12,..,20 denoting zones in the Region
- p is an index over positions in the household (p=1,..,7; with p=1: child; p=2: single; p=3: head 2p household; p=4: head 3p household; p=5: head 4+p household; p=6 partner; p=7: non-household position).

Variables

Variables are represented in the following list of symbols, together with their indices. In general lowercase symbols in boldface indicate variables representing population numbers, and uppercase symbols indicate household variables. There are two exceptions: **K**(x,s,y,z) indicates the population cross-classified by age x, household category (s,y) and zone z; **T**(p,p',x,x') denotes the number of persons in household category p and age x primo year t, who are in household category p' and age x' ultimo year t. **K** corresponds to the **population distribution matrix K** which is described in Chapter 7. **T** is the **population transition matrix** also described in Chapter 7. Another notational convention used here is an aggregation symbol. If **D**(s,y,j,z,j',z') is the number of households of type (s,y) who live in a dwelling of type j in zone z (housing submarket (j,z)) and prefer to move to submarket (j',z') then **D°**(j,z,j',z') is the summation over household types (s,y). So, the symbol ° denotes summation over household categories. Further, **D°°**(z,z') denotes aggregated household preferences over household and dwelling types between zone z and z'. Unless otherwise stated all variables are endogenous. Some variables are **test variables:** these are both observed from census data and predicted by the model. The following list introduces all the variables used in the accounting framework:

A(x,s,y,z) The number of persons of age x who live in a household of size s (s=1,..,4) and age of head y in zone z; is used to link the population by age to the household composition;

Å(x,s,y,z) The **household composition matrix** derived from **A** (see also Chapter 3);

B (s',y',j',z') Internal (originating within the study area) immigration of households type (s',y') into submarket (j',z');

B°(j',z') Internal (originating within the study area) immigration of households into submarket (j',z'); derived through aggregation over origin submarkets from **M°**(j,z,j'z');

b(x,z') Internal population immigration to zone z' by age category; **test variable;**

C(j,z) Internal (i.e. originating within the study area) emigration of households from submarket (j,z); derived through aggregation over destination submarkets from **M°**(j,z,j'z');

c(x,z) Internal population emigration from zone z by age category; **test variable;**

D(s',y',j,j',z,z') The number of households of type (s',y') who live in submarket (j,z) and prefer a dwelling in submarket (j',z');

D°(j,j',z,z') Demand **D**(s',y',j,j',z,z') aggregated over (s',y');

d(x,z) Deaths by age x and zone z

E(s',y',j,z) External emigration of households type (s',y') originating in submarket (j,z);

e(x,z) External population emigration by age x from zone z; exogenous;

E°(j,z) Vacancies in submarket (j',z') through external migration;

F(s',y',j',z') External immigration of households type (s',y') into submarket (j',z');

f(x,z') External population immigration by age x into zone z; exogenous;

G(s,y,z) Household distribution by type (s,y) and zone z (see also Chapter 7); **(partly) test variable;**

H(s',y',z) New household formations by household type (s',y') and zone; derived from **Q**, the occupancy status after household transitions and before migration;

I(j',z') Initial vacancies primo year t in submarket (j',z');

J(s',y',j',z') Total external plus internal immigration of households type (s',y') into zone (j',z');

J°(j',z') Total external plus internal immigration of households into zone (j',z');

K(x,p,z) The population distribution status, denoting the number of persons of age x and are in a household position p in zone z; referred to in Chapter 7 as the **population distribution matrix**;

K*(p′,x′,z) The population distribution matrix after demographic transitions and before migration; derived from **K** and **T**;

l(x,z) Population of age x in zone z primo year t; **test variable**;

M(s′,y′,j,j′,z,z′) Migration flow of households type (s′,y′) who originate in submarket (j,z) and move to a dwelling in submarket (j′,z′);

M°(j,j′,z,z′) Aggregated migration flow **M** over household categories between submarkets;

M°°(z,z′) Aggregated migration flow **M**° over household categories and dwelling types between zones; **test variable**;

N(j′,z′) New housing construction of dwelling types j′ in zone z′; exogenous;

O(s,y,j,z) **Occupancy matrix** of households type (s,y) who live in a dwelling in submarket (j,z);

O°(j,z) total number of households in submarket (j,z) primo year t;

O*(s,s′,y,y′,j,z) Occupation status of households after demographic transitions and before migration of households of type (s′,y′) ultimo year t who were of type (s,y) and live in submarket (j,z) primo year t;

Q(s′,y′,j,z) Number of households of size s′ and age y′ ultimo year t, living in a dwelling in submarket (j,z) wo are willing to move to another dwelling in year t;

R(s,s′,y,y′,z) Number of household transitions in zone z of households of type (s,y) primo year t and of type (s′,z′) ultimo year t; in Chapter 7 referred to as the **Household Projection matrix**;

S(j′,z′) Supply of dwellings through new constructions **N** plus vacancies through outmigration **C** (internal) and **E** (external) plus initial vacancies **I** plus vacancies through household dissolutions **V**°);

$\mathbf{s}_i$ average household size of households of type i; used in the derivation of **Å** from **A**;

T(p,p′,x,x′,z) Probability matrix for zone z of persons age x and position in the household p primo year t to be alive and of age x′in position p′ ultimo year t: the **Individual Transition Table**;

U(s′,y′,j,z) Total demand of households type (s′,y′) originating in submarket (j,z); derived from **Q** and **H**;

U°(j,z) Total aggregated demand **U** over household types originating in submarket (j,z);

V(s,y,j,z) Household dissolutions of type (s,y) in year t and living in submarket (j,z);

V°(j,z) Total number of household dissolutions in submarket (j,z) in year t; also the total number of dwellings available through household dissolution;

W(s',y',j',z') Demand exerted by households type (s',y') for a dwelling in submarket (j',z'); derived from **D** plus **F**;

W°(j',z') Total aggregated demand over household types for dwellings into submarket (j',z');

Z(s,y,j,z) Households of type (s,y) who are forced to move due to housing demolitions in submarket (j,z); derived from **Z°**(j,z);

Z°(j,z) Housing demolitions in submarket (j,z) in year t; exogenous.

Phase One: The initial State of the Model

Starting at the beginning of each year t, we have the occupancy matrix **O**(s,y,j,z), of households classified by household category (s,y) and dwelling type j in zone z. As described above, j is a shorthand notation of the three-dimensional dwelling distribution. Parallel to the household occupancy status we also have the population distribution over ages x and positions in the household p: the population distribution matrix **K**(x,p,z).

On the housing side we have the initial supply **S**(j',z') for every submarket, consisting of new dwellings constructed in year t: **N**(j',z') plus initial vacancies **I**(j',z'). New construction is input for every yearly run of the model and the number of initial vacancies is calculated by the model at the end of the previous year.

Phase Two: Household and Population dynamics

In the model it is assumed that demographic transitions within each year t take place before housing market decisions. This is in line with the assumption stated in Chapter 1 that migration decisions are taken in response to life cycle changes. In reality this will not always be the case. Demographic changes may take place after a move to another dwelling if households anticipate the change. For the situation ultimo year t the order is unimportant but, as will be shown in Chapter 8, for the derivation of housing demand it is crucial to estimate life cycle transitions before housing demand.

Demographic transitions can be evaluated at the population level and at the household level. In Chapter 7 it is shown that household events (transitions) can be derived from individual events, so we start at the population level with the population distribution **K**. The dynamic element is contained in the probabilities **T**(p,p',x,x',z). The elements **T** denote the conditional probability that an individual in zone z aged x with a position in the household p primo year t is alive and aged x' with position in the household p' ultimo year t. The probability of child bearing is also included (with p the position of the mother) and the number of deaths can be calculated from :

$$\mathbf{d}(x,z) = \mathbf{l}(x,z) - \sum_{p,p',x'} \mathbf{T}(p,p',x,x',z) * \mathbf{K}(p,x,z)$$

$$(p,\ p'=1,..,7;\ x,\ x'=1,..,14;\ z=1,..,20) \qquad (5.1)$$

For more information see Chapter 7. Combining **K** and **T** gives the **population distribution matrix** after demographic transitions and before migation:

$$\mathbf{K}^*(p',x',z) = \sum_{p,x} \mathbf{K}(p,x,z) * \mathbf{T}(p,p',x,x',z)$$

$$(p,\ p'=1,..,7;\ x,\ x'=1,..,14;\ z=1,..,20) \qquad (5.2)$$

Individual transitions in position in the household can be translated to household transitions. There are three types of transitions relevant for the household level, viz. (1) transition from a non-head (single or head) to a head position; (2) transition from a head to a non-head position; and (3) transitions between head positions. The first type of transition is a household formation while the second type is a household dissolution (although there are some well defined exceptions to these rules, as will be shown in Chapter 7). The third type of transition is a change in household size of existing households. In Chapter 7 this is described in more detail. These transitions can be aggregated to the household level, resulting in the household projection matrix $\mathbf{R}(s,s',y,y',z)$, with s=1,..,4 denoting heads of households by size primo year t, and s=5 denoting new household formations in year t. Likewise, s'=1,..,4 denotes household size ultimo year t and s'=5 denotes household dissolutions in year t. **R** can be combined with the occupancy matrix **O** to arrive at the occupancy status after demographic transitions and before migration $\mathbf{O}^*$:

$$\mathbf{O}^*(s,s',y,y',j,z) = \mathbf{R}(s,s',y,y',z) * \mathbf{O}(s,y,j,z) \ / \ \mathbf{O}^\circ(j,z)$$

$$(s=1,..,4;\ s'=1,..,5;\ y,\ y'=1,..,6;\ j=1,..,12;\ z=1,..,20) \qquad (5.3)$$

$\mathbf{O}^*$ contains all relevant household information needed in the housing demand model. However, it contains only information about existing households. Two other household groups are also important with respect to housing demand, viz. starting households and dissolving households. The first group can be calculated readily from the household projection matrix **R**, as will be shown in Chapter 7. The size index s indicates both existing households primo year t (s=1,..,4) and new households (s=5). Likewise, s' indicates both existing households ultimo year t (s'=1,..,4) and dissolved households in year t (s'=5). By summing over the relevant cells of **R** we arrive at the table of new households:

$$H(s',y',z) = \sum_y R(5,s',y,y',z)$$

$$(s'=1,4;\ y,\ y'=1,6;\ z=1,..,20) \quad (5.4)$$

Note that here the index y (age of the head of the household primo year t) for new households relates to the age of the person before entering the state of head.
The number of dissolved households **V** can be calculated form O^*, since these households occupy a dwelling at the beginning of year t:

$$V(s,y,j,z) = O^*(s,5,y,y',j,z)$$

$$(s=1,..,4;\ y,y'=1,..,6;\ j=1,..,12;\ z=1,..,20) \quad (5.5)$$

Note that here the index y' (age of the head ultimo year t) relates to the age of the head if the household would still exist. The number of vacancies that are created through household dissolution is simply $V^{\circ}(j,z)$.

Phase Three: The Generation of Housing Demand

The occupancy matrix O^* after demographic transitions and before migration provides all the input for the housing demand model. It contains:

- Household dynamics (s,s')
- present life cycle (s',y')
- dwelling characteristics (j, which includes size, buy/rent and single/multi-family indicators)
- prsent zone of residence

In Chapters 8 and 9 the housing demand model is developed based on these characteristics. In these Chapters parameters are estimated that are related to the probability, or relative frequency of the propensity to relocate and the probability or relative frequency of prefering a dwelling in a specified submarket and zone. If we define the probability for a household to be willing to move as p^M and the probability of prefering a certain dwelling submarket as p^D then the occupancy matrix O^* (and hence O) can be related to housing demand. The generation of Q, the number of households who are willing to move is simply, given p^M :

$$Q(s',y',j,z) = \sum_s \sum_y p^M_{s,s'y',j,z} * O^*(s,s',y,y',j,z)$$

$$(s,s'=1,..,4;\ y,y'=1,..,6;\ j=1,..,12;\ z=1,..,20) \quad (5.6)$$

Note that we sum over s, the original household size so that from now on household characteristics are indexed by their values ultimo year t. Total internal housing demand, originating in submarket (j,z) can now be calculated:

$$\mathbf{U}(s',y',j,z) = \mathbf{Q}(s',y',j,z) + \mathbf{H}(s',y',j,z) + \mathbf{Z}(s',y',j,z) - \mathbf{E}(s',y',j,z)$$

$$(s'=1,..,4;\ y'=1,..,6;\ j=1,..,12;\ z=1,..,20) \quad (5.7)$$

Thus, total internal housing demand equals demand exerted by existing households **Q** plus new household formations **H** plus forced moves through housing demolitions **Z** minus external migrations **E**. $\mathbf{Z}(s',y',j,z)$ is calculated from $\mathbf{Z}°(j,z)$, the number of demolished dwellings in submarket (j,z) in year t. $\mathbf{E}(s',y',j,z)$ is calculated from $\mathbf{e}(x,z)$, the number of out-migrants from zone z by age x (see the last subsection).

Given **U** we can calculate the relative preferences for alternative dwelling submarkets (j',z') by applying the probabilities $\mathbf{p}^D$ to the cells in the table **U**:

$$\mathbf{D}(s',y',j,j',z,z') = \mathbf{p}^D{}_{j'z'/s'y'jz} * \mathbf{U}(s',y',j,z)$$

$$(s'=1,..,4;\ y'=1,..,6;\ j,j'=1,..,12;\ z,z'=1,..,20) \quad (5.8)$$

Note that $\mathbf{p}^D{}_{j'z'/s'y'jz}$ is a conditional probability of preferring submarket (j',z') given (s',y',j,z). As will be shown in Chapter 8 the preferences for the various submarkets are determined, among other things, by the supply in that submarket $\mathbf{S}(j',z')$:

$$\mathbf{p}^D{}_{j'z'/s'y'jz} = \text{Funct}[\ldots.,\ \mathbf{S}(j',z')] \quad (5.9)$$

where Funct[.] is a suitable function (see Chapter 8) and $d\mathbf{p}^M / d\mathbf{S} > 0$. For the allocation within one year this implies that the preferences over the various submarkets change as **S** changes.

The resulting table **D** is a complete origin-destination preference table broken down by household type. Aggregating **D** over household type gives $\mathbf{D}°(j,j',z,z')$ the total number of households who prefer a dwelling in (j',z') and live in (j,z).

Total demand for dwellings in submarket (j',z'), **W** is the sum of internal demand **D** plus external demand **F**:

$$\mathbf{W}(s',y',j',z') = \sum_j \sum_z \mathbf{D}(s',y',j,j',z,z') + \mathbf{F}(s',y',j',z')$$

$$(s'=1,..,4;\ y'=1,..,6;\ j,j'=1,..,12;\ z,z'=1,..,20) \quad (5.10)$$

$\mathbf{F}(s',y',j',z')$ is estimated from $\mathbf{f}(x',z')$, the total number of immigrants from outside the study area into zone z', broken down by age x' (see the last subsection). This completes the accounting framework for the housing demand model.

Phase Four: Generation of Housing Supply

Housing supply **S**(j,z) is the sum of a number of variables:

- new housing construction **N**(j,z)
- initial vacancies at the beginning of year t **I**(j,z)
- vacancies through household dissolutions **V°**(j,z)
- vacancies through external emigration of households **E°**(j,z)
- vacancies through internal emigration of households **C**(j,z)

At the start of year t only **N** and **I** are nonzero. New supply in year t is then generated through vacancy chains in the allocation submodel. A migration movement of an existing household originating in submarket (j,z) creates a vacancy of either type **E°** or type **C**, depending on the destination of the movement.

Phase Five: Housing allocation

Allocation is the matching of total demand **D**(s',y',j,j',z,z') with supply **S**(j',z'). In Chapter 9 the structure of the allocation mechanism is explained. It entails the scaling of total demand for submarket (j',z'): **W**(j',z') with a factor $\alpha_{j'z'}$ such that:

$$\alpha_{j'z'} = \mathrm{Min}[1, \mathbf{S}(j',z') \;/\; \mathbf{W}(j',z')\;] \tag{5.11}$$

Migration flows **M** can then be calculated form the scaled **D**. First, total demand **W** into (j',z') is scaled:

$$\mathbf{J}(s',y',j',z') = \alpha_{j'z'}\; \mathbf{W}(s',y',j,j',z,z') \tag{5.12}$$

W consists of both external and internal demand (**F** + **D**), so external demand **D** is also scaled. On the other hand we have a constraint, viz. the requirement that $\mathbf{F}^{exp} = \mathbf{F}^{obs}$ (or rather: $\mathbf{f}^{exp} = \mathbf{f}^{obs}$ since observed external immigration is on the person level). By giving external immigants priority in the alloction mechanism (see below) this requirement is fulfilled.

The allocation submodel iterates in a number of rounds until the calculated number of internal migration movements $\mathbf{M}^{exp}$ equals the observed number of internal migration movements $\mathbf{M}^{obs}$. In each round new vacancies are generated through **E°** and **C** and thus **S** changes every iteration. From (5.9) it is clear that as a consequence the preference structure changes within one year. This can be interpreted as the household response to the aggregate market situation.

Before the first iteration of the allocation model, supply consists of new construction **N** plus initial vacancies **I**. In the first iteration external outmigration **E** is treated which results in vacancies **E°**. External immigration **F** is exogenous. In order to guarantee a 100 percent allocation of this group they are given priority in the allocation. The same is true for **Z** and **H** (forced moves and starting households). More details concerning the priorities are given in Chapter 10. Iteration stops if $\mathbf{M}^{exp}$ equals $\mathbf{M}^{obs}$. For the accounting framework **M** and **B**, **C**, **E** and **F** are treated as the sum of the allocations over all iterations in year t. This results in **M**(s',y',j,j',z,z'), the complete breakdown of migrating households by type of household (s',y'), origin submarket (j,z) and destination submarket (j',z'). **B**(j,z) and **C**(j,z) are total internal in- and outmigration of households respectively. **F** and **E** are their external counterparts. **B** and **C** and **M** are transformed to population numbers **b**, **c** and **m** respectively. For these figures observed population data are available to test the model outcomes. This test is extensively done in Chapter 10.

Phase Six: Updating Households Dwellings and Population

After demographic transitions and household relocations we arrive at the household and population status at the end of year t. The next accounting rules identify the link between the state ot the system primo and ultimo year t. First the updating of households is treated which is a set of simple accounting equations. Population is slightly more complicated and involves a modelling step. Starting from **O** we have shown how demographic transitions take place to form $\mathbf{O}^*$, the occupancy matrix after demographic transitions and before migration. By adding immigration and subtracting emigration we arrive at **G**(t+1), the household distribution primo year t+1:

$$\mathbf{G}(s',y',z';t+1) = \sum_s \sum_y \sum_{j'} \mathbf{O}^*(s,s',y,y',j',z';t) +$$

$$\sum_{j'} \mathbf{B}(s',y',j',z';t) + \sum_{j'} \mathbf{F}(s',y',j',z';t) -$$

$$\sum_{j'} \mathbf{C}(s',y',j',z';t) + \sum_{j'} \mathbf{E}(s',y',j',z';t) \qquad (5.13)$$

Note that we have added the time-index t and t+1 for clarity. Note also that a prime over an index now relates to the characteristics primo year t+1 (which equals the situation ultimo year t). The occupancy matrix **O**(s',y',j',z';t+1) can be calculated from the same variables $\mathbf{O}^*$, **B**, **C**, **F** and **E** without summing over j'.

The housing stock at the end of year t consists of occupied dwellings plus vacancies. From $\mathbf{O}^*$(t+1) the occupied dwellings can be calculated by summing over household types. Vacancies at the end of year t form the initial vacancies at year t+1: **I**(t+1) and this forms the remaining supply in the last iteration in year t. Let $\mathbf{S}^-$(j',z') be the supply at the beginning of the last iteration in year t, $\mathbf{B}^-$ (j',z') the allocated households into submarket (j',z') in the last iteration and $\mathbf{C}^-$ (j',z') the total allocated outmigration from submarket (j',z'). There is no remaining external migration in the last iteration since these are allocated in the first iterations. Total initial vacancies primo year t+1 is the remaining supply after the last iteration and equals:

$$\mathbf{I}(j',z';t+1) = \mathbf{S}^{-}(j',z') + \mathbf{C}^{-}(j',z') - \mathbf{B}^{-}(j',z') \tag{5.14}$$

Population by age category per zone $\mathbf{l}(x,z)$ can be calculated easily:

$$\mathbf{l}(x',z';t+1) = \sum_{p'} \mathbf{K}^{*}(x',p',z';t) + \mathbf{b}(x',z') + \mathbf{f}(x',z';t) - \mathbf{c}(x',z';t) - \mathbf{e}(x',z';t) \tag{5.15}$$

Finally, the new **population distribution matrix** $\mathbf{K}(x',p',z',t+1)$ has to be calculated. This is not as easy as the previous accounting equations. We have only incomplete information concerning the changes in population by position in the household. From $\mathbf{l}(t+1)$ we have the new population by age and from $\mathbf{G}(t+1)$ we have information about singles and heads by age y, which contains only 6 classes, whereas the population age categories x contain 14 classes. To solve this problem a technique can be used that estimates the most probable table $\mathbf{K}(x',p',z';t+1)$ taking into account all pieces of information that we have from this table. This includes the population age-vector $\mathbf{l}(x',z';t+1)$, which is one marginal total of the table $\mathbf{K}$, and $\mathbf{G}(s',y',z',t+1)$, which constrains 4 * 6 = 24 groups of cells for singles and heads to equal certain values. For instance the household vector $\mathbf{G}$ specifies that the number of heads of two person households in the age category 25 to 34 is 1,000. This means that the sum of persons with position 'head of a two person household' (p=3) and age between 25 and 34 (x=6 and x=7) also equals 1,000. Finally we can add a probability distribution in the estimation that is as close as possible to the table to be estimated (a prior distribution). For our purposes such a table is available. It is simply the population distribution table $\mathbf{K}^{*}$ after demographic changes and before migration. So the missing information on the zonal net change in the number of persons by age and position in the household due to migration flows is estimated by this procedure. In Chapter 6 a technique and a computer program is developed to estimate these tables.

Mathematically, the new **population distribution** $\mathbf{K}(x',p',z';t+1)$ is estimated using $\mathbf{l}(t+1)$, $\mathbf{G}(t+1)$ and $\mathbf{K}^{*}(t)$. To show how this is done we give the formula. For more detailed information concerning the estimation technique the reader is referred to Chapter 6. Before doing so, a slightly different notation is helpful at this point. Let $\mathbf{k}(x,y,p,z)$ be the (unknown) table of persons of 5-year age category x and 10-year age category y (the categorisation used for the heads) who have a position in the household p. It is clear that y is redundant if x is known but it simplifies the notation that follows. Let $\mathbf{l}(x,z)$ be the (known) number of persons in age category x and zone z. Further, let $\mathbf{g}(y,j)$ be the (known) number of people who are in the 10-year age category y (although x is not known) and have position in the household p, where p runs from 3 to 6 (the singles and heads). Finally, let $\mathbf{k}^{*}(x,y,p,z)$ be an observed table of persons by age, position in the household and zone that is 'close' to the table to be estimated. The estimation procedure entails finding multipliers β and γ such that the sum over the cells i of the ratios $\sum_i \mathrm{Log}(\mathbf{k}_i/\mathbf{k}^*_i)$ is as small as possible. This is the Minimum Information principle (see also section 6.2). The estimated multipliers ensure that:

$$\mathbf{k}(x,y,p,z) = \beta_x \gamma_{y\ ,\ p=3\ \mathrm{to}\ 6}\ \mathbf{k}^*(x,y,p,z) \qquad (5.16)$$

is the optimal table in the Minimum Information sense within the set of tables that can be formed given the constraints **l** and **g**.

This completes the description of the accounting framework. In the final subsection the transformation from persons to households is discussed.

From Persons to Households

One step that occurs frequently in the model has not been discussed yet. That is the transformation of persons to households. From households to persons and dwellings is straightforward and need not be discussed here.
In section 3.3 the Akkerman model was introduced. Equation (3.11) gives the mapping of population into households and vice versa using the **Household Composition Matrix A**. For our purposes we use a variant of the household composition matrix that contains persons by age and household type: **A**(x,s,y,z). Following (3.11) we can write:

$$\underline{\mathbf{G}}(z) = \mathbf{\mathring{A}}(z)\ \underline{\mathbf{l}}(z) \qquad (5.17)$$

where $\underline{\mathbf{l}}(z)$ is the population vector for zone z and $\underline{\mathbf{G}}(z)$ the household vector (note that here explicit matrix notation is used). $\mathbf{\mathring{A}}(z)$ is the 14 * 24 household composition matrix for zone z derived from **A**(x,s,y,z), the table of persons by age x and household type. If we denote an element of $\mathbf{\mathring{A}}(z)$ as $\mathbf{\mathring{a}}_{xi}$, where i is the combined index (s,y) of household types, the average household size in household category i as $\mathbf{s}_i$, and an element of $\underline{\mathbf{l}}(z)$ as $\mathbf{l}_x$ then:

$$\mathbf{\mathring{a}}_{xi} = \mathbf{a}_{xi}\ /\ [\mathbf{l}_x * \mathbf{s}_i] \qquad (5.18)$$

gives the entries in the household composition matrix $\mathbf{\mathring{A}}$. If $\underline{\mathbf{l}}$ is known then (5.17) gives an estimate of the household composition $\underline{\mathbf{G}}$. For migration in and out of each zone z this estimate is used to derive households by type from population age distributions. Of course this procedure is only valid under the assumption that the household distribution of migrants is proportional to the household distribution of the resident population. The translation from households to persons is straightforward given a zone specific matrix **A**.

The presentation of the accounting framework in this section has been extensive but can serve as a source of reference when the various submodels are discussed in the next chapters.

CHAPTER 6. DATA NEEDS AND ASSESSMENT OF MISSING INFORMATION

6.0 Introduction

One of the major problems inherent in designing and estimating dynamic disaggregate models is the lack of data. Often the necessary data are only available at one point in time and commonly only available in the form of aggregate totals. For instance, in our case we need a complete breakdown of population by age and by specific types of households, but there are only data available on the age-distribution and for some given household types. Another common situation is the availability of a survey sample that covers all the data needs but which needs to be updated or expanded using census information.

Common solutions to such data problems are to resort to simulation modelling or to aggregate models, while stressing the need for more and better data in the future. Modellers in many fields face similar problems and have developed methods and solutions with varying degrees of success. In transportation science for instance, it is common practice to estimate a complete traffic matrix of origin-destination flows using partial information from screen lines, total zonal trip-production aggregates and survey information. In economic input-output modelling the base-year input-output table is updated for each time-period using aggregate production- and consumption totals, while employing the RAS or IPFP-method (see section 6.2). A third field is migration research (Willekens, 1980; De Jong, 1985). Here, the problem is to estimate migration flows between zones using partial knowledge of total in- and outmigration and some flow characteristics. Given the breadth of experience with these problems and the range and results of the methods which have been applied, there is a priori no reason why such data estimation cannot be used in dynamic household and housing market models.

The aim of this chapter is to describe the information needs of our household relocation model and to discuss in some detail a method for the estimation of missing data in population and household tables. Due to the categorical nature of many variables used in the model, most information is available in (cross-)tabular form. This property leads to the use of models for frequencies (counts). In section 6.1 the information needs of the model are described. The gap between data supply and demand is bridged using an adjusted data estimation method. Section 6.2 contains a short survey of these methods. In section 6.3 a method is introduced that combines most of the advantages of the existing methods. The next two sections (6.4 and 6.5) give some empirical results using the 1971 census information to estimate two important matrices for our model: the household composition matrix and the occupancy matrix. The last section (6.6) contains a short summary and conclusion.

6.1 The Data Needs for the Housing Market Model

Before we give an account of the various forms of data it has to be noted that the model has both a zonal and a temporal component. This means that for every datum x in principle a two-dimensional matrix **X** can be formed, with elements x_{zt}, where z is a zonal index and t is a time indicator. In our case, z runs from 1 to 20, and time runs from 1971 to 1984 and from 1985 to 1999. The various components of the model, that were introduced in Chapter 5, have their own data needs and we shall discuss each of them separately.

For every submodel a basic distinction can be made between non-survey (census) information and survey information. The census information for the base year 1971 is the national census (CBS, 1971) which gives detailed tabular information for every zone in the study area. However, it is not a complete breakdown of all relevant variables. In addition there is yearly information available on a more aggregate level. The amount of information for the city of Amsterdam and the rest of the zones is different, since the central city has its own Census Bureau and a large Planning department which collect their own data sources. The survey information used is of two kinds, i.e. (1) a large cross-sectional one percent sample held in 1981 in the Netherlands on housing needs (WBO, 1981) that contains detailed information on households and housing market characteristics, and (2) a retrospective survey held in 1980 in the Amsterdam region that contains retrospective data on households, housing market and labor market behaviour from the period 1975 - 1980 (NEI, 1982). Although these data were designed for other research projects, they could meaningfully be used for our project to estimate basic model parameters on household transitions and housing demand.

Following the overall model framework introduced in Chapter 5, the data needs can be separated into a number of components corresponding to each model. Each component is discussed separately below.

The Household Submodel

At the heart of the household submodel is the household composition matrix. This matrix was introduced in Chapter 3 and its position in the overall model framework was described in Chapter 5. The household composition matrix is the link between population age structure and household composition, but complete data are not available from the census tables. To estimate this matrix we need information on the age distribution of the total population and on the distribution of households. Also some estimate of the interdependence between age distribution and household structure is required. The population age distribution is available from official records for every year per zone and the household distribution can be observed from the 1971 national census. For the interaction between the two variables the 1981 WBO sample was used. Section 6.5 describes in more detail the structure of the household composition matrix.

Another important element in the household model is the household projection matrix. This concept was introduced in Chapter 5 and is explained in Chapter 7 in more detail. The basic transition probabilities are derived from the retrospective survey but they depend on a number of demographic events, i.e. births, deaths, marriage and divorce (including cohabitation and breaking up of unmarried households) and leaving the parental home to become independent. These events can in principle be derived from official records or estimates and so the estimation problem is then to update the sample transition matrix to be consistent with the exogenous demographic population figures. These demographic figures are available on a yearly basis for every zone.

The Housing Demand Model

In the housing market model the demand side is modelled using the concepts of "willingness to move" and housing preferences. The basic parameters of the demand model are estimated using the housing needs survey of 1981. The retrospective survey 1975 - 1980 allows an estimation of the effect of household transitions on willingness to move (see Chapter 8). In order to aggregate the model outcomes to total demand per market segment the occupancy matrix is used. This matrix, introduced in Chapter 5, is the core of the accounting framework for the model. It is the detailed cross-classification of households by household category and dwelling category. The cell entries of this table are not directly available from published material and so we had to rely on data estimation using the 1971 census tables. This contains the most important bivariate tables for all variables included and these were used to estimate the base year table. Section 6.5 describes the estimation process in more detail. For later years this table can be updated using more aggregate information on household structure and dwelling stock.

The Housing Supply

Housing supply information is composed of data on new construction, housing vacancies and migration outside the study area. For housing construction there is information available on the key variables (size, tenure status and type) on a yearly and zonal basis, but the total cross-classification has to be estimated from these aggregate data. Here, use is made of the WBO sample distribution of new houses. The housing vacancies are endogenous in the model except for the base year 1971. Here, we use the 1971 census data on vacancies and a data estimation method (see section 6.5) to derive detailed figures. The third component, i.e. the migration data to and from the zone are exogenous and are available at an aggregate level. Total external in- and outflow is known from published records per age category and for heads of households, single people and other persons in families. This information can be used to estimate household type and dwelling status at a more detailed level.

The Allocation Model

Virtually every transaction in the housing market involves a move and thus the migration data give a more or less complete (yet aggregate) record of the housing market clearance. The total number of transactions broken down by household category and dwelling status is the final outcome of the model, these figures are validated using the observed migration data. Before validation the model outcomes are aggregated in various ways to be consistent with observed migration data. Thus, these migration data are used solely for validation and no data estimation is performed on these figures. These observed migration data take various forms.

Firstly, there is a total flow matrix between every pair of zones in the region, per year, with Amsterdam aggregated to one zone. This matrix also gives the intra-zonal flows per zone. This means that we do not know the total number of people who move from, for example the centre of Amsterdam (zone 1) to Purmerend (a zone in the Region). But we do know the total number of people who move from Amsterdam as a whole to Purmerend.

At a second level, the total intra-municipal flow matrix between the zones in Amsterdam is known, also for each year. This allows the distinction per zone in Amsterdam between three types of migration, i.e. migration within the same city-zone, migration to other zones in the city, and third, the migration to zones outside Amsterdam. The total flow matrix could be viewed as a block-diagonal matrix with one block containing intra-urban migration and one block containing inter-zonal flows except between the Amsterdam zones. The blocks are related through aggregates of the total flows in the two blocks. Besides this flow information there are data available on the total age-composition and the number of heads of families that in- or outmigrate for every zone in the area.

Given these data needs for the housing market model we now turn to methods for data estimation. In the next section an overview is presented of existing methods.

6.2 Data Estimation Methods: an Overview

The first application of a method for inferring missing data from given marginal totals is due to Kruithof (1937). He estimated telephone communication flows from aggregate information on total incoming and outgoing calls by means of "iterative proportional fitting procedure" (IPFP). This involves finding scalars α_i and β_j such that

$$n_{ij} = \alpha_i \beta_j m_{ij}, \quad (i=1,..,I;\ j=1,..,J) \tag{6.1}$$

are consistent with the marginal totals $\{n_{i.}, n_{.j}\}$. Ireland-Kullback (1968) showed that (6.1) can be derived by minimizing the information statistic $I = \Sigma_i \Sigma_j n_{ij} \log (n_{ij} / m_{ij})$ subject to the marginal constraints and the non-negativity condition.(see also Batten, 1983, p.114). The Fratar method (1954) and the Furness algorithm (1962) are based on the same bi-proportional relation and are frequently used in transportation science.

Another minimization-criterion is the Pearson Chi-square statistic or the modified version $X^2 = \Sigma_i \Sigma_j (n_{ij} - m_{ij})^2 / m_{ij}$. This leads to the function that is used by Stephan (1942):

$$n_{ij} = m_{ij} + \alpha_i m_{i.} + \beta_j m_{.j} \tag{6.2}$$

The RAS method, developed by Stone (1962) is equivalent to the Furness-Fratar method and the doubly constrained model of minimum information gain. It was further developed by Bacharach (1970) and is often used in updating input-output tables for economic research.

In the seventies some new methods were developed independently in regional modeling and in statistics which were closely related. In 1966 the concept of entropy was introduced in spatial analysis by Medvedkov (1966) and shortly afterwards Wilson published a book on the subject (1970). In 1975 some new methods for multivariate discrete data analysis, i.e. loglinear models for analysis of contingency tables, became popular through the work of Bishop et al.(1975). These publications had a different scope but involved both the estimation of interaction models and the prediction of cell frequencies in interaction tables. There are many similarities between the various methods. The equivalence between entropy maximization (EM) and information gain minimization (IGM) is well known (see, among others, Wilson, 1970; Snickars and Weibull, 1977). Nijkamp (1975, p.209) compares linear programming (LP) and EM methods and concludes that the balancing factors (i.e. the Lagrange multipliers of the constrained optimization problem) are related to the dual variables of the LP problem. (see also Nijkamp, 1978). Wilson (1983, p.127) observes that "the LP model can be converted to a corresponding EM model by taking the objective function and converting it to be a constraint but taking a suboptimal value; or vice versa". It appeared that the fitting of loglinear models was also closely related to these methods (Willekens,1980; Batten,1983), although some differences remained. The similarities are obvious if one compares the models for a two-way interaction table $\{T_{ij}\}$ with I rows and J columns.

First we give the standard method of writing the doubly-constrained entropy maximizing model :

$$T_{ij} = A_i B_j O_i D_j F_{ij} \qquad (6.3)$$

where T_{ij} is the expected interaction flow from zone i to zone j, given the model and O_i and D_j are total zonal outflow and inflow respectively. The balancing factors A_i and B_j ensure that the total set $\{T_{ij}\}$ is consistent with the set of marginal totals $\{O_i\}$ and $\{D_j\}$. The term F_{ij} is an interaction function that describes friction of movement from i to j .

The loglinear model for a two-way contingency table is :

$$\log T_{ij} = \mu + \mu_1(i) + \mu_2(j) + \mu_{12}(ij) \qquad (6.4)$$

where $\mu = (\Sigma_{ij} \log T_{ij})/IJ$ is a scaling factor for the table. The terms $\mu_1(i)$ (= $((\Sigma_j \log T_{ij})/J) - \mu$))and $\mu_2(j)$ (= $((\Sigma_i \log T_{ij})/I) - \mu$)) denote the deviation of origin i (destination j) from the grand mean μ . Finally the interaction term $\mu_{12}(ij)$ represents the interaction effect between levels i of O and j of D . It is easily verifiable that the log transformation turns equation (6.3) into (6.4) (see Willekens, 1980, p.188). In fact, $\mu_1(i) \equiv \log A_i O_i$, $\mu_2(j) \equiv \log B_j D_j$ and $\mu_{12}(ij) \equiv \log F_{ij}$.

With regard to the main effects μ_1 and μ_2 (O and D) there is no special reason to prefer one method to the other. From a statistical viewpoint both imply essentially the same result. Some differences occur, however, regarding the interaction term. In the standard saturated loglinear model (6.4) we have as many interaction parameters as there are cells in the table, whereas in an EM model F_{ij} is usually a one- or two-parameter function with unknown coefficients. The standard loglinear model is not capable of estimating these coefficients unless these values are fixed in advance. Incorporating interaction functions in the standard loglinear model is only possible using prior values, but it is questionable whether this is still a function (see also Batten, 1983, p.162). The use of prior values is also typical for IGM methods (see Snickars and Weibull, 1977 for a theoretical account and application of this method) and can be incorporated in EM models without problems. So it can be concluded that the EM or the IGM method is preferable to the standard loglinear model because they can handle more types of interaction functions, including prior values.

In the seventies, however, a new statistical technique for the estimation of (log)linear models was developed. In 1972 Nelder and Wedderburn published a paper on "Generalized Linear Models" (GLM's) and since then this method has become very popular through its implementation in the computer program GLIM. The method is very flexible and captures all kinds of linear models with an error term of the exponential family, including standard loglinear models (see Nelder, 1974; Payne, 1977; McCullagh and Nelder, 1983; Nijkamp et al., 1985). GLM's are models that can include both qualitative terms and quantitative terms ("mixed models") and allow full flexibility in the specification of the main and interaction effects through the use of the design matrix. Willekens (1985) uses the term "hybrid loglinear model" for these non-standard specifications. Thus the GLM's provided the missing link between EM and IGM on the one hand and contingency table analysis on the other hand. An application of GLM's in the estimation of migration flows is given in Brouwer et al. (1983) and Scholten and Van Wissen (1985). The estimation of missing data for the housing market model is done using a specific form of a GLM. The model will be elaborated in the next section.

6.3 The Data Estimation Model

GLM's

A GLM is defined by specifying three components :

1. A random component , i.e. a dependent variable Y with a distribution: $E(Y) = \pi$ and $Var(Y) = D(.)$, where D is an exponential distribution.
2. The systematic component, i.e. the independent variables x_k which can be both covariates and factors(dummies) : $\eta = \Sigma_k \beta_k x_k$.
3. The link between the random and the systematic components through a link function g(.) : $g(\pi) = \eta$.

Various models can be derived by choosing the appropriate combination of link function and error structure, including the regression model, the logit and the probit model. Our concern is here with loglinear models and they can be formed by specifying the log-link : $\log \pi = \eta$ and a Poisson error structure: $var(Y) = \pi$. If the systematic component takes the form of the right hand side of equation (6.4) then a standard loglinear model is specified. More complex structures can be specified by inclusion of covariates, or terms with known (fixed) parameter values. In this way a set of prior values can be incorporated in the model. For example, the Fratar-Furness model has the following form as a GLM :

$$\log \pi_{ij} = \alpha_i + \beta_j + m_{ij} , \qquad (6.5)$$

where m_{ij} is the prior variable and the α's and the β's are the growth factors. The EM model of spatial interaction (6.3) is in GLM form :

$$\log \pi_{ij} = \mu_1(i) + \mu_2(j) + \log O_i D_j + f_{ij} \qquad (6.6)$$

where f_{ij} is a suitable interaction function in the log scale, $O_i D_j$ is the prior value that corresponds to the total effect of aggregate number of origins and destinations in i and j respectively and the μ's are the log's of the balancing factors (the term $O_i D_j$ is not necessary for the estimation of T, but is included as a biproportional scaling factor for the μ's).

The log-likelihood function for a two-way interaction table without interaction terms is given by:

$$L = \Sigma_{ij}\, n_{ij} \log \pi_{ij} = \Sigma_i n_{i.}\mu_1(i) + \Sigma_j n_{.j}\mu_2(j) \qquad (6.7)$$

from which it can be seen that the observed marginal totals $n_{i.}$ and $n_{.j}$ are sufficient statistics for parameter estimation. Together with the property that the observed marginal totals are equal to the ML estimates of their expectations this forms the basis for the use of log-linear models for estimation of missing observations from given aggregate figures. This result can be generalized to higher order data structures and hybrid loglinear models.

The Design Matrix

In specification and estimation of a GLM the design matrix plays a key role. It allows for all possible forms of factors, covariates, prior values and incomplete tables (including structural zeros). The design matrix is the link between the (unknown) cell entries and the constraints given by the data. The following examples show how various forms of hybrid models can easily be formulated using the design matrix framework. We start with the specification of the basic model without interaction term for a 3 x 3 contingency table with cell entries n_{ij} of observations cross-classified by two variables A and B with levels i (i=1,2,3) and j (j=1,2,3) respectively. Written out in matrix format the model is:

$$\begin{bmatrix} \log n_{11} \\ \log n_{12} \\ \log n_{13} \\ \log n_{21} \\ \log n_{22} \\ \log n_{23} \\ \log n_{31} \\ \log n_{32} \\ \log n_{33} \end{bmatrix} = \begin{bmatrix} 1 & 0 & 0 & 0 & 0 \\ 1 & 0 & 0 & 1 & 0 \\ 1 & 0 & 0 & 0 & 1 \\ 1 & 1 & 0 & 0 & 0 \\ 1 & 1 & 0 & 1 & 0 \\ 1 & 1 & 0 & 0 & 1 \\ 1 & 0 & 1 & 0 & 0 \\ 1 & 0 & 1 & 1 & 0 \\ 1 & 0 & 1 & 0 & 1 \end{bmatrix} \cdot \begin{bmatrix} \beta_1 \\ \beta_2 \\ \beta_3 \\ \beta_4 \\ \beta_5 \end{bmatrix} \qquad (6.8)$$

$$Y \quad = \quad X \quad \beta$$

Each row of the design matrix X corresponds to one cell in the table, and each column corresponds to one coefficient and one constraint for the fitted values. The first column corresponds to the overall constraint $\Sigma_{ij}n_{ij} = N$ (the total number of observations). Column two and three correspond to the constraints on level two and three of variable A ($\Sigma_j n_{2j} = n_{2.}$ and $\Sigma_j n_{3j} = n_{3.}$ respectively). Since $n_{1.} = n - n_{2.} - n_{3.}$, the specification of a separate term for level one of variable A is redundant. Column four and five of X correspond to variable B in the same way. So given the marginal distribution of the observations on variables A and B model (6.8) is appropriate to fit the cell entries.

Now suppose the following information is additionally available to predict the cell entries more accurately: (1) a survey that gives sample information on level one and two of A and B, and (2) the population total for cell n_{33}. Then the following hybrid model can be specified :

$$\begin{bmatrix} \log n_{11} \\ \log n_{12} \\ \log n_{13} \\ \log n_{21} \\ \log n_{22} \\ \log n_{23} \\ \log n_{31} \\ \log n_{32} \\ \log n_{33} \end{bmatrix} = \begin{bmatrix} 1 & 0 & 0 & 0 & 0 & \log m_{11} & 0 \\ 1 & 0 & 0 & 1 & 0 & \log m_{12} & 0 \\ 1 & 0 & 0 & 0 & 1 & \log m_{13} & 0 \\ 1 & 1 & 0 & 0 & 0 & \log m_{21} & 0 \\ 1 & 1 & 0 & 1 & 0 & \log m_{22} & 0 \\ 1 & 1 & 0 & 0 & 1 & \log m_{23} & 0 \\ 1 & 0 & 1 & 0 & 0 & 0 & 0 \\ 1 & 0 & 1 & 1 & 0 & 0 & 0 \\ 1 & 0 & 1 & 0 & 1 & 0 & 1 \end{bmatrix} \cdot \begin{bmatrix} \beta_1 \\ \beta_2 \\ \beta_3 \\ \beta_4 \\ \beta_5 \\ 1 \\ \beta_6 \end{bmatrix} \qquad (6.9)$$

$$Y \quad = \quad X \quad \beta$$

In addition to model (6.8) there are two extra columns in X. Column six contains the sample information on the elements of n. Since this prior information is the basic level that has to be scaled to be consistent with the population figures of A and B, the corresponding coefficient is fixed as 1. The last column corresponds to the exact information we have for cell (3,3) and β_6 guarantees that actual and fitted value for this cell match completely.

Other possibilities within the design matrix method are:

- Specification of a functional form for the interaction term in the model. This can be accomplished by adding the covariate(s) as (an) extra column(s) to the design matrix

- Specifying structural zeros (prior values for cells to be zero). This is done by giving the structural zeros a weight 0 and the remaining cells a weight 1. The effect is that these cells are removed from the fit and that the row-dimension of **Y** and **X** is reduced accordingly

The Algorithm

Finney (1952) found that for probit analysis maximization of the log-likelihood using the Newton-Raphson method is equivalent to a weighted least squares method (WLS) on a transformed dependent variable. Nelder and Wedderburn generalized this result to GLM's. Since for a Poisson error distribution the weights are equal to the (unknown) fitted means the estimation process must be iterative (IWLS).

The fitting algorithm takes the following form:
Let X be the n x p design matrix and c the p x 1 vector of constraints, given by the data. Let y be an initial estimate of the data that is feasible within the constraint set. The problem is then to find the vector of coefficients β such that

$$\pi = X\beta \tag{6.10}$$

gives the maximum likelihood solution for the table and by definition,

$$c = X^T\pi = X^Ty \tag{6.11}$$

X^Ty is the sums of cross-products in linear models, Σxy, and for qualitative terms it is equal to the marginal total as well. So the least squares fit takes the form of choosing β such that fitted marginals and actual constraints are equal for all terms in the model. Given an estimate π^1 a new estimate π^2 is found by regressing the transformed dependent variate $\log \pi^{*1} = \log \pi^1 + (y - \pi^1)/\pi^1$ on the X with weights π^1. After every iteration the π's are updated and the process is continued until (6.10) holds within a certain specified limit.

To start the process a vector of initial values y is needed that is feasible given the constraints. For small tables with simple constraints this can be done by hand. For large tables this is more difficult, and some method is needed to compute the initial values. One possible solution is the use of the SIMPLEX algorithm (Willekens and Baydar, 1985) for LP problems. However, the non-negativity condition implies that for every cell a 'slack' variable has to be introduced. For large tables like the applications in the next section this would be very inefficient. An alternative is to specify the problem in its dual form $c = X^T\pi$. This is a system of p linear equations in n unknowns (with usually $n >> p$) so that there are multiple solutions of π that fit the constraints. A simple least squares solution can then be applied. If a negative value is found this element is constrained to be zero and the process is repeated until all elements are non-negative. Although this method can break down theoretically, it performs very well in most situations and is very fast.

The computer program RIWILS was written to estimate unknown cell frequencies given some aggregate information on the data. The user has to specify the known information and the design matrix. The program first computes the initial values using the OLS solution in the dual form and next computes the ML solution using the IWLS algorithm.

In the next two sections the empirical results of the data estimation procedures will be presented for two basic tables in the model: the household composition matrix and the occupancy matrix.

6.4 Empirical Results on the Household Composition Matrix

The specific structure of the household composition matrix is given in table 6.1.

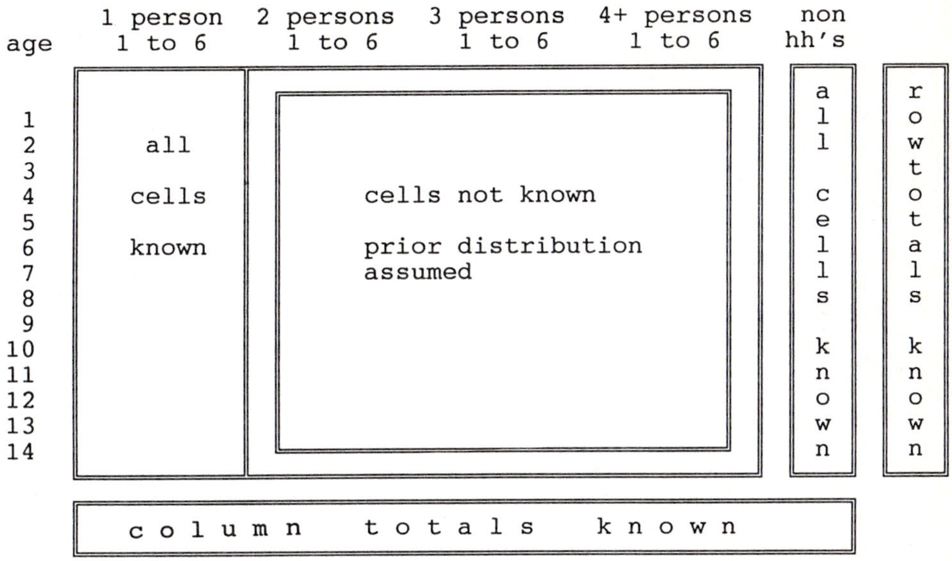

Table 6.1. Structure and data availability for the household composition matrix

Every cell entry in the matrix a_{xi} denotes the average number of persons in age category x (x=1,..,14) that live in a household type i (i is the combined index of household size s (s=1,..,4+) and age of head y (y=1,..,6)). This is a transformation of a matrix with counts of individuals n_{xi} in age category x and household type i which we call the untransformed household composition matrix. It is clear that the transformed and untransformed matrix are merely alternative ways of expressing the same information. For data estimation purposes we are concerned with the untransformed matrix of counts, which has the following properties:

- the matrix is a cross-classification of the total population, both for households (column 1-24) and for non-households (column 25),
- the row totals give the total age distribution of the population in 5-year classes (total 14 classes),
- the column totals give the total population distribution over the household categories including the group non-households,
- some cell entries are zero by definition. In the first 6 columns corresponding to the one-person households there are only 14 non-zero entries,
- The matrix is non-negative.

This matrix contains 14 x 25 = 350 cells. Since there is a basic distinction in the census between singles and households, the age distribution of singles is directly observable. The same holds for the non-household population (persons in homes for the elderly, boarding houses, monasteries). For the remaining cells, i.e. the cells corresponding to households with size 2+, the age distribution is known as well as the marginal totals for the household categories. This information corresponds to the hypothesis of no interaction between individual age and household type membership and it is not very likely that this is actually the case. Therefore it was decided to use sample information to introduce an interaction term in the matrix. The sample taken was the 1981 one percent national survey of housing needs (WBO, 1981).

Table 6.2 gives the weighted number of persons in every cell. These were taken as the prior values for biproportional adjustment. Using this information the program RIWILS was run for every zone (the program took about 110 system seconds on a Cyber 170 system per zone).

hhtype dwelling type	1	2	3	4	5	6	7	8	9	10	11	12	13	14	15	16	17	18	19	20	21	22	23	24	24
1	1	1	1	1	1	1	1	1	1	1	1	1	2	2	2	2	2	2	3	3	3	3	3	3	1
2	1	1	1	1	1	1	1	1	1	1	1	1	2	2	2	2	2	2	3	3	3	3	3	3	1
3	1	1	1	1	1	1	1	1	1	1	1	1	2	2	2	2	2	2	3	3	3	3	3	3	1
4	1	1	1	1	1	1	2180	1175	100	50	1	1	664	100	100	1	1	1	184	304	100	1	1	1	1
5	1	1	1	1	1	1	22545	19635	353	166	50	1	3923	6250	620	50	1	1	686	2643	572	100	1	1	1
6	1	1	1	1	1	1	752	39085	2118	253	50	1	100	19443	2050	91	1	1	347	23133	1727	236	101	1	1
7	1	1	1	1	1	1	100	17067	5804	174	50	50	1	13913	5977	310	50	1	100	28650	22194	1987	100	1	1
8	1	1	1	1	1	1	100	401	8082	452	90	100	1	337	9660	1295	100	1	50	2049	43596	3280	100	50	1
9	1	1	1	1	1	1	100	190	5080	2878	211	150	1	119	6849	3579	442	50	1	120	8315	14204	815	89	1
10	1	1	1	1	1	1	100	100	402	9417	1194	264	1	100	233	2901	1516	122	1	50	446	29203	1274	377	1
11	1	1	1	1	1	1	50	225	122	10988	9713	786	1	1	125	9485	6099	434	1	1	100	13065	6082	554	1
12	1	1	1	1	1	1	50	50	148	499	27875	3152	1	1	100	328	13039	846	1	1	1	101	6934	524	1
13	1	1	1	1	1	1	0	50	100	94	21806	11473	1	1	1	125	5023	2519	1	1	1	1	3054	1338	1
14	1	1	1	1	1	1	0	0	141	226	1353	68790	1	1	1	50	92	6427	1	1	1	1	3243	3478	1

Table 6.2. Prior distribution matrix (14 x 25) for the 1971 household composition matrix (source: WBO, 1981)

In table 6.3 the estimated untransformed household composition matrix is shown for zone 7 in Amsterdam.

hhtype dwel. type	1	2	3	4	5	6	7	8	9	10	11	12	13	14	15	16	17	18	19	20	21	22	23	24	25	Tot.
1	0	0	0	1	0	0	5	15	78	169	101	80	29	173	271	508	299	227	43	549	1379	1586	610	188	0	6311
2	0	0	0	2	0	0	6	18	92	200	120	95	35	204	320	600	354	269	51	649	1631	1875	721	222	0	7464
3	0	0	0	2	0	0	6	17	85	184	110	87	32	187	294	552	325	247	46	596	1499	1723	663	204	0	6859
4	63	0	0	0	0	0	392	639	275	298	4	3	344	303	476	9	5	4	92	1952	1615	19	7	2	25	6527
5	398	0	0	0	0	0	348	914	83	85	15	0	174	1622	253	38	0	0	29	1454	791	159	1	0	60	6424
6	0	440	0	0	0	0	3	396	109	28	3	0	1	1099	182	15	0	0	3	2771	520	82	13	0	5	5670
7	0	385	0	0	0	0	0	76	131	9	1	1	0	347	234	23	2	0	0	1515	2952	166	6	0	5	5853
8	0	0	350	0	0	0	0	1	129	16	2	2	0	6	268	67	3	0	0	77	4100	355	4	1	5	5386
9	0	0	280	0	0	0	0	1	87	106	5	3	0	2	202	198	14	1	0	5	2835	1635	36	1	5	5416
10	0	0	0	265	0	0	0	0	8	381	29	5	0	2	8	782	54	3	0	2	49	3685	62	6	5	5346
11	0	0	0	265	0	0	0	1	3	565	299	19	0	0	5	731	277	15	0	0	14	2096	375	11	5	4681
12	0	0	0	0	305	0	0	0	6	47	1573	141	0	0	8	46	1087	54	0	0	0	30	785	18	5	4105
13	0	0	0	0	455	0	0	1	5	10	1446	601	0	0	0	21	492	187	0	0	0	0	406	55	5	3684
14	0	0	0	0	0	2210	0	0	9	31	112	4513	0	0	0	10	11	598	0	0	0	0	540	178	480	8692
Tot.	461	825	630	535	760	2210	760	2079	1100	2129	3820	5500	615	3945	2521	3600	2923	1605	264	9570	17385	13411	4229	886	605	82418

Table 6.3. Estimated 1971 household composition matrix for zone 7 in Amsterdam

6.5 Empirical Results on the 1971 Occupancy Matrix

The occupancy matrix is the core matrix of the model. It keeps track of all transitions that take place both within the households and within the housing stock. The matrix is in fact the intersection of two tables, a household cross-classification by household and dwelling status and a dwelling cross-classification by type and occupancy status. This situation is visualized in figure 6.1.

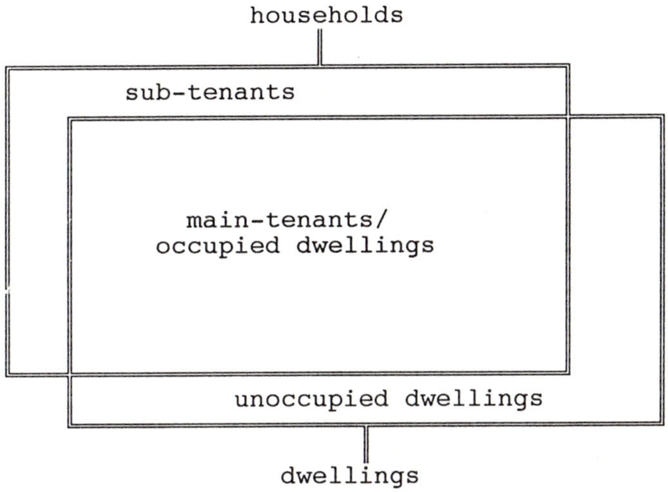

Figure 6.1. Households and dwellings by occupancy status

The largest category is the category of main-tenants (from a household perspective) or occupied dwellings (from a dwelling perspective); these are the observations to be stored in the occupancy matrix. No distinction is made between dwellings and other units for residential purposes. The sub-tenants and the unoccupied dwellings are stored in separate vectors and are important for determining housing demand and supply. For data estimation it is of importance to know whether the available information concerns households, or dwellings, or both. In our case we used both sources of information from the 1971 census which led to the simultaneous estimation of the occupancy matrix and the vectors of sub-tenants and vacancies.

The household categorization is the same as the one used for the household composition matrix. Dwellings are classified in 11 categories (see Chapter 5). These 11 dwelling types originate from the cross-tabulation of three variables with 4 x 2 x 2 = 16 basic cells. So the occupancy matrix has 24 x 11 = 264 cells but for estimation purposes the original 16 dwelling categories are used.

The 1971 census contains the following relevant information for our estimation purpose:

1. For all households:
   -age of head **[A]** x household size **[H]**;
2. For main-tenants:
   -age of head **[A]** x dwelling size **[S]**;
   -age of head **[A]** x tenure status **[E]**;
   -household size **[H]** x dwelling size **[S]**;
   -household size **[H]** x tenure status **[E]**;
3. For all non-single households:
   -tenure status **[E]** x dwelling type **[T]**;
4. For all dwellings:
   -dwelling type **[T]**;

The table **[E]** x **[T]** for non single households can also be viewed as a three way interaction between **[E]**, **[T]** and **[H*]**, where **H*** is the simplified household size categorization 1 vs. 2+ persons. Thus the corresponding loglinear model for the table can be expressed in shorthand loglinear notation (see Payne, 1977) as: **[A.H][A.S][A.E][H.S][H.E][E.T.H*][T]** (note that the table is an incomplete table). Specification of a loglinear model with these interaction terms will give the most likely cell frequencies given the marginal information.

Validation

A major weakness of data estimation methods is often the lack of a validation phase. Usually the data at hand are used for estimation purposes and there is nothing left to assess the fit of the model. For the occupancy matrix, unlike the household composition estimation procedures, 1971 census information is available. This allows the use of the 1981 WBO data for validation purposes. However, this is not a validation in a strict sense. Firstly, there is a time difference of 10 years and it is likely that the structure of the occupancy matrix has changed in that period. Secondly, the full table cannot be reproduced by the sample, owing to both the sampling scheme (the sampling unit is the individual) and to sample size considerations. Therefore the validation was performed on a simplified table that contained only main tenants in independent housing units. A separate analysis was performed for the city of Amsterdam and for the region.

Table 6.4 gives the input for a loglinear model to test the hypothesis that the interaction terms included in the data estimation model give a good approximation to the observed frequencies (N.B.: sfu = single family unit). Table 6.5 gives the results of the hypothesis testing in a number of steps. The fit criterion is given by the scaled deviance (SD), or log-likelihood ratio : $-2\sum_z y_z \log(y_z/\pi_z)$, and is approximately chi-square distributed. This statistic is -2 times the information gain statistic and can be interpreted as a measure of information loss. Here it is used to test the overall model fit (the null-hypothesis is that the model is a good approximation of the data) by comparing it with the chi-square distribution, although for large samples the deviance is likely to be larger than the expectation, even for good-fitting models (see Baker and Nelder, 1978), The statistic can also be used to measure the difference in fit between various models (this is possible if the models are nested). By comparing the SD value of a fitted model with that of a 'null-model' (i.e. the minimal model with as few parameters as possible) an assessment can be made of the proportion of the dispersion in the table that is 'explained' by the model.

	1-2 persons			3+ persons		
	< 35 y.	35-64 y.	65+ y.	<35 y.	35-64 y.	65+ y.
<u>Amsterdam</u>						
rented flat:						
1-3 rooms	120	231	210	65	140	11
4+ rooms	25	107	95	64	299	24
rented sfu:						
1-3 rooms	2	11	20	3	6	1
4+ rooms	6	21	20	2	48	9
own.occ. flat:						
1-3 rooms	11	19	5	6	9	0
4+ rooms	1	13	4	7	12	0
own.occ. sfu:						
1-3 rooms	4	5	1	1	0	0
4+ rooms	3	7	7	1	22	1
<u>Region</u>						
rented flat:						
1-3 rooms	15	30	31	4	11	1
4+ rooms	18	33	20	29	55	2
rented sfu:						
1-3 rooms	4	8	16	3	6	2
4+ rooms	5	49	50	54	244	11
own.occ. flat:						
1-3 rooms	8	7	1	3	1	0
4+ rooms	1	2	3	4	3	0
own.occ. sfu:						
1-3 rooms	11	19	4	6	11	2
4+ rooms	22	72	29	86	290	14

Table 6.4. The 1981 sample occupancy matrix for Amsterdam and the Region (source : WBO, 1981)

The first model in table 6.5 is the null-model and contains only a constant. The corresponding SD values give the total dispersion in the table. The second model is the model with all two-way interaction terms; the SD statistic indicates that for both Amsterdam and the Region this model is a close approximation for the observed table (the critical chi-square value with 27 degrees of freedom at the 95 percent confidence level is 41.34 and this is well above the SD values of the models). This result indicates that if we would had had all bivariate tables this would have been sufficient for the estimation. The third model is actually the model used for the data estimation described above.

The SD values indicate that there is a significant difference between the model outcomes and the observed data (the critical chi-square value with 32 degrees of freedom is 46.2), but that in terms of 'explained' dispersion in the table we still have a good fit. It is also evident that the model is more consistent with the Amsterdam data than with the Region data. Next, some models were tested in order to assess the relative information content of the interaction terms.

	Amsterdam			Region		
Model	S.D.	d.f	expl.var	S.D	d.f.	expl.var
1.Null-model	3589.00	47	-	2620.00	47	-
2.All two-way interactions	32.70	27	.991	36.21	27	.986
3.Data estimation model	112.80	32	.969	219.90	32	.916
Terms in model 3:						
4.Model 2 - [A.H]	279.80	29	.922	215.90	29	.918
5.Model 2 - [A.S]	66.23	29	.982	41.90	29	.984
6.Model 2 - [A.E]	54.86	29	.985	67.70	29	.974
7.Model 2 - [H.S]	208.10	28	.942	120.60	28	.954
8.Model 2 - [H.E]	37.11	28	.990	37.79	28	.986
9.Model 2 - [E.T]	101.10	28	.972	226.50	28	.914
Terms not in model 3:						
10.Model 2 - [A.T]	46.25	29	.987	62.95	29	.976
11.Model 2 - [H.T]	32.81	28	.991	70.35	28	.973
12.Model 2 - [S.E]	33.41	28	.972	39.43	28	.985
13.Model 2 - [S.T]	84.32	28	.976	105.00	28	.960

Table 6.5. Results of loglinear hypothesis testing on the 1981 sample occupancy matrix

Therefore the basic model with all two-way interaction terms was taken and a sequence of models was tested each having one interaction term less than the basic model. The increase in SD indicates the loss of information caused by the removal of the term concerned.

Inspection of table 6.5 shows that in general the interaction terms included in the data estimation model have the highest information content. For both Amsterdam and the Region the three most important interaction effects (although in a different order) are **[A.H]** (age of head x household size), **[H.S]** (household size x dwelling size) and **[E.T]** (tenure status x dwelling type). The most important term <u>not</u> included in the model is **[S.T]** (dwelling size x dwelling type). The other interaction terms not included in the data estimation model are of minor importance, with the exception of the term **[H.T]** (household size x dwelling type) for the Region. It also appears that the table **[H.E]** (household size x tenure status) does not add information to the full table.

From this analysis it can be concluded that the amount of information supplied by the observed bivariate tables is not satisfactory to describe all the interactions in the table. It may be argued, however, that the null-hypothesis used is not too strong an assumption for the data and that a less close approximation is 'close enough' for modelling purposes. It can also be concluded that the most important interactions are included and that no higher order interactions are necessary. In terms of explained variance within the table the data estimation model covers 96.9 percent of the dispersion in the Amsterdam data and 91.6 percent of the dispersion in the Region data. Given these results it was concluded that the model used for data estimation was 'good enough' for our purposes.

(1) Total number of dwellings for 4 dwelling classes:

rented flat:	6695
rented single family unit:	5505
owner occupied flat:	770
owner occupied single family unit:	5070

(2) Number of households for 4 household size classes and 6 age classes:

	1 pers.	2 pers.	3 pers.	4+ pers.
< 25 year	1870	320	135	35
25-34 year	715	965	1075	1640
35-44 year	450	490	570	3350
45-54 year	415	825	975	2830
55-64 year	595	1295	835	825
65+ year	965	1345	305	145

(3) Number of rented and owner occupied dwellings for 6 age classes and 3 household size classes:

	ago						household size		
	< 25	25-34	35-44	45-54	55-64	65+	2 p.	3 p.	4+ p.
rented	50	790	1740	1710	1305	1105	1620	1090	3145
own.occ	360	3010	2980	3260	2155	1545	3330	2675	5620

(4) Number of dwellings of 3 dwelling size classes for 6 age classes and 3 household size classes:

	age						household size		
	< 25	25-34	35-44	45-54	55-64	65+	2 p.	3 p.	4+ p.
3 rooms	60	175	190	170	195	330	345	45	40
4 rooms	65	520	390	415	420	450	870	485	390
5+ rooms	280	3080	4125	4370	2820	1825	3725	3225	8325

(5) Total number of flats and single family units:

flats:	11625
single family units:	8650

Table 6.6. 1971 census information for estimation of the occupancy matrix for zone 12 (Amstelveen)

Results of the Data Estimation

A design matrix was drawn up to estimate both the occupancy matrix and the vectors of sub-tenants and vacancies. This involved the specification of 72 constraints for 414 cells (size of the occupancy matrix before aggregation to 11 dwelling types : 16 x 24 = 384; 384 + 24 sub-tenant categories + 6 aggregated dwelling types = 414 cells). The program RIWILS was run for every zone (one run costs approximately 150 system seconds on a Cyber 170) and the results were aggregated to the appropriate dimensions. Table 6.6 gives as an illustration the input for zone 12 (Amstelveen, a suburban zone); the resulting occupancy matrix is presented in table 6.7.

hhtype / dwel.type	1	2	3	4	5	6	7	8	9	10	11	12	13	14	15	16	17	18	19	20	21	22	23	24	Total
1	6	4	1	1	5	9	7	4	1	1	3	4	1	1	0	0	1	0	0	1	1	0	0	0	51
2	5	26	59	59	98	185	4	24	20	34	62	74	1	25	24	39	39	16	1	50	172	139	47	9	1212
3	19	36	42	35	42	78	17	30	13	16	21	26	1	6	3	3	2	1	0	4	6	3	1	0	405
4	2	8	20	16	24	54	5	14	13	15	24	37	0	3	3	3	3	1	0	2	7	4	1	0	259
5	14	34	43	36	40	73	14	32	15	19	22	28	1	6	3	4	2	1	0	3	6	3	1	0	400
6	6	28	26	27	35	56	20	88	31	48	67	71	5	73	29	42	32	12	1	38	52	37	9	2	835
7	6	27	25	25	34	53	16	72	26	39	55	59	4	60	23	34	26	10	1	31	43	30	8	1	708
8	1	6	12	11	19	36	4	34	25	35	62	81	1	26	21	28	27	13	0	18	52	34	11	2	559
9	11	47	53	68	97	131	68	281	122	232	346	317	26	376	180	327	261	86	17	627	1064	936	249	40	5962
10	10	45	51	65	92	124	56	231	100	190	284	260	22	309	148	268	215	71	14	515	873	768	205	32	4948
11	1	10	24	29	51	85	15	107	96	170	321	362	5	134	132	223	225	92	5	303	1061	870	292	57	4670
subten.	1790	444	96	43	59	82	95	23	2	1	2	2	68	55	5	3	3	1	22	47	15	5	1	0	2864
Total	1871	715	452	415	596	966	321	940	464	800	1269	1321	135	1074	571	974	836	304	61	1639	3352	2829	825	143	22873

Table 6.7. The estimated 1971 occupancy matrix for zone 12 (Amstelveen)

6.6 Summary

In this chapter an overview is given of the various data needs of the model and the ways to overcome data deficiencies. A short survey is given of existing models for data estimation and a method is presented that combines most advantages of these existing methods (i.e. flexibility, ease of use and cost-effectiveness). Two elaborate examples were then described, including a test of goodness of fit for the occupancy matrix.

This result concludes the chapter on data estimation methods. The household relocation model as developed, relies to some extent on data estimation procedures performed on exogenous (input) variables for the model. Our assumption is that the estimated data give a 'good' approximation to the real world and can therefore be used to build an operational model for the Amsterdam housing market.

CHAPTER 7. A DYNAMIC HOUSEHOLD MODEL FOR THE AMSTERDAM REGION

7.0 Introduction

In this chapter the first module of the Amsterdam model, the household model, will be described in detail. As pointed out in the overview of the entire model in Chapter 5 this model predicts the dynamics in the number of households and household composition in the Amsterdam region. These events are considered to be the major driving force for the housing demand. The following three types of events are modelled:

1. new household formation, generating new demand for dwellings
2. household dissolution, generating vacancies on the market
3. changes in household composition, defined in terms of household size and age of the head, that may lead to a re-evaluation of the current housing situation of the household, and eventually to a move to another dwelling in the same or another zone of residence

The model developed below predicts these events, using the methodology of multistate demography, a technique already introduced in Chapter 3. It uses observed transition rates, derived from secondary analysis of a retrospective survey held in the area in 1980 and covering the period 1975-1980. The final outcome of the model is a population projection matrix **T**, that allows a complete projection of individuals by age and position in the household, and a household projection matrix **D**, containing the expected numbers of households generated and dissolved by size and age of the head, and the changes in size and age composition of existing households. Following the general model structure discussed in Chapter 5, the **R** matrix and the household occupancy matrix **O** together generate the input for the housing demand model. The next three chapters will turn to the housing market consequences of the demographic processes modelled here. In the present chapter the presentation will mainly focus on demographic modelling of household events.

The application of the household model in a housing market context makes a longitudinal household definition necessary. Every household is attached to a dwelling unit. If we take a small time interval dt short enough to allow at most one transition event, the following events can occur in an occupied dwelling between t and t+dt:

1. The household changes its composition from a type g to type g'
2. The household dissolves, thus leaving the dwelling vacant

3. The household moves out, which also results in a vacancy
4. The house is demolished, resulting in a household without a dwelling

If none of these events occur the same household with the same characteristics occupies the house at time t+dt. Therefore, the household model must determine whether a household dissolves, or changes its composition. New household generations must be defined too. According to McMillan and Herriot (1985) a set of accounting principles or continuity rules is necessary in order to define these transitions. These definitions are always to a certain extent arbitrary (Keilman and Keyfitz, 1987).

For the household model developed in this chapter a set of accounting rules was adopted where, admittedly, some strong assumptions had to be made. Much theoretical and empirical work has to be done on this matter in the future. The aggregation procedure adopted in our model can be motivated by the need to define the household as the basic decision unit. For the housing demand model the household is the unit of analysis, i.e. households, not individuals, make housing decisions. The housing decision process within one housing market area is induced by household transitions and this is exactly what the household model is developed for.

In section 7.1, we continue the introductory notes, given in Chapter 3, on multistate demographic methodology. The main result of this section is an explicit formula for the calculation of the transition probabilities in terms of the observed rates. Next we turn to the model itself in section 7.2. Here the explicit forms of the individual projection matrix **T** and -through aggregation- of the household projection matrix **R** are derived. Next we turn to the empirical stage. Section 7.3 gives an account of the retrospective survey used, and explains what can and cannot be inferred from the data. In section 7.4 the coefficients of the model are estimated and in section 7.5 some results are described in terms of the stationary distribution and expected numbers of transitions. The final section (7.6) summarizes the main results of this chapter, and provides the link with the subsequent chapters, which are dominated by housing market processes.

7.1 The Methodology of Multistate Demography

Multistate demography was already introduced in section 3.7, and it was concluded there that this technique is a very useful instrument for micro demographic modelling. The mathematical theory of the method can be found in a number of references (Rogers, 1973, 1975; Rogers and Ledent, 1975; Ledent, 1980; Willekens, 1980; Willekens et al., 1980, Willekens and Drewe, 1984). In this section a summary is presented of the basic ideas, continuing the introduction given in Chapter 3, and leading to the required formula for empirical estimation of the transition probabilities. The exposition in this section serves mainly to provide the necessary theoretical background for the subsequent sections.

Demographic Events in a Multistate System

The following example is taken from Ledent (1980, pp.537-8). Suppose we define a system with two states, i and k, where k stands for all states except i. A simple accounting framework shows how the system develops from time x (=t+y) to time x+dx (dx=dy) for persons of age x:

$$l_i(x+dx) = l_i(x) - m_{i\delta}(x) - m_{ik}(x) + m_{ki}(x) \qquad (7.1)$$

where $m_{ik}(x)$ is the number of moves from state i to state k (k=1,..,r, k≠i) made by those members of the population who were in state i at age x, $l_i(x)$, in the small time interval dt=dx, and $m_{i\delta}$ is the number of deaths in the same time interval in this group. If we treat the state of death as the (r+1)th state of the system, and substitute for k the summation over all states j except i, (7.1) can be rewritten as:

$$l_i(x+dx) = l_i(x) - \sum_{\substack{j=1 \\ j\neq i}}^{r+1} m_{ij}(x) + \sum_{\substack{j=1 \\ j\neq i}}^{r+1} m_{ji}(x), \quad i=1,..,r \qquad (7.2)$$

This accounting equation can be transformed into a function of rates. In general, there are two options that are commonly used to define the rates μ:

1. the rates are constant over the interval dx
2. the rates are linearly dependent on time in the interval dx

If m_{ij} is the number of events in the small time interval dx, and $l_i(x)$ is the number of individuals at the beginning of the time interval, then, taking the option of constant rates, the rate of transition can be written as:

$$\mu_{ij}(x) = \lim_{dx \to 0} \frac{m_{ij}(x)}{l_i(x)dx}, \quad i=1,..,r;\ j=1,..r+1;\ j\neq i \qquad (7.3)$$

It can be shown that the matrix of transition probabilities **P** can be found by:

$$\mathbf{P}(t) = \exp(-\mu t) \qquad (7.4)$$

where μ is a matrix of transition rates as defined in (3.7) and **P**(t) is of the same form with elements $p_{ij}(x,x+t)$. The ML estimator of μ is the set of occurrence/exposure rates o/e. However, the exposure rates can only be observed when complete life histories of all individuals are available. Usually these are not known and have to be estimated. Keilman and

Gill (1987) propose a method for estimating exposure times in the case of population registration data and use (7.4) to arrive at an 'exact' solution for the transition matrix **P**. Another alternative is to adopt the linear option for the transition rates in μ. This option is an integrated part of the linear integration model, the most frequently used model for estimation of multistate demographic models and presented below. However, there is a theoretical drawback in applying this method. In their paper Keilman and Gill have shown that this model is not compatible with a Markov process. One of their findings is also that the differences between the 'exact' solution (7.4) and the linear solution is more of a theoretical than a practical value. Numerical estimates show that the differences between model outcomes are small. This means that the linear integration model described below can be used as a working approximation of the theoretical underlying Markov model.

If equation 7.3 is substituted in 7.2 and generalized to matrix notation, we arrive at the multistate form of the life table:

$$\frac{d}{dy} \underline{l}(x) = -\mu(x)\, \underline{l}(x) \tag{7.5}$$

where $\underline{l}(x)$ is a vector with elements $l_i(x)$, and $\mu(x)$ is the r x r matrix of transition rates given in equation (3.7). The Markovian assumption that the instantaneous rates depend only on the individual's present state and not on its previous states, allows the generalization of (7.5) into:

$$\frac{d}{dx}\, {}_y\mathbf{l}(x) = -\mu(x)\, {}_y\mathbf{l}(x) \tag{7.6}$$

where ${}_y\mathbf{l}(x)$ is a r x r matrix with elements ${}_yl_{ij}(x)$, being the number of persons of age x surviving in state j who were in state i n years ago (n=x-y). The age y denotes the cohort.

The solution of the differential equation (7.6) has the following form:

$$ {}_y\mathbf{l}(x) = {}_y\Omega(x)\, {}_y\mathbf{l}(y) \tag{7.7}$$

where ${}_y\Omega(x)$ is a probability matrix describing the evolution of the system from time t+y to t+y+n = t+x.

<u>The Solution of $\Omega(x)$</u>

The conditional probability $p_{ij}(x)$ that a person alive in state i at age x is in state j at age x+h can be found from equation (7.7). The matrix **P**(x) can also be written as ${}_x\Omega(x+h)$ and then from (7.7) we have:

$$\mathbf{P}(x) = {}_x\Omega(x+h) = {}_y\mathbf{l}(x+h)\ [{}_y\mathbf{l}(x)]^{-1}, \tag{7.8}$$

assuming non-singularity of ${}_y\mathbf{l}(x)$.
It can be shown (Willekens, 1980, p.570) that ${}_y\mathbf{l}(x+h)$ can be written as:

$$ {}_y\mathbf{l}(x+h) = {}_y\mathbf{l}(x) - \int_0^h \mu(x+s)\ {}_y\mathbf{l}(x+s)\ ds \tag{7.9}$$

Combining (7.8) and (7.9) gives:

$$\mathbf{P}(x) = \mathbf{I} - \int_0^h \mu(x+s)\ {}_y\mathbf{l}(x+s)\ [{}_y\mathbf{l}(x)]^{-1}\ ds \tag{7.10}$$

The number of years lived in each state between ages x and x+h for a person at age y in each state can be interpreted as the exposure measure for the calculation of the rates, and is denoted as ${}_y\mathbf{L}(x)$, i.e.:

$$ {}_y\mathbf{L}(x) = \int_0^h {}_y\mathbf{l}(x+s)\ ds \tag{7.11}$$

The matrix of age-specific life table rates is given by (see Willekens, 1980, p.571):

$$\mathbf{m}(x) = \left[\int_0^h \mu(x+s)\ {}_y\mathbf{l}(x+s)\ ds \right] [{}_y\mathbf{L}(x)]^{-1} \tag{7.12}$$

here, $\mathbf{m}(x)$ has the same form as the $\mu(x)$ matrix. Combining (7.10) and (7.12) gives an explicit formulation of the transition probabilities in terms of the rates:

$$\mathbf{P}(x) = \mathbf{I} - \mathbf{m}(x)\ {}_y\mathbf{L}(x)\ [{}_y\mathbf{l}(x)]^{-1} \tag{7.13}$$

<u>Calculation of **P**(x) from Observed Data</u>

If complete life histories of individuals were available, exposures and occurrences could be measured exactly and no problems would exist in deriving $\mathbf{P}(x)$ given $\mathbf{M}(x)$, the observed counterparts of $\mathbf{m}(x)$ and $\mathbf{L}(x)$. If the data are only available at fixed time intervals $\mathbf{L}(x)$ has to be estimated. In the linear model the linear integration hypothesis is used, implying a uniform distribution of events over the interval x to x+h:

$$ {}_y\mathbf{L}(x) \sim \tfrac{1}{2}\, h\ [\ {}_y\mathbf{l}(x) + {}_y\mathbf{l}(x+h)\ ] \tag{7.14}$$

Combining (7.13) and (7.14) gives the final result:

$$\mathbf{P}(x) = \left[\mathbf{I} + \frac{h}{2}\mathbf{M}(x) \right]^{-1} \left[\mathbf{I} - \frac{h}{2}\mathbf{M}(x) \right] \tag{7.15}$$

with the theoretical rates **m** replaced by the observed **M**.

7.2 Description of the Household Model

The purpose of this section is to describe the empirical derivation of the transition matrix **R**, as introduced in section 7.1. Starting at the individual level, a number of 'system' states or positions in the household can be defined, together with a number of basic individual demographic events, which are the transitions from one position in the household to another. The intensity, or rate, of these transition processes has to be measured from empirical data. This will be described in detail in the next two sections. It was already shown in the previous section that multistate demographic methods allow the estimation of transition probabilities from observed rates. Using this methodology, this leads to an individual age specific transition probability matrix **T**(x) (where x is the age). The next step is then to aggregate the individual transition probability matrix to the household level. The matrix **R**(x) describes the changes in household composition. Since **R**(x) is derived through aggregation from **T**(x), household projections are consistent with population projections.

The Definition of the Individual Household States

The start of a new household involves the individual transition of a non-head to a head position (including singles). The termination of a household involves the change of a head (or single) to a non-head position or death. Thus, in order to describe the process of entering or leaving the housing market, it seems appropriate to make a distinction between non-heads and heads (including singles). However, these states alone are not enough to describe changes in existing households. We need household size explicitly in the definition of the household positions since a change in this variable is the key input variable explaining the behaviour of existing households on the housing market. The impact of this variable on housing demand will be shown explicitly in Chapter 8 where willingness-to-move functions are being estimated using demographic input variables.

Combining the head-non-head and size categories leads to the following definitions of household positions:

- child
- single person
- head of a 2 person household
- head of a 3 person household
- head of a 4+ person household
- partner (household members who are not a child or head)
- person in non-household positions

The motivation for this classification scheme can only fully be understood by reference to the housing demand model, to be described in the next chapter. The transition events between states generated by the household model fit exactly into the housing demand model. Another advantage of the model is its flexibility. The generality of the definition allows for all possible types of household units, including various forms of non-family units, which have significantly grown in importance in Amsterdam in the past decade (see also Chapter 2).

From a purely demographic viewpoint, this definition scheme is somewhat unsatisfactory. There is no direct link between these states and published census data on fertility or marriage (since the household state is not explicitly related to the number of children). The definition is also less detailed compared to a number of recently developed household models (see Chapter 3). Despite these differences, due to a different scope and objective, some transitions included in our model are common to most dynamic household models, viz. the transition from child to single or the transition to a non-household position.

The Individual Transition Table **T**(x)

Using the previously defined 7 household positions a 7 x 7 transition table can be formed. Table 7.1 depicts the 49 theoretical transitions and classifies them according to their logical and empirical state. Some transitions are very rare, for instance the transition from a non-child to a child. These are marked with a dash (-). Other transitions are not rare, but still infrequent. For instance, the transition from single or child to head of a 4+ household does happen sometimes, but it is not a common event. These events are marked with an asterisk (*). Very common transitions are child to single (C,S), child to head of a two person household (C,H2), or to partner (C,P); from single to head of a two person household (S,H2) or to partner (S,P); finally, the transitions between all pairs of heads of adjacent household size categories. The state of death is implicitly included in the table since it is the difference between the total number of persons in state i at time t, N_i, and the summation of row i in the table, $\sum_j T_{ij}$:

$$d_i = N_i - \sum_j T_{ij} \tag{7.16}$$

Note that **T** does not contain migration. So all transition probabilities, including the transition to death, apply to the cohort of individuals present in the system at the beginning of the time period and irrespective of a migration movement or not.

	t = 2						
t = 1	child	single	head 2p	head 3p	head 4+p	partner	non-hh
child		(C,S)	(C,H2)	*	*	(C,P)	(C,N)
single	-		(S,H2)	*	*	(S,P)	(S,N)
head 2p	-	(H2,S)		(H2,H3)	*	(H2,P)	(H2,N)
head 3p	-	*	(H3,H2)		(H3,H4)	*	(H3,N)
head 4p	-	*	*	(H4,H3)		*	(H4,N)
partner	-	(P,S)	(P,H2)	(P,H3)	(P,H4)		(P,N)
non-hh	-	(N,S)	(N,H2)	(N,H3)	(N,H4)	(N,P)	

Table 7.1. Individual transition table of household positions
- : transition not taken into account
* : infrequent transition

Individual transition rates can be converted into transition probabilities using formula (7.15). This results in an age specific probability matrix **T**(x). A complete projection population projection model consists of the set of **T**(x) matrices (x = 1,..,highest age category) and fertility rates F(x) organized in a matrix **T** that satisfies the equation:

$$\underline{K}(t+1) = \mathbf{T}\ \underline{K}(t) \qquad (7.17)$$

where $\underline{K}$ is a stacked vector of the form

$$\underline{K}(t) = \{\underline{k}(1),\underline{k}(2),\underline{k}(3),...,\underline{k}(x),\ ..,\underline{k}(X)\}' \qquad (7.18)$$

and $\underline{k}(x)$ is a vector with the number of persons classified by position in the household in age group x (x=1,..,X) as elements, i.e.,

$$\underline{k}(x)=\{k_c(x),k_s(x),k_{h2}(x),k_{h3}(x),k_{h4+}(x),k_p(x),k_{nh}(x)\}' \qquad (7.19)$$

The stacked vector K is the population distribution table introduced in Chapter 5. So equation 7.17 describes the transition of household positions of the population from time t to time t+1. Matrix **T** is formed of all age-specific transition tables **T**(x), where x is an index of 5-year age intervals (x=1,..,14). In order to arrive at a complete population projection model it also contains fertility rates. Willekens (1980) proposes this complete projection matrix in the analysis of working life tables and his idea is incorporated in the present model.

The full matrix **T** has the following form:

$$
\begin{bmatrix}
0 & \cdots & 0 & \mathbf{B}(a) & \cdots & \mathbf{B}(b) & 0 & 0 & \cdots & 0 \\
\mathbf{T}(1) & 0 & \cdots & 0 & \cdots & 0 & & & \cdots & 0 \\
0 & \mathbf{T}(2) & & & & & & \cdot & & \cdot \\
\cdot & & & & & & & \cdot & & \cdot \\
\cdot & & & & & & & \cdot & & \cdot \\
\cdot & & & & \mathbf{T}(x) & & & \cdot & & \cdot \\
\cdot & & & & & & & \cdot & & \\
 & & & & & & & & & 0 \\
0 & & \cdots & & \cdots & & 0 & 0 & \mathbf{T}(13) & \mathbf{T}(14)
\end{bmatrix}
$$

The **T**(x) matrices are the age-specific transition matrices and the **B**(x) matrices give the total probability of child-bearing of the population in age category x in the time period x to x+h (Willekens, 1980, p. 595). These fertility matrices have the following form:

$$\mathbf{B}(x) = \tfrac{1}{2}\, h \,[\, \mathbf{F}(x) + \mathbf{F}(x+h)\, \mathbf{T}(x) \,] \tag{7.20}$$

The a and b are the lowest and highest age categories of child bearing, respectively. Note that the fertility rate matrix **F**(x) is a matrix of zeros except for the first column which is a vector of the following form:

$$\{f_c(x), f_s(x), f_{h2}(x), f_{h3}(x), f_{h4+}(x), f_p(x), f_n(x)\}' \tag{7.21}$$

F(x) allows the specification of state dependent fertility rates.

In the presentation until now it was assumed that the length of the age-interval and the projection period are equal. This is not the case in the household model however. The household model projects household transitions one year ahead, while the age-interval is assumed to be five years. The model assumes that transition probabilities are constant within each five-year age interval. If we denote the probability of staying in the same age interval x in the period t to t+1 by p_x, and the probability of moving to the next age interval by q_x (= $1-p_x$) , then, under the assumption that a change in age category and a change in household position are conditionally independent given age x, the matrix **T** has the following form:

$$
\begin{bmatrix}
p_1\mathbf{T}(1) & \cdots & \mathbf{B}(a) & \cdots & & \mathbf{B}(b) & 0 & \cdots & 0 \\
q_1\mathbf{T}(1) & p_2\mathbf{T}(2) & \cdots\ 0 & \cdots & & 0 & & \cdots & 0 \\
0 & q_2\mathbf{T}(2) & & & & & & & \cdot \\
\cdot & & & & & & & & \cdot \\
\cdot & & & & & & & & \cdot \\
\cdot & & q_{x-1}\mathbf{T}(x-1) & p_x\mathbf{T}(x) & & & & & \cdot \\
\cdot & & & q_x\mathbf{T}(x) & p_{x+1}\mathbf{T}(x+1) & & & & \\
 & & & & & & & p_{13}\mathbf{T}(13) & 0 \\
0 & & \cdots & \cdots & \cdots & 0 & & q_{13}\mathbf{T}(13) & \mathbf{T}(14)
\end{bmatrix}
$$

Inferring Household Events from Individual Transitions

The matrix **T** describes the individual events associated with changes in household position. In general it is true that any household formation, dissolution or change in composition involves a change in individual household membership status of one or more persons. The reverse argument, that a change in household position implies an event at the household level is not always true. Some problems of definition play an important role in this respect. For instance, if two persons (head and partner) split up, it is uncertain who is the old household and who starts a new household. Or, should this be interpreted as one household dissolution and two new household formations? Decisions have to be made and some may be slightly arbitrary, due to the lack of empirical evidence on this matter. We shall discuss each of the household positions and related events in turn below.

Child (C)
Possible transitions involving a new household position are (C,S), (C,H) (where H is H2, H3 or H4+). Typical events in this respect are children leaving the parental home to become single or to start a multi-person household. It also includes the transition of a child to S or H due to death of the head.

Possible transitions involving no household event: (C,P),(C,N),(C,d) (d is the state of death).

Single (S)
Possible transitions involving the termination of the household are (S,P),(S,N),(S,d). Note that (S,C) is assumed to be zero. The only possible transition involving a change in the composition of the household is (S,H). So it is assumed that if the head of the new formed multi-person household was single before the event, it is merely the continuation of the former single-person household.

Heads (H2, H3, H4+)
Possible transitions that result in the termination of a household are (H,P),(H,N). The transition to death is not considered to be the loss of a household. A basic assumption made throughout the model is that the identity of the household is linked to the head. So any transition between the states of S or H is only a change of an existing household. Whether these events also involve household formation or dissolution depends on the behaviour of the other individual(s) involved in the event. So the transition from H to P is considered to be the dissolution of one household. There is one important exception to this rule. We assume that the death of a head does not involve the dissolution of the household, but a change in household composition. In conventional marital status tables, a common assumption is that the rate of transition from marriage to widow is equal to the death rate of the spouse. If a similar assumption is made here we could treat a part of the transitions of partners to head as a change in existing households (see below). This excludes the possibility of children becoming the head after

the event (for instance in the case of single-parent households). Another assumption made here is that the transition to a non-household position involves the loss a household. It could be argued that this is the same case as a transition to death, and for younger ages this may be the case. But the most important event associated with this transition is the movement of older households to homes for the elderly.

Partner (P)
As described above, the change from partner to H or S may or may not result in the formation of a new household, depending on the type of event that caused the transition. If the total number of transitions from P to H2, say, is n[P,H2], then we assume that n[H3,d] out of these n[P,H2] involve a change due to death of the head (of a 3 person household) and thus may be considered as a change in existing household composition. The remaining n[P,H2] - n[H3,d] are then new household formations. Similar relations hold for (P,S), (P,H3) and (P,H4+). The examples in table 7.2 make clear what the consequences of the individual events are, under the assumptions stated above. Loss or gain of a household is denoted as -/+ 1, while the transitions that do not involve a change in the number of households are denoted by 0.

Type of event:	Individual transitions	Household transitions
Two children starting a two person household	(C,H)	+ 1
	(C,P)	0
	result:	+ 1
Two singles starting a two person household	(S,H2)	0
	(S,P)	- 1
	result:	- 1
Splitting up of a three person household	(H3,S)	0
	(P,H2)	+ 1
	(C,C)	0
	result:	+ 1
Death of head of a four person household	(H4+,d)	0
	(P,H3)	0
	(C,C)	0
	(C,C)	0
	result:	0

Table 7.2. Some examples of household formation, dissolution and change

The Household Projection Matrix **R**

With the assumptions stated above we are now in a position to derive the projection matrix **R** from the individual transition matrix **T**. First, the matrix **R**(x) is derived from **T**(x), where **R** is given in terms of the expected number of events given the probabilities in **T**. If we denote the expected number of individual transitions, given by the transition probabilities in **T**, by n[x,y], the expected number of household events is given in table 7.3. Note the consequence of the assumption on death of heads of households. From the total number of transitions of partners to singles or heads to an m-size household the total number of deaths of heads of a household of size m+1 is subtracted to give the number of new household formations. The number of deaths of heads is added to the transitions of existing households from size m+1 to size m. Thus the matrix still fulfils the logical conditions that the sum of the rows and columns gives the total number of households by category at time t = 1 and t = 2 respectively. A minor annoyance in adopting this procedure is that, in order to know how many transitions occur from category four to three due to the death of a head of a four person household, we have to distinguish between four and five+ person households.

t = 1	t = 2				
	single	head 2p	head 3p	head 4+p	dissolution
single	n[S,S]	n[S,H2]	n[S,H3]	n[S,H4]	n[S,d] + n[S,P] + n[S,N]
head 2p	n[H2,S] +n[H2,d]	n[H2,H2]	n[H2,H3]	n[H2,H4]	n[H2,P] + n[H2,N]
head 3p	n[H3,S]	n[H3,H2] +n[H3,d]	n[H3,H3]	n[H3,H4]	n[H3,P] + n[H3,N]
head 4+p	n[H4,S]	n[H4,H2]	n[H4,H3] +n[H4,d]	n[H4,H4] +n[H5,d]	n[H4,P] + n[H4,N]
new households	n[C,S] +n[P,S] +n[N,S] -n[H2,d]	n[C,H2] +n[P,H2] +n[N,H2] -n[H3,d]	n[C,H3] +n[P,H3] +n[N,H3] -n[H4,d]	n[C,H4] +n[P,H4] +n[N,H4] -n[H5,d]	0

Table 7.3. The matrix **R**(x) of expected number of household transitions derived from **T**(x)

From every age-specific **T**(x) matrix a corresponding **R**(x) matrix can be derived following the aggregation scheme given above. The next step is then to form the full **R** matrix of expected household transitions from the age-specific **R**(x) matrices. This involves the aggregation of 14 age categories into 6 age categories used in the classification of heads of households (see Chapter 5), and taking care of the consequences of the difference in projection period and age interval already noted in the construction of the **T** matrix.

If we assume that the partner who becomes head after the death of the householder falls in the same age category as the former head, this aggregation is straightforward and then we arrive at the matrix **R** of expected number of household events (formation, dissolution and change) with the following form:

$$\begin{bmatrix} p_1\mathbf{R}(1) & 0 & 0 & 0 & 0 & 0 \\ q_1\mathbf{R}(2) & p_2\mathbf{R}(2) & 0 & 0 & 0 & 0 \\ 0 & q_2\mathbf{R}(2) & p_3\mathbf{R}(3) & 0 & 0 & 0 \\ 0 & 0 & q_3\mathbf{R}(3) & p_4\mathbf{R}(4) & 0 & 0 \\ 0 & 0 & 0 & q_4\mathbf{R}(4) & p_5\mathbf{R}(5) & 0 \\ 0 & 0 & 0 & 0 & q_5\mathbf{R}(5) & \mathbf{R}(6) \end{bmatrix}$$

p_y $(y = 1,..,6)$ is the probability of remaining in the same age interval in the period t to t+1, given that one will be a head at time x+1, and $q_y = 1 - p_y$ is the complementary probability of moving to the next age interval between t and t+1. The household vector at time t can be calculated from **R** by summing over the columns; by summation over the rows we arrive at the household vector at time t+1. Thus,

$$\underline{G}(t) = \mathbf{R}\,\underline{i} \tag{7.22}$$

and

$$\underline{G}(t+1) = \underline{i}'\,\mathbf{R} \tag{7.23}$$

where $\underline{i}$ is a (30x1) column vector of 1's and $\underline{G}$ is a stacked column vector:

$$\underline{G}(t) = \{\underline{g}(1),\underline{g}(2),..,\underline{g}(y),..,\underline{g}(6)\}' \tag{7.24}$$

with

$$\underline{g}(y) = \{g_s(y), g_{h2}(y), g_{h3}(y), g_{h4+}(y), g_o(y)\}' \tag{7.25}$$

$g_o(y)$ in equation (7.25) is the number of new formed households or dissolved households in the period t to t+1, depending on usage.

Having now specified the methodology and the specific form of the dynamic household model we turn to various issues of empirical estimation in the next sections. We have to come up with individual transition rates to calculate the matrix **T** and the following sections focus on that topic. Section 7.3 describes the data used for the empirical estimation and in section 7.4 the estimation results are presented.

7.3 Secondary Analysis of Longitudinal Survey Data

The Sample

The data used for the estimation of the parameters of the household model were taken from a retrospective survey, held in the so-called 'North wing' (Noordvleugel) of the Rim-city in 1980 (see Chapter 5). The area of the Noordvleugel-study (NVS) overlaps the present study area with the most notable exclusion of the ZIJP. It also includes a number of other regions, viz. 'Het Gooi' (Hilversum and surroundings) to the south-east, and Haarlem and IJmond, some larger urbanized and industrialized areas to the west near the North Sea. The delineation of the study area was based on observed commuting patterns to the major working districts in the region (Amsterdam, Zaanstad, Hoofddorp (including Schiphol airport), IJmond, Haarlem and Hilversum. The goal of the NVS was to provide insight into the determinants of relocation of labour, residence and changes in commuting travel modes simultaneously (see NEI, 1980, 1981, 1983a, 1983b and Verster, 1986).

The total sample comprised 3,821 responding households, cross-stratified by degree of urbanization, commuting time, household type (single versus multi-person households) and mobility class. Four mobility classes were distinguished based on a two by two cross-classification of movers and non-movers in the housing market and the labour market in the period 1978-1980. After weighting, the sample was representative of the population of households with at least one working member in the period 1978 - 1980. So this delineation excluded non-working households (students, senior citizens, unemployed).

The Questionnaire

Since the scope of the study was to focus on interrelations between changes in location of work place, residence and mode to work, a retrospective form of questionnaire was chosen. Two types of questionnaires were mailed out: a major questionnaire to be filled in by the main employee in the household (and, if present, a second worker) and a smaller type of questionnaire for every individual present in the household in 1980.

In the major questionnaire detailed information was collected on a quarterly basis for every main and second employee in the household since 1975, concerning the following topics:

- place of work
- place of residence
- position in the household
- car ownership
- mode usage for work trips

A significant part of the questionnaire was devoted to labour market and mode choice questions. In our study only attention is paid to the demographic and housing market sections. A number of questions was asked about present and former household and residential characteristics. Among these variables were:

- size of the household
- main reason for starting or entering the present household
  Possible causes included:
  . leaving parental home
  . marriage or cohabitation
  . parents' divorce or partners' breaking up
  . death
  . move in with parents
- number of rooms
- type of dwelling (buy/rent; single/multi-family)
- propensity to change residence in the next two years

In addition to these household questions some information was collected in the major questionnaire on former household members, viz.:

- period of departure
- sex and age
- position in the household at the time of departure

No information on the cause of leaving the household or on new household position (if any) was asked. The smaller questionnaire was filled in by every other member of the household. Only a small number of questions was relevant for demographic purposes. First, it was asked since when the person was a member of the household. If this had occurred after 1-1-1975, the main reason for entrance was asked. Possible answers included:

- birth
- marriage or cohabitation
- parents' divorce
- former cohabitant's death or death of parents

No information on former household position or composition was collected from these persons.

In the present study the NVS is used in a secondary demographic analysis in order to estimate representative transition rates for each of the events defined in section 7.2. Since the data have a longitudinal character and span a period of five years, individual transitions can be measured, and rates defined in terms of occurrences/exposures, can be calculated. Despite the longitudinal character of the data there are a number of drawbacks in the use of these data for the present purpose. When using secondary data in empirical analysis the conclusions drawn form such an analysis should be carefully evaluated.

For the present study the problems stem from the following sources:

(a) the sampling scheme
(b) the questionnaire

The first type of problems restricts the representativeness of the sample. The theoretical populations of the NVS and the present study do not entirely coincide. The second type of problem relates to the amount of information collected in the survey. We shall discuss each type of problem below and try to find solutions to them.

Restrictions Due to the Sampling Scheme

Both the number of occurrences (events) and the exposure measure have to be calculated from the data. This means that we had to reconstruct the population distribution over the household positions at the beginning of the time interval (1975) from the observed distribution at the end of the time interval (1980) and the number of events in the time interval. If the 1980 distribution is biased, the exposure measure will be biased too if no corrections are made. Some sources of bias can easily be corrected however. We shall first discuss the differences between the NVS sample and our theoretical population, which is the total population alive at some point in time in the Amsterdam region between 1971 and 1986. The following differences with the NVS population are relevant:

- The study areas do not overlap completely. This is not a major problem **per se** since most of the present study area (that is, the Amsterdam housing market) is included in the NVS area, the ZIJP being the only exclusion. Moreover, it is not very likely that the NVS area outside the Amsterdam housing market is very different from the suburban zones in the Amsterdam region in terms of demographic behaviour. Larger differences can be expected between the city of Amsterdam and the rest of the study area, and ideally one would like to estimate separate models for the city of Amsterdam and the Region. However, the sample size for Amsterdam is only 385 (10 % of the total NVS) which is too small to estimate separate household models

- The research period of the NVS is 1975-1980, and this is exactly the mid five-year interval between 1971 and 1984, the relevant period for the present study. So, if there exist stable monotonic temporal trends in demographic processes between 1971 and 1984, it is likely that the observed demographic intensities in the NVS are central moments for the process in the period 1971-1985

- The NVS excludes non-working households and non-household units. Thus, some groups are excluded, viz. students and senior citizens, who form a significant part of the population in Amsterdam. This means that without suitable correction procedures, our results are likely to be biased both at the entrance and at the exit side of the housing market. For retired households there is no major problem since only two types of events are relevant with respect to the housing market, viz. death and movement to a non-household unit. External data sources, even at the appropriate regional level, can be used to fill the information gap for these events. For young non-working households there are strong objections in transferring data or model-results from the national level to the Amsterdam regional level. Fortunately, regional data exist on the number of children who leave the parental home for study reasons. Detailed discussion of this topic is deferred until section 7.4

Under the assumption that the marginal distribution of the sample over the household positions in 1980 is representative of the population, the distribution at an earlier time period can be reconstructed, with one important exception: any transition of a household out of the household population in the region between 1975 and 1980 is not observable by the sample. This group includes outmigrants to other regions, deaths and moves to non-households. External data sources can be used to reconstruct the total number of transitions of these types and so the total household distribution in 1975 can be reconstructed.

Figure 7.1 depicts some differences in household composition between the NVS and the WBO (National Survey on Housing Needs, see Chapter 6). This is a large scale cross-sectional survey held periodically by the Central Bureau of Statistics both for demographic and housing market purposes.

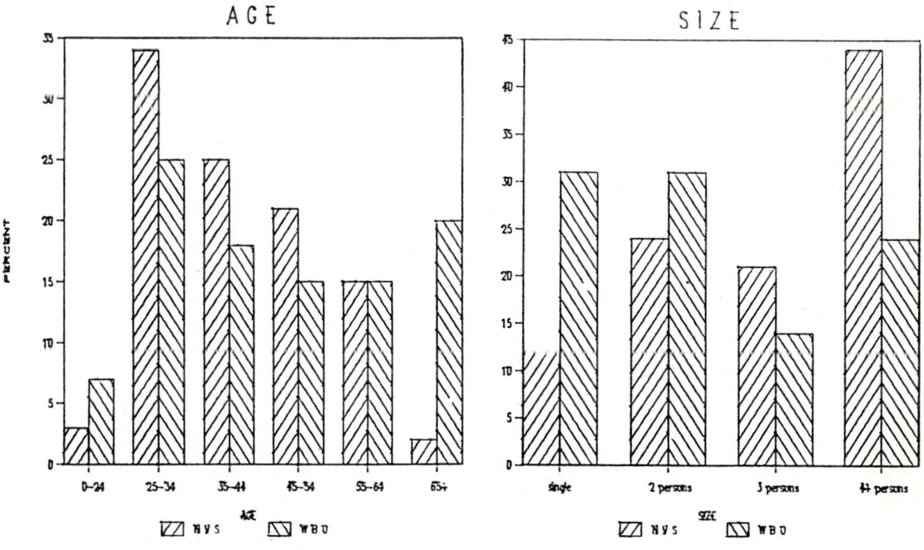

Figure 7.1. Age of head and household size in the WBO and NVS samples compared

In accordance with the differences stated above we find that both young and retired households are strongly underrepresented in the NVS compared with the WBO sample.

Restrictions Due to the Questionnaire

Since the NVS was not intended to be used for demographic purposes **per se** the questionnaire did not cover the total amount of information needed for a complete description of all individual demographic careers in terms of position in the household and household size. In order to see what kind of information can be derived from the NVS demographic data three types of groups can be distinguished, viz.:

1. persons who were in the same household since 1975
2. persons who entered/started the household since 1975
3. persons who left the household since 1975

The first group is a stable group. A change in household position for persons in this category is not observable by the data so there is no possibility of observing a change from child or partner to head of the same household. As described in section 7.2, the model allows one possibility of including this type of transitions, i.e. if the event is due to death of the head of the household. The second group is more important in terms of household events. If the person involved is a head or single, the corresponding change in position in the household can be observed, since both the present and former household position and composition is known. If the person is a partner or child after the transition the situation is different. Table 7.4 helps to clarify this point. For ease of presentation, we assume that cell entries only relate to persons of group 2. Transitions are possible between child, single, head, partner and non-household (denoted, as before, by C, S, H, P, and N respectively). All entries in the columns relating to singles and heads are covered by the sample. Re-entrance into the position of a dependent child is not possible in the model. All births in the sample are reported in the non-worker questionnaires so this leaves only the origin of the new-entered partners unknown to us, although the total number of transitions is known as well as the timing of the transitions.

For new entered partners there is also some information on the main reason to become a member of the household, but this does not help us very much, since 92 percent answered 'marriage or cohabitation'. So some additional assumptions have to be made here, using the known information on heads. In particular, it is assumed that the distribution of the partners over the origin positions in the household equals the distribution of heads over the origin positions. So, if the percentage of new heads who were child before the transition is 52.5 percent (from table 7.4) it is assumed that the same percentage of partners was child before. Another assumption is that the percentage of heads who were partner before transition equals the percentage of partners that were head.

1975	1980 child	1980 single	1980 head	1980 partner
child	-	66	259	466
single	0	-	181	
head	0	16	35	
partner	0	8	18	
birth	1118	0	0	
total subsample group 2	1118	82	493	466

Table 7.4. Observed household transitions in the NVS sample for respondents who entered or started a household since 1975 (weighted numbers)

Conclusion

At this point it is worthwhile to put the main results of this section together. Our goal is to estimate transition rates between household positions using the NVS data. Rates are defined in terms of occurrences/exposures (o/e) and so we need information on both the number of events and the exposure measure (i.e. the total population at risk in a fixed time interval). Since the survey is retrospective, we have to reconstruct the total population at risk at the beginning of the time period from the prior household positions and taking into account the non-observable transitions out of the household population (death, non-households). For children, singles and heads this is not a problem (as can be seen from table 7.4) since we know what their former situation was. For partners the questionnaire gives insufficient information to reconstruct their prior household positions. Instead, we have to make some strong assumptions here. The procedure of reconstructing the population from retrospective data is only valid if the sample itself is representative. This is not the case since non-working households are not included, and it can lead to a serious bias in the results for starting households. In order to come up with reliable estimates for young starting households, the data on persons leaving the household (group 3) are used, assuming that these are unbiased observations of the same event at the origin side.

7.4 The Estimation of Transition Rate Functions from the NVS Sample

This section deals with the empirical estimation of the age-specific transition rates **M**(x) to be used for the calculation of the individual probability matrix **T**(x). The necessary steps taken in the empirical analysis will be elaborated below in detail. First, the data were transformed in order to be able to estimate one-year transition events. Second, from the number of transition events reported and introducing a number of assumptions stated in the last section, the population at the beginning of the time interval was reconstructed. Third, age-specific (five-year interval) sample rates were calculated. However, these rates contain sampling error and this can lead to large variations over the age categories. Moreover, for some age categories no observations were available and interpolation was necessary. Thus, instead of using the observed rates directly, rate functions were estimated in order to smooth the data and to make interpolations. For a number of not frequently observed transitions simple sample means were taken since the data did not allow any curve fitting procedures.

Using One-Year Projection Intervals

The time period of the NVS ranges from the first quarter of 1975 to the first quarter of 1980. Due to the underlying Markovian assumption of the household model the transition probabilities depend only on the state presently occupied, and so we may break down this five-year period into five one-year periods and pool them together to derive a one-year time transition interval, which results in a sample size of 5N (N being the original sample size). This might cause a downward bias in the estimated rates, since the change of one household to the other could only be reported once. In general however, even a five-year period is considered short enough to allow only one transition in most cases (see Ledent, 1980; Willekens, 1980). Table 7.5 gives the total pooled matrix of one year transitions to different household positions.

Calculating Exposure-Occurrence Rates

Age-specific rates were calculated by dividing each number of events per age category of the population by the average number of persons in that age category in each time period. This number was found by applying formula (7.14) to the data.

t =1	t = 2						
	child	single	head 2p	head 3p	head 4+p	partner	non-hh
child	+	66	240	11	8	266	-
single	-	+	153	28	0	194	-
head 2p	-	34	+	429	2	10	-
head 3p	-	17	105	+	428	10	-
head 4+p	-	15	14	130	+	10	-
partner	-	8	18	2	0	+	-

Table 7.5. Observed individual transition table of household positions
- : transition not taken into account
+ : no transition

Adjusting the (C,S) Transitions

We assume that the bias, introduced by the NVS sampling scheme, only seriously affects the transition rates for children to single (C,S; for instance the event of students leaving the parental home) and for elderly to non-household units. For this last group data can be used on the number of beds in homes for the elderly and other non-household units. For the transition of child to single more problems arise.

Transition Rates of Students Leaving their Parental Home

The NVS sample contains singles and heads who were child before the transition to their 1980 positions only if they are employee. Transitions from child to a student household are not included. Therefore, additional information was gathered with respect to the group of children who leave their parental home for study reasons. This group is of considerable interest in Amsterdam because of the large possibilities in higher education (a large number of colleges and two universities) in Amsterdam. Using some additional data-sources the demand for dwellings in Amsterdam of students living in the study area was calculated. These data-sources can be found in the following publications:

- The College Student (De HBO-student, 1983)
- The Dutch Youth and the Secondary Education (De Nederlandse Jeugd in het Voortgezet Onderwijs, 1977)
- The Demand for Higher Education (Kodde and Ritzen, 1986)
- Regional figures on university students (CBS, 1985)

From these data-sources it can be inferred that in 1971 3.5% of all students in the age group 15-19 in the Amsterdam region demanded a dwelling (or room) in Amsterdam. This percentage is calculated in the following way.

Of all persons aged 17, 18 or 19 15.3% had a degree in secondary education on the A-level and 26.8% on the B-level. Of all persons educated on the A-level 58.5% went to university and 27.5% to college, while 48% of the persons educated on the B-level went to college. This means that 9% (58.5% of 15.3%) of all persons aged 17,18 or 19 started a study at university and 17% (26.8% of 48% plus 15.3% of 27.5%) entered a college. 72.0% of all persons who went to university and were living in the Amsterdam region choose for academic education at one of the two universities in Amsterdam and 53.3% of all persons choosing a college and living in Amsterdam or surroundings received their professional education in the city of Amsterdam. This means that in 1971 6.5% (72% of 9%) of all persons aged 17,18 or 19 went to university and 9.1% (53.3% of 17%) attended college in Amsterdam. The percentage of students aged 17,18 or 19 leaving their parental home was 50 for those going to university and 24 for those going to college. This results in a percentage of students leaving home in 1971 at the age of 17, 18 or 19 and going to higher education in Amsterdam of 5.4% (50% of 6.5% plus 24% of 9.1%). Of all persons in the age group 15-19 65% is aged 17,18 or 19. This results in a percentage of students leaving home in the age group 15-19 and going to study in Amsterdam in 1971 of 3.5%. The same calculations have been made for the following years but it turned out that although the different percentages change all the time the final outcome of 3.5% is stable. So this percentage is used for the whole validation period 1971-1984. Consequently, the transition rate from child to single in the age category 15-19 was increased with 0.035.

The Form of the Transition Rate Functions

The calculated age-specific transition rates were used to fit a number of transition rate functions. Two types of functions were used, viz. the log-normal and the negative-exponential form. These are frequently used functions in demographic analysis of fertility, marital status and other age-dependent processes (see e.g. Castro and Rogers, 1981; Hoem et al., 1982). Gordijn and Heida (1985) showed that these functions perform equally well in modelling household transition rates. The log-normal functional form used was:

$$m(x) = \tau * \exp\left[\frac{[\log(x-x_o) - \log(\alpha - x_o)]^2}{2 * \sigma^2}\right] \qquad (7.26)$$

where $m(x)$ is the age-specific expected rate, τ is the maximum expected rate value, x_o is the minimum age at which the process starts, α is the age at which the value τ is attained, and σ is the dispersion parameter. The negative-exponential function used had the following form:

$$m(x) = \tau * \exp\left[\frac{\log(0.5) * (x - x_0)}{\beta}\right] \tag{7.27}$$

The parameter τ is the maximum expected rate, to be attained at age x_0, and β is the half-life of the function. Since the negative exponential function is continuously decreasing, the starting age x_0 coincides with the age of maximum intensity. Both functions were estimated with a weighted non-linear least squares technique. The data used for the estimated were grouped in five-year intervals, and for each group the average rate was used. Each data point (x,y; with x = 1,..,14 denoting the transformed age and y = [0,..] the mean rate) was weighted with the number of observations. An alternative option is to make the weights proportional to the reliability resulting in weights equal to the variance. This method led to convergence problems in some instances and to small differences with the other method in cases where convergence was reached. So it was decided to use the weights equal to the group size for all functions (for this estimation the NAG-routine F04GDF was used). The functions were evaluated using the R^2-measure for overall model performance and the t-statistic to obtain individual coefficient confidence regions. The R^2 was used to measure the percentage improvement of the optimal model over the so-called null-model with one constant τ_c and to choose between alternative model specifications (for a detailed account of these non-linear regression models, see Amemiya, 1983).

Results of the Estimations

Nine transition rate functions were estimated in our analyses. The results will be given below for every position in the household.

Children: (C,S),(C,H2),(C,P)

From inspection of the observed rates it is clear that the functional form underlying all of these three transition processes is the same and can be approximated with a log-normal curve. Resulting coefficients are given in table 7.6 together with the corresponding t and R^2 statistics. The age scale is in five year intervals, so a value for α of 7 means 32 years (being the mid-point of the seventh age interval). Comparison of the maxima of the functions (the τ's) reveals that the transition to head of a two person household has the highest peak rate of 0.0766 at an age of approximately 27 years followed by the transition to partner at about the same age. The transition to single has a peak rate which is almost half of the transition to head, and is attained some ten years later (slightly under 37 years of age). Comparing the dispersion parameters shows that the dispersion of the (C,S) rate is much larger than the other two. Comparing the curves (Figures 7.2, 7.3 and 7.4) reveals the differences in form and gives an impression of the model fit through the observed data points. In interpreting these curves one has to take into account that the state of dependent child is numerically not very important after the age of 30, so large differences in rates after this age have relatively little impact on the resulting numbers.

parameter	(C,S)-model value	(C,S)-model t-statistic	(C,H2)-model value	(C,H2)-model t-statistic	(C,P)-model value	(C,P)-model t-statistic
τ	0.0766	-17.67**	0.1691	-14.90**	0.1368	-12.55**
α	7.9389	5.98	5.9676	23.11	5.8105	12.51
σ	0.7668	12.91	0.3745	27.56	0.4759	13.57
x_0	3.0*	-	3.0*	-	3.0*	-
N (df)	5 (1)		5 (1)		5 (1)	
R^2	0.9974		0.9981		0.9884	

Table 7.6. Estimated coefficients for the transition rate functions from child to single (C,S), head of a 2 person household (C,H2) and partner (C,P)
* parameter values for this coefficient were fixed at various integer values
** t-statistic based on log-transformation results

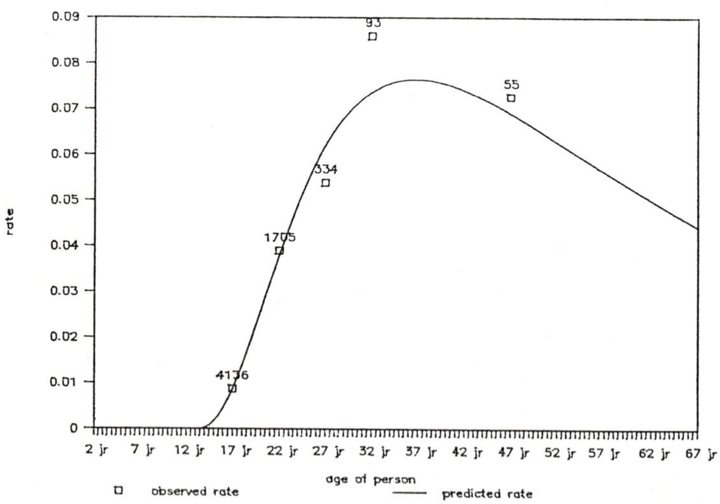

Figure 7.2. Rate function for child to single

The fit of the models is reasonably good. The t-statistics for all coefficients except the α for the (C,S) model are well beyond the critical level of the 95% confidence interval, with one degree of freedom (df). The R^2 values confirm the graphical impression that the curves fit well.

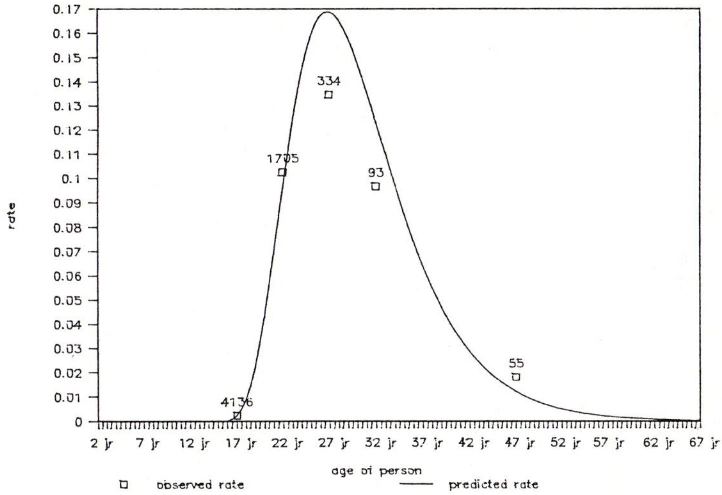

Figure 7.3. Rate function for child to head of a 2 person household

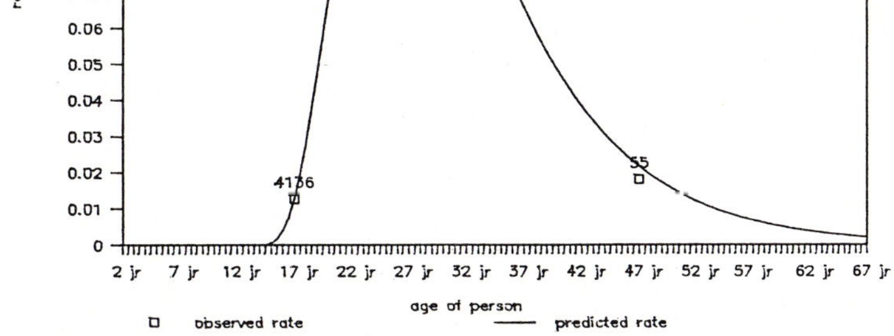

Figure 7.4. Rate function for child to partner

Singles: (S,H2),(S,P)
These transitions are very important in the age categories between 20 and 30, and decrease afterwards, although the exact form of the curve for the partners is less clear. Both a log-normal and an exponential form were tried and a choice was made on the basis of the R^2 statistic. Table 7.7 gives the log-normal and table 7.8 the negative-exponential model results. The curves for both types of functions are depicted in figure 7.5 and figure 7.6.

parameter	(S,H2)-model value	t-statistic	(S,P)-model value	t-statistic
τ	0.1411	-5.10**	0.5324	-0.13**
α	4.6171	2.05	3.4269	0.21
σ	0.7460	3.83	1.0445	0.94
x_0	3.0*	-	3.0*	-
N (df)	9 (5)		9 (5)	
R^2	0.8580		0.6748	

$t_{.95,5} = 2.015$

Table 7.7. Log-normal model results for the functions from single to head of a 2 person household (S,H2) and partner (S,P)
* parameter values for this coefficient were fixed at various integer values
** t-statistic based on log-transformation results

parameter	(S,H2)-model value	t-statistic	(S,P)-model value	t-statistic
τ	0.1437	-8.39*	-1.0252	-1.42*
β	1.8637	6.07	1.5400	3.35
x_0	3.8114	-	3.0122	-
N (df)	9 (6)		9 (6)	
R^2	0.8403		0.6500	

$t_{.95,6} = 1.943$

Table 7.8. Negative-exponential model results for the functions from single to head of a 2 person household (S,H2) and partner (S,P)
* t-statistic based on log-transformation results

Since the log-normal model uses one extra degree of freedom, the fit as measured by the R^2 should be higher. The results for both types of events are in the same direction. On the basis of the t statistic and the R^2 the negative-exponential form is preferred in the both cases.

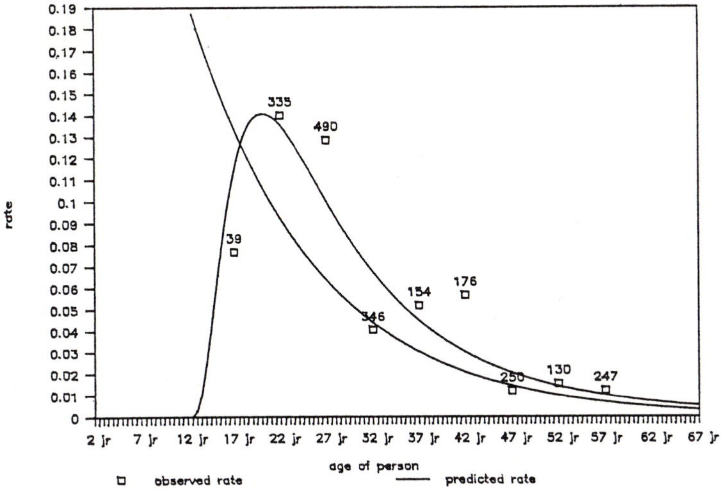

Figure 7.5. Alternative rate functions for single to head of a 2 person household

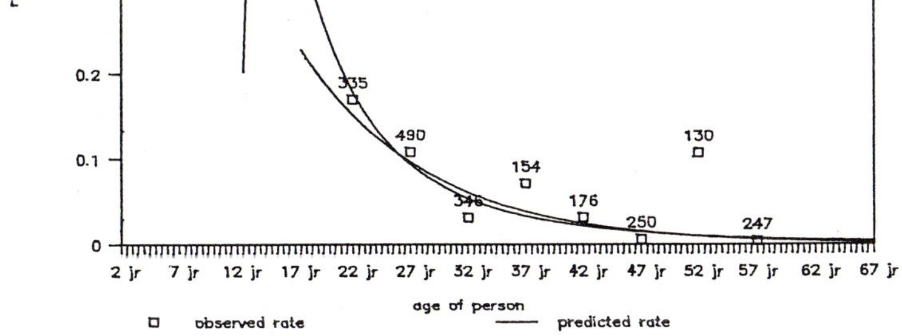

Figure 7.6. Alternative rate functions for single to partner

Heads: increasing household size (H2,H3),(H3,H4+)
The models for these transitions could be approximated relatively straightforward with the log-normal functional form. The results of these estimations are given in table 7.9 and the corresponding curves are drawn in figures 7.7 and 7.8. The peak-value for the transition from 3 to 4 is somewhat higher than for 2 to 3 and is attained at an age slightly lower than the corresponding age for transitions from 2 to 3. The curve for the 3 to 4+ transition performs better, as can be seen both from the t-values and the R^2's. A graphical inspection (Figures 7.7 and 7.8) reveals that this is mainly due to the outlier in the curve for 2 to 3 persons in the age-category 30-34.

parameter	(H2,H3)-model value	t-statistic	(H3,H4+)-model value	t-statistic
τ	0.1859	-13.16**	0.2496	-7.82**
α	6.2736	24.10	5.9383	12.84
σ	0.2668	11.25	0.2756	8.37
x_o	1.0*	-	2.0*	-
N (df)	6 (2)		6 (2)	
R^2	0.9632		0.9674	

$t_{.95,2} = 2.920$

Table 7.9 Log-normal model results for the functions for heads from 2 to 3 person households (H2,H3) and 3 to 4+ persons (H3,H4+)
* parameter values for this coefficient were fixed at various integer values
** t-statistic based on log-transformation results

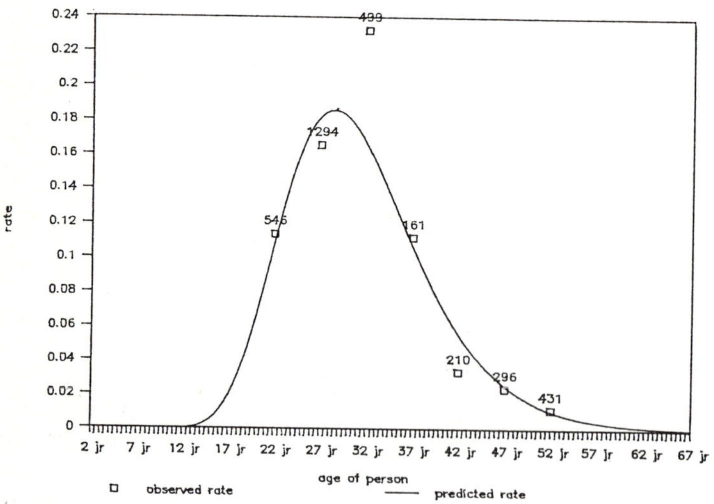

Figure 7.7. Rate function for heads of 2 to 3 person households

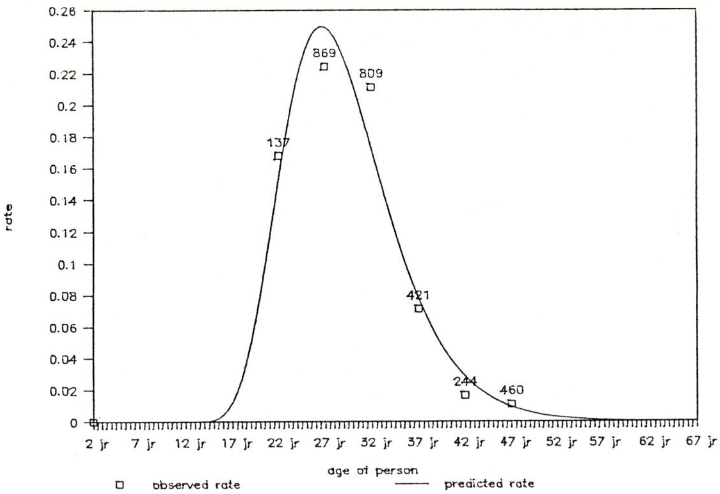

Figure 7.8. Rate function for heads of 3 to 4+ person households

Heads: decreasing household size (H3,H2),(H4+,H3)
We have two functions here: from size 3 to 2, and from 4+ to 3. Inspection of the data shows that a single log-normal curve is not appropriate in these cases (Figures 7.10 and 7.11). Both functions have in common that there is a lower tail at ages prior to the log-normal curve. The nature of the transitions is such that there exist two different causes for household decline, each with a separate functional form, viz. (1) divorce and splitting up of head and partner(s) and (2) dependent children leaving home. With the first type of transition one can associate the negative-exponential form responsible for the lower left and the second cause results in the log-normal curve at later ages. Consequently, a stepwise procedure was followed in the estimation of the curves:

(1) Estimate a log-normal curve on the total data set
(2) Calculate the residuals and fit a negative-exponential model on them

Table 7.10 shows the results of the estimations of the log-normal, and table 7.11 the results of the negative-exponential model. Figures 7.10 and 7.11 give the resulting curves. Both log-normal curves perform reasonably well, although the results for the negative-exponential residual models are somewhat less satisfactory, due to the higher variability in the observed rates. The R^2 denotes the improvement over the alternative null-model, and this is still judged to be a satisfactory improvement.

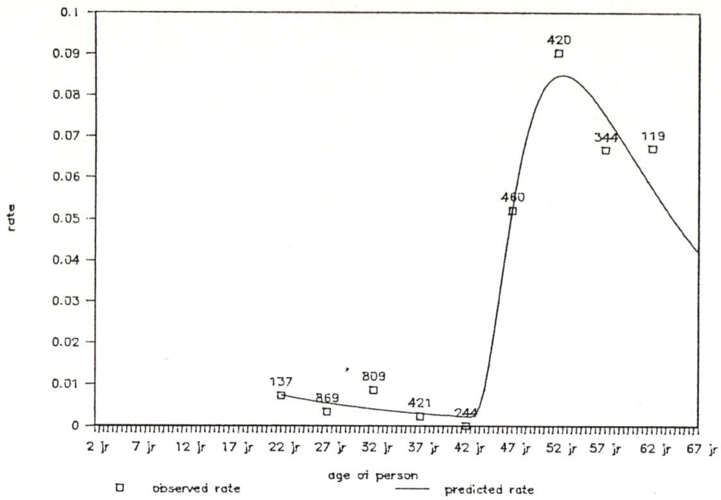

Figure 7.9. Rate function for heads of 3 to 2 person households

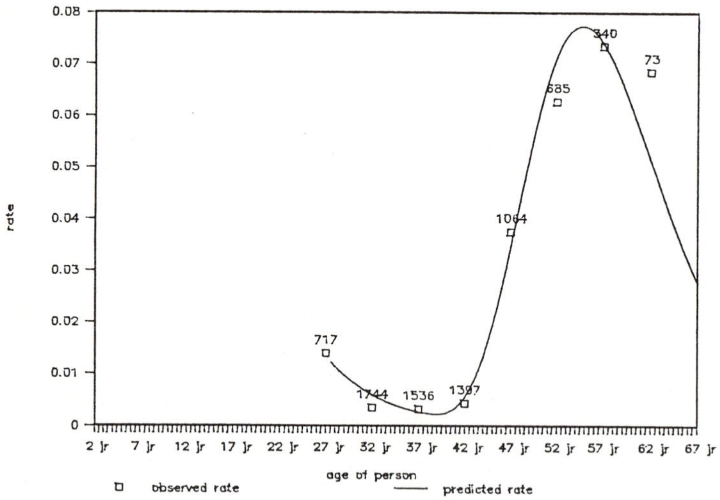

Figure 7.10. Rate function for heads of 4+ to 3 person households

parameter	(H3,H2)-model value	t-statistic	(H4+,H3)-model value	t-statistic
τ	0.0838	-18.45**	0.0773	-24.24**
α	11.0850	8.53	9.4269	23.01
σ	0.7376	4.02	0.2560	14.54
x_o	9.0*	-	4.0*	-
N (df)	5 (1)		5 (1)	
R^2	0.8649		0.9950	

$t_{.95,1} = 6.314$

Table 7.10. Log-normal model results for the functions for heads of 3 to 2 person households (H3,H2) and 4+ to 3 persons (H4+,H3)
* parameter values for this coefficient were fixed at various integer values
** t-statistic based on log transformation

parameter	(H3,H2)-model value	t-statistic	(H4+,H3)-model value	t-statistic
τ	0.0051	-9.55*	0.0134	3.09*
β	7.9293	0.20	2.9085	0.85
x_o	5.7131	-	6.2498	-
N (df)	5 (2)		4 (1)	
R^2	0.0200		0.2569	

$t_{.95,2} = 2.920$; $t_{.95,1} = 6.314$

Table 7.11. Negative-exponential model results for the functions for heads of 3 to 2-person households (H3,H2) and 4+ to 3 persons (H4+,H3)
* t-statistic based on log transformation

Other Transitions: Sample Means

For a number of less frequent transitions functions could not be estimated, and therefore simple sample means were inserted in these places. These are given in table 7.12.

t = 1	t = 2						
	child	single	head 2p	head 3p	head 4+p	partner	non-hh
child		(C,S)	(C,H2)	.00049	.00036	(C,P)	(C,N)
single	-		(S,H2)	.01251	.00000	(S,P)	(S,N)
head 2p	-	.00763*		(H2,H3)	.00045	.00217	(H2,N)
head 3p	-	.00443	(H3,H2)		(H3,H4)	.00217	(H3,N)
head 4p	-	.00198	.00191	(H4,H3)		.00217	(H4,N)
partner	-	.00436	.00017	.00020	.00014		(P,N)
non-hh	-	(N,S)	(N,H2)	(N,H3)	(N,H4)	(N,P)	

Table 7.12. Calculated sample means used in the household model for infrequent transitions
* transition due to death of head not included

Transitions from and to Non-Household Units

The NVS data do not allow the estimation of senior citizens to non-household units. Below the age of 55 other types of transitions from and to non-household units are very infrequent (change to and from the military service is not treated as a household transition). We assume that below the age of 55 there is a very low rate of in- and outflow between household and non-household positions. After this age the rate of inflow to non-households increases. The rate of inflow to non-household positions was calculated from given statistics on deaths in non-household units, plus the annual change in the total number of non-household units. This rate of inflow was calculated in order to compensate for the death rate in these non-household institutions and the changes in capacities.

7.5 Calculation of the Probabilities and Evaluation of the Results

The age-specific transition rates were organized in M(x) matrices, and transition probability matrices were calculated using formula (7.15), with the theoretical m(x) matrix replaced by the observed M(x).

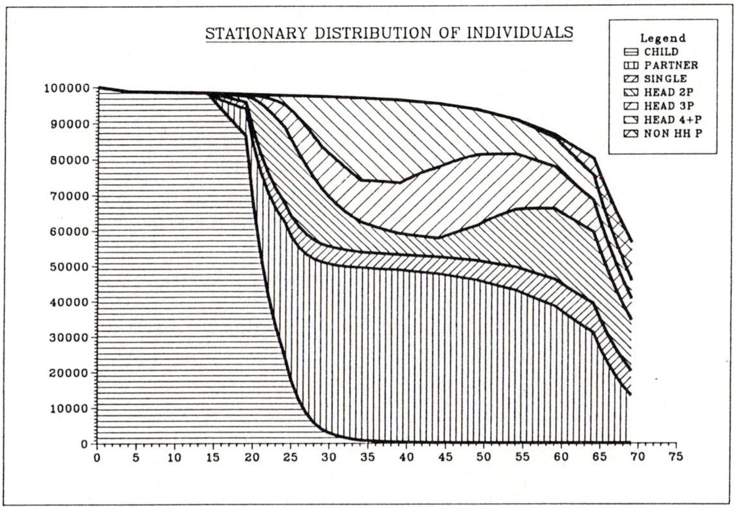

Figure 7.11. Stationary population distribution by position in the household calculated from the NVS data.

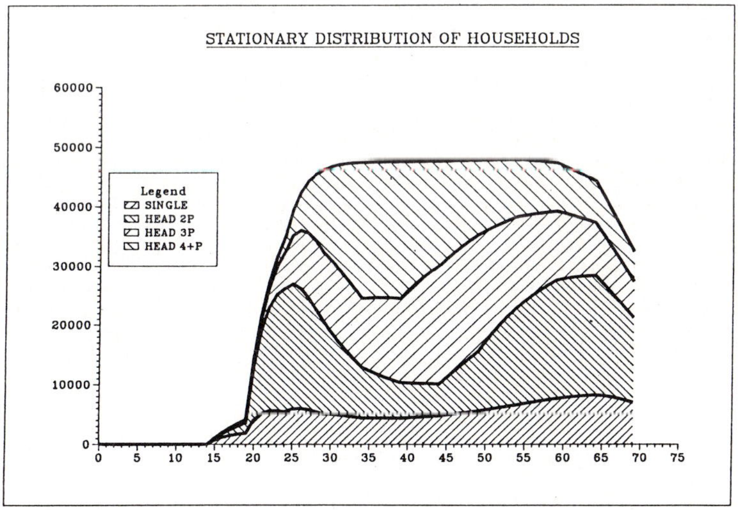

Figure 7.12. Stationary household distribution calculated from the NVS data

<u>The Stationary Distribution</u>

These results can be evaluated in a number of ways. Various statistics can be calculated from the life table, e.g. the total years lived in each state, the mean age of entering a stage (see Ledent, 1980). In the present context these descriptive measures are less relevant. Instead we will present a graphical result of the life table in terms of the stationary population. The stationary population can be calculated from the probabilities if we start with a radix $_0\mathbf{l}(0)$ of babies born who are all in one state. According to equation (7.8) we find this cohort in the next time interval distributed over the states as:
$_0\mathbf{l}(1) = \mathbf{P}(0)\ _0\mathbf{l}(0)$; $_0\mathbf{l}(2) = \mathbf{P}(1)\ _0\mathbf{l}(1)$. The resulting distribution of the population is the stationary distribution. Figure 7.11 displays this population distribution, starting from an initial radix of 100,000 babies and figure 7.12 shows the corresponding stationary household distribution, by looking only at singles and heads. Two person households dominate the distribution at younger and older ages. In between we find a large fraction of three and four+ person households, while the group of singles is becoming relatively more important at the older ages.

	1972						
1971	child	single	head 2p	head 3p	head 4+p	partner	non-hh*
child	239865	2208	4159	292	58	5065	284
single	0	89967	3797	1325	52	4071	3747
head 2p	0	673	87588	3004	285	203	3817
head 3p	0	215	1796	45673	3206	113	831
head 4p	0	142	177	2938	69289	159	475
partner	0	2554	578	232	146	210990	3836
non-hh*	6764	5	6	6	6	6	13236
tot.1972	246629	95764	98101	53470	73042	220607	787613
tot.1971	251931	102959	95570	51834	73180	218336	793810

*: population in non-household units and number of deaths in 1971

Table 7.13. Expected number of individual transitions in Amsterdam in 1971-1972

Expected Numbers of Transitions

Another way of evaluating the derived transition probabilities is to apply them to real world data. We have taken the 1971 population of the city of Amsterdam and calculated age-specific transitions. The results will be presented in two aggregate transition tables; table 7.13 gives the expected numbers of transitions of persons by household position.

Since the Amsterdam population is not closed we cannot observe directly whether or not these transitions have taken place. The observed 1972 population distribution in Amsterdam reflects both migratory effects and household dynamics effects. These results indicate that the pure household dynamics effects of the resident population in Amsterdam show an increase in the number of multi-person households and partners, and a decrease in the number of singles. Since the observed trend in Amsterdam since 1971 has been a trend towards singles, this implies strong redistribution effects of migration in order for the household model to be a true representation of the household dynamics. As will be seen in the next chapters, this is true in some zones in Amsterdam but the result is questionable for the total city of Amsterdam. The results also indicate that some adjustments of the parameter values may be necessary for the Amsterdam case. However, the total impact of the household dynamics on zonal household distributions can only be evaluated in an integrated framework with migration data. This will not be done in the present chapter but deferred until the chapters on housing market transactions. The aggregation of person transitions to household transitions gives the matrix of expected household events, and this matrix is shown in table 7.14

	1972				
1971	single	head 2p	head 3p	head 4+p	dis-solution
single	88337	3769	1307	53	9494
head 2p	661	86348	3002	285	5274
head 3p	214	1787	45454	3210	1170
head 4+p	142	177	2847	69300	715
formation	2285	4405	328	161	-

Table 7.14. Expected number of household transitions in Amsterdam in 1971-1972

7.6 Conclusion

The presentation of the household model in this chapter has been purely from a demographic point of view. Still, household dynamics is incorporated in the model to serve as input for housing market relocation behaviour. So, the model should be evaluated in the light of the housing market modelling goals set. Some decisions taken in the design and estimation of the model may be questionable from a purely demographic point of view. The rationale for these decisions will hopefully be made clear in the next chapters where the model is used to generate housing demand at a zonal level in the Amsterdam housing market on a yearly basis. The final evaluation of the household model can only be made in an integrated context with migration. This integration will be done in the framework of the allocation model, which is the subject of Chapter 9. The conclusion that can be drawn at this point is that the basic model is able to generate a dynamic pattern of household development in terms of household distributions over the ages, that seems realistic. It can also be concluded that the basic model coefficients presented in this chapter can only be seen as starting values, both for the time dimension and possibly also for the zonal dimension. The results found for the 1971 Amsterdam situation indicate that some adjustments in parameter values may be necessary for Amsterdam as opposed to the region. Statistical support cannot be given from this point on, simply because there are no data available to estimate time- or zone varying transition parameters. This will be taken up in more detail in the testing of the model in Chapter 10.

CHAPTER 8. THE ESTIMATION OF THE COEFFICIENTS IN THE LOGIT MODELS

8.0 Introduction

In this chapter the estimation procedure for the parameter values to be used in the model for the housing market demand model is described. As mentioned in Chapter 5 we use both the binomial logit model and the multinomial nested logit model. The structure of the estimation procedure which is actually used, is depicted in figure 8.1. From a theoretical point of view a four level estimation procedure would be more preferable. We will return to this dilemma between theory and practice in section 8.1.

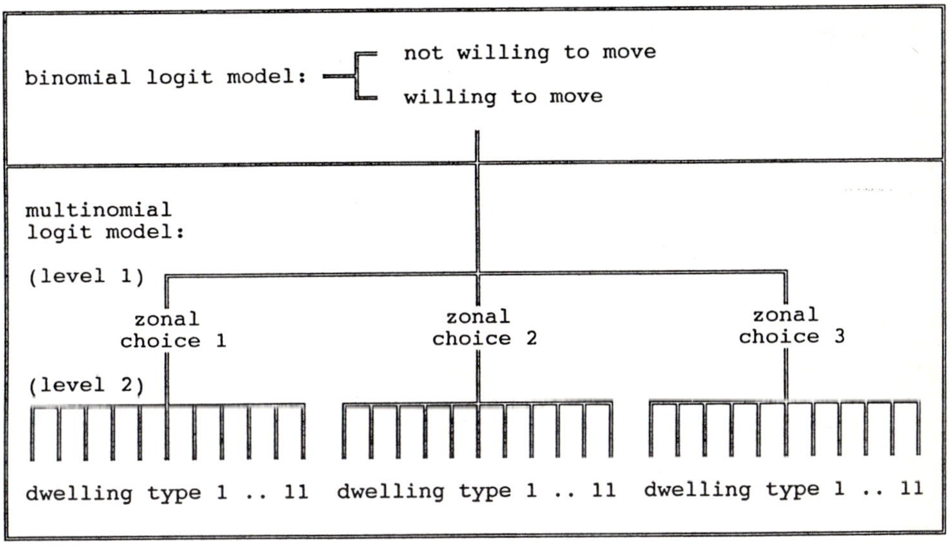

Figure 8.1. The decision tree of willingness-to-move and household preferences by zonal choice and dwelling type

In section 8.1 some theoretical aspects of the use of the logit model are discussed. The coefficients used for the willingness-to-move submodel and the submodel of household preferences per zone and dwelling type are estimated in section 8.2 and section 8.3, respectively. The results of this chapter are very important since these coefficients will be used in Chapter 9 in the calculation of the potential demand for housing differentiated by household type and dwelling type. Some concluding remarks are given in section 8.4.

8.1 Description of the Logit and Nested Logit Model

When a researcher has an individual or household-based data set, but only wants to use probabilities of a specific event for certain classes (and thus of a more aggregate level like as in our case), there are two possible alternatives:

- using the observed frequencies of the classes
- calculating the probabilities by means of a choice model

Choosing the first alternative, the frequencies of the specific event for the classes can be simply extracted from the disaggregated data set by dividing the number of persons (households) in a class for which this event occurs by the total number of persons (households) in this class.

Using the second alternative, first the exogenous variables which have an impact on the event are investigated and the corresponding coefficients are estimated, for instance by means of the multinomial logit model by using the individual or household data. Secondly, the probabilities of the classes are calculated by multiplying the coefficients, which are determined at a disaggregate level, with the mean class values of the exogenous variables.

Although, the first alternative is certainly much less time consuming then the second, we preferred the second alternative for calculating the probabilities in the housing demand model for two reasons:

- modelling allows the probabilities to become time-dependent since the exogenous variables may change over time,
- the calculation of frequencies for every combination of household type and dwelling type class is not possible, given the data size of the available samples.

The willingness-to-move coefficients using a simple logit model with two alternatives are estimated as follows. The assumption is made that on the basis of individual value judgments and satisfaction or (utility) levels, the decision to consider a move is made. If, for an individual household i the satisfaction level at time t is U_t, we assume that this level will influence the decision to move at time t (N.B.: the subscript i for households is omitted for the sake of simplicity):

$$P_t = F(U_t) \qquad \text{with } 0 \le F(.) \le 1. \tag{8.1}$$

The satisfaction or utility level itself is the result of both household and housing conditions:

$$U_t = U(s_t, h_t), \tag{8.2}$$

with s_t a vector of household characteristics and h_t a vector of housing characteristics.

Suppose there is a change in household conditions in the period between t and t+1, denoted by $\delta s_{t,t+1}$. The satisfaction level will change accordingly with an amount of:

$$\delta U_{t,t+1} = \delta U(\delta s_{t,t+1}). \tag{8.3}$$

It is assumed that the willingness to move, p_t^M is influenced by both the initial satisfaction level U_t and the change in satisfaction $\delta U_{t,t+1}$, and thus:

$$p_t^M = \exp(U_t,\ \delta U_{t,t+1})/(1 + \exp(U_t,\ \delta U_{t,t+1})). \tag{8.4}$$

Our central hypothesis is that households try to adjust their housing situation to changes in household structure, and hence changes in household composition have a stronger effect on housing demand than static household variables.

The set of variables s_t, $\delta s_{t,t+1}$ and h_t are contained in the definition of the 1056 household types (see Chapter 5). This generates the variables listed in table 8.1.

	number of classes
age of head	6
household size at time t	4
change of household size between t and t+1	4
dwelling size (number of rooms) at time t	4
tenure status of the dwelling (rent/buy)	2
dwelling type (flat/single family unit)	2

Table 8.1. Variables used in the estimation procedures

The first two variables are the s_t variables. Variable 3 is the δs_t variable and the last three variables are the h_t variables. These variables are used in various forms as input to the binomial logit model (see section 8.2).

Next, household preferences for residential zone and dwelling types are estimated with the help of the multinomial logit framework. For this model three main structures can be distinguished (see Hensher and Johnson, 1981, p. 78):

- the independent structure,
- the sequential or recursive structure, and
- the simultaneous structure.

These structures are not necessarily consistent with real behaviour of households, but are mainly chosen for analytical convenience. The first two structures are examples of the conditional decision structure. In the simultaneous structure no assumptions are made about independence or the decision tree structure; thus it is assumed that all decisions are made simultaneously by the households. Although in most cases the simultaneous structure will be superior to the conditional decision structure because it is difficult to find a 'true' sequence, in many empirical situations (i.e. when the variables defining the probabilities of the alternatives are not independent and mutually exclusive) this structure is not realistic. The conditional decision structure should be preferred in these cases. Another disadvantage of the simultaneous structure is the large number of alternatives which can cause computational problems. The independent structure is the simplest of the two conditional decision structures. The households are assumed to make their decisions independent from each other and there are no interactions or feedbacks between the decision levels. In many empirical situations the assumption of independence is not realistic and a extension is needed by means of the sequential or recursive structure.

In these structures the choices at a lower decision level are conditional on the higher decision level. The feedback between the decision levels is taken into account with the help of the 'inclusive value' or 'expected maximum utility'. Estimation begins with the latest decision and then moves back to the initial decision, taking into account the inclusive values L of the lower level decisions: the logarithm of the summation over the exponential utilities U of the lower level, i.e.:

$$L_m = \log \Sigma_n \exp(U_{mn}), \qquad (8.7)$$

with m and n the indices for the alternatives at the two decision levels. The inclusive values L enter the utility function of the higher level and their coefficients are simultaneously estimated together with the other exogenous variables.

Since the results of the estimated models are influenced by the sequence of the decision tree, testing of the sequential assumptions is necessary (Hensher and Johnson, 1981). The concept of decision-making embodied in the nested logit model is only limited to the random utility formalism and fitting the model cannot reveal anything about a hierarchy in the real-world decision-making process. Consequently, the nesting depends on correlations among the unobserved attributes of the alternatives, while the coefficients of the inclusive values in the nested model reveal something about the similarity across sets of alternatives but nothing about any decision tree in a real-world choice process.

From the above mentioned advantages and disadvantages of the decision structures we concluded that the most suitable model for our decision structure for the combined zone and dwelling type preferences is one of the most commonly used examples in the field of recursive structures: the multinomial nested logit model.

In mathematical terms the two-level nested logit model for the dwelling and zonal choices looks as follows.
The utility function for dwelling type k in zone z for a household k can be specified as:

$$U^D_z = U(s,h), \tag{8.8}$$

with s and h defined as above, and where the subscript i for individual households and the subscript t for time are left out for the sake of simplicity. The probability of choosing dwelling type k in zone z is equal to:

$$P^D_{k/z} = \exp(U^D_{kz})/\Sigma_{k'} \exp(U^D_{k'z}) \tag{8.9}$$

where Σ is the summation over all different dwelling types k'.

The inclusive value of the dwelling types over the zones can now be defined as:

$$L_z = \log \Sigma_k \exp(U^D_{kz}), \tag{8.10}$$

The utility for zonal choice z is:

$$U^Z_z = U(s,h,L_z), \tag{8.11}$$

and the probability of choosing zone z is:

$$P^Z_z = L_z^{\tau_z} \exp(U^Z_z)/\Sigma_{z'} L_{z'}^{\tau_z} \exp(U^Z_{z'}), \tag{8.12}$$

with Σ the summation over the preferred zones z' and τ_z the estimated coefficient of L_z.

The probability of the willingness to move to dwelling type k in zone z is by definition equal to:

$$P_{kz} = P^D_{k\backslash z} \, . \, P^Z_z . \tag{8.13}$$

From a theoretical viewpoint it is argued by Clark and Onaka (1985, see figure 4.1) that it would be preferable to extend the decision structure for dwelling choice with another level above level 1, i.e. the extension to incorporate the willingness-to-move decision by taking into account the inclusive value of the zonal choice. However, estimation of this model structure was not possible given the sample data, since households which were not willing to move were not asked about their preferred dwelling type and zonal choices.

Clark and Onaka also argued that another level should be added below level 2, because individuals and households do not choose just a dwelling of a specific dwelling type in a certain zone, but one <u>unique</u> dwelling. At this level, given the zonal and dwelling type choice, the individual dwelling unit will be chosen. Unfortunately, these individual dwelling utilities cannot be observed (see Anas, 1983), and therefore the approximation for the utilities on this level suggested by Quigley (1984, p. 48) is applied here.

If we assume that all individual dwellings w in a specific dwelling class k and zone z are completely homogeneous with respect to dwelling attributes, i.e. the individual dwelling units belonging to a given dwelling type k and zone z are highly similar and consequently have the same utility level. This means that the probability of choosing an individual dwelling w of dwelling type k and zone z is equal to:

$$P_{w/kz} = 1/N_{kz}, \qquad (8.14)$$

with N_{kz} the number of dwellings within class k and zone z at the beginning of the period. Now the inclusive value for the expected maximum utility of all dwellings within class k and zone z is equal to:

$$L_{kz} = \log(N_{kz}), \qquad (8.15)$$

This means that the inclusive value calculated from the decision level of choosing an individual dwelling unit is equal to the (logarithm of the) supply of dwellings per dwelling type and zone.

This inclusive value or supply must be incorporated in the dwelling type decision (level 2 in figure 8.1). The utility function (8.8). is consequently extended and the utility function for dwelling type k in zone z for a household k can now be specified as:

$$U^D_z = U(s,h,\log(N_{kz})), \qquad (8.16)$$

Then the probability of choosing dwelling type k in zone z now becomes:

$$P^D_{k/z} = N^{\tau_d}_{kz} \exp(U^D_{kz})/\Sigma_{k'} N^{\tau_d}_{k'z} \exp(U^D_{k'z}) \qquad (8.17)$$

with τ_d the estimated coefficient of N_{kz}.

So the household decision process is modelled as follows: first, a household decides to be willing to move. Second, given that the household wants to move, it decides upon the preferred zone. In this decision an aggregate dwelling type measure is taken into account. Third, given the preferred zone, the housing type is chosen, taken into account the supply per dwelling type and zone. The results of the estimation procedure with respect to the nested logit model described above, are given in section 8.3.

With respect to the value of τ, the coefficient of the inclusive value, we note the following. In case of a nested logit model with more than two decision levels there are two sufficient and necessary conditions for the model to be consistent with stochastic individual utility maximisation (McFadden, 1978, p. 287:

- the coefficients of each inclusive value fall in the unit interval. For our model this means that both τ_d and τ_z must fall between 0 and 1.
- the coefficients of the inclusive value do not decline as one moves up in the decision tree. For our model this means that τ_z must be larger than or equal to τ_d.

If the necessary and sufficient condition $0 \leq \tau \leq 1$ is satisfied, we can consider τ as a measure of correlation between the different levels in the decision tree. When τ is equal to 0, there is no correlation between the two levels in the nested logit model. In this case nesting is not necessary and therefore the coefficients of the exogenous variables which influence the alternatives can be estimated in a logit model with only one level. When τ is equal to 1, the correlation between the two level is at its maximum. In this case sequential estimation is necessary. If τ is in the unit interval, the structure is recursive. In some literature (for instance in Fischer and Aufhauser, 1986) the coefficient of the inclusive value is defined as $1-\tau$.

8.2 The Estimation of the Willingness-to-move Coefficients

For the estimation of the willingness-to-move coefficients, a data-set is needed containing information with respect to housing market characteristics on the individual or household level, i.e. current dwelling type of household, age of head of household. Two data samples satisfying the data needs were available: the Noordvleugel (NVS) data (NEI, 1982) and the Woningbehoefte onderzoek (WBO) data (WBO, 1981). Both data sources contain the outcomes of interviews held in 1980 and 1981 respectively (see also Chapter 6). In the interviews questions are asked with respect to past and present household composition, dwelling type, but also with respect to preferred dwelling type and location in the future. For the estimations of the logit parameters the computer program Chimp/Choice (see Van Essen, 1977, for a description of the model) was used.

An individual household was considered to wish to move, if in response to the question "do you want to move within two years" one of the following three answers was given:

- definitely yes,
- probably yes,
- has already found a new house.

Also households which have moved the past year are considered to be willing-to-move, because then the effect of household changes in the past year on the willingness-to-move is measured more precisely.

An advantage of the NVS-data is that from the interviews held all household changes in the past year can be deducted. In the WBO-data only increases in the households (mostly births) can be deducted. However, the WBO-data contain more households than the NVS sample and the data of the former seem to be more reliable than the latter, probably due to the stratification of the NVS-data survey into movers and non-movers (see Chapter 7). So unfortunately we cannot estimate all the necessary coefficients with the WBO-data since household dynamics cannot properly be estimated with this data set and we need the NVS-data to estimate the coefficient of the variable representing household dynamics. Therefore we will concentrate the estimation procedure on the NVS-data set for variables related to household dynamics and on the WBO-data set for the other variables.

After screening the data for the study area, the WBO sample contains 2979 households of which 587 (19.7%) are considering a move, while the NVS set contains 816 households of which 210 (25.7%, weighted sample) are willing to move. From table 8.2 it can be seen that in both data sets the willingness-to-move in Amsterdam is about 10% higher than in the Region.

A variety of household and dwelling characteristics is used as exogenous variables, e.g. age, tenure status, duration of stay. Also combinations of variables such as number of rooms related to household size, and log-transformations of variables are used. In the end, only variables which have a significant influence on the willingness-to-move remain in the model.

	NVS-data	WBO-data
Amsterdam:		
number of households	248	1679
willing to move	34.5%	23.7%
Region:		
number of households	568	1300
willing to move	21.9%	14.5%
Total study area:		
number of households	816	2979
willingness-to-move	25.7%	19.7%

Table 8.2. Number of households and willingness-to-move in Amsterdam and the Region for the NVS- and WBO-data

Although the WBO-data contains many variables that could be included in the model such as income, rent, the only variables used were those which can be directly calculated from the class-characteristics of dwellings and households (see Chapter 5). The reason being the need to only use data which can be collected every year from existing data sources. Naturally this can only be done if the results of using these 'simple' variables are satisfactory. Only the results with respect to the final choice of variables are presented here. To check whether one model was suitable for all zones in the study area zone-dummies were incorporated in the estimation procedures. From the results it was clear that a division between Amsterdam and the rest of the study area (already defined as the "Region") was necessary.

The variables and coefficients which gave the best results in the logit estimations using the WBO-data are listed in table 8.3 for Amsterdam as well as for the Region.

WBO-data	Amsterdam		Region	
(household size t=2-number of rooms)/number of rooms	0.660 (0.153)	(*)	0.474 (0.204)	(*)
single family unit/flat (flat=1)	0.657 (0.232)	(*)	1.741 (0.187)	(*)
tenure status rent/buy (buy=1)	-0.546 (0.257)	(*)	-0.524 (0.202)	(*)
log(household size t=1/ household size t=2)	-1.495 (1.002)		0.011 (1.321)	
age	-0.027 (0.004)	(*)	-0.025 (0.006)	(*)
Likelihood-value	-860.294		-461.957	
Rho-square	0.405		0.655	

(*): significant at the 5% level
standard-errors between brackets

Table 8.3. Final results of the logit estimations for Amsterdam and the Region using the WBO-data

From table 8.3 the following conclusions can be drawn. As mentioned before, we have concentrated on the WBO-data for all coefficients except the variable with respect to household dynamics, because this variable could not be calculated with the data in the WBO sample. So we have chosen the model with the best fit (maximum likelihood value), in which the coefficients of all variables (except the household dynamics variable) are significantly different from zero. All coefficients calculated with the WBO-data have the expected signs: households with a relatively small number of rooms compared with their household size are more frequently willing to move than households with a relatively large dwelling with more rooms. Also households living in a flat, non-owners of dwellings and young households want to move more often than households living in a single family unit, own their dwelling and are older. It turned out that the proxy for household dynamics (i.e. only an increase in household size instead of both increase and decrease) was not significant for both the Amsterdam model and the Region model. The constant term was not significant in both zones, which implies that the independent variables capture most of the variance in choice behaviour.

The values of the coefficients from the WBO-data indicate interesting differences in willingness-to-move between Amsterdam and the Region. The relation between household size and dwelling size is clearly more important in Amsterdam than in the Region, while households in the Region living in a flat are much more willing to move than similar households in Amsterdam. The willingness-to-move of house-owners is nearly equal in the Region and Amsterdam. Also the influence of age in Amsterdam is almost the same as in the Region. All these outcomes can easily be explained and are intuitively clear.

Also other variables has been used as exogenous variables, such as "duration of stay", income, etc., but the coefficients of these variables turned out to be not significantly different from zero and the models with these variables had a lower fit than the model listed in table 8.3.

In contrast to the appealing results of the WBO-data the comparable model outcomes using the NVS-data were less satisfactory (see table 8.4).

NVS-data	Amsterdam		Region	
(household size t=2-number of rooms)/number of rooms	1.343 (0.433)	(*)	0.182 (0.424)	
single family unit/flat (flat=1)	-0.698 (0.732)		0.978 (0.298)	(*)
tenure status rent/buy (buy=1)	-0.064 (0.504)		0.113 (0.286)	
log(household size t=1/ household size t=2)	-3.703 (1.607)	(*)	1.284 (0.758)	
age	-0.025 (0.012)	(*)	-0.055 (0.013)	(*)
Likelihood-value	-155.751		-249.351	
Rho-square	0.163		0.456	

(*): significant at the 5% level
standard errors between brackets

Table 8.4. Final results of the logit estimations for Amsterdam and the Region using the NVS-data

Inspection of the results and the data showed that in particular the data on dwelling characteristics were highly unrepresentative for the population in the study area. So with respect to the results of the NVS-data we concentrate only on the dynamic household variable, which is not significant in the Region model but very significant in Amsterdam. This result is not surprising: households in the Region are relatively larger than in Amsterdam and live in larger dwellings so they can cope easier with changes in household composition (especially with respect to increases in household size).

To use the proper coefficients to calculate the willingness-to-move for the housing market demand model the coefficient of the household-variable of the NVS-data is transferred to the coefficients calculated with the WBO-data (see figure 8.2). Since the household variable in the Region is not significant, this is only necessary for the coefficient for the model concerning Amsterdam.

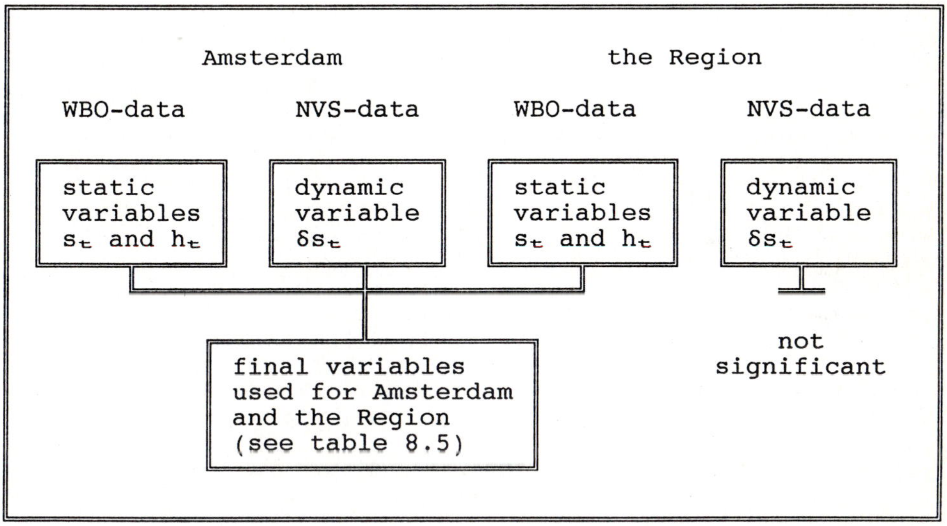

Figure 8.2. Scheme of used variables in the calculation of the willingness-to-move

To see whether a combination of the different coefficients gives a good fit we fixed all but the dynamic household coefficient from the WBO-data, and estimated the value of the household dynamic variable with the NVS-data. Fixing of parameter values is not possible with the logit-program Chimp/Choice; so the computer-program Chomp (Daganzo and Schoenfeld, 1978) was used, in which the likelihood function can be specified within the program. This resulted in a coefficient of the household dynamics variable of -3.99 and a likelihood-value of -159.498. Because the model with the fixed values and the original model are nested, we can calculate with the help of the likelihood ratio test (Mood et al,

1974, p. 419) that the model with fixed values is not significantly different from the original model for Amsterdam with the NVS-data. Also the values of the coefficients of the household dynamics variable of -3.99 with a standard error of 1.62997 and -3.70 with a standard error of 1.67719 are not significantly different from each other (tested with the Chi-square test, Mood et al, 1974).

	Amsterdam	Region
(household size t=2-number of rooms)/number of rooms)	0.66028	0.47463
single family unit/flat (flat=1)	0.65677	1.74084
tenure status rent/buy (buy=1)	-0.54641	-0.52429
log(household size t=1/ household size t=2)	-3.70322	0.00000
age	-0.02733	-0.02480

Table 8.5. Coefficients used in the calculation of the probabilities of the willingness-to-move in the demand side model of the housing market

So it is concluded that the coefficients of the estimations with the WBO- and NVS-data sets can be combined according to the scheme presented in figure 8.2. In table 8.5 the coefficients used in the calculation of the probabilities of the willingness-to-move in the housing market demand model are summarized. This is established by multiplying the coefficients estimated by means of the household-based data sets, with the class mean values of the combined dwelling type and household type classes. Since all the variables which distinguish the dwelling classes or household classes play a role as an exogenous variable in the estimation procedure the willingness to move will be different in all classes, except in the Region in which households will have the same willingness to move, independent of the changes in the household composition. Some results concerning the calculations of the probabilities to consider moving can be found in Chapter 9.

8.3 The Estimation of the Coefficients of the Zone and Dwelling Type Preference Model

Before starting with the actual estimation procedure the definitions and frequencies of the dwelling and zonal alternatives as well as the definition of the supply per dwelling type and zone are given.

Definitions of the alternatives and the supply variable

For the estimation of the coefficients of the preference model of the zones in our study area and the defined dwelling types (Chapter 5), we used the WBO-data exclusively, because the necessary data are not available in the NVS-data set. In the WBO-interviews held, questions were asked about preferred zones and dwelling types. Unfortunately households in Amsterdam were not asked whether they want to stay in their own neighbourhood, but only whether they want to stay in Amsterdam, so we could only discriminate between 10 zones (Amsterdam and the 9 zones in the Region) instead of 20. Most households wanted to stay in their own zone and the percentage of households which prefer another zone is very small or even zero (see table 8.6). Therefore aggregation of alternatives is necessary in order to estimate a meaningful choice model. As can be seen in table 8.6, households living in Amsterdam (zone 1) prefer to stay in Amsterdam and if they go to the Region they prefer to go to the ZIJP (originally zone number 20). This preference is not surprising taking into account the stimulus given by the municipality of Amsterdam to encourage households living in Amsterdam to move to this satellite town (see Chapter 2).

Households living in the Region also prefer to stay in their own zone and if they move out of their zone they mostly prefer to go to Amsterdam rather than to zones in the Region. Based on the previous analysis the 10 preferred zones were aggregated into 3 zonal choices which are different for households living in Amsterdam and households living in the Region (see table 8.7). The difference in definition of the alternatives between Amsterdam and the Region implies a separate estimation procedure for the dwelling type and zonal choices for the two areas.

preferred zone / present zone	1-11	12	13	14	15	16	17	18	19	20
1-11	85.7	5.5	18.5	7.1	4.1	4.0	.0	4.5	6.9	3.1
12	1.9	89.0	.0	.0	.0	.0	.0	.0	.0	.0
13	1.5	1.4	77.8	.0	.0	.0	.0	.0	.0	.0
14	.4	.0	.0	92.9	.0	1.3	.0	.0	3.4	.0
15	1.6	2.7	.0	.0	93.2	.0	.0	.0	.0	.0
16	1.2	.0	0	.0	.0	94.6	.0	.0	3.4	.0
17	.4	1.4	.0	.0	2.7	.0	100.0	.0	.0	.0
18	.4	.0	.0	.0	.0	.0	.0	86.4	6.9	.0
19	2.9	.0	.0	.0	.0	.0	.0	9.1	79.4	.0
20	4.0	.0	3.7	.0	.0	.0	.0	.0	.0	96.9

Table 8.6. Percentages of preferred zones by present zones (n=1527)

Amsterdam (number of households is 1082)	
zonal choice 1: staying in Amsterdam	85.7%
zonal choice 2: going to the Region except ZIJP	10.3%
zonal choice 3: going to the ZIJP	4.0%
Region (number of households is 445)	
zonal choice 1: staying in zone	91.5% *
zonal choice 2: going to Amsterdam	5.2% *
zonal choice 3: going to another zone in Region	3.3% *
*: average percentage over all zones in the Region	

Table 8.7. Definition of zonal choices and corresponding percentages

As input for the allocation model the demand per dwelling type is needed for every zone. Therefore the 3 zonal choices need to be transformed back into the original 20 zones of the study area. The scheme for this disaggregation procedure can be found in figure 9.1 of Chapter 9. From a theoretical viewpoint the aggregation of zones is not problematic within the nested logit structure (see McFadden, 1979, p. 91).

The variation in the dwelling types was large enough to continue with the 11 dwelling types already defined. In table 8.8 the percentages of households preferring the dwelling types are listed. From this table it is clear that households in Amsterdam have a greater preference for the smaller rented flats (class 1, 5 and 6) and households in the Region prefer larger rented flats (class 6) and the larger rented and owner-occupied single family houses (class 10 and 11).

		Amsterdam	Region
alt. 1)	flat/rent: 1 or 2 rooms	26.9	7.6
alt. 2)	flat/buy: 1-5+ rooms	2.9	4.3
alt. 3)	single fam. unit/rent: 1-3 rooms	1.6	4.5
alt. 4)	single fam. unit/buy: 1-3 rooms	.4	2.5
alt. 5)	flat/rent: 3 rooms	35.7	9.9
alt. 6)	flat/rent: 4 rooms	23.8	26.4
alt. 7)	single fam. unit/rent: 4 rooms	1.8	9.9
alt. 8)	single fam. unit/buy: 4 rooms	.4	9.7
alt. 9)	flat/rent: 5+ rooms	5.5	2.5
alt.10)	single fam. unit/rent: 5+ rooms	.8	10.6
alt.11)	single fam. unit/buy: 5+ rooms	.2	12.1

Table 8.8. The percentages of households per dwelling type

According to the overall model framework (see Chapter 5) the supply of dwellings is composed of the following three components:

- vacancies for more than one year
- vacancies resulting from outmigration during the year
- newly built and renovated dwellings during the year

Some of these data were available in statistical yearbooks, but sometimes we had to construct the data on the basis of known figures (see Chapter 5). In Amsterdam supply of dwellings is mainly the result of outmigration. In the Region this is also true, but here new construction is much more important than in Amsterdam (see table 8.9).

	Amsterdam	Region
vacancies	16.5%	9.7%
outmigration	77.8%	65.8%
new and renovated dwellings	5.7%	24.5%

Table 8.9. Percentages in contribution of total supply in Amsterdam and the Region

<u>Nesting: Dwelling Type Choices conditional on Zonal Choices</u>

Starting at the lowest decision level as depicted in figure 8.1, first the coefficients of the exogenous variables which determine the choice of the 11 dwelling type alternatives are estimated. As mentioned before, the logarithm of the supply per dwelling type for the preferred zones is one of the exogenous variables (see formula 8.13). Secondly, we calculated the logarithm of the summation over the dwelling types (inclusive values) for the 3 zonal choices, while, finally, the coefficients of the inclusive values together with the other exogenous variables are estimated.

The final results of the nested logit estimation procedure for Amsterdam can be found in tables 8.10 and 8.11. As can be seen here, the choice functions are the same for all alternatives (see formula (8.16), but for some alternatives the coefficients of the exogenous variables are not significantly different from zero. In the latter case the coefficient is not included in the table and a "-" is put in place of the value of the coefficient.

Because there is already a large variation in the inclusive values between the 11 alternatives, the coefficient of the inclusive value is restricted to be equal for all 11 dwelling type choices (i.e. being estimated as an abstract variable). The estimated coefficient of the log(supply) is high in Amsterdam, indicating that households do take into account the supply of dwellings in their decision-process.

Amsterdam	constant term	age	tenure status (rent=0)	preferred household size	logarithm of supply
alt. 1)	3.466 (0.391)	-	-	-	0.854 (0.071) (abstr.)
alt. 2)	-	-	3.847 (0.496)	1.808 (0.259)	
alt. 3)	-	0.023 (0.006)	-	2.057 (0.249)	
alt. 4)	-	-	3.672 (0.090)	1.504 (0.342)	
alt. 5)	-	0.014 (0.005)	-	1.941 (0.234)	
alt. 6)	-	-0.047 (0.007)	-	2.905 (0.241)	
alt. 7)	1.191 (0.353)	-0.051 (0.009)	-	3.049 (0.246)	
alt. 8)	-	-0.047 (0.012)	2.859 (0.637)	2.855 (0.281)	
alt. 9)	-	-0.093 (0.011)	-	3.462 (0.255)	
alt. 10)	-	-0.083 (0.010)	-	3.621 (0.251)	
alt. 11)	-	-0.074 (0.015)	3.942 (0.510)	2.935 (0.286)	

Likelihood-value: -1766.380
Rho-square: 0.790

standard-errors between brackets

Table 8.10. Variables and coefficients for dwelling type choices for Amsterdam with dwelling type choices conditional on zonal choices

The coefficient of the variable 'preferred household size' is always positive. This means a positive correlation between this variable and the dwelling type choice relatively compared to the reference alternative 1) (rent/flat with 1 or 2 rooms) and increases when the number of rooms of the alternative is larger.

The variable with respect to the tenure status is in Amsterdam only significant and positive for the alternative dwelling types in the owner-occupied classes. This means that households owning their house intend to continue to do so when they move. The age-coefficient is sometimes positive but mainly negative which is probably the result of a strong correlation between this variable and the other exogenous variables.

Using the 3 inclusive values for dwelling types in the logit estimation for zonal choice, gives the results listed in table 8.11.

Amsterdam	constant term	tenure status (rent=0)	number of rooms	inclusive value of dwelling types
alt. 1)	-	-	-	0.988 (0.139)
alt. 2)	-	-	0.336 (0.090)	0.916 (0.139)
alt. 3)	-	-	-	0.946 (0.146)

Likelihood-value: -527.266
Rho-square: 0.794

standard-errors between brackets

Table 8.11. Variables and coefficients for zonal choices for Amsterdam with dwelling type choices conditional on zonal choices.

The signs of the coefficients are not counter-intuitive: households in Amsterdam living in larger dwellings have a higher willingness-to-move to the Region.

The coefficients of the inclusive values are very close to one. In Amsterdam dwelling type choices and zonal choices have a significant influence on each other, primarily because of the influence of supply on the decisions on the housing market made by households living in Amsterdam.

The results of the nested logit estimation procedure for the Region can be found in tables 8.12 and 8.13.

The coefficient of the supply variable is close to zero, from which it can be concluded that the influence of supply on housing market decisions in the Region is small. The fact that the coefficient is high in Amsterdam where the supply of housing does not match demand and is low in the Region where supply and demand are more in agreement with each other, indicates that households do take into account the discrepancy between demand and supply on the housing market in their decision-process.

The relation between 'preferred household size' and the dwelling type choice is more clean in the Region than in Amsterdam. Also in the Region households owning their house want to keep it this way when they move. 'The present dwelling type' dummy (which is 1 if the present dwelling type is equal to the preferred dwelling type and 0 otherwise) is only significant in the Region and not in Amsterdam, indicating that households in the Region are more inclined to choose the same dwelling type as households living in Amsterdam.

Region	constant term	age	tenure status (rent=0)	preferred household size	present dwelling type	logarithm of supply
alt. 1)	4.483 (0.993)	-	-	-		
alt 2)	-	-	2.579 (0.496)	2.316 (0.654)		
alt. 3)	-	0.039 (0.007)	-	2.410 (0.640)		
alt. 4)	-	-	3.440 (0.774)	1.752 (0.704)		
alt. 5)	-	0.057 (0.008)	-	1.715 (0.648)		
alt. 6)	-	-	-	2.641 (0.646)	0.434 (0.137) (abstr.)	0.178 (0.062) (abstr.)
alt. 7)	-	-	-	3.222 (0.641)		
alt. 8)	-	-0.030 (0.012)	2.849 (0.408)	2.962 (0.649)		
alt. 9)	-	-0.086 (0.035)	-	3.532 (0.713)		
alt.10)	-	-0.055 (0.013)	-	3.605 (0.650)		
alt.11)	-	-0.072 (0.014)	2.990 (0.373)	3.441 (0.651)		

Likelihood-value: -735.471
Rho-square: 0.781

standard-errors between brackets

Table 8.12. Variables and coefficients for dwelling types choices for the Region with dwelling type choices conditional on zonal choices

The use of the inclusive values of the dwelling type choices in the logit model for the zonal choice results in the model specification listed in table 8.13.

Owners of dwellings are more willing to move to other regions, probably because they have more opportunity to leave their region, while renters have less flexibility due to institutional constraints which make them more likely to be captive to their zone. The coefficient of age for alternative 2 (going to Amsterdam) is negative, as expected: young households are more likely to go to Amsterdam.

The inclusive value of the dwelling types is not significantly different from zero for alternative 3: going to another zone. Probably other factors play a role here, such as changing work place. The influence of dwelling choice is most important for staying in the same region (alt. 1).

Region	constant term	age	tenure status (rent=0)	inclusive value of dwelling types
alt. 1)	-	-	-	0.359 (0.039)
alt. 2)	-	-0.028 (0.013)	-	0.206 (0.058)
alt. 3)	-	-	2.183 (0.520)	0.195 *) (0.453)

Likelihood-value: -153.157 *) not significant
Rho-square: 0.876

standard errors between brackets

Table 8.13. Variables and coefficients for zonal choices for the Region with dwelling type choices conditional on zonal choices

To test whether the specified decision structure -dwelling choice conditional on zonal choice- gives is better than vice versa the alternative decision sequence was tried also. The results -not reported here- were not in agreement with utility maximising principles.

8.4 Conclusions

In this chapter we have estimated the coefficients for both the willingness-to-move model and the nested logit model for the dwelling and zonal choices. Two models have been constructed, which give a good fit for the disaggregated data-sets used. With respect to the interpretation of the estimation results, we must bear in mind that the main purpose of the estimation procedure is not to construct an explanatory model for household behaviour on the housing market, but to predict the probabilities for the different classes used in the housing demand model given the exogenous variables.

Of course, it is vitally important that the coefficients can be used to calculate reliable probabilities. In this respect the values of the coefficients belonging to the inclusive values are especially important, since they play an important role among the exogenous variables. When the estimated coefficients of the inclusive values are outside the unit interval, one can consider this as evidence of a specification error in the nested logit model (Fischer and Aufhauser, 1986).

	Amsterdam	Region	
inclusive value of supply (level 3) for dwelling types (level 2):			
dwelling type choice 1-11	0.854	0.178	
inclusive value of dwelling types (level 2) for zonal choices (level 1)			
zonal choice 1)	0.948	0.359	
zonal choice 2)	0.916	0.206	
zonal choice 3)	0.946	0.195	*)

*): not significant

Table 8.14. The inclusive values coefficients of the nested logit model

The coefficients of the inclusive values of supply and the dwelling type decision level, are summarized once more in table 8.14. From the outcomes listed in this table, we can conclude that all coefficients of the inclusive values fall in the unit interval and that their parameter estimates increase as one goes up in the decision tree structure. This means that the nested logit model specification fulfills the necessary and sufficient conditions to be consistent with stochastic individual utility maximization (see section 8.1).

The coefficients listed in tables 8.10-8.13 can be used in the calculation of the class-probabilities of the willingness-to-move to the preferred zones and dwelling types in the housing market demand model. So for every household/dwelling class and zone we have 33 (11 x 3) probabilities for choosing a specific dwelling type in a specific zone. An example will make this probably more clear. Consider a household in household class 6 (two-persons, age of head between 25-34 years old) living in a dwelling belonging to dwelling type 5 (rented flat with 3 rooms) in Amsterdam. Furthermore, the household did not experience a change in household composition. The values of the exogenous variables for this household are (see table 8.5):

- (household size t=2 - number of rooms)/ number of rooms = (2-3)/3 = -0.333
- single family unit/flat 1
- tenure status rent/buy 0
- log(household size t=1/ household size t=2) log(2/2) = 0
- age (class average) 30

The utility of the willingness to move of this household is now equal to (see formula (8.2) and the coefficients in table 8.5):

$$U = 0.660 \times -0.333 + 0.657 \times 1 + -0.546 \times 0 + -3.703 \times 0 + -0.027 \times 30 = -0.373$$

The probability of the willingness to move of this household is now equal to (see formula (8.4):

$$P^{M} = \exp(-0.373/(1+\exp(-0.373)) = 0.689/1.689 = 0.41$$

In a similar way the probabilities can be calculated for all household types, living in different dwelling types and zones. Various results regarding these probabilities will be given in Chapter 9.

CHAPTER 9. THE HOUSING DEMAND MODEL AND THE ALLOCATION MODEL

9.0 Introduction

In this chapter the housing demand and allocation models are described. First, in section 9.1 the different steps, in which the demand for the 11 dwelling types per zone is calculated, are discussed in detail. Then some selected results with respect to the probabilities of the zonal and dwelling type choices are given in section 9.2, while a description of the allocation model can be found in section 9.3. Finally, some concluding remarks can be found in section 9.4.

9.1 The Housing Demand Model

In the housing demand model the number of households preferring to move to a specific zone and dwelling type is calculated. The structure of the demand model used for all 20 zones of the Amsterdam area is depicted in figure 9.1. The different steps in which the calculation of demand takes place are described below.

Step 1: reading the data needed

The input for the housing demand model is:

- the coefficients of the willingness-to-move variables (from table 8.5 in section 8.2.)
- the exogenous variables of the household classes with respect to household and dwelling type characteristics (defined by the class definitions in Chapter 5)
- the number of households of the occupancy matrix after household changes and before migration (from the demographic model in Chapter 7) per household type and dwelling type
- subtenants, i.e. households living together with other households, new households, households forced to move because of demolition, and households migrating into the study area from outside (from the demographic model in Chapter 7)
- supply in the beginning of the period per dwelling type and zone (partially known from published data sources and partially calibrated; see Chapter 6)
- the coefficients of the preference variables of zones and dwelling types (tables 8.17-8.20 in section 8.3)

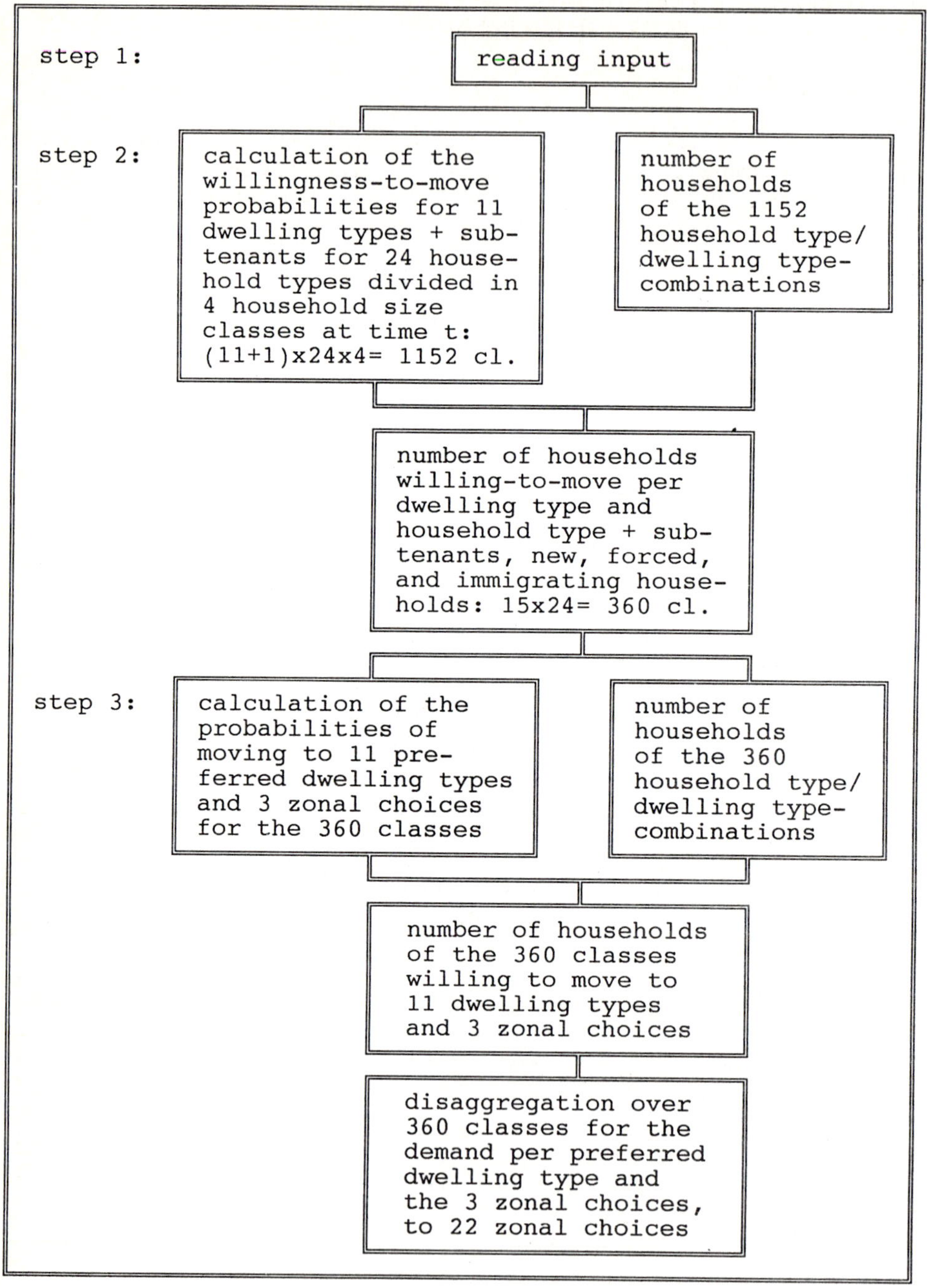

Figure 9.1. The structure of the housing demand model

Step 2: calculation of the number of households willing to move

First the probabilities of the willingness-to-move are calculated for all 20 zones and all household type/dwelling type combinations by multiplying the parameter values with the corresponding exogenous variables. Since the willingness-to-move is dependent on the changes in household size between time period t and t+1, the 24 household types defined in Chapter 5 are distinguished by their household size at time t. Therefore the same classification of household size as in figure 5.1. is used.

These changes in household compositions are known because of the multiplication of the occupancy matrix with the transition matrix (see Chapter 7). Thus, the calculation of the willingness-to-move probabilities is carried out for 4 x 24 = 96 household classes in 11 dwelling types = 1056 household type/dwelling type combinations per zone. The coefficients of table 8.5 for Amsterdam and the Region are used for the zones in Amsterdam (1-11) and for the zones in the Region (12-20), respectively. The willingness-to-move for 4 x 24 subtenants is also calculated, assuming their dwelling characteristics to be equal to households in a rented flat with 1 or 2 rooms (dwelling type 1), because this class has the highest probability to move. Multiplication of the number of households per class by the corresponding probability of the willingness-to-move results in the number of households willing to move. Since the household size at time t is not needed anymore as a class characteristic, the households in the 4 household size classes are aggregated into (1056+96)/4 = 288 household type/dwelling type combinations.

Furthermore it is assumed that the probability of the willingness-to-move for new households (24 classes), 'forced' movers (24 classes) and immigrating households (24 classes) to be equal to one. So as a result of the willingness-to-move model the number of households willing to move for all 20 zones and 360 classes is known (for the definition of the 360 classes, see table 9.1.).

11 dwelling types x 24 household types	
	(4 hhold size classes and 6 age classes)
1 x 24 hhold classes living together with other hholds	
	(class 12)
1 x 24 hhold classes of newly formed hholds (class 13)	
1 x 24 hhold classes of hholds forced to move (class 14)	
1 x 24 hhold classes of hholds migrating into the zones	
	(class 15)
15 x 24 household classes = 360 household classes	

Table 9.1. Definition of the 360 household (hhold) classes

The number of households in the 360 household classes form the input for the calculations in step 3.

Step 3: calculation of the number of households preferring a specific zone and dwelling type

Per household type and zone the 33 probabilities of the preference to move to the 11 dwelling types and 3 zonal choices have been calculated using the nested logit structure of section 8.3. and the coefficients of tables 8.17 and 8.18 for the 11 zones in Amsterdam and of tables 8.19 and 8.20 for the 9 zones in the Region and the exogenous variables resulting from the class characteristics. For classes 12 to 15 (see table 9.1 for their definitions) it is assumed that the households in these classes have the same characteristics as households in dwelling type 1 (rented flat with 1 or 2 rooms), and that the dummy of the present dwelling type is zero for dwelling types 14 and 15, i.e., there is no preference for a specific dwelling type. For the subtenants (class 12), new households (class 13) and the forced movers (class 15) both the zonal and dwelling type preferences are calculated. For the immigrating households (class 14) only the preferred dwelling type is estimated, because the preferred zone is already known.

Multiplication of the output of step 2, the number of households per zone and class which are willing to move, with the 33 probabilities, gives the number of households willing to move per preferred zone and dwelling type. Before this demand can be used in the allocation model the 3 zonal choices must be disaggregated into 20 preferred zones. This will be the subject of the last part of this section.

Since the 3 zonal preferences are known for all 20 present zones, they can be extended towards 20 preferred zones according to the scheme in figure 9.2.

Now the demand for moving to the 11 dwelling types in Amsterdam and the 9 zones in the Region is known. The demand of the households wishing to move within in Amsterdam, is divided over the zones in Amsterdam using a distance function. Also the demand of the households in the Region wishing to move to another zone in the Region is divided over the Region with the use of a distance function. The procedure with respect to the two distance functions is described below. Since the migration flows between the zones in Amsterdam and the zones in the Region are not known, this procedure cannot be followed for the households in the Region which want to migrate to Amsterdam and for households in Amsterdam which want to move to the Region, so two extra zones are added: zone 21, which consists of the demand of the Region for migrating to Amsterdam and zone 22, which consists of the demand of Amsterdam for migrating to the Region.

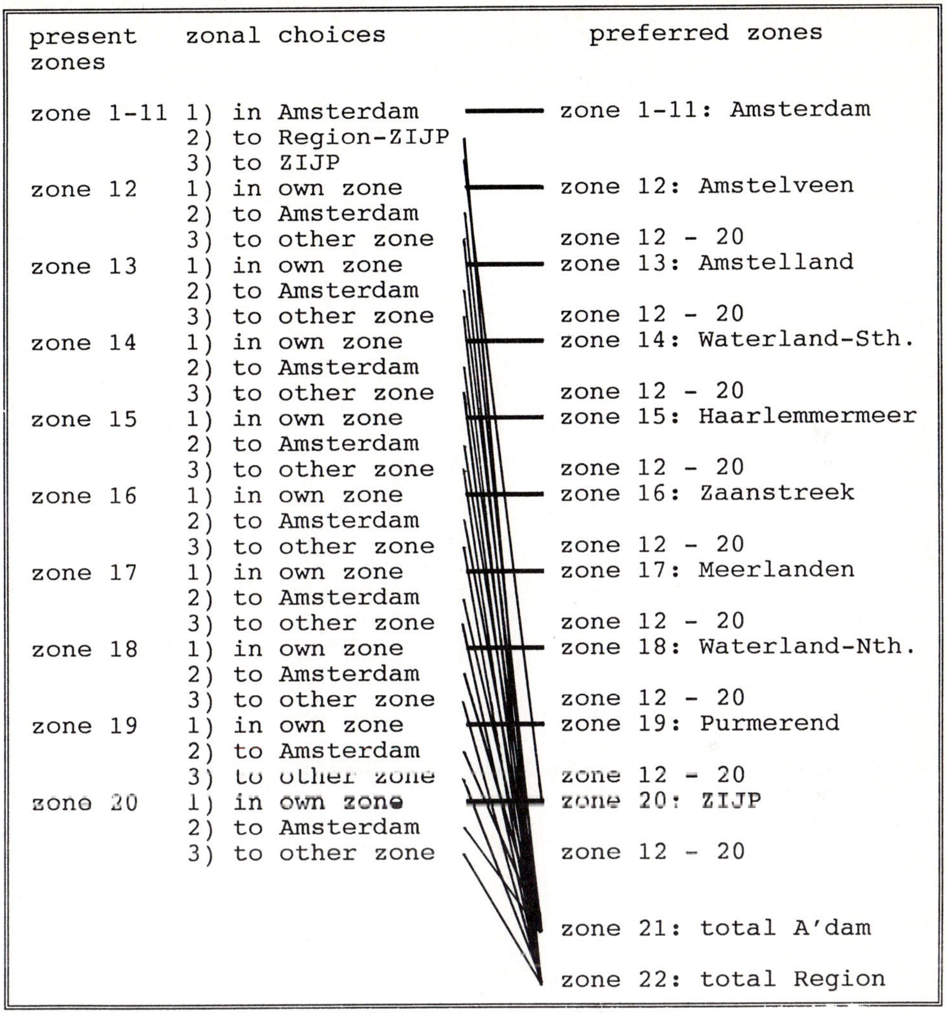

Figure 9.2. Clustering scheme of the 3 zonal choices to the 20 (+2) zones

Distance functions for Amsterdam and the Region

On the basis of observed migration flows within Amsterdam and within the Region a distance parameter has been estimated. In the computerprogram GLIM the following function was defined:

$$T_{ij} = c\, \alpha_i\, \beta_j\, d_{ij}^{\tau} \qquad (9.1)$$

with T_{ij} the observed migration between zone i and zone j, c a constant, d_{ij} the distance between zone i and zone j, and α_i, β_j, τ the parameters to be estimated. The results with respect to the estimate of τ for both Amsterdam and the Region are depicted in figure 9.3.

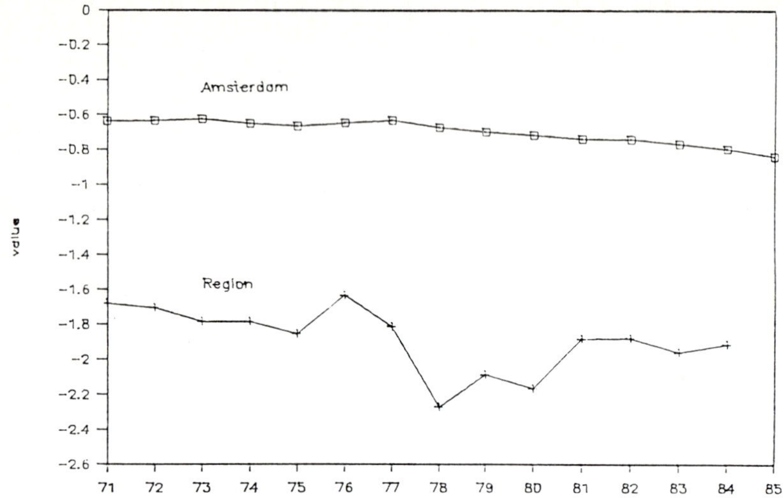

Figure 9.3. The estimate of the distance parameter τ, 1971-1984

As expected, the value of τ is negative, implying that households move more often to a zone which is closer to their present zone. The values for Amsterdam are more stable in time than the values in the Region.

The values of τ for each year are incorporated in the housing demand model to calculate probabilities of choosing between the zones within Amsterdam for households willing to move within Amsterdam and between the zones within the Region for households living in the Region which want to move to another zone in the Region. The probability function has the following form:

$$P_{j|i} = \exp(U_{ij}) / (\textstyle\sum_k \exp(U_{ik})), \qquad (9.2)$$

and

$$\exp(U_{ij}) = A_j \, d_{ij}^{\tau}, \qquad (9.3)$$

with $P_{j|i}$ the probability of choosing zone j when living in zone i, U_{ij} the attractivity of zone j when living in zone i. U_{ij} depends on the supply in zone j (A_j) and the distance between zone i and zone j (d_{ij}), with τ the estimated distance parameter.

For Amsterdam the calculated probabilities are multiplied by the households which want to move within Amsterdam. For the Region the calculated probabilities are multiplied by the households which want to move to another zone in the Region.

Before describing the allocation model, in the following section results are given for the probabilities of both the willingness-to-move and the household preferences of the dwelling types and zones using the supply and household data of the base-year 1971.

9.2 Some Results for the Probabilities used in the Demand Model

As mentioned above, some results for the probabilities used in the demand model will be given in this section. The purpose of presenting these outcomes is to show that the probabilities are realistic. Of course this can also be seen from the results of the coefficient estimation in Chapter 8, but the comparison on the basis of the probabilities is easier to interpret and also the differences between zones can be taken into account by means of the inclusive values and supply per zone and dwelling type (since these elements are used as exogenous variables in the model).

A comparison will be made here between classes which have large differences in the probabilities. The probabilities will be discussed according to the sequence of the nested logit structure (see figure 8.1), so first the willingness-to-move probabilities, then the zonal preferences and finally the preferences per dwelling type. The willingness-to-move probabilities per class differ only for Amsterdam and the Region, since two different models have been estimated in Chapter 8. The probabilities per preferred zone and dwelling type differ for all zones due to the differences in supply. For the comparison three zones have been chosen: Amsterdam, and two zones in the Region, one with a large supply per dwelling class (Amstelveen: zone 11) and one with a low supply per dwelling class (Waterland-South: zone 14). The housing supply per dwelling class is listed in table 9.2.

dwelling class	1	2	3	4	5	6	7	8	9	10	11
Amsterdam	8128	2985	1905	657	16477	14796	1694	557	4280	1172	1799
Amstelveen	527	540	645	137	799	872	436	358	109	683	1433
Waterland-South	20	20	112	54	9	1	172	176	122	54	603

Table 9.2. The supply per dwelling class for Amsterdam, Amstelveen and Waterland-South

Willingness-to-Move Probabilities

In figures 9.4 and 9.5 the willingness-to-move for the 6 age classes is shown; in figure 9.4 for the households with a large change in household composition (from size 1 at time t to size 4 at time t+1), living in a rented flat with 1 or 2 rooms (dwelling type 1), and in figure 9.5 for households with no change in composition (size 4 at time t and t+1), living in an owner-occupied single family unit with more than 4 rooms (dwelling type 11). In both figures the probability of moving is declining with age (due to the negative value of the age coefficient in table 8.5). The households defined for figure 9.4 are much more willing to move than the households of figure 9.5. This is obvious, since the first households experience large changes while the latter household composition is stable and these households are already living in a large dwelling. The willingness-to-move probabilities in figure 9.4 are higher for Amsterdam than for the Region as a result of the absolutely higher coefficients of the 'household size/dwelling size' and 'household size change' variables in Amsterdam (see table 8.5). The probabilities in figure 9.5 are slightly higher for the Region than for Amsterdam (the coefficient for Amsterdam of the tenure status dummy (rent=0) is more negative than for the Region).

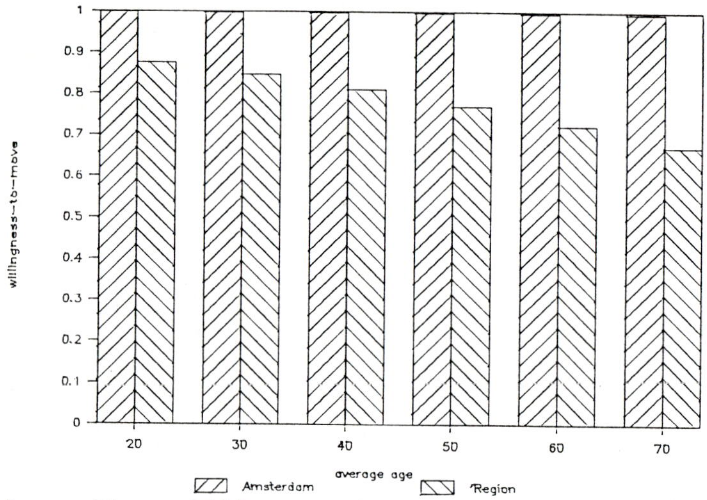

Figure 9.4. The willingness-to-move per age-class for households with large changes in household composition and living in dwelling type 1

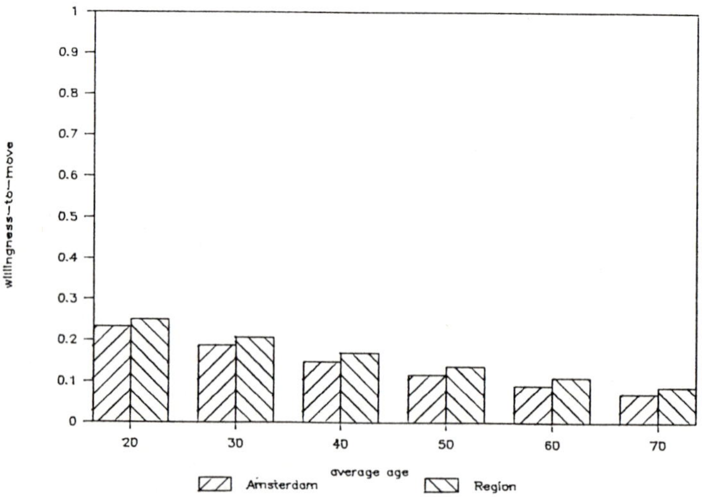

Figure 9.5. The willingness-to-move per age-class for households with no changes in household composition and living in dwelling type 11

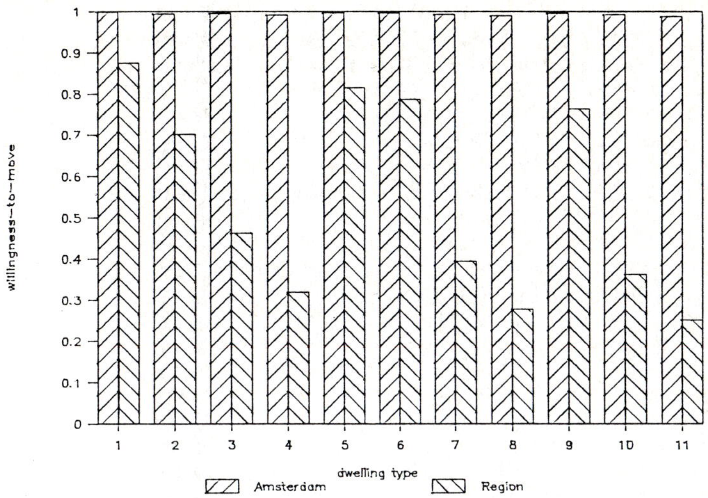

Figure 9.6. The willingness-to-move per dwelling type for households with large changes in household composition and age of head 20

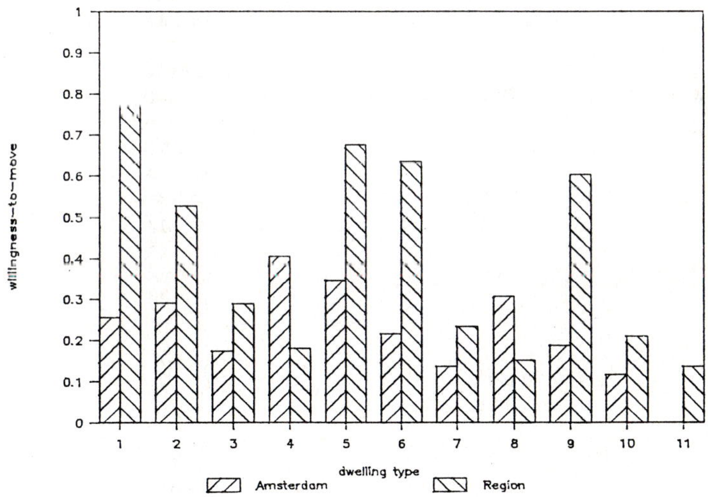

Figure 9.7. The willingness-to-move per dwelling type for households with no changes in household composition and age of head 20

Figures 9.6 and 9.7 give the willingness-to-move for Amsterdam and the Region per dwelling class of households with large household size changes and average age of head 20, and of households with no household size changes and average age of head 50 respectively. The probabilities in figure 9.6 for Amsterdam are all higher than those for the Region, and in figure 9.7 vice versa (Amsterdam lower than the Region). Again the willingness-to-move is much higher for younger households with large changes in household composition. In both figures the fluctuations due to the dwelling type definitions can be clearly seen. Households in rented flats (class 1, 5, 6 and 9) are those with the strongest intention to move, then the households in owner-occupied flats (class 2) and in rented single-family units (class 3, 7 and 10), and finally the households in owner-occupied single family units (class 4, 8 and 11).

Probabilities of Zonal Choices

In figure 9.8 and 9.9 the zonal preferences for the 24 household types in Amsterdam (9.8.a and 9.9.a), Amstelveen (9.8.b and 9.9.b) and Waterland-South (9.8.c and 9.9.c) are presented. The preferences of households living in dwelling type 1 (rented flat with one or two rooms) are given in figure 9.8, and of households living in dwelling type 11 (owner-occupied single family unit with more than 4 rooms) in figure 9.9. For the sake of clarity in table 9.3 the zonal choices defined in Chapter 8 are listed again for Amsterdam, Amstelveen and Waterland-South.

	zonal choice 1	zonal choice 2	zonal choice 3
Amsterdam:	staying in Amsterdam	going to the Region except the ZIJP	going to the ZIJP
Amstelveen:	staying in Amstelveen	going to Amsterdam	going to another zone in the Region
Waterland-South:	staying in Waterland-South	going to Amsterdam	going to another zone in the Region

Table 9.3. Zonal choices of households in Amsterdam, Amstelveen and Waterland-South

Most households in dwelling type 1 (figure 9.8:a-c) want to stay in the zone they presently live in. Households living in small dwellings (household size 1-6) are more likely to stay in Amsterdam. The probability of the zonal choice for Amsterdam, i.e. going to the ZIJP is very small (or even 0) in 1971 since large construction of new dwellings started in 1973. Of course the probabilities of the three zonal choices sum up to one for all households and dwelling types. The fluctuations between the age classes is the result of taking into account the inclusive value of preferred dwelling types. For Amstelveen and Waterland-South the histograms are almost the same. The differences are the result of taking into account the supply by means of the inclusive value of preferred dwelling types. Since the supply in Amstelveen is higher than in Waterland-South, the probability of staying in Amstelveen is higher than in Waterland-South. Also here the fluctuations between the age classes are visualized. Households living in a large owner-occupied dwelling (type 11) in Amsterdam prefer to move to the Region (figure 9.9.a). The probability of going to Amsterdam of households living in dwelling type 11 in Amstelveen and Waterland-South is naturally much lower (figure 9.9.b and c) than of households living in dwelling type 1. However, households living in dwelling type 11 are likelier to move to other zones in the Region (as a result of the positive coefficient for the 'tenure status' variable for zonal choice 3 in table 8.20).

In figure 9.10 for Amsterdam, Amstelveen and Waterland-South the probabilities of the 3 zonal choices is given per dwelling type. More than 50% of the households living in small (less than 5 rooms) rented dwellings (class 1, 3, 5, 6 and 7) prefer to stay in Amsterdam (figure 9.10.a). Households living in Amstelveen and Waterland-South living in owner-occupied dwellings (class 2, 4, 8 and 11) are more likely to move to other zones in the Region than households living in other dwelling types.

Probabilities of Dwelling Type Preferences

The probabilities per preferred dwelling type are depicted in the histograms of figures 9.11 and 9.12, presenting the probabilities of the preferred dwelling types per present dwelling types for households of type 1 (singles aged 20) living in dwelling type 1 and living in dwelling type 11 respectively. Again the probabilities of the 11 dwelling types sum up to one, but now we are not primarily interested in the absolute values but in the relative differences for one specific dwelling type between the three zonal choices.

Young singles living in a small rented flat in Amsterdam who want to stay in Amsterdam (zone 1 of figure 9.11.a) prefer to move to a small or medium size rented flat (class 1, 5 and 6), probably because of the large supply of these dwelling types in Amsterdam. However, when these single people want to move into the Region (zone 2) they prefer to live in a rented single family-unit with 4 rooms (class 7) because of the higher supply of this dwelling type outside Amsterdam. For young singles living in a small rented flat in Amstelveen or Waterland-South (figure 9.11.b and c) the effect of preferring to stay in the same dwelling type (see abstract dummy coefficient in table 8.19) is clearly present, although there are some differences between the 3 preferred zones.

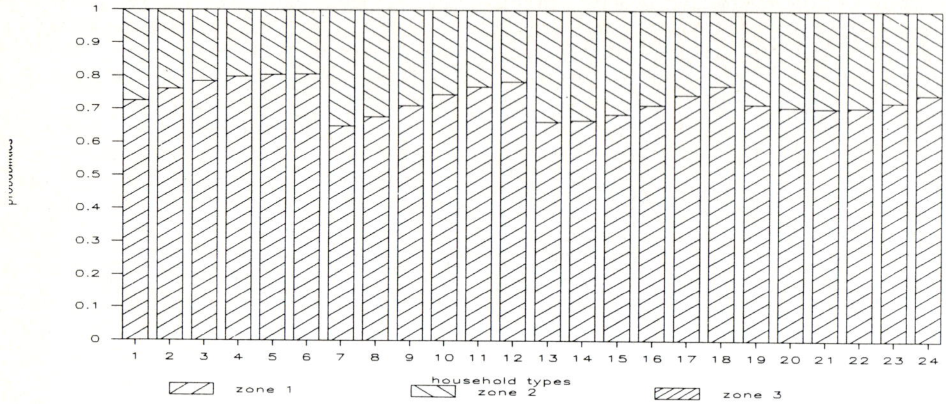

9.8.a. Probabilities for Amsterdam

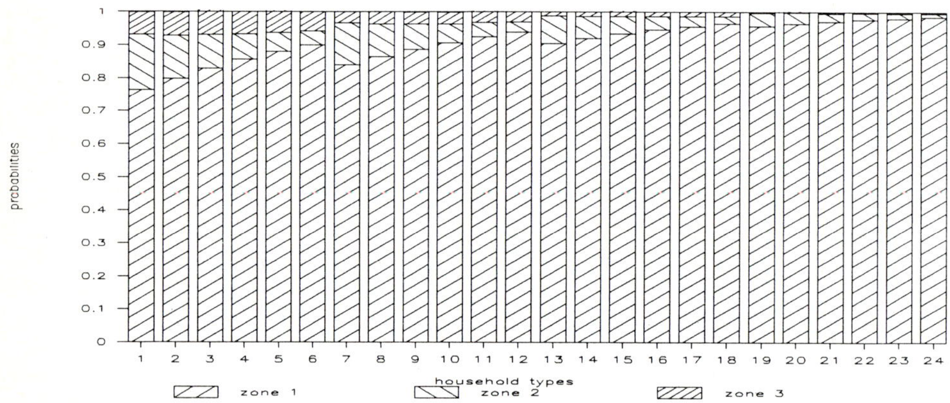

9.8.b. Probabilities for Amstelveen

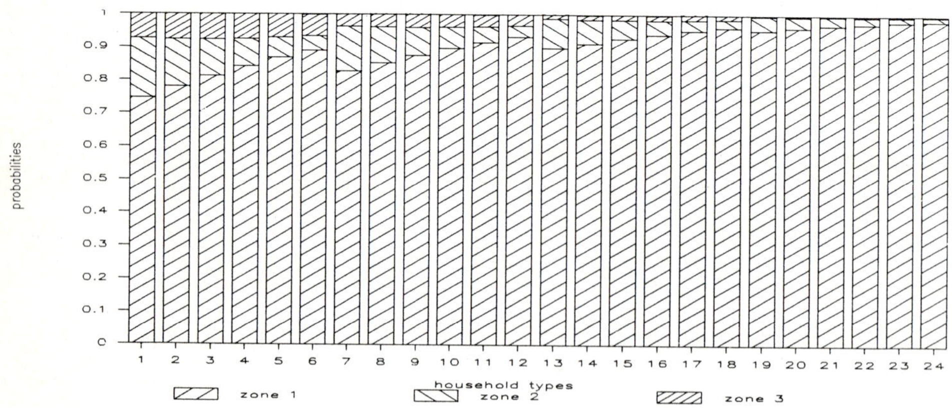

9.8.c. Probabilities for Waterland-South

Figure 9.8. Probabilities of zonal choices per household type of households living in dwelling type 1

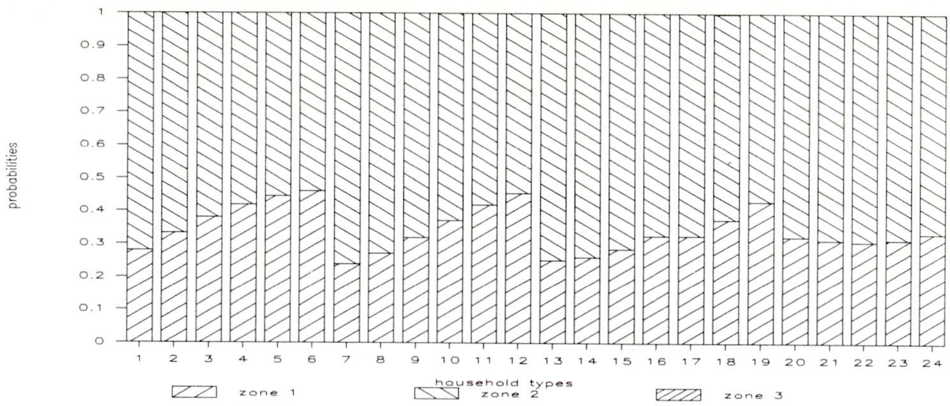

9.9.a. Probabilities for Amsterdam

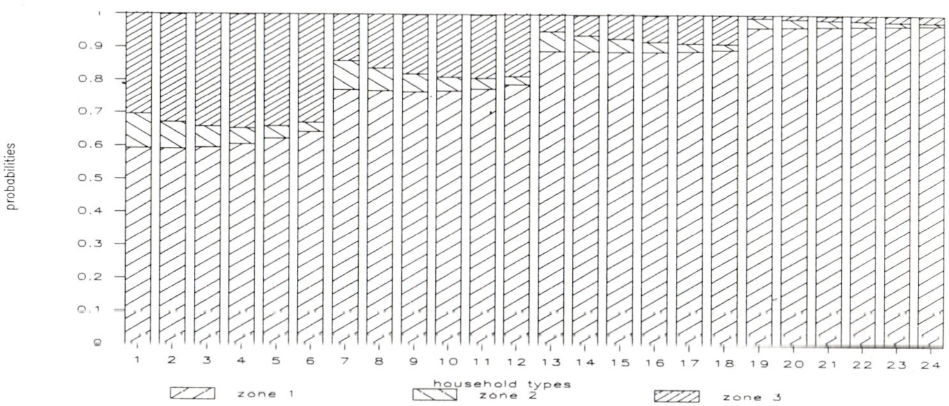

9.9.b. Probabilities for Amstelveen

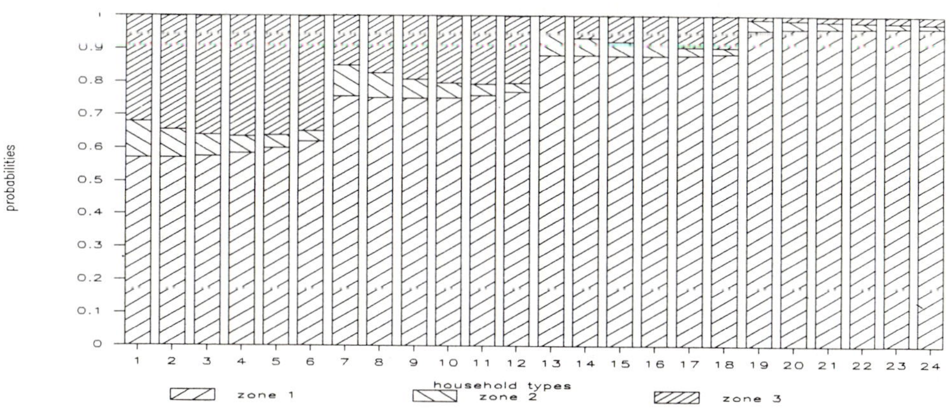

9.9.c. Probabilities for Waterland-South

Figure 9.9. Probabilities of zonal choices per household type of households living in dwelling type 11

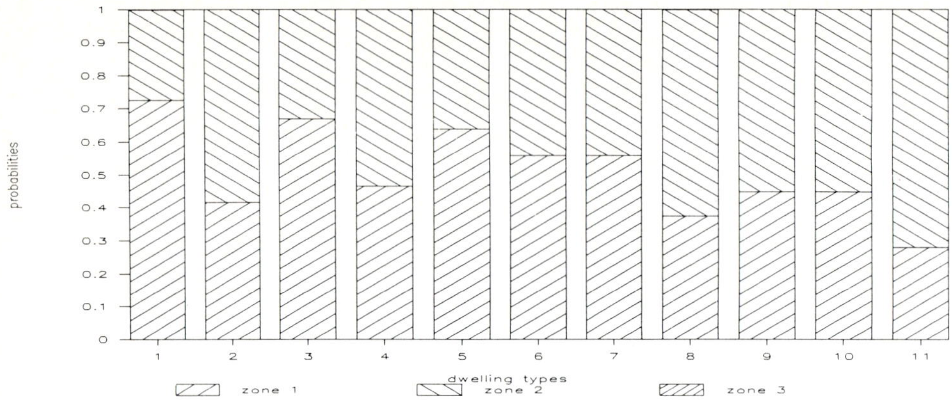

9.10.a. Probabilities for Amsterdam

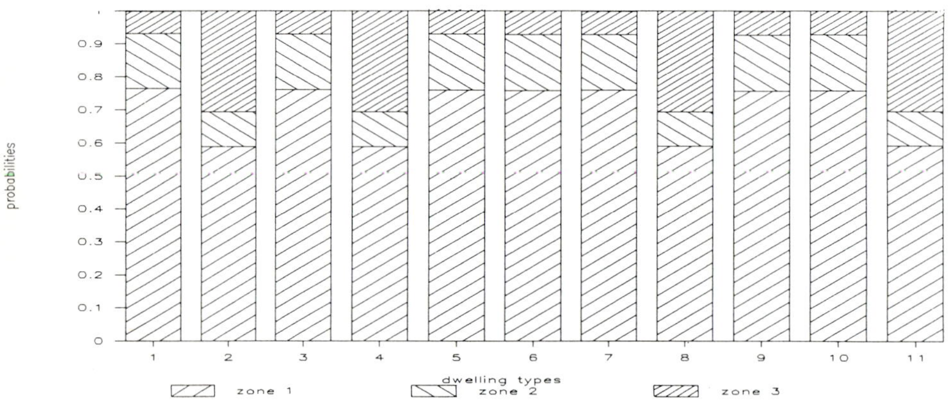

9.10.b. Probabilities for Amstelveen

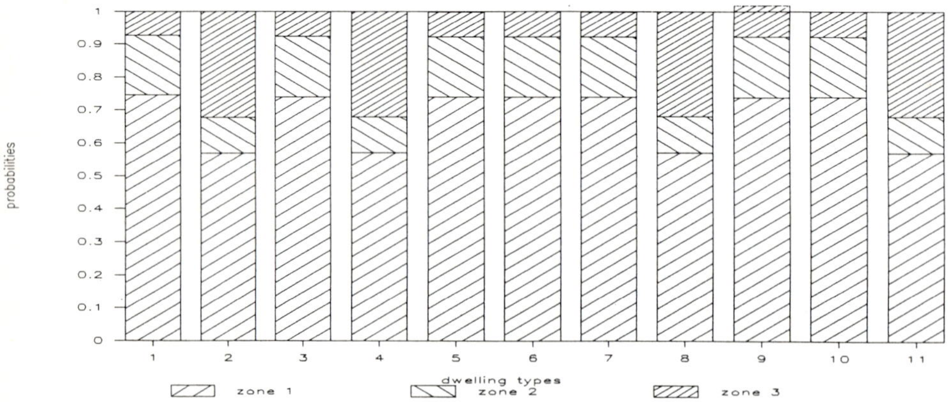

9.10.c. Probabilities for Waterland-South

Figure 9.10. Probabilities of zonal choices per dwelling type of households in household class 1

Young singles owning a large single-family unit (class 11) in Amsterdam (figure 9.12.a) who want to stay in Amsterdam (zone 1) prefer to move to an owner-occupied flat (class 2). When they move to the Region (zone 2) they prefer to stay in their original dwelling type (class 11) or to buy a smaller single-family unit (class 8). The effect of preferring to stay in the same dwelling type is for young singles living in Amstelveen or Waterland-South in a dwelling of type 11 not as important as for households living in dwelling type 1. Regardless of the zone they want to move to they also want to move to other dwellings they can buy (class 2, 4 and 11).

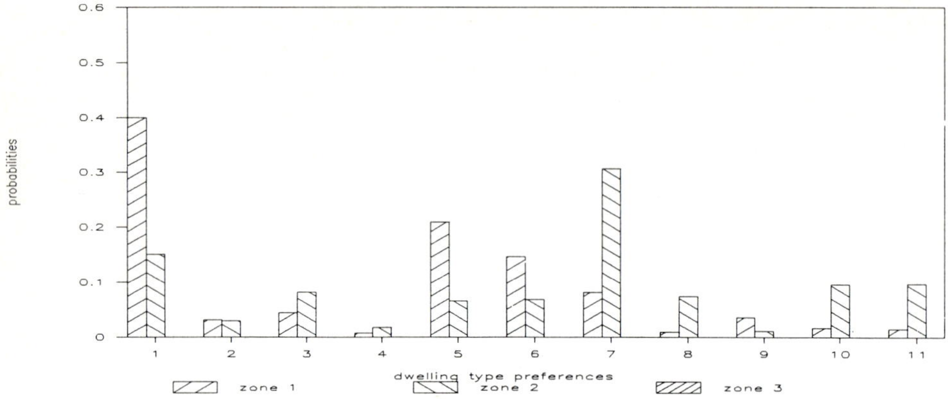

9.11.a. Probabilities for Amsterdam

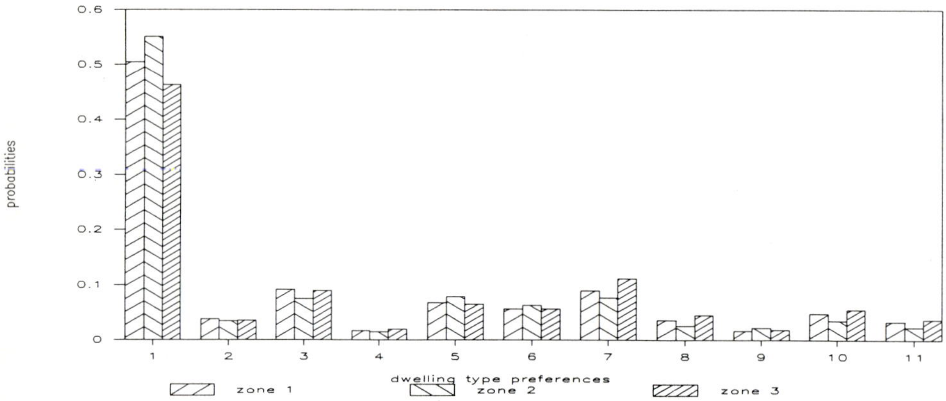

9.11.b. Probabilities for Amstelveen

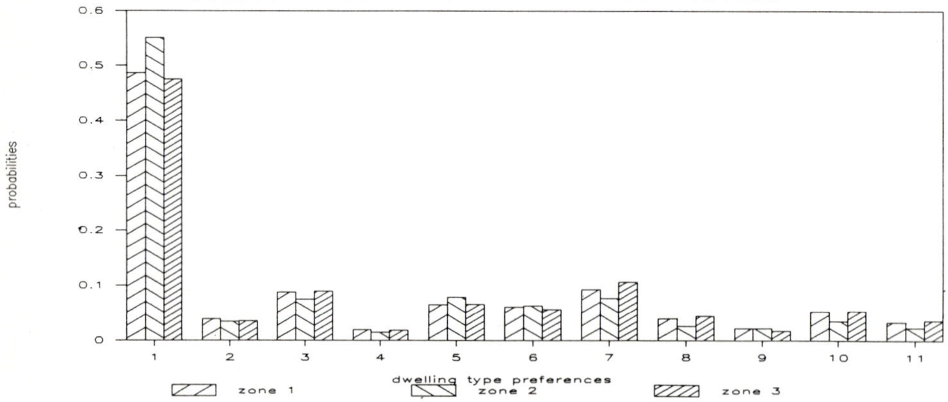

9.11.c. Probabilities for Waterland-South

Figure 9.11. Probabilities of dwelling type preferences per present dwelling type for households of type 1, living in dwelling type 1

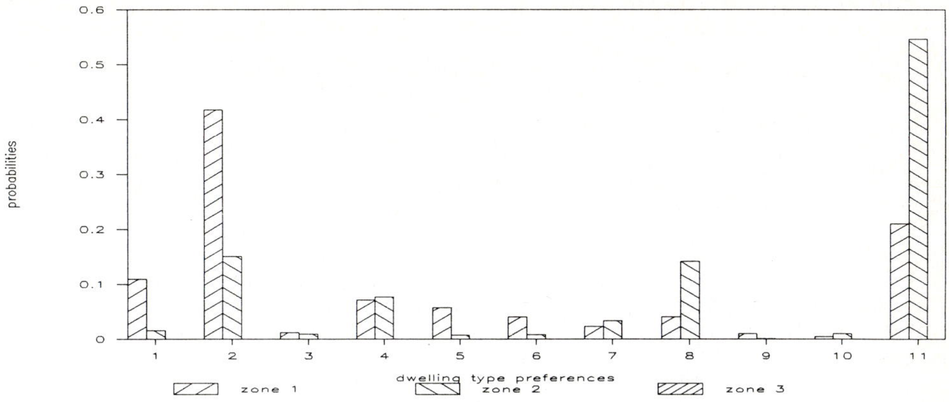

9.12.a. Probabilities for Amsterdam

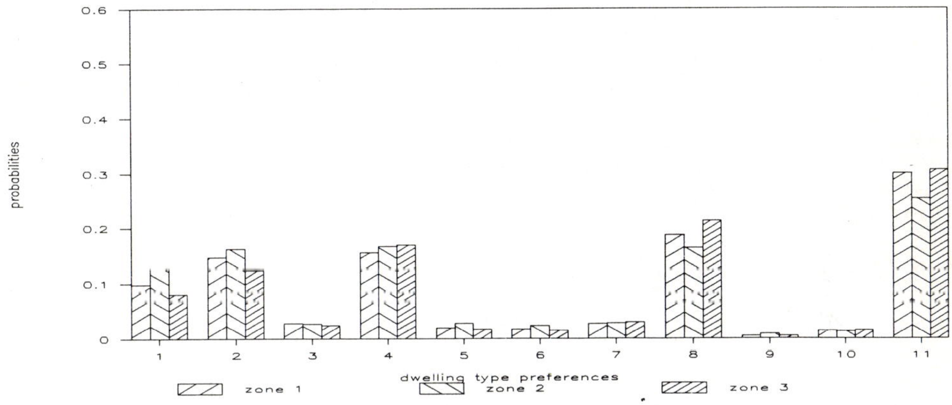

9.12.b. Probabilities for Amstelveen

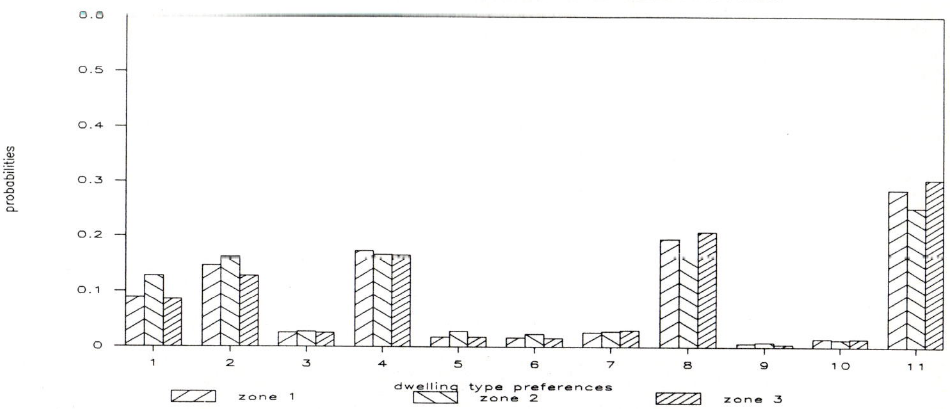

9.12.c. Probabilities for Waterland-South

Figure 9.12. Probabilities of dwelling type preferences per present dwelling type for households of type 1, living in dwelling type 11

9.3 The Allocation Model

In the allocation model the market clearing process is described, i.e. demand is matched with supply.

A typical demand element D is indexed by household category g after demographic changes, present dwelling type k and zone z, and preferred dwelling type k' and zone z': $D_{gkk'zz'}$. Supply of houses S is specified by dwelling type and zone: $S_{k'z'}$.

The allocation of households to dwellings is achieved through a simple proportional scaling process where demand is distributed over available supply. Within one time period a number of iterations take place in order to simulate a simplified vacancy chain process. The process stops if the calculated total number of re-allocations equals the observed number of allocations in the Amsterdam region for a given year.

For ease of presentation of the allocation process the household index g will be dropped, and one index i or j represents each possible submarket at the origin or destination side. Thus a typical simplified demand element is D_{ij}, and supply is given by S_j. In addition b_j is defined to be the total demand to submarket j from households without an origin submarket within the region (external immigrants, starters, households whose dwelling is being demolished. So total demand to zone j is:

$$U_j = \Sigma_i D_{ij} + b_j = D_{.j} + b_j \tag{9.4}$$

where summation over an index is denoted as a dot.

Allocation of the households b_j is denoted by e_j and reduces the number of housing vacancies because there is no vacancy chain generated by these moves. Their counterparts are given by a_i, the number of households who leave the housing market (outmigration, death, doubling up). The events associated with the generation of a_i are outside the allocation model, and it is assumed that these households leave the market at the beginning of the period. Also given is the number of vacancies H_j at the beginning of the period.

Next define M_{ij} to be the realized allocation from i to j. So total outmigration from submarket i is:

$$V_i = \Sigma_j M_{ij} + a_i = M_{i.} + a_i \tag{9.5}$$

and total immigration to zone j is:

$$W_j = \Sigma_i M_{ij} + e_j = M_{.j} + e_j \tag{9.6}$$

The allocation process involves a number of rounds. Every variable is therefore also indexed by the number of the round r. The general structure is as follows:

Step 1: Calculate initial vacancies at beginning of period:

$$S_j^1 = H_j^1 + a_j^1 \qquad (9.7)$$

Step 2: Calculate demand by origin and destination submarket:

$$D_{ij}^1 = N_i^1 \; F(S_j^1) \qquad (9.8)$$

where N is the total demand generated in submarket i and F(.) is the nested logit function that calculates probabilities for alternatives j as a function of supply S_j, as described in Chapter 8.

Step 3: Match demand with supply:

$$M_{ij}^1 = \alpha_j^1 \; D_{ij}^1 \qquad (9.9)$$

and

$$e_j^1 = \alpha_j^1 \; b_j^1 \qquad (9.10)$$

where α is defined as:

$$\alpha_j^1 = \begin{cases} 1 & \text{if } U_j^1 \geq S_j^1 \\ 1 \,/\, U_j^1 & \text{if } U_j^1 < S_j^1 \end{cases} \qquad (9.11)$$

So α_j^1 is the proportion of demand that is allocated in j in the first round. Total inflow in j in round 1 is thus:

$$W_j^1 = \alpha_j^1 \; U_j^1 \;\; \leq S_j^1 \qquad (9.12)$$

because inflow cannot exceed total supply in j.

Step 4: Calculate new supply for zone j after allocation:

$$S_j^2 = S_j^1 - \Sigma_i \; M_{ij}^1 - e_j^1 + \Sigma_i \; M_{ji}^1 \qquad (9.13)$$

Total new supply for the region is:

$$S_.^2 = S_.^1 - M_{..}^1 - e_.^1 + M_{..}^1 = S_.^1 - e_.^1 \qquad (9.14)$$

Equation (9.14) gives the obvious result that the vacancies in round 2 equal vacancies in round 1 minus the number of starters in the first round.

Since $S_.^1$ is H. + a. (eq. 9.7) and thus $S_.^2$ = H. + a.- $e_.^1$. it depends on the relative sizes of a and e whether vacancies increase or decrease in the study area.

Step 5: Calculate new demand:

$$N_i^2 = N_i^1 - M_{i.}^1 \tag{9.15}$$

and

$$D_{ij}^2 = N_i^2 \; F(S_j^2) \tag{9.16}$$

Go back to step 3 to allocate demand in round 2 until $M_{..}$ equals T, the total number of observed migrations in the study area in the year.

Specifying Allocation Rules: The Incidence Matrix Z

The above mentioned allocation is very simple. The probability of moving to j, α_j, is equal for every subgroup with a preference for a dwelling in j. This is not very likely however since the probability of a successful call on the market varies among groups. Starters on the market obtain a housing unit by definition (subrental units are included in the supply), so for all j: $e_j = b_j$. Another distinction is local versus inter-local demand. Local demand (moves within the municipality) has a higher probability of success than inter-local demand, unless specific housing submarkets are available for inter-local moves, as is the case with new towns (Purmerend, ZIJP). The so-called Incidence-matrix Z_{ij} of all combinations of origin and destination submarkets captures these distribution rules by specifying a 0 or 1. If the entry is 0, the allocation of demand in this round is not possible, due to the distribution rules. Since Z is round-specific, allocation-priorities can be introduced reflecting the institutional constraints on the market. So, in every round demand D_{ij} is replaced by $Z_{ij}D_{ij}$.

Although the use of the Incidence matrix gives only an approximate image of the household distribution rules, a number of existing mechanisms in the market, as described in Chapter 2 can be simulated, viz.:

1. Forced mobility due to housing demolitions can be given priority;
2. Local demand can be given priority over interlocal demand. This reflects the current policy of many municipalities of first providing the local inhabitants with adequate housing;
3. Households already living in a housing unit are usually given priority because this generates new supply. Since there is no queuing system in the model, the effect of duration of stay in the allocation-probability cannot be simulated.
4. New towns (e.g. Purmerend, ZIJP) are built primarily for suburban demand originating in Amsterdam. This can easily be captured in the Incidence Matrix.
5. The Amsterdam allocation rules specify a strict relation between household size and dwelling size. Since both variables are included in the model, this can easily be taken into account.

This simple allocation model is a heuristic device that captures part of the institutional setting of the market. Since the institutional arrangements are highly complex it can only be an approximation of a number of rules, related to rationing. However, some effects of these regulations can be simulated. This will be done in the next chapters.

9.4 Conclusion

This chapter concludes Part II: the theoretical description of the various submodules of the housing market model. Following the theoretical background and the intermediate results of the housing market model, in Part III the results of applying the model will be described and analysed. Chapter 10 is devoted to the presentation and discussion of the empirical results for the years 1971-1984. On the basis of the results of Chapter 10 the housing market model will be used to predict future developments after 1984 using different scenarios. The results of these scenarios will be given in Chapter 11.

Part III
Simulation

CHAPTER 10. MODELLING RESULTS FOR THE PERIOD 1971 - 1984

10.0 Introduction

In the previous chapters of Part II all the submodels have been set up and coefficients have been estimated both for the demographic and the housing market processes. The submodels are linked in a consistent accounting framework described in detail in Chapter 5. In Part III the results on the total model performance will be presented. In this chapter a validation test is conducted using observed data in the period 1971 - 1984. This validation test will determine if the model is capable of reproducing observed developments in household number and relocation behaviour. First, the allocation submodel is tested and an optimal allocation rule is found in section 10.1. Next, in section 10.2 a small set of aggregate data is presented, covering the situation at the beginning of 1982, that contains in a nutshell the most important information to determine the overall model performance. The basic version of the model, hereafter called <u>model I</u>, is tested and evaluated against these data in section 10.3. A number of possible refinements are given in the next section, in order to 'fine-tune' the model. An improved version of the model, called <u>model II</u>, with adjusted parameter values is treated in detail in the remainder of this chapter. Model II is also used in Chapter 11 for the simulation of two housing market scenarios in the area.

10.1 Specifying Allocation Rules

The allocation model described in section 9.3 simulates a process, where demand and supply are matched in a number of iterations and where in each round households are relocated and new vacancies are generated, thus creating a new supply structure over the submarkets in the subsystem. The iterations create a sequential structure in the allocation process and a number of alternative procedures can be adopted to direct this process in a desired direction. These allocation rules can be seen as a means to introduce some elements of government control over the housing market in the model in a simplified way. Government control in Amsterdam over housing distribution is highly complex, as shown in Chapter 2. For instance, detailed rules exist specifying limits on the number of rooms in relation to household size in the distribution sector. In the model this is not taken into account explicitly. However, inspection of the results of the demand functions reported in Chapter 8 shows that households are very realistic in their housing preferences and usually prefer a dwelling within the permitted size range. The allocation rules introduced in the model distinguish between local demand and interzonal demand, including suburbanization. In the suburban zones housing quota are reserved for Amsterdam residents (see Chapter 2 for more details) and this should be taken into account in the allocation process. Forced moves due to housing demolition (i.e. urban renewal) are given highest priority in housing distribution in Amsterdam. Although not all forced moves have to relocate within the area most of them will relocate in their original zone. For starters the situation is somewhat similar. They have to relocate but not within the area by definition. External immigrants have to find a dwelling in the area and their probability of being allocated is therefore 1.

A number of alternatives were tried on the 1971 data in order to find the optimal allocation structure. The following groups were distinguished:

1. Starters and forced moves
2. External immigrants
3. Immigrants from the Region to Amsterdam
4. Outmigrants from Amsterdam to the Region

In table 10.1 a number of alternative sequences are specified. In the table the number of the iteration is specified for each group where priority is given over other groups.

Groups	Priority alternatives 1	2	3	4
1. Starters and forced moves	-	1	1+4	1+3
2. External immigrants	-	1	1+4	1+3
3. Migrants from Amsterdam to Region	-	2	3	4
4. Migrants from Region to Amsterdam	-	2	3	4
5. Intrazonal moves in Amsterdam and Region	-	3	2	2

Table 10.1. Priority in allocation rounds for alternative specifications

In the <u>first</u> alternative all groups have equal priority in all allocation rounds. So demand per subgroup is simply scaled each round with the ratio of supply over demand per preferred submarket. The resulting allocation pattern reflects strongly the demand structure, with a high percentage of intrazonal moves. Table 10.2 shows that interzonal flows are seriously underestimated in this alternative and intrazonal flows dominate the allocation pattern. Moreover, external immigrants have the same probability of being matched as movers within the area resulting in only 30 percent being allocated.

Statistics	Observed (x 100)	Priority Alternatives 1	2	3	4
1. Total migration to Amsterdam	44	12	36	52	51
2. Total migration from Amsterdam	126	89	207	288	134
3. Intra-urban moves in Amsterdam	831	1120	951	794	783
4. Interzonal migrations	209	115	196	185	132
5. Percentage of group 2 allocated	100	31	81	98	99

Table 10.2. Results for various alternative priority sequences

In the <u>second</u> alternative the forced movers, starters and external immigrants are given first priority in the first iteration. Since total supply at the beginning of each annual run exceeds the total number of households in these starters' groups most households in these groups are allocated in the first round. Per submarket the situation can be quite different with housing shortage in the highly preferred submarkets and excess supply in the less favoured parts of the market. After the first round total initial supply is reduced significantly, since none of the moves generated in the first iteration creates a vacancy. In the second round interzonal demand to and from Amsterdam is matched with remaining supply and in the third round intrazonal demand is given first priority. In the remaining iterations all groups are given equal priority and the process stops when the total number of moves observed in that year in the system is reached, or (hypothetically) when all demand is allocated. This alternative results in a strong overestimation of interzonal flows to and from Amsterdam, while still not all external immigrants are allocated leaving a relatively high supply level open for suburban moves. Migration to Amsterdam is still too low. Inspection of the results shows that this flow is highly associated with the number of starters in the Region being allocated.

In the <u>third</u> alternative even more priority is given to new demand on the market. This leads to almost 100 percent of external immigrants being allocated. The reduced number of vacancies compared to alternative 2 reduces the number of intrazonal moves in Amsterdam but has no effect on the overestimation of suburban moves. This suggests that groups 1 and 2 should be allocated before suburban demand is given priority.

In the fourth alternative priorities are reversed in iteration three and four leading to a reduced supply level in the Region and a lower level of outmigration from Amsterdam to the suburbs. This alternative treats withdrawals and entrances in the market equally: since external outmigrations and household dissolutions are withdrawn from the market at the beginning of the period it is natural to add their counterparts to the market at the same time. The figures in table 10.2 show that the results of this alternative are superior to the others. On the basis of these results it was decided to run the model for the whole time period according to the rules specified in alternative four.

10.2 Observed Household Data in 1982

The starting year of the model is 1971. The 1971 census data are used to specify the initial data for the modél. In order to evaluate model performance the outcomes have to be compared with observed data on age and household structure and observed migration data. A simple way to evaluate the overall model performance over the whole time period is to compare the predicted household structure with observed data at the end of the simulation period. Since data on household structure are not available annually, a natural 'checkpoint' is the situation at the end of 1981 as measured in the WBO-sample (WBO, 1981, 1984). The Amsterdam estimates can be compared with data on cohabitation-units made available through linking of person records with real estate records since 1983 (Werkgroep Koppeling Vastgoed-Bevolking, 1983, 1984). In the Region only the WBO estimate is available. In table 10.3 the main variables on population and household numbers for Amsterdam and the Region are given.

Year	Amsterdam		Region	
	Population	Households	Population	Households
1971	820	324	410	126
1982	701	337 (330)	534	185
1984	676	334	563	n.a.
1985	676	342	577	n.a.
1986	679	351	n.a.	n.a.

Table 10.3. Observed population and household figures (x 1000) 1971 - 1986 in the study area (Source: WBO 1981, 1984; Werkgroep Koppeling Vastgoed-Bevolking, 1984, 1985, 1986)

The Amsterdam data show a somewhat lower figure in 1984 than the WBO estimate for 1982. Both are estimates. One is a stratified sample (WBO) and the Amsterdam data are estimates based on the (almost) complete occupancy status of persons at addresses. Given the level of detail in these data the Amsterdam estimate seems more accurate than the WBO. In order to arrive at an estimate for 1982 based on the Amsterdam data the trend in households can be related to the increase in the number of dwellings. In 1982 there were 303,000 dwellings in the city, rising to 311,000 in 1984 and further to 323,000 in 1986: an increase of 20,000 units in four years, against only 15,000 in the whole period 1971-1982. In line with this dwelling stock development an estimate of 330,000 households in 1982 is reasonable. This is well within the 95 percent confidence limits of the WBO estimate (336,000 +/- 11,000).

Household size	Amsterdam			Region	
	1971	1982	1984	1971	1982
single	31	39(42-44)	46	13	17
2 persons	30	33(31-33)	31	25	29
3 persons	16	13(12-13)	12	19	16
4+persons	23	15(12-14)	12	44	39

Table 10.4. Size composition of Households 1971, 1982 and 1984 in Amsterdam and the Region (Source: CBS;

Table 10.4 shows the change in the observed size distribution of households since 1971. For Amsterdam both the WBO and the Amsterdam estimates are given. For the region only the WBO distribution is available for 1982. The WBO estimate of the percentage of singles is relatively low compared to the Amsterdam data. The 95 percent confidence limits of this percentage are 39 +/- 1.25 so, even taking into account a further increase in the percentage of singles from 1982 to 1984 there is a significant difference between the estimates. Again the Amsterdam estimate can be considered to be more accurate in this respect giving an estimate of the percentage of singles in 1982 of slightly under 45 percent.

The final table (10.5) of this section gives the 1971 and 1982 observed figures on the age distribution of heads of households in Amsterdam and the Region. The linked person-real estate records for Amsterdam give no reliable estimate of this information since the resident with the longest duration of stay in the dwelling is considered to be the main resident. This leads to a serious overestimation of the number of heads in the age categories 55-64 and 65+. The data in the table show an increase in the number of heads in the age

25-34 for Amsterdam together with a reduction in the number of middle-aged heads (45-64). The stable figure for heads under 25 in the city can be criticized however. The severe underestimation of singles in the WBO may well result in an underestimate of the group heads under 25. In the Region the pattern is quite stable showing no clear tendency except for a reduction in the share of the youngest heads.

Age of head	Amsterdam 1971	Amsterdam 1982	Region 1971	Region 1982
0 - 24 year	9	9	6	4
25 - 34 year	17	25	24	25
35 - 44 year	15	15	22	23
45 - 54 year	17	13	19	17
55 - 64 year	18	15	15	15
65 + year	24	24	14	16

Table 10.5. Age distribution of heads in 1971 and 1984 in Amsterdam and the Region (Source: CBS; WBO,

The tables presented in this section are used in the superficial test of overall model performance. In the next section the results for the basic model (model I) are given.

10.3 Model I Results: Fixed Coefficients

Model I is the model with parameter values for the household and the housing demand model fixed at their sample estimate values (in Part II). Two remarks should be made at the start:

- Recall that the household model was estimated for the whole study area, thus making no distinction between central city and suburban households transition rates. The housing demand model was specified separately for Amsterdam and the Region. This gave plausible differences in urban and suburban housing market behaviour.
- The data sets for the estimation of the households model and of the housing demand model did not allow for time-varying parameter values. This is less a problem in the housing demand model since some of the exogenous variables in the demand functions vary over time (viz. supply per submarket). So even with fixed coefficients housing market behaviour is time dependent. This does not apply to the household model. Transition intensities are state and age specific and variation over time is not introduced in the model specification. It is very likely that these intensities have changed since 1971.

The conclusion to be drawn from these remarks is that model I should be considered as a 'baseline' model and that some refinements have to be made to calibrate the model for the whole time period. The results of model I serve two purposes. First we have to judge whether the overall model framework is valid. Second, on the basis of model I results, adjustments in parameter values may be necessary to improve model performance.

In the next subsections the model I results are compared with the data described in section 10.2.

Population and Households

Results on total population and total number of households for Amsterdam and the Region are presented in table 10.6.

	Amsterdam		Region		Total	
	Model I	Obs.	Model I	Obs.	Model I	Obs.
Population	666	701	569	534	1235	1235
Households	289	330	184	185	473	515

Table 10.6. Predicted and observed persons and households in Amsterdam and the Region (1982) for model I

Looking at the population figures, it is clear that too many people are allocated from Amsterdam to the Region. (approximately 35,000 persons, corresponding with 12,000 households). Since external migration flows to and from the total area are treated exogenous in the model total population in the model should correspond closely to total observed population. The excess outmigration to the Region does not result in an overestimate of the number of households in the suburbs. This indicates that household generation in the Region has been somewhat too low. This is compensated by outmigrants from Amsterdam who moved into the dwellings that would otherwise have been occupied by local demanders in the Region. The Amsterdam estimate of the number of households is far too low, even after compensating for the excess outmigration of 12,000 households to the Region there is still a gap of 29,000 households. This is clearly due to a specific Amsterdam household generation effect that is not included in the coefficients of the household model. So from the superficial results of model I on total population and households the validity of the first remark made above is shown, i.e. that Amsterdam-specific household transition intensities are necessary. Inspection of the size and age distribution of households shows which groups are underestimated.

Household Size Distributions

In table 10.7 the observed and predicted size distributions of households in Amsterdam and the Region are compared. For the 1982 observed distribution in 1982 in Amsterdam a range is given combining the findings in the WBO and the Amsterdam data.

Household size	Amsterdam		Region	
	Model I	observed	Model I	observed
single	29	42-44	17	17
2 persons	31	31-33	27	29
3 persons	20	12-13	24	16
4+persons	20	12-14	32	39

Table 10.7. Predicted and observed size distribution of households in Amsterdam and the Region in 1982 for model I.

As can be seen in the table the singles in Amsterdam are seriously underestimated while larger households (three and four+ persons) are overestimated. For singles there is even a relative decline compared to the 1971 situation. The estimates for two person households are close to the observed figures, both in Amsterdam and in the Region. The Region estimate for singles is also very accurate. Here, some discrepancy exists between observed and predicted shares for three and four person households. About 8 percentage points of the three person households should be a four person household in order to make the total distribution for the Region equal to the WBO distribution.

Clearly, the trend shown by the model results in what could be called an 'average' household development pattern with some characteristics related to urban and others to more suburban household developments. The model trend for small households is accurate for the Region but too low for the city while the trend towards large households is too high for the city and too low for the Region.

Age Distribution of Heads

The results on the age distribution of households are somewhat less clear, as shown in table 10.8. In Amsterdam the picture is quite accurate, with the exception of the age category 25-34 which is underestimated by 6 percentage points. Taking into account the bias in the WBO sample giving an underestimate of the number of singles the estimated 10 percent of heads in the youngest age category could be an underestimate too. A plausible explanation for the resulting age distribution of heads is that household generation in the age group 25-34 is too low. Typical processes in this age category are splitting up and divorces resulting in an increase in the number of singles. Another possible explanation is a difference between urban and suburban lifestyles for singles. In the city singles are less inclined to change to a multi-person household position than in the Region. This leads to more singles in the next-to-youngest age category.

In the Region an overestimate of the youngest age group is accompanied by an underrepresentation of heads in the next two age groups. This might be caused by the household composition of immigration flows from the city to the Region. Figures 10.26 and 10.27 give evidence of this proposition. Here, the observed and predicted age distribution of migrants between Amsterdam and the Region in 1971 and 1984 are depicted. The age categories under 25 are overestimated and the reverse is true for the ages between 25 and 34.

Age of head	Amsterdam		Region	
	Model I	observed	Model I	observed
0 - 24 Y.	10	9	10	4
25 - 34 Y.	19	25	20	25
25 - 44 Y.	16	15	19	23
45 - 54 Y.	15	13	18	17
55 - 65 Y.	15	15	15	15
65 + Y.	26	24	18	16

Table 10.8. Expected and observed age distribution of households in Amsterdam and the Region in 1982 for model I.

Conclusions: Model I Performance

The results presented in this section are of a highly aggregate level but they can illustrate the overall validity of the model. If one model component is erroneous then the total household distribution after a simulation over 11 years is not valid either. A discussion of model performance on a lower level is only relevant if the aggregate outcomes are within an acceptable range around the observed values. Model I will be discussed based on the aggregate outcomes presented in this section.

The first question concerns the overall validity of the model. This question should be placed in the proper context. The model parameters were not estimated from the data used in the simulations, except for a distance parameter in the housing preference function. The only constraint in the model is to match the total observed number of moves per year in the system. So the resulting age distributions, household distributions and the migration flows by age and household category are almost completely free in the model. Moreover, after the specification of initial values for the 1971 situation and the annual updating of the dwelling stock and the input of population flows to and from the system the system path is completely endogenously determined. Within one year, four submodels are linked and run sequentially, and the output of year t is input for year t+1. Therefore the model simulation does not fit in the family of singly or doubly constrained spatial interaction models frequently used in location models. Rather, interactions are the result of endogenously determined basic demographic transitions, housing preferences and (partially endogenous) housing supply.

The results achieved with model I indicate that the model is able to reproduce 'average' behaviour in household developments and household relocation. The predicted household development in the Region is quite accurate and shows the same explosive growth in the number of households as observed in reality. The results for Amsterdam are somewhat less accurate, showing a decrease in the number of households instead of the observed modest growth in the period from 1971 to 1982. However, these differences in outcomes can be explained in terms of plausible differences in intensities in household transitions between city and suburbs.

The general conclusion the model is able to reproduce 'average' household behaviour is also relevant for the second question to be answered: do the results give guidelines for improvement of the model through suitable parameter adjustments ? The answer, given implicitly in this section is affirmative and the next section will treat this topic in more detail.

10.4 Adjustments in Parameter Values of the Household Model

The corrections implicitly suggested in the previous section are summarized below. They can be classified in two types:

- Introduction of zone specific transition rates. The basic distinction to be made is between city and suburbs.
- Introduction of time dependent parameter values.

These two types of adjustments will be discussed below. The final values of the adjusted parameters are given at the end of this section.

Zone Specific Transition Rates

The results of model I suggest the following corrections to be made in the transition rates for Amsterdam:

1. A lower rate of transition and at a later age from single to a multi-person household position. This results in an increase in the number of singles most likely in the age category 25-34;
2. A higher rate of transition from child to single, combined with a lower rate from child to partner and from child to head;
3. A reduced transition rate from smaller to larger household sizes combined with a higher rate of transition from larger to smaller households. This higher rate of transition to smaller households reflects both the higher rate of splitting up and the increased rate of children becoming independent. The transition rate functions to a reduced size household were split in two additive parts (see Chapter 7), one part related to splitting up (the negative exponential form) and one part related to children leaving the parental home. So the adjustments were made in the parameters for both parts.

Time Varying Transition Rates

Figure 10.1 shows the development in divorce rates for the Netherlands as a whole and for Amsterdam.

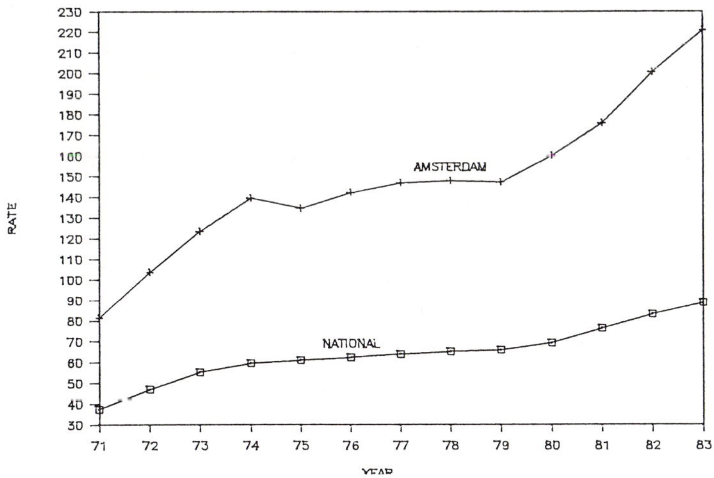

Figure 10.1. Observed divorce rates (number of divorces per 10000 married men) in Amsterdam and the Netherlands 1971 - 1983 (Source: CBS; Yearbooks Amsterdam)

This figure illustrates both the need for separate intensities for Amsterdam and the Region and for time dependency. This trend can be translated to the following types of transitions:

4. An increasing rate of transition from a two person head position to single;
5. An increasing rate of transition from partner to single. In the household model it is assumed that when households split up the partner starts a new household (single) while the existing household is reduced in size. So this also gives rise to the next adjustment:
6. An increasing rate of transition from head of a four to a three person household and of a three to a two person household.

Next, it is assumed that the rate of leaving the parental home is increasing in the study period. It is also assumed that this only affects the transition to single. This leads to the following adjustment:

7. An increasing rate of transition from child to single in Amsterdam.

Adjusted Parameter Values

A number of models were run with changes made along the lines given above. On the basis of different trails on the 1971 data superficial sensitivity analyses of parameter values were tried and a number of models was run for the whole period 1971 - 1984. One complete run of the model takes approximately 3,000 seconds Central Processor Unit (CPU) time on a Cyber 750 system, corresponding with 6 hours total Input-Output (IO) time. Budget constraints allowed only a limited number of model trails for the whole period. The final outcome of this process is model II and the results of this model are described in detail in the following sections. The final parameter values for the model are presented below.

Child to Single

In figure 10.2 the final curves for Amsterdam and the Region are drawn. The Region curve is unchanged but for Amsterdam the maximum value is doubled resulting in a maximum rate of transition of 0.15, and increasing to 0.20 in 1984. At the same time the age of maximum rate of transition is reduced to 25 years.

Child to 2p Head and to Partner

Although an increase in transition rate for child to single could have a reducing effect on these events the results for the number of two person households and partners were unsatisfactory, so these rates were left constant.

<u>Single to 2p Head</u>
The adjusted curve for Amsterdam is shown in figure 10.3 together with the -unchanged- curve for the Region. For Amsterdam the lognormal curve was preferred, with a maximum rate of transition of 0.05. The curve for Amsterdam was also shifted 5 years so that singles change to another household position at a later age.

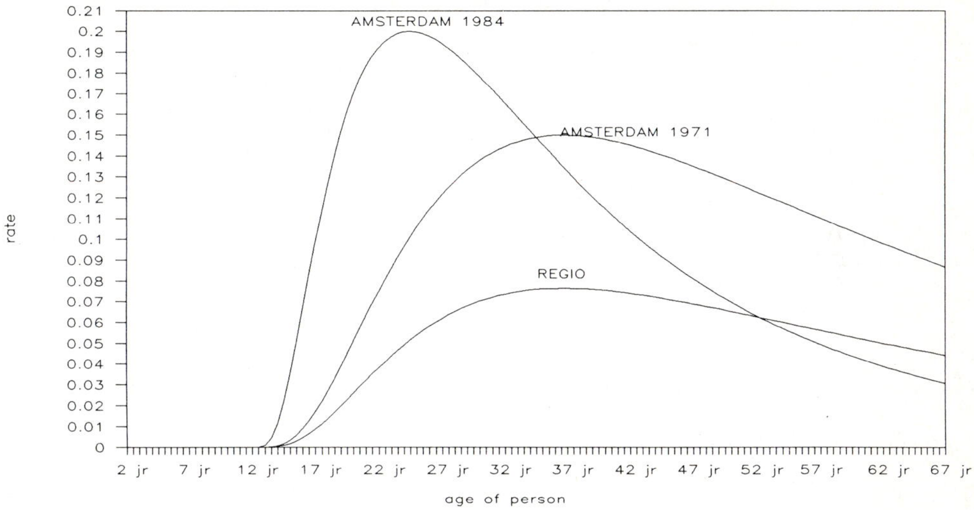

Figure 10.2. Adjusted transition rate curves for child to single for Amsterdam and the Region

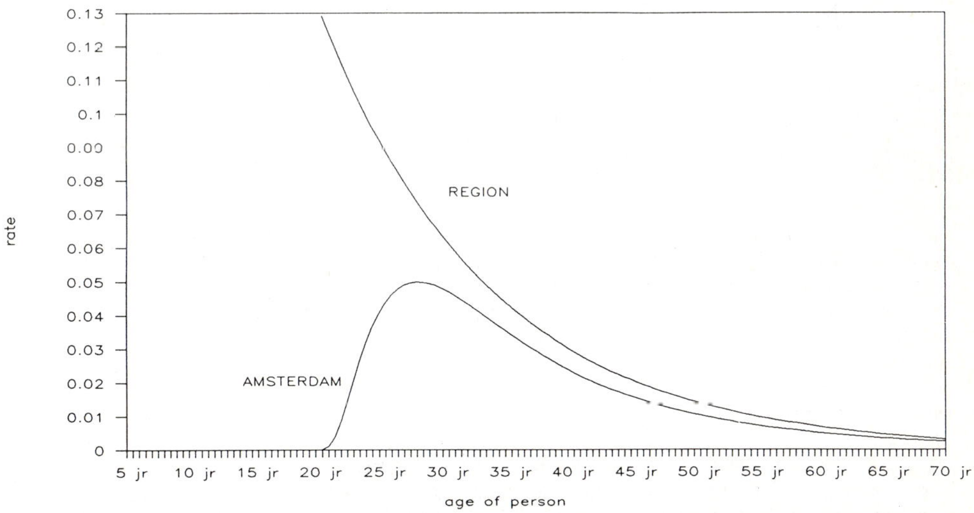

Figure 10.3. Adjusted transition rate curves for single to 2p head for Amsterdam and the Region

Single to Partner
Similar to the transition from single to 2p head the log-normal curve was preferred for Amsterdam, with a maximum value of 0.06 and the starting age of the process was increased with 5 years, while the dispersion σ was reduced to 0.30. Figure 10.4 shows the resulting curves.

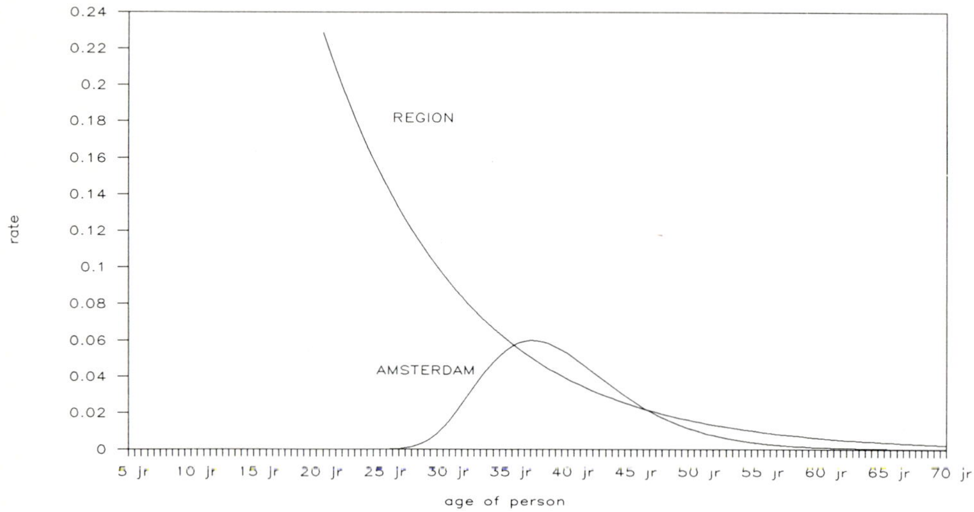

Figure 10.4. Adjusted transition rate curves for single to partner for Amsterdam and the Region

2p Head to 3p Head
For Amsterdam the maximum value of this transition rate function was reduced with 20 percent.

3p Head to 4p Head
The value of the maximum rate of transition was changed in opposite directions for Amsterdam and the Region: an increase in the Region with 20 percent against a decrease with the same amount for Amsterdam.

4p Heads to 3p Heads and 3p Heads to 2p Heads
The maximum values of the exponential curves representing household breaking up were doubled for Amsterdam and gradually increased over the period with a factor of three for the total area. Initially it was assumed that the sample estimates, taken from data in the period 1975 - 1980 could be taken as the mid-points of these curves, but results of the trails showed that they had to be taken as the lower bounds. Figure 10.5 shows the resulting curves for the assumed maximum level of splitting up of four- and three person households for Amsterdam and the Region. Since the rates for leaving the parental home were not changed no change was made in the lognormal curves for transition from 4p to 3p and 3p to 2p households.

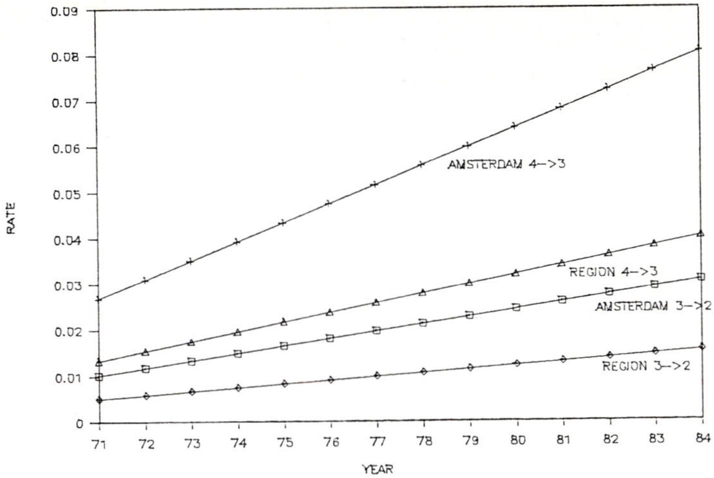

Figure 10.5. Assumed time path for splitting up rates from 4p to 3p and from 3p to 2p households for Amsterdam and the Region

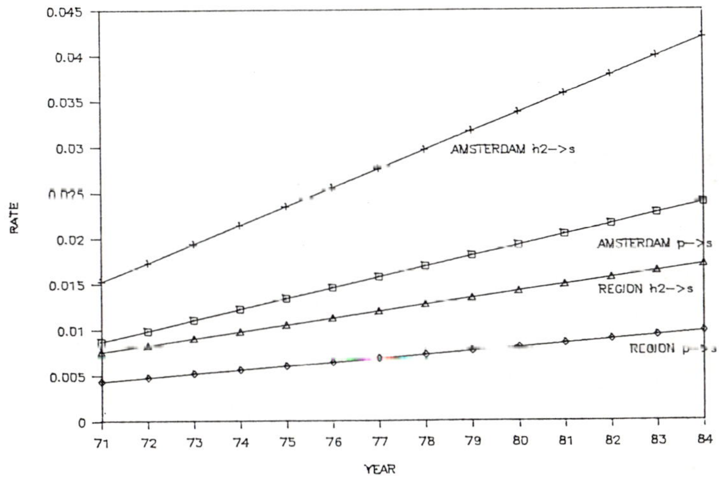

Figure 10.6. Assumed curves for transition rates from partner to single and from head 2p to single for Amsterdam and the Region.

Partner to Single and Head 2p to Single

A distinction was made between Amsterdam and the Region. Since these transition rates were simply estimated using sample means a time path for these means was specified using the slopes of the observed trend in divorce rates for

Amsterdam and the Region. Moreover, the difference in the level of the curves between Amsterdam and the Region was adjusted according to the observed level difference between the Netherlands and Amsterdam, taking the sample estimate for the Region equal to the national level. The resulting curves are given in figure 10.6.

10.5 Model II Results: Introduction

In this and the following sections the detailed results of simulations with model II will be presented. First, the overall tests performed in section 10.3 will be repeated for model II in the next subsection. The following sections deal with partial results per submodel. Section 10.6 gives results on household dynamics in the area. Section 10.7 deals with housing demand and housing supply and in 10.8 the resulting migration flows are treated in more detail. The following section gives results on the combined impact of household dynamics and migration on household developments. Next, in 10.10 the resulting outcomes of population and household figures is presented. The final section 10.11 summarizes and evaluates the results achieved for the period 1971 - 1984.

Overall Test of Model II

Tables 10.9 to 10.11 give the tentative results of model II for the 1982 situation. The form of these tables is identical to the tables used for testing model I so a comparison between model I and model II can also be made.

The performance in terms of total numbers of households and population levels in Amsterdam and the Region has improved considerably (table 10.9). The total population estimate is now slightly under the observed figure and there is only a gap of 5,000 households in Amsterdam. The household estimate for the Region is now slightly higher than in model I, indicating a modest overestimation of households generation in this area. Predicted total household level for the entire study area is approximately equal to the observed total of 515,000 in 1982.

	Amsterdam		Region		Total	
	Model II	Obs.	Model II	Obs.	Model II	Obs.
Population	697	701	537	534	1235	1235
Households	325	330	188	185	513	515

Table 10.9. Predicted and observed persons and households in Amsterdam and the Region in 1982 for model II

The improved results in terms of total household and population figures were achieved through a selective process of parameter adjustments. Consequently, household distributions over size and age categories have changed also. In table 10.10 the model II results for household size are reported. The results for Amsterdam are very good. All predicted percentages are close to the observed shares. The results for singles have greatly improved over model I outcomes (where a 29 percent estimate for singles was predicted). Two person households are underestimated by two percentage points and three person households are slightly overestimated. The regional outcomes are less satisfactory. Singles are highly overestimated and large households are seriously underestimated.

Household size	Amsterdam		Region	
	Model II	observed	Model II	observed
single	43	42-44	23	17
2 persons	29	31-33	25	29
3 persons	15	12-13	22	16
4+persons	12	12-15	30	39

Table 10.10. Predicted and observed size distribution of households in Amsterdam and the Region in 1982 for model II.

The changes in parameter values of the household model have not resulted in an improved size distribution of households in the Region. The changes in favour of larger households have not resulted in higher shares of four+ person households. Moreover, the number of singles has grown too much.

The changed age distribution of households is shown in table 10.11. Again there is an improvement for Amsterdam in the age structure compared to model I. The youngest age category is somewhat overpredicted but, as noted before, the population estimate is biased downwards. Households in the next-to-youngest age category are still underestimated, despite the changes in favour of this group in parameter values. The remaining age categories are closely approximated by the model. For the Region there is a larger variation around the observed data. The youngest age category is highly overestimated, even more than in model I. Except for this group the other categories are slightly better predicted than in model I.

Age of head	Amsterdam		Region	
	Model II	observed	Model II	observed
0 - 24 Y.	13	9	13	4
25 - 34 Y.	19	25	21	25
25 - 44 Y.	15	15	19	23
45 - 54 Y.	14	13	17	17
55 - 65 Y.	14	15	14	15
65 + Y.	24	24	16	16

Table 10.11. Predicted and observed age distribution of households in Amsterdam and the Region in 1982 for model II.

The two models can be compared using a fit-measure to summarize overall goodness of fit. The statistic used here is the relative mean square error RMSE (Bovy, 1982) which is given by formula 10.1 :

$$RMSE = sqrt(\Sigma_i (F_i - f_i)^2) \qquad (10.1)$$

with F the observed value and f the model estimate. The average error AE is based on the RMSE and is given by:

$$AE = RMSE / \overline{F} \qquad (10.2)$$

where $\overline{F}$ is the average value per cell in the table. The AE is a standardized value and can be used for comparison of different tables. A value of 1 means that the RMSE is equal to the mean cell value and a value between 0 and 1 indicates a relative error smaller than the average cell value. The RMSE or AE is especially useful in analyzing the absolute differences between the observed and calculated values. A comparison of model I and model II using the AE statistic (table 10.12) shows that the Amsterdam results have greatly improved through parameter adjustments. The results for the Region have become somewhat less accurate. As will be shown in detail in the next sections the impact of suburbanization in this area on household structure is large and so household developments in the city have an indirect but strong effect on household developments in the Region.

	Household Size		Age of Head	
	model I	model II	model I	model II
Amsterdam	1.48	0.26	0.92	0.74
Region	0.67	0.98	1.06	1.12

Table 10.12. Average error statistic for predicted household size and age of head distributions of model I and model II

10.6 Model II Results: Household Dynamics

The first module in the overall accounting framework is the household model. At the beginning of each year this submodel predicts the total number of household transitions relevant for housing market behaviour per zone. The result is a time- and zone specific household transition matrix. In this section some main characteristics of these yearly transition matrices will be presented for various zones in the system.

The total number of household formations and dissolutions for Amsterdam are depicted in figure 10.7.

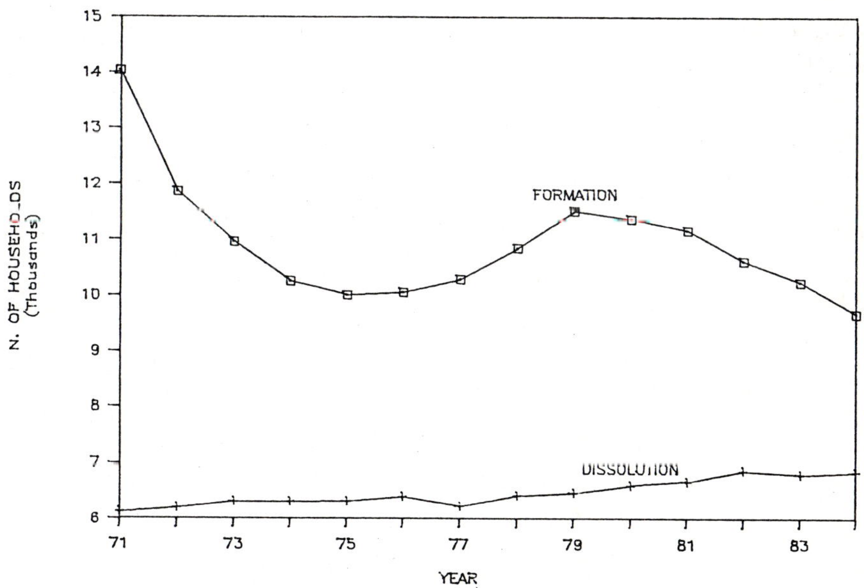

Figure 10.7. Predicted total number of household formations and dissolutions in Amsterdam 1971 - 1984 with model II

The pattern for the number of new households per year is highly interesting. Starting in 1971 a sharp decrease sets in until 1975, followed by an increase until 1979. After 1979 the trend is reversed again. Household dissolutions show a slightly upward trend throughout the whole period. The net effect of the household transition process is an increase in the number of households, although the two curves approach each other fast after 1980.

The net effect of the internal household dynamics for Amsterdam is positive, but on the zonal level within Amsterdam large differences occur. Looking at figure 10.8 it can be seen that the average Amsterdam pattern is more or less representative for zones 4 (shown), 6, 7, 8, 9 and 10, which are mainly the established residential zones outside the centre. In zones 1, 2 and 3 (the inner city zones) a entire different picture emerges. Household dissolution exceeds household formation although sometimes the wavelike pattern of the household formation curve exceeds the dissolution curve.

In zone 5 the household formation curve drops rapidly and crosses the dissolution curve in 1983. In zone 11, Amsterdam South-East (the Bijlmermeer), where most of the new housing construction takes place, household formation and dissolution increases as the total population increases.

The predicted trend is the result of a number of factors. Firstly, parameter values of the household transition process vary over time. This leads to an increase in the generation of new households over time. Secondly, population decreases in Amsterdam, predominantly the households with children, giving a downwards trend in the number of household generations over time. Thirdly, the distribution of persons over household positions changes and this has a strong impact on new household generations. An increase in the share of singles in the population reduces the rate of new household formations since a single can only move in with another household leading to a loss of households. The downwards movement of the formation curve in the period 1971 - 1975 is mainly due to the combined effect of the population drain and a changing household composition in the city. The upward shift from 1975 to 1979 is caused by the combined effect of reduced outmigration and higher rates in household transition processes. After 1980 the impact of a changing population distribution with a strong tendency to singles is predominant leading to a downward shift in the formation process.

The pattern for the region is more straightforward. Both household formation and dissolution numbers increase steadily over the whole time period. This increase is mainly due to the general increase in population in the time interval.

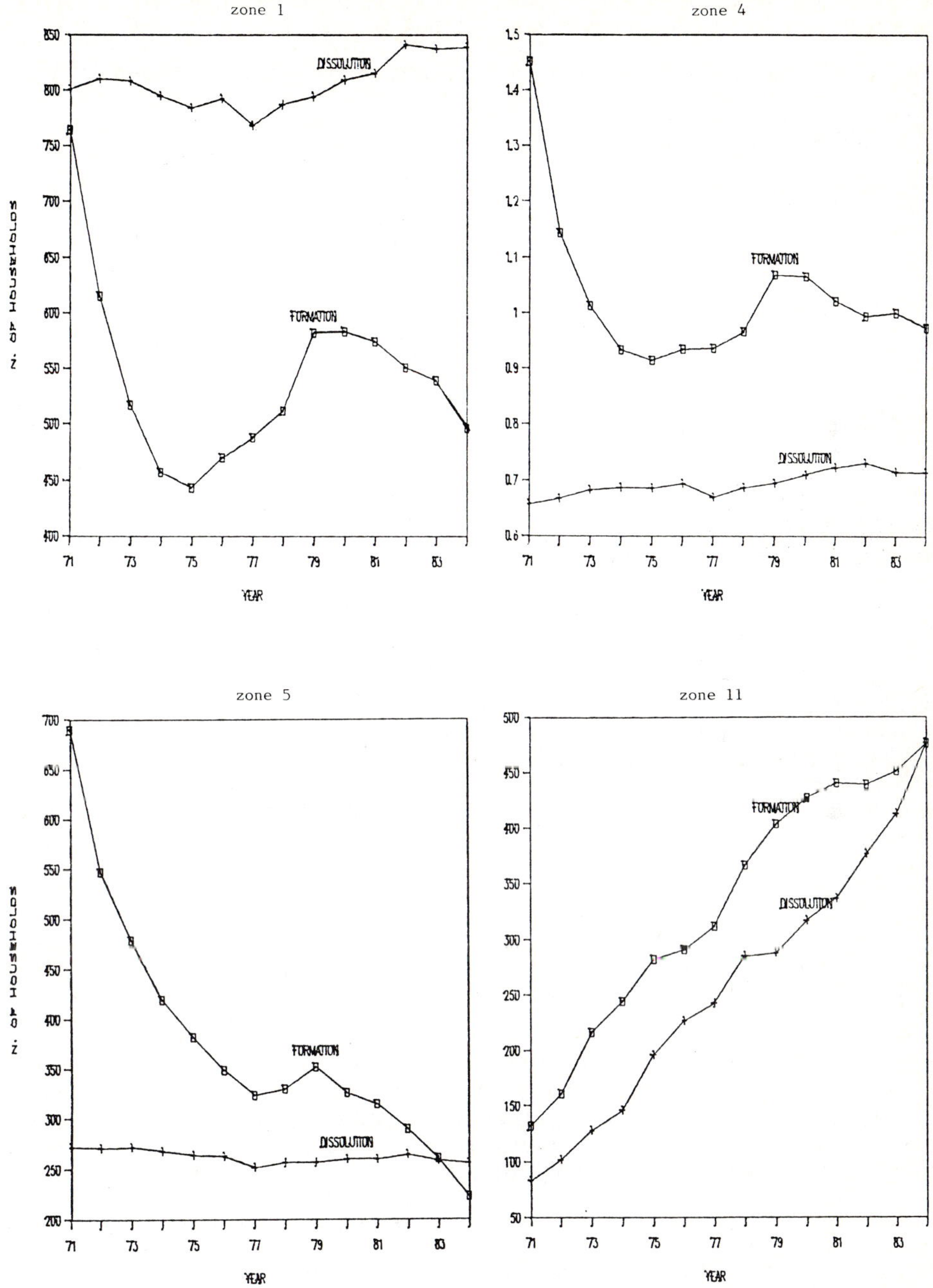

Figure 10.8. Predicted total number of household formations and dissolutions for selected zones in Amsterdam 1971 - 1984 with model II

After correction for the number of households the formation curve shows a negative slope (figure 10.9) that is mainly attributable to ageing and the corresponding changing distribution of persons over the household positions. The average picture for the Region as a whole is representative for all zones in the Region, except the new towns: zone 19 (Purmerend) and zone 20 (ZIJP) which show a steady increase in the number of household transitions. After correction of these numbers for the population increase a more or less flat household formation rate curve results.

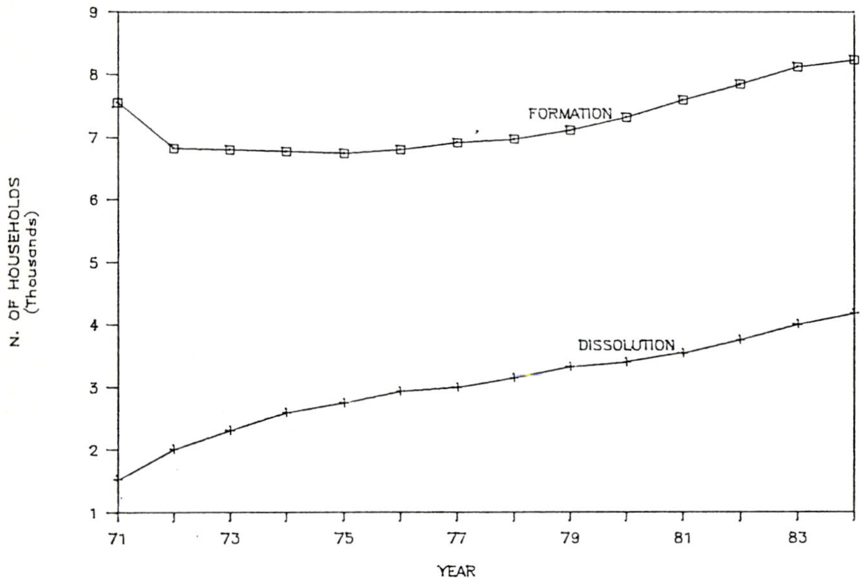

Figure 10.9. Predicted number of household formations and dissolutions in the Region 1971 - 1984 with model II

New households are predominantly singles. In Amsterdam the percentage of starting singles in 1971 is 77.0 percent. This figure increases to 83.1 percent in 1984. The figures for the Region are somewhat lower. The predicted percentage of starting singles in 1971 is 66.0 percent, this increases to 79.4 percent in 1984.

10.7 Model II Results: Housing Demand and Housing Supply

The relocation of households in the model is the result of the matching of (notional) demand and supply. This notional demand is not observable in reality and therefore it cannot be confronted with realized figures. The notional demand, which is dependent on the supply structure in the market, is approximately three times as large as the total supply available in Amsterdam and the Region (see table 10.13 and figure 10.10). Total supply increased in the period 1971-1984 with 33 % which is mainly due to outmigration from the study area. There are large differences of demand and supply between dwelling types and zones. In the Region the demand for dwelling type 7 (rented single family unit with 4 rooms) is 10 times as much as supply, while the demand/supply ratio for dwelling type 11 (owned single family unit with more than 4 rooms) is almost 2. In Amsterdam the demand for rented flats is 4 times the supply, while the supply for dwelling type 11 nearly equals the demand. In the Region the discrepancy between demand and supply is in general larger than in Amsterdam (demand/supply ratio of 5 versus 2), but there is a large difference in scale of demand between Amsterdam and the surrounding zones.

year	(notional) demand	supply	supply/demand ratio
1971	144148	47676	0.33
1972	144497	49127	0.34
1973	144364	52903	0.37
1974	147310	56149	0.38
1975	154103	58269	0.38
1976	151401	55625	0.37
1977	153292	56986	0.37
1978	154822	55198	0.36
1979	160399	51464	0.32
1980	163782	48483	0.30
1981	165476	46997	0.28
1982	167640	50542	0.30
1983	170613	55739	0.33
1984	175686	63354	0.36

Table 10.13. Total demand and supply in the study area 1971-1984

Figure 10.11 depicts the supply/demand ratio for Amsterdam and the Region and for the total area. This ratio is substantially higher in the city than in the suburbs. However, this graph only depicts relative numbers. In absolute terms the gap between demand and supply is much larger in Amsterdam than in the Region. The curve for Amsterdam shows a steep decline in the second half of the seventies. In this period housing construction was reduced significantly in the city, while total external outmigration reduced also as a result of the general downward trend in the housing market conditions.

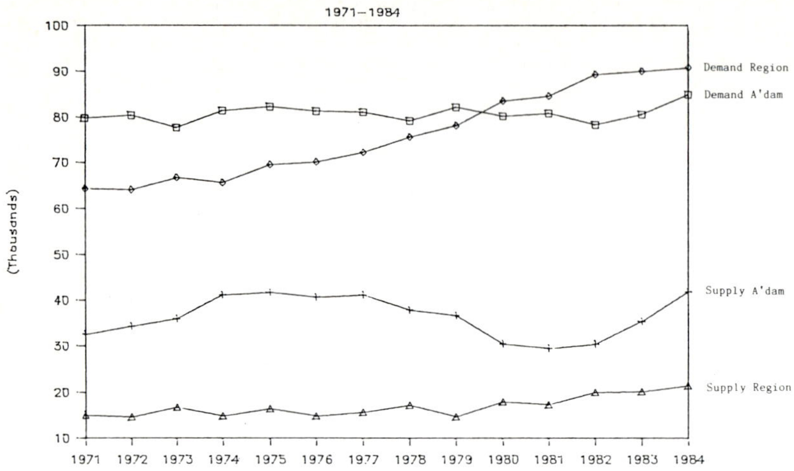

Figure 10.10. Demand and supply in Amsterdam and the Region

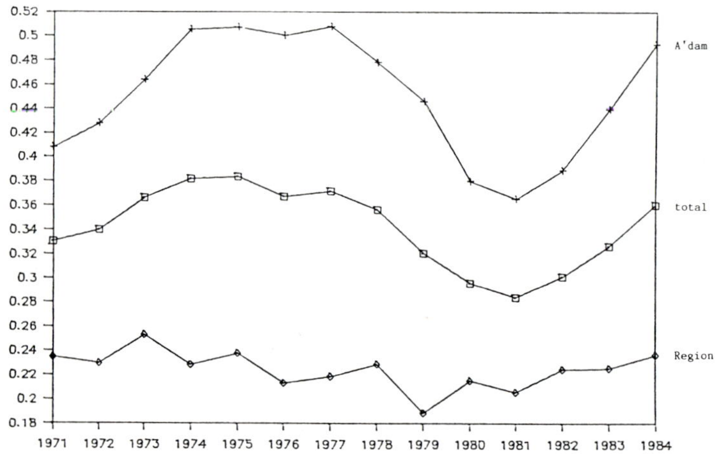

Figure 10.11. The supply/demand ratio, 1971-1984

There are large differences in demand and supply situations between the zones. This is especially true for Amsterdam. In figure 10.12 the supply/demand ratio for some specific zones in Amsterdam are presented. The separate position of zone 11 (Bijlmermeer) is striking. This is the only zone in the total area with a supply/demand ratio close to 1. As described in Chapter 2 this zone with mainly high rise newly constructed apartments has experienced a large vacancy rate since the seventies.

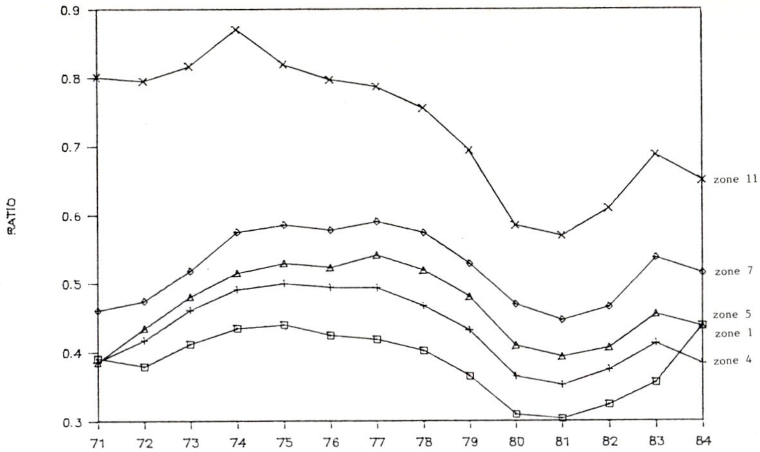

Figure 10.12. Supply/Demand ratios for selected zones in Amsterdam 1971 - 1984

While the total supply/demand rate for this zone is still below 1, supply exceeds demand for various dwelling types in this zone. The development of the supply/demand ratio of selected dwelling types in zone 11 is depicted in figure 10.13. Especially for larger rented apartments (type 6: 4 rooms; type 9: 5+ rooms) in this zone there is not enough demand to fill these dwellings, while lower ratios apply for the rented single family houses. The results indicate that the supply/demand ratio for owner-occupied dwellings in this zone is higher than in the rented sector. The ratio for dwelling type 10 (rented single family 5+ rooms) is approximately 0.30 while the corresponding owner-occupied type 11 has a ratio of 1.07 (in 1971) to 0.71 (1984). These results show that the high vacancy rates in submarkets in this new zone, which were indeed observed in this period, can be explained wholly in terms of housing market mechanisms.

Between 1971-1984 both Amsterdam and the Region experienced a shift in supply, and therefore also in demand, towards owner-occupied dwellings (see table 10.14). In general these latter dwellings have more rooms than the rented dwellings.

The shift towards a somewhat better tuning between demand and supply in the period 1971-1984 can also be seen in the following two figures of this section. The ratio between notional demand and realized demand gives an indication of the probability of realizing an intended move on the housing market of Amsterdam and the Region (figure 10.14). A slight improvement can be noticed for both Amsterdam and the Region after 1979.

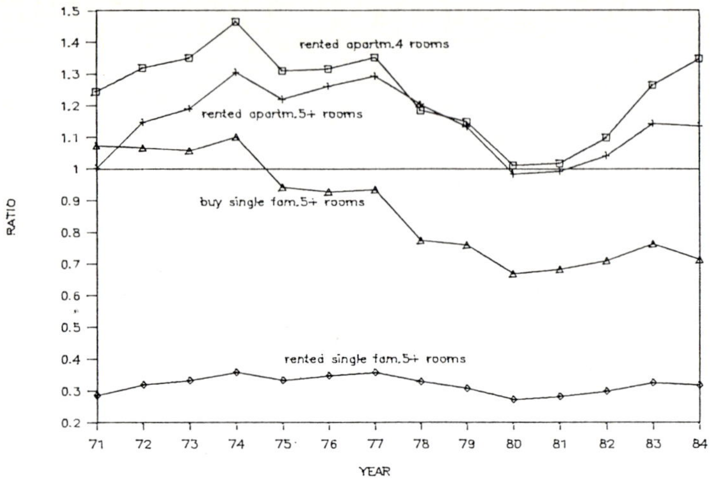

Figure 10.13. Supply/demand ratios for selected dwelling types in zone 11 (the Bijlmermeer)

	rented flat	owned-flat	rented single family unit	owned-single family unit	rent	buy	total
1971							
supply	68%	4%	20%	8%	88%	12%	100%
demand	45%	2%	46%	7%	91%	9%	100%
1984							
supply	66%	7%	19%	8%	85%	15%	100%
demand	41%	4%	45%	10%	86%	14%	100%

Table 10.14. Demand and supply of rented and owner-occupied dwellings in 1971 and 1984

When demand and supply are fully geared to one another the supply/realized demand ratio should be equal to one. Of course this will seldom be the case in reality due to time lags and changing preferences. However, in figure 10.15 it can be seen that the supply/realized demand ratio is increasing fast from 1982 onwards after a steep decrease in the last years of the seventies. In figures 10.14 and 10.15 the effects of the supply conditions in Amsterdam can be seen. Between 1978 and 1981 new housing construction in Amsterdam dropped considerably due to the economic recession. In the eighties a new urban policy was adopted that aimed at a revitalization of the city and a reversal of the population drain outwards. This resulted in a large new construction programme. The upward shift of the curves can be explained in terms of this new 'Compact City' policy.

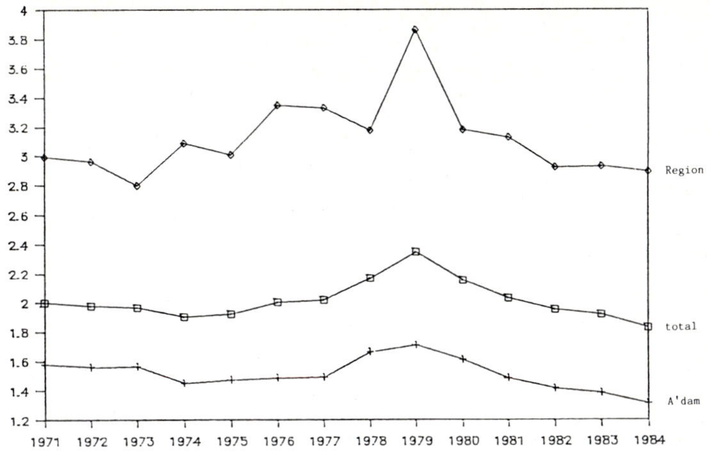

Figure 10.14. The notional/realized demand ratio, 1971-1984

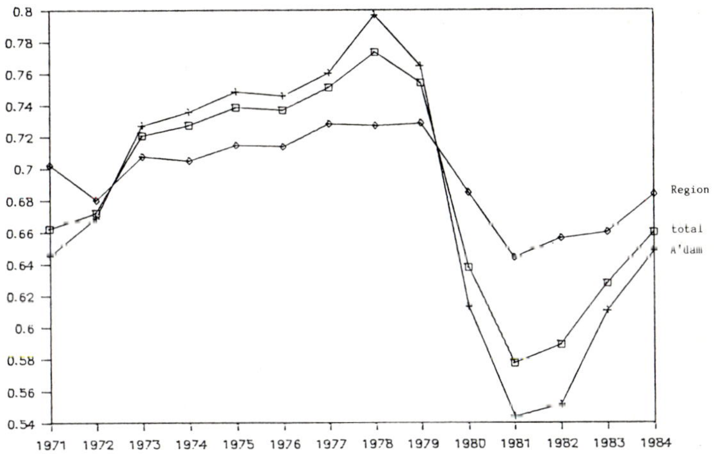

Figure 10.15. The supply/realized demand ratio, 1971-1984

Although the results of the housing market demand model can not be compared with observed values the outcomes presented in this section give evidence that the demand is modelled in a realistic way. It can also be concluded from this section that the level of detail of the model makes a number of interesting observations possible as was shown in the developments of the supply/demand ratio at the zonal level and at the dwelling type level.

10.8 Household Relocation Behaviour

In the allocation model each year the (notional) demand of dwellings is matched with the supply of dwellings per zone resulting in relocation of households. Since the number of migrations within the total study area in the allocation model is set equal to the realized number of migrations, the summation over the flows between zones in Amsterdam and the Region equals the observed number of migrations (see figure 10.16). As can be seen the mobility within the study area increased considerably from 131,000 in 1971 to 165,000 persons in 1984.

However, real world and modelling outcomes can be different from each other if total migration is disaggregated to the zonal level and to subcategories of the population in the study area. Whether the modelling results give a good impression of the actual migration flows will be discussed below. Analysis of the migration flows in relation with the observed migration flows will be done by means of goodness-of-fit indicators and by means of figures.

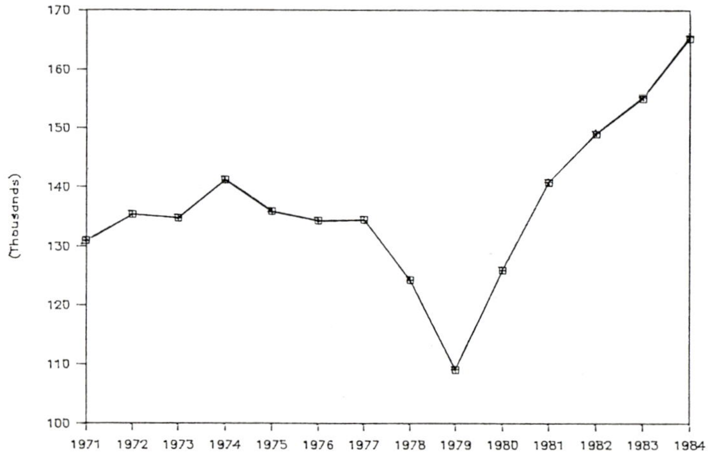

Figure 10.16. The observed and calculated total migration flows within the study area, 1971-1984

For the comparison between the estimated and observed flows many goodness-of-fit statistics are available, each with their own advantages and disadvantages (see e.g. Scholten and Van Wissen, 1985). In our analysis we make use of two statistics: the well-known R^2, the square of the correlation coefficient, and the relative mean square error RMSE and its standardized equivalent, the average error AE which was already introduced in section 10.5.

In table 10.15 the AE statistics of the migration matrices per year within Amsterdam and between the zones in the Region (Amsterdam included) are listed.

year	migration flows within Amsterdam AE	migration flows within the Region (Amsterdam included) AE
1971	0.58	0.37
1972	0.57	0.27
1973	0.61	0.31
1974	0.63	0.38
1975	0.70	0.55
1976	0.69	0.50
1977	0.67	0.52
1978	0.69	0.66
1979	0.69	0.59
1980	0.67	0.27
1981	0.75	0.39
1982	0.72	0.28
1983	0.70	0.37
1984	0.78	0.24

Table 10.15. The average error statistic for the migration matrices of Amsterdam and the Region 1971 - 1984

The average error is always lower than the mean cell value in the transition matrices. The results for the Region are clearly better than for the intra urban flow matrix of Amsterdam. This is mainly due to the good estimates of the intra-zonal migrations by the model, including the total number of intra-zonal migrations for Amsterdam. It can also be noted that the overall level of the results is quite stable in the Region for the whole period, while the Amsterdam results have a tendency to become less accurate.

In figures 10.17 to 10.20 some time-series with respect to migration flows from and to Amsterdam and from and to the Region are shown according to the following classification:

	from Amsterdam	from the Region
to Amsterdam	figure 10.17	figure 10.19
to the Region	figure 10.18	figure 10.20

Table 10.16. Migration flows depicted in figures 10.17-10.20.

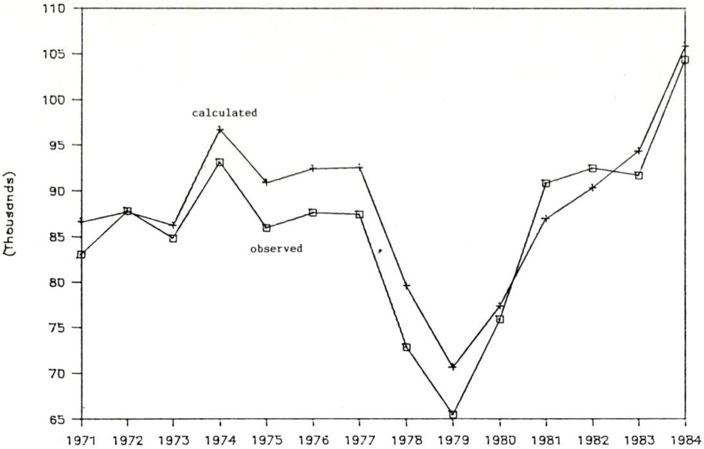

Figure 10.17. Intra-zonal migration within Amsterdam, 1971 - 1984

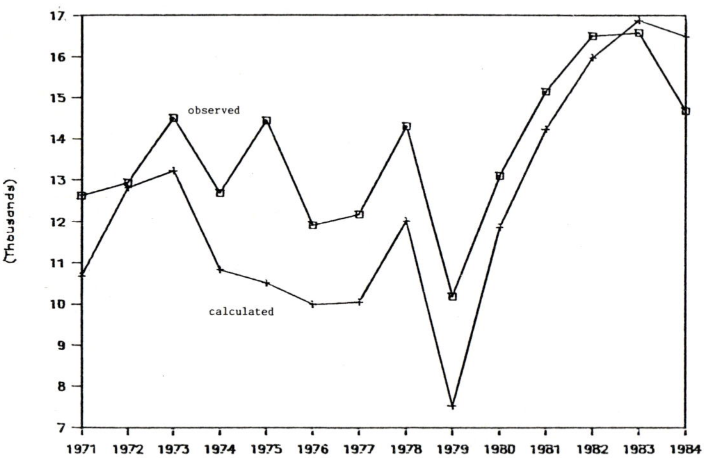

Figure 10.18. Migration flows from Amsterdam to the Region, 1971 - 1984

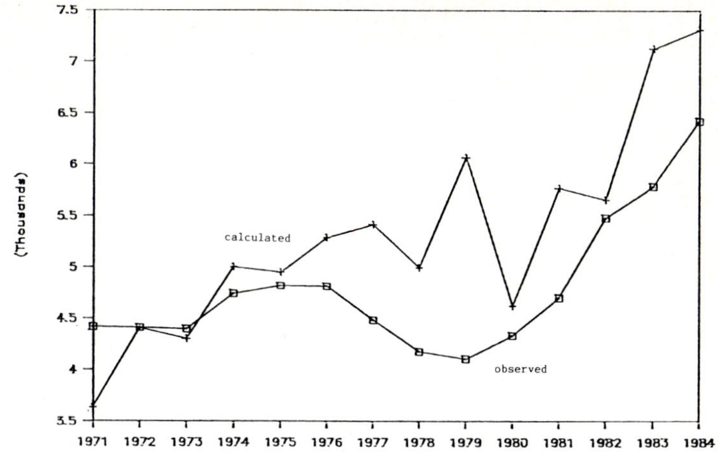

Figure 10.19. Migration flows from the Region to Amsterdam, 1971 - 1984

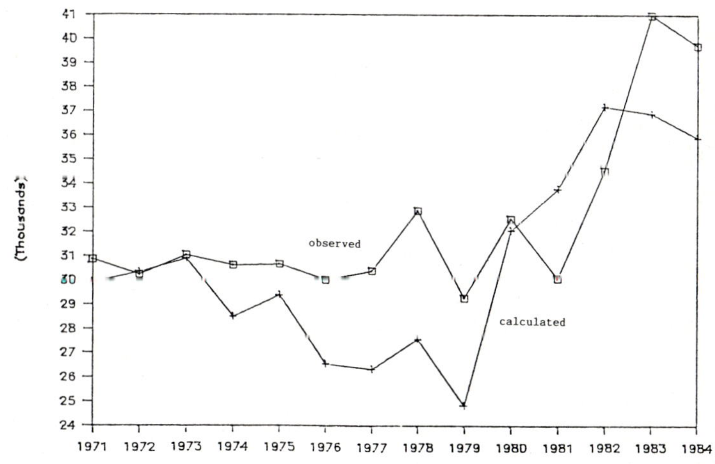

Figure 10.20. Intra-zonal migration within the Region, 1971 - 1984

Especially the calculated flows of total intra-zonal migration within Amsterdam correspond very well with the observed migration flows (figure 10.17). The match between the model outcomes and observed flows between Amsterdam and the Region and the intra-zonal migrations in the Region are not that good but still acceptable bearing in mind that these outcomes are solely the result of the allocation model and not constrained by observed values. The observed trends in the migration flows can also be found in the calculated flows, although the yearly fluctuations in the observed flows are not reproduced by the model outcomes, which show a smoother pattern. In the period 1979-1983 all migration flows increased, but since 1983 a marked change occurred in both the observed and calculated values where the mobility within Amsterdam and the migration to Amsterdam started to increase, with a corresponding downward shift in the Region. In Chapter 11 it will be seen if these initial trends are continued after 1984.

After concluding that the results with regard to the overall migration flows are satisfying, we will look in more detail to the migration results for zones and age classes. In figure 10.21 the migration flows between the zones within Amsterdam and within the Region in 1971 are visualized. The interpretation of this figure is as follows. Observed figures are drawn on the x-scale while predicted values are marked on the y-scale. The closer the points lie to the line which makes a 45° angle with the x-axis and the y-axis the better the fit.

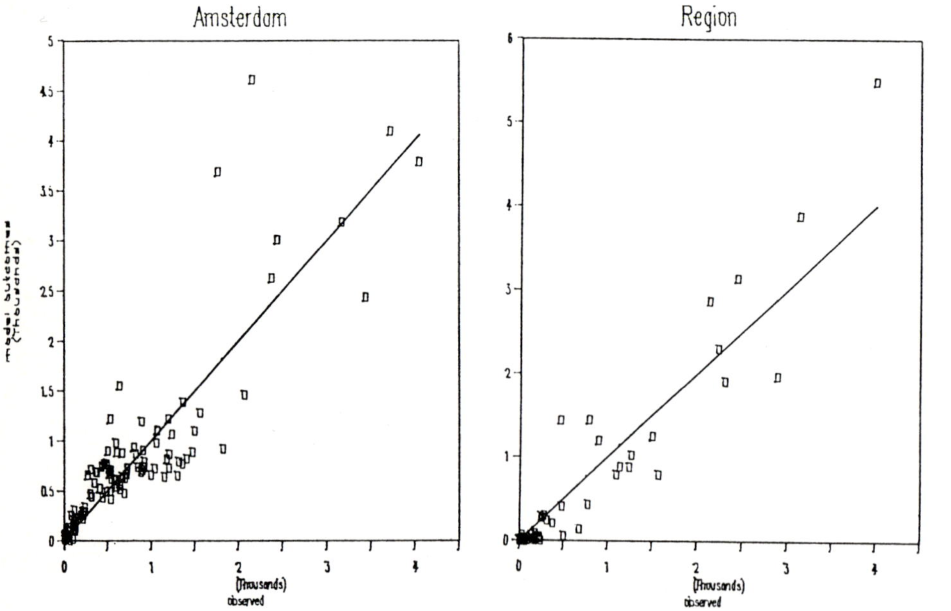

Figure 10.21. Migration flows in Amsterdam and the Region, 1971

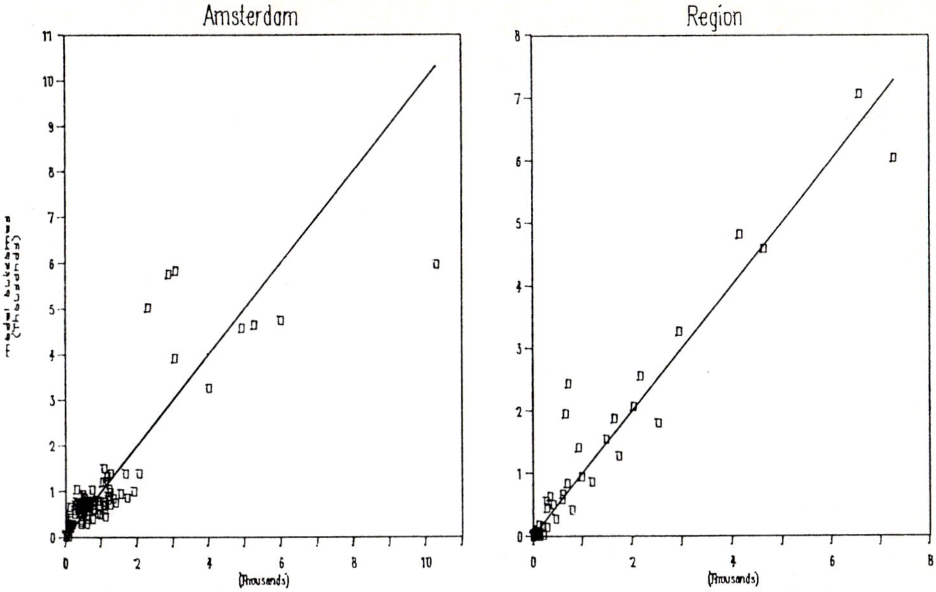

Figure 10.22. Migration flows in Amsterdam and the Region, 1984

The results in 1971 are better for the Region than for Amsterdam (especially the intra-zonal flows within zone 3 and 5 are overestimated). For the Region the results in 1984 are even better (see figure 10.22), but in Amsterdam the intra-zonal migration within one zone (the Bijlmermeer, zone 11) is underestimated.

Age Distributions of Migration Flows

On a lower level of disaggregation the model predicts flows between zones per household type. This can be transformed into persons by age category. Since the observed migration flows of household types classified according to age of head and household size are unknown, we will restrict ourselves for validation purposes to the person-age level. Observed figures are available per zone of total in and outmigration by age-category.

Especially for Amsterdam the age distribution of immigrants differs from the age distribution of outmigrants which results in an overrepresentation of specific age classes in the population of Amsterdam. Of course, the latter phenomenon has its influence on the demand and supply of specific dwelling types in Amsterdam. The age distribution and total numbers in 1971 and in 1984 of immigrants and outmigrants of Amsterdam can be seen in figures 10.23 and 10.24 respectively. In 1971 the number of immigrants in the age classes 20-24 and 25-29 and the number of outmigrants in the age class 25-29 are underestimated, while the number of outmigrants in the age class 15-19 is overestimated.

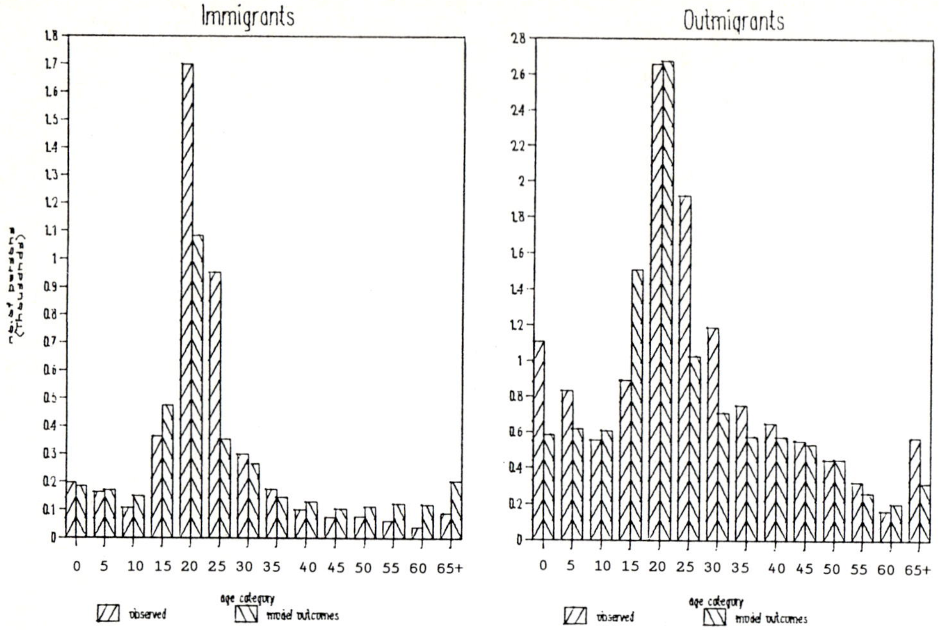

Figure 10.23. Number of immigrants and outmigrants per age class of Amsterdam, 1971

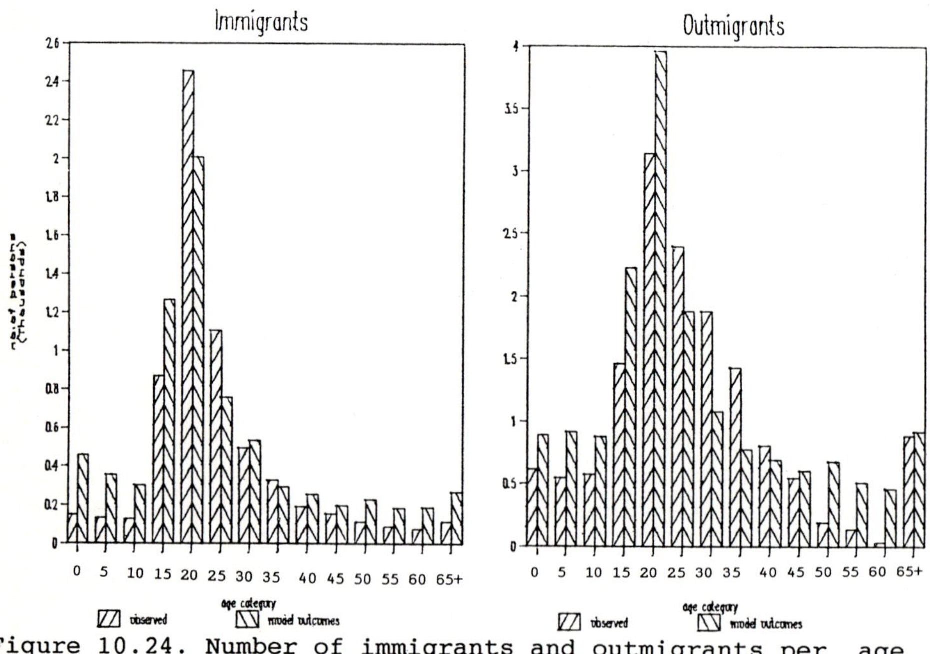

Figure 10.24. Number of immigrants and outmigrants per age class of Amsterdam, 1984

The estimate for the number of outmigrants in the age class which is the most mobile, age class 20-24, is very good. In 1984, the observed age distributions and the model outcomes still match very well, although the total number of children migrating to Amsterdam and the number of persons older than 50 years who leave Amsterdam is slightly overestimated.

The age-specific figures and the goodness-of-fit statistics listed in table 10.17 show that the model outcomes are also satisfactory on the more detailed level. The distribution of total in and outmigration for Amsterdam as a whole are good predicted by the model. For the zones in the Region the results are somewhat lower for immigration. Results for 1984 are better than for 1971 and this could be due to the sample that was used for the estimation of the housing demand functions (WBO). It was taken at the end of 1981 and so it is likely that it resembles the 1984 housing market preferences more than the 1971 situation. The total picture over the whole time period is nevertheless reasonably stable and from this it can be concluded that housing preference functions are relatively invariant over time.

zone	immigration flows		outmigration flows	
	1971	1984	1971	1984
Total Amsterdam	0.87	0.91	0.74	0.73
Zone :				
12	0.67	0.75	0.62	0.78
13	0.66	0.56	0.59	0.89
14	0.41	0.43	0.54	0.87
15	0.64	0.55	0.60	0.90
16	0.60	0.74	0.70	0.83
17	0.64	0.66	0.70	0.80
18	0.41	0.68	0.64	0.92
19	0.53	0.56	0.71	0.83
20	0.52	0.49	0.39	0.54

Table 10.17. R^2 measures for observed and predicted age distributions of in and outmigrants per zone in 1971 and 1984 (Amsterdam aggregated to one zone)

10.9 Components of Household Change

In the previous sections household dynamics and migration were described on a detailed level and for each process separately it was shown that they contribute to the change in the population and household structure of the zones. In this section these two components of zonal change are combined and by comparing the two their total impact and relative importance in the total household developments can be inferred. For instance, for some zones both processes may work in the same direction, thus leading to a large growth rate of households. In others the processes may work in opposite directions.

Looking first to the Amsterdam and Regional totals (figure 10.25), the differences are predominantly in the migration component. The total effect of the household demographic component is positive and in the same order of magnitude for both areas. Taking into account the differences in population size between Amsterdam and the Region this means that the net rate of reproduction of households in the Region is considerably higher. Large differences exist in the impact of the migration component. Its impact in Amsterdam is almost always negative although the general trend in the curve is upwards, while the development in the Region is exactly the opposite.

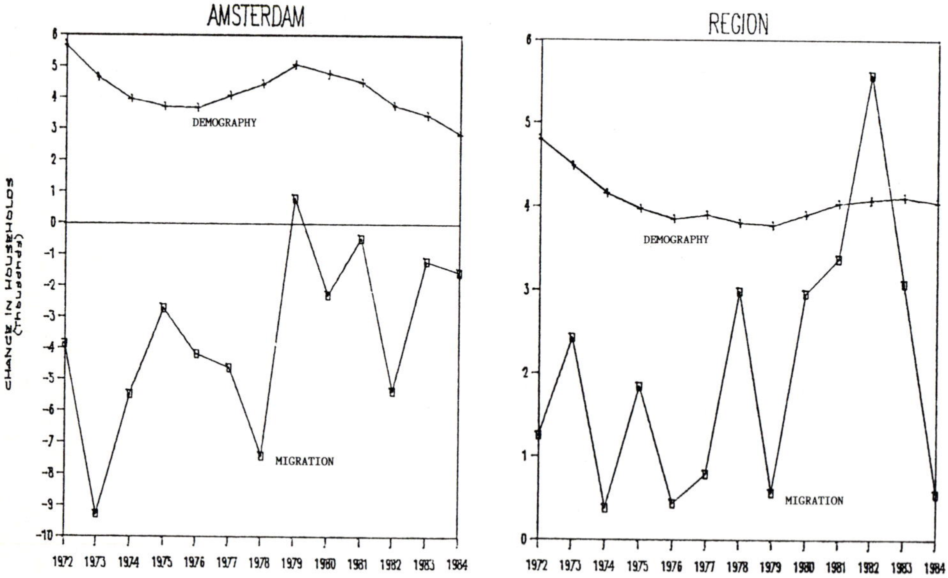

Figure 10.25. Components of household change in Amsterdam and the Region, 1972 - 1984

Comparing the two components in Amsterdam it can be seen that the decrease due to outmigration exceeds the increase caused by the demographic component in Amsterdam in the first half of the seventies and that a net gain of households starts in the second half of the seventies. In the Region both the demographic and the migration component work in the same direction, leading to an explosive growth of households. However, the migration component drops steeply after 1982, corresponding with an upward shift of the curve in Amsterdam. This trend indicates that the mid-eighties could be a turning point in the household development in the area. If the migration curve is extrapolated a situation occurs where Amsterdam gains households both through internal (although diminishing) household generation and immigration, while in the Region the increase in households due to the internal demographic component is reduced by a negative migration effect. In Chapter 11 this topic will be investigated in more detail.

Disaggregation of these components of household change to the zonal level leads to some interesting differences for Amsterdam. In figure 10.26 a number of representative zones are depicted. In zone 1, the inner city, internal household dynamics is negative, but the impact of migration is positive, leading to a net increase in households after 1974. In zone 2, which is part of the old residential areas around the inner city, the demographic component is in general slightly negative. The migration component adds to the number of households after 1978. A similar pattern can be found in zone 3 (not shown). In zone 7, a 20th century extension west of zone 2, the gain in households due to internal demographic developments is exceeded by the loss of households due to migration. The other zones follow more or less the general Amsterdam trend, with the exception of zone 11 (the South East, or the Bijlmermeer) which experiences high levels of immigration as the result of large scale housing construction.

All zones in the Region show the same positive demographic trend (figure 10.27). Some differences occur in the relative impact of the migration component. Zone 12 (Amstelveen) has a negative migration component after 1974, zones 14 (Waterland South) and 15 (Haarlemmermeer) are in general positive but fluctuating and zones 19 and 20 (Purmerend and the ZIJP, the new towns) have a large positive migration effect. The other zones are in general similar to the Region trend, with a positive, but decreasing migration component.

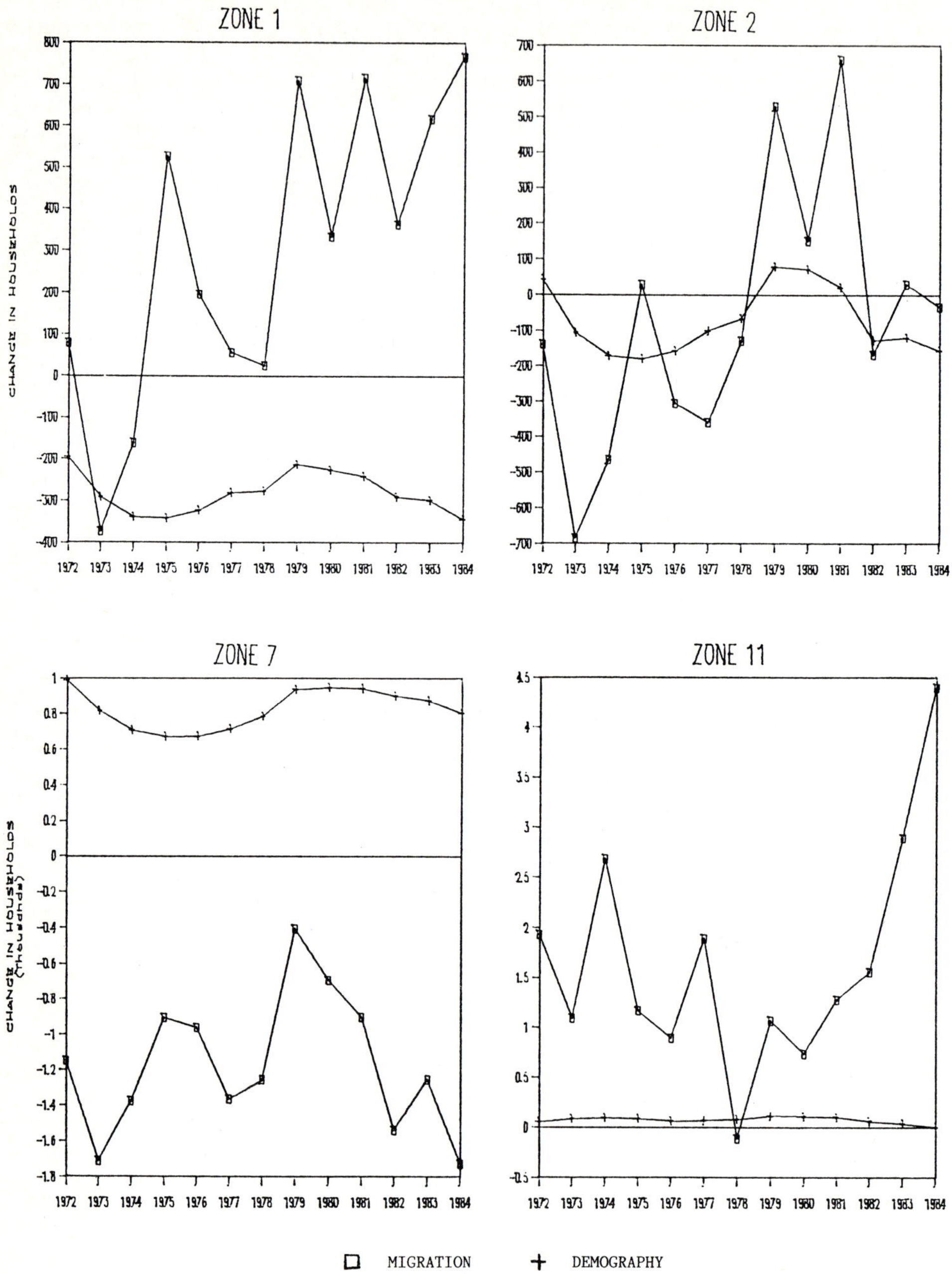

Figure 10.26. Components of household change in selected zones in Amsterdam, 1972 - 1984

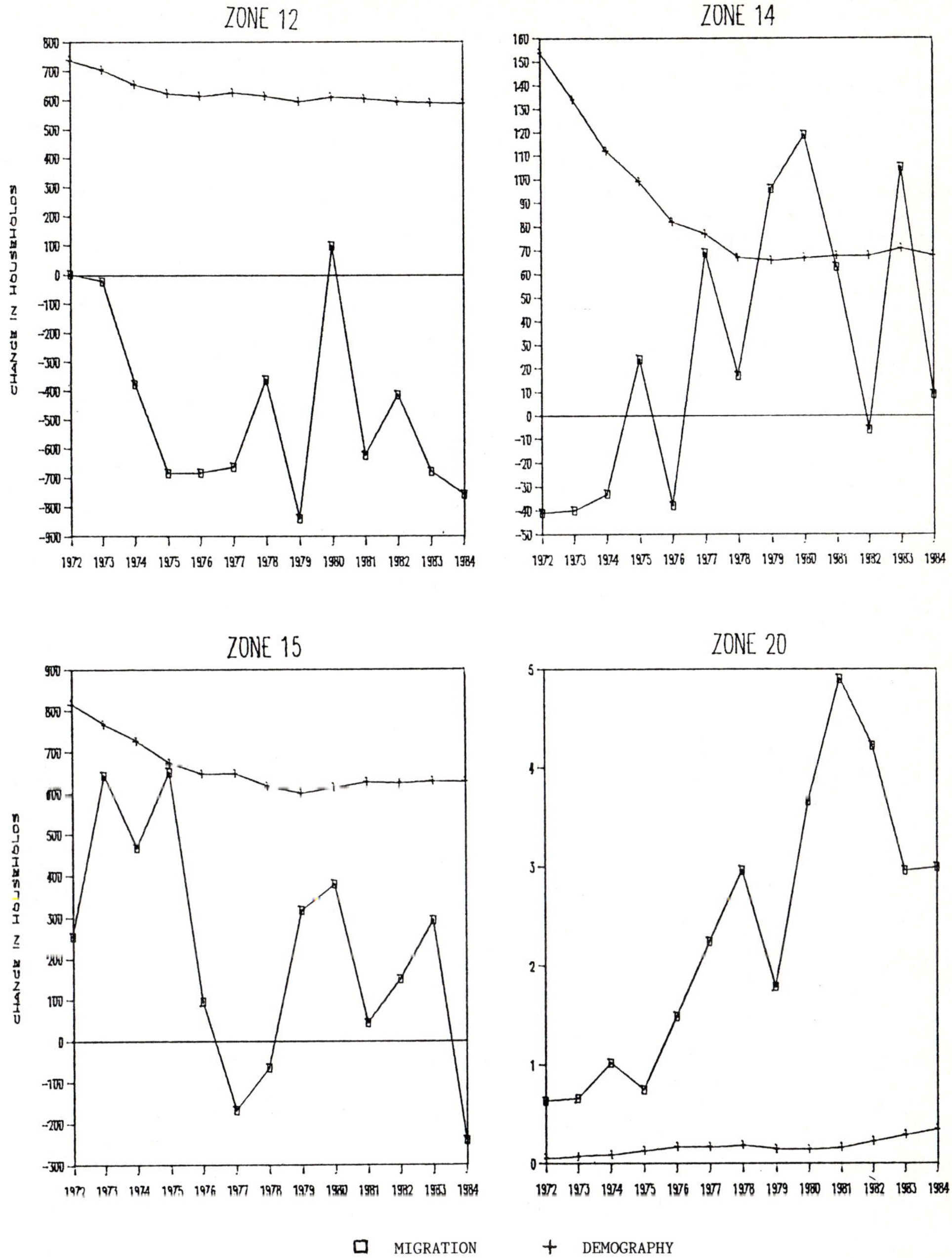

Figure 10.27. Components of household change in selected zones in the Region, 1972 - 1984

10.10 Total Population and Household Developments

Population

The final result of household dynamics and relocation is a new population vector for every zone every year. In this section we will concentrate on the total population development per zone as predicted by the model and compare it with observed population figures. Figure 10.28 presents the total observed and predicted population developments in Amsterdam and the Region. The curves for both areas almost exactly mirror each other, with Amsterdam loosing 120,000 inhabitants and the Region increasing with almost the same number after 1971. Predicted trends for Amsterdam and the Region conform very well with the observed pattern, although there is some divergence after 1982. In terms of goodness-of fit the Amsterdam curve fits somewhat better.

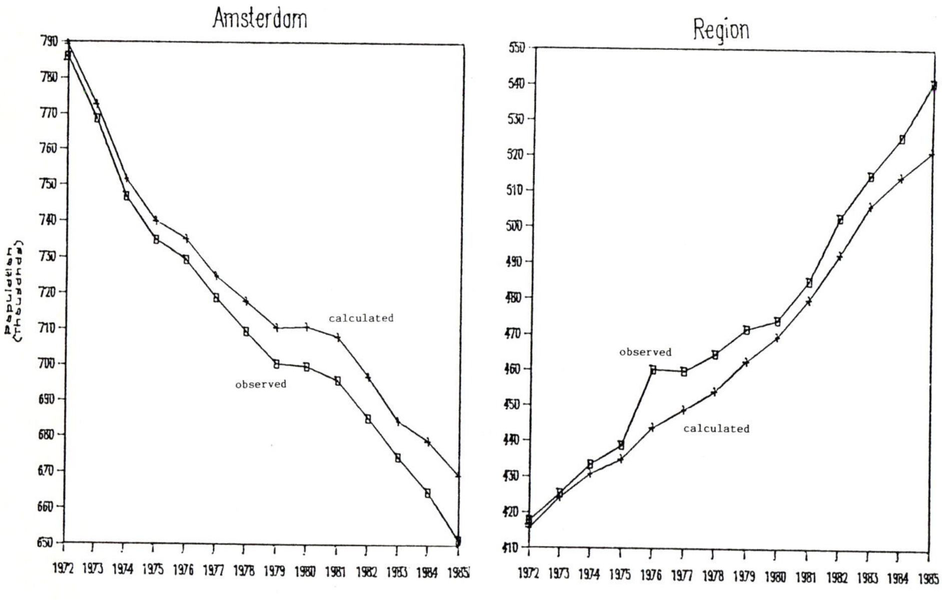

Figure 10.28. Total predicted and observed population developments in Amsterdam and the Region, 1972 - 1984

Table 10.18 gives the results of linear regressions of the model outcomes on the observed values. The R^2 measure for Amsterdam is 0.998 against 0.987 for the Region.

	Model = α + β Obs			
Zone:	α	β	σ_{est}	R^2
1	10532	0.839	2711	0.577
2	22140	0.773	1445	0.964
3	26075	0.698	789	0.977
4	16230	0.794	610	0.992
5	5984	0.800	236	0.984
6	53814	0.400	836	0.902
7	20811	0.785	821	0.977
8	-42993	1.434	2935	0.622
9	15122	0.846	1745	0.948
10	-768	0.901	122	0.934
11	8924	0.479	1612	0.949
Amsterdam	82253	0.897	1656	0.998
12	58234	0.192	707	0.526
13	559	0.932	377	0.954
14	4279	0.713	311	0.276
15	-475	0.987	1205	0.952
16	104447	0.243	1695	0.078
17	18498	0.511	513	0.487
18	41927	0.211	980	0.525
19	5660	0.817	985	0.954
20	665	0.863	1197	0.998
Region	38317	0.902	4058	0.987

Table 10.18. R^2 results of linear regression of model outcomes on observed population totals per zone

Zonal results for Amsterdam and the Region are depicted in figure 10.29. Within Amsterdam the results for zones 2, 3, 4, 5 and 7 are highly satisfying, with R^2 measures in general close to 1. However, the slope of the curve is always less then 1 and the intercept positive (except zone 8) indicating that the model outcomes tend to be biased downward at the end of the projection period. The results for zone 1 and zone 8 are less satisfactory. In zone 1 the observed increase in population after 1980 has not been taken up by the model. In zone 8 (North of the Y-river) the outmigration has been overestimated considerably. Presumably the attractiveness for this zone is higher than indicated by the model. The special geographical position of the zone might cause this special pattern and this is not taken into account in the model. The picture for model 11 shows that predicted total population is considerably lower than observed in reality (an estimated β of 0.479). So the immigration to this zone has been larger than predicted by the model.

One possible explanation of this pattern is the fact that the high observed vacancy rate in this zone in the seventies stimulated the local government to open this submarket for immigrants thus removing a number of institutional thresholds for potential movers. This is not taken into account in model II.

The variation in results over the Regional zones is even larger. The R^2 measures are in general lower than in the city, although the value for the Region as a whole is still 0.987. The closest approximation is found in zones 19 and 20 which are the new towns north and south-east of Amsterdam respectively. So the model is capable of reproducing these concentrated suburbanization processes. For zones 13 and 15 similar results are achieved. Both zones experienced large housing construction programmes in the seventies and eighties. Results are less satisfying for zones 12, 14, 16, 17 and 18. These areas are characterized more by an independent development with more emphasis on consolidation than growth. Zones 12 (Amstelveen) and 16 (Zaanstad) received large suburban inflows in the sixties. Zones 14, 17 and 18 have a partially rural character and are less integrated in the Amsterdam housing market system. The model is driven totally by demographic and housing market factors. This is reflected in the model outcomes for these zones.

<u>Households</u>

Finally, some results are presented on household developments in Amsterdam and the Region. In figure 10.30 total predicted household developments in Amsterdam and the Region are drawn. In Amsterdam a reversal of the downward trend in the number of households occurred in the mid-seventies. As noted in the previous section this was mainly the result of the upward shift in the (negative) migration component. The growth in the Region has been explosive, as both migration and the internal household dynamics contributed to an increase in the number of households. However, as can be seen, in the eighties this curve is flattening due to a decrease in the migration component.

The number of singles is Amsterdam is increasing rapidly (figure 10.31), while the relative growth in the Region of this group is lower, but still positive. In the presentation of the first results of model II it was noted that the predicted household distribution in the Region was not as good as in the city giving a serious overestimation of singles accompanied by a similar underestimation of large households. Therefore, the downward curve for large households in the Region should be less steep. On the other hand, the same trend in Amsterdam is more in line with reality, which is equally true for the predicted curve for two and three person households.

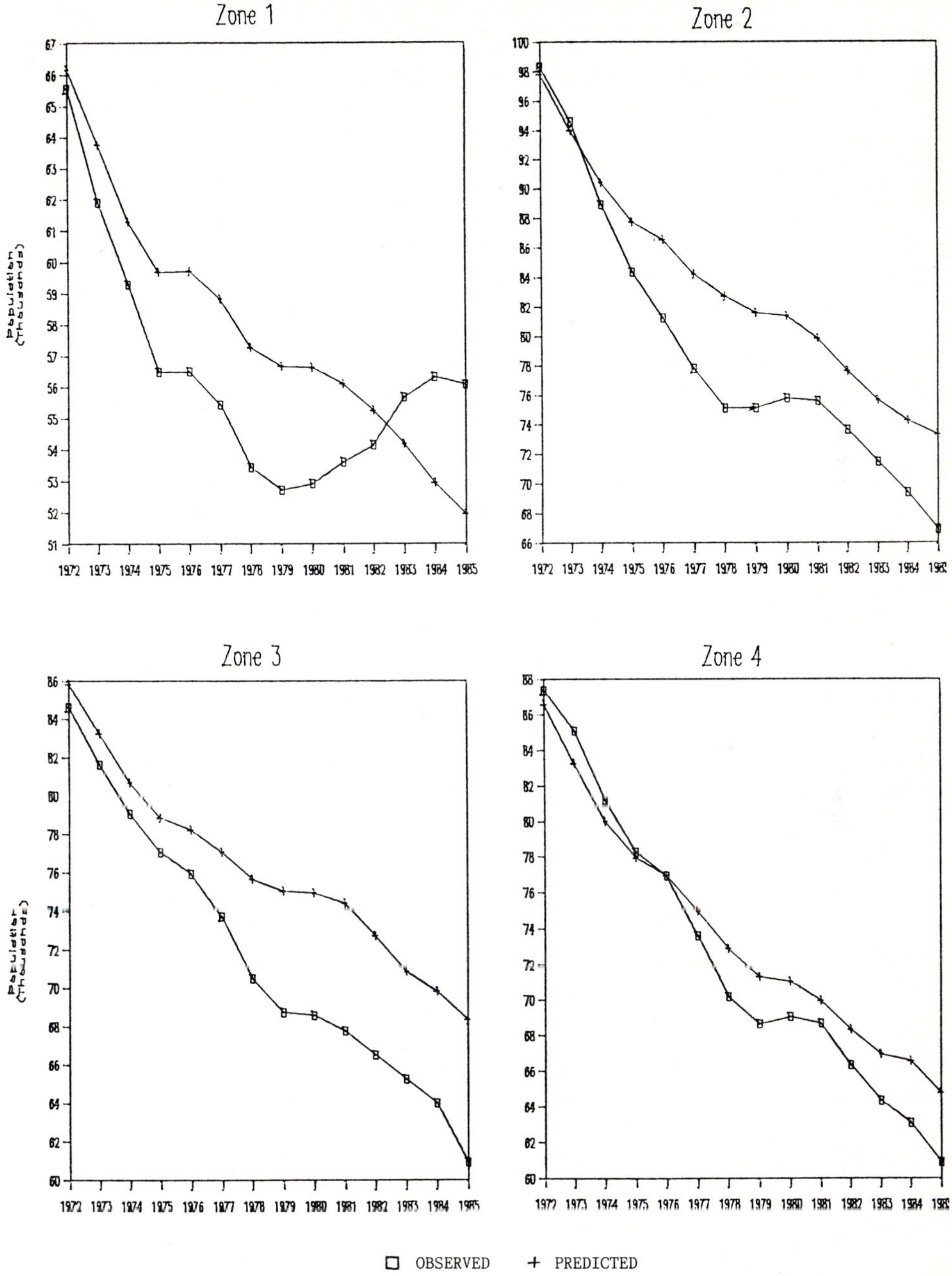

Figure 10.29. Observed and predicted population per zone, 1972 - 1984: zones 1 - 4 (continued)

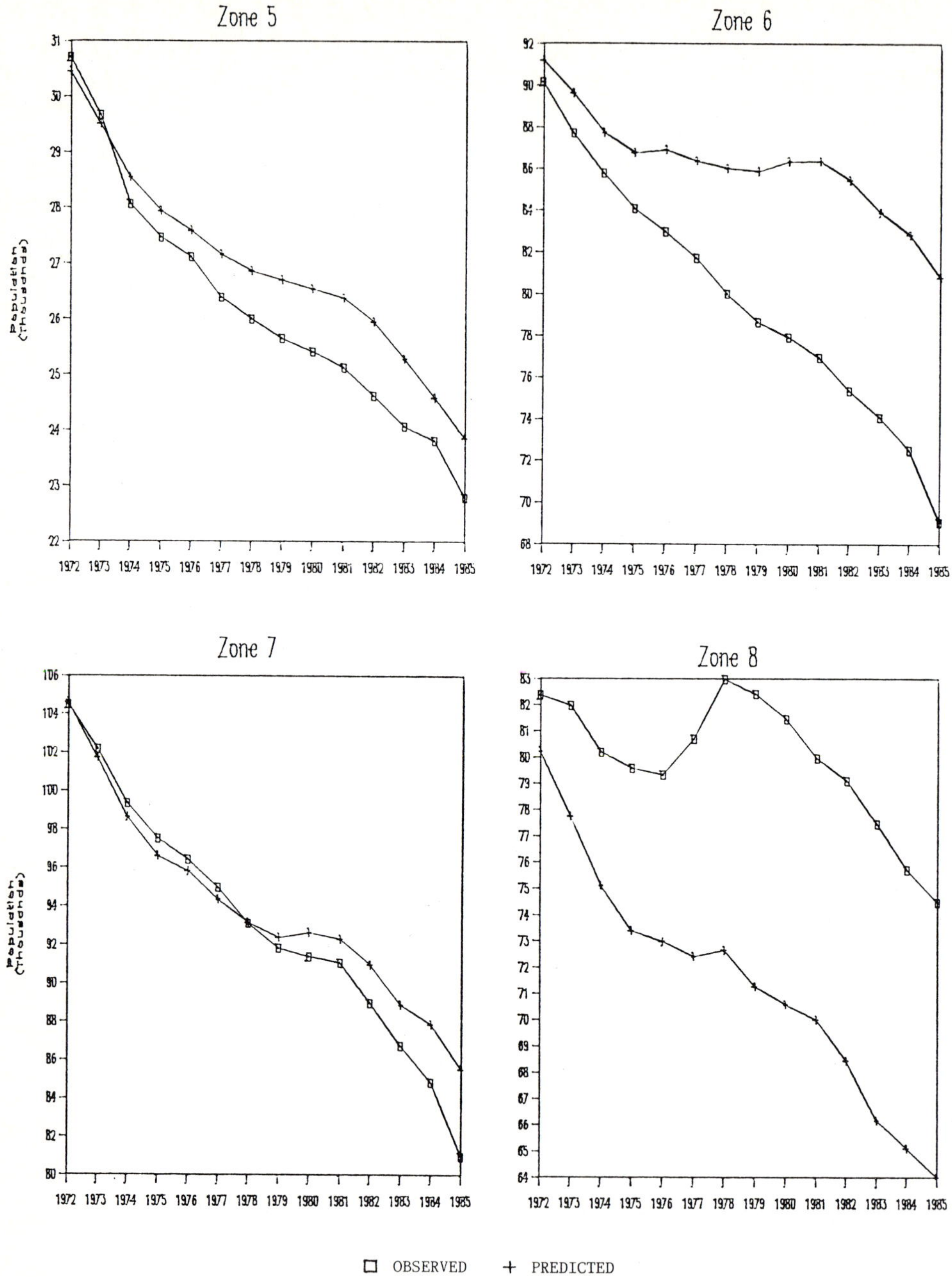

Figure 10.29. Observed and predicted population per zone, 1972 - 1984: zones 5 - 8 (continued)

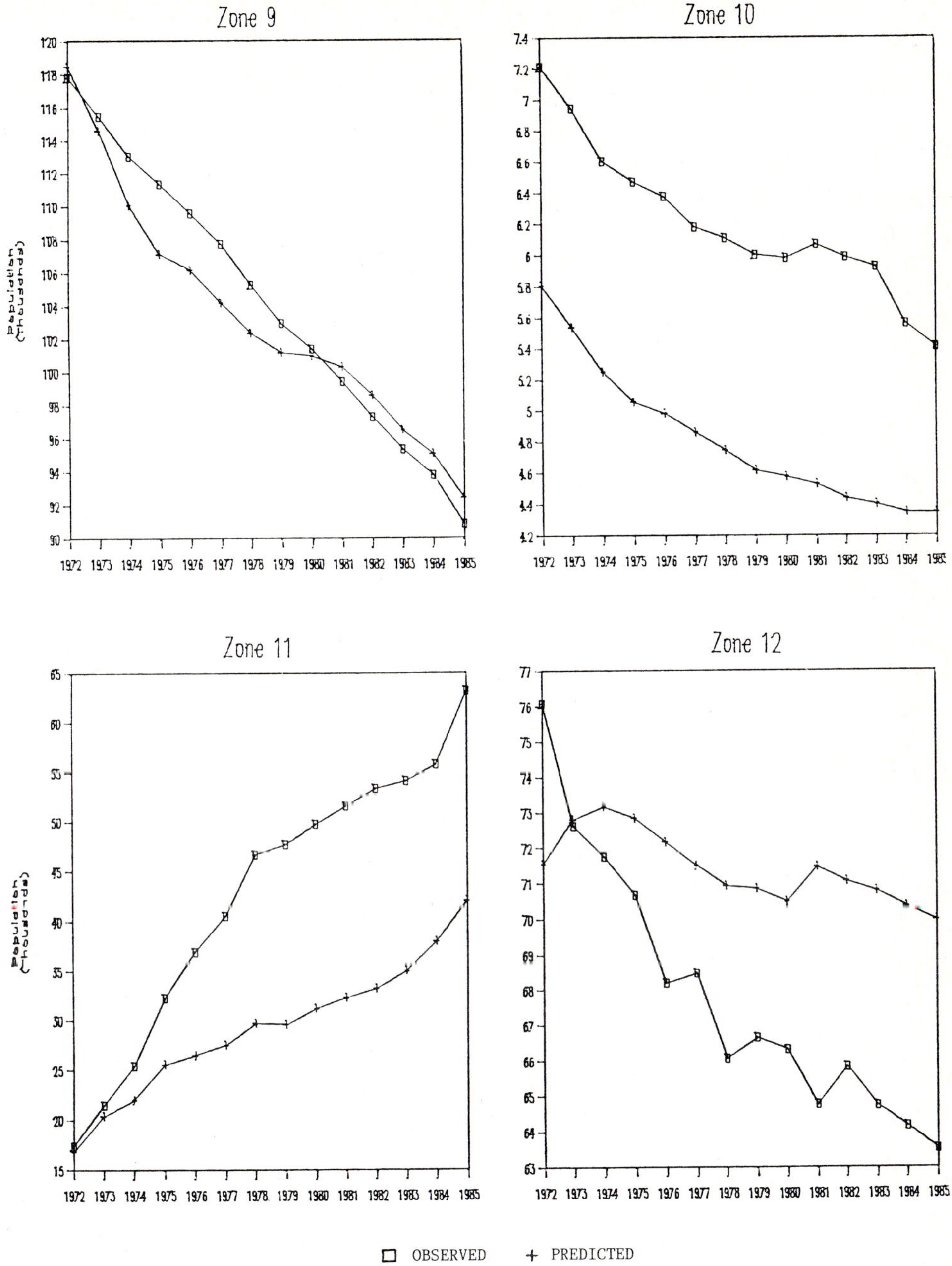

Figure 10.29. Observed and predicted population per zone, 1972 - 1984: zones 9 - 12 (continued)

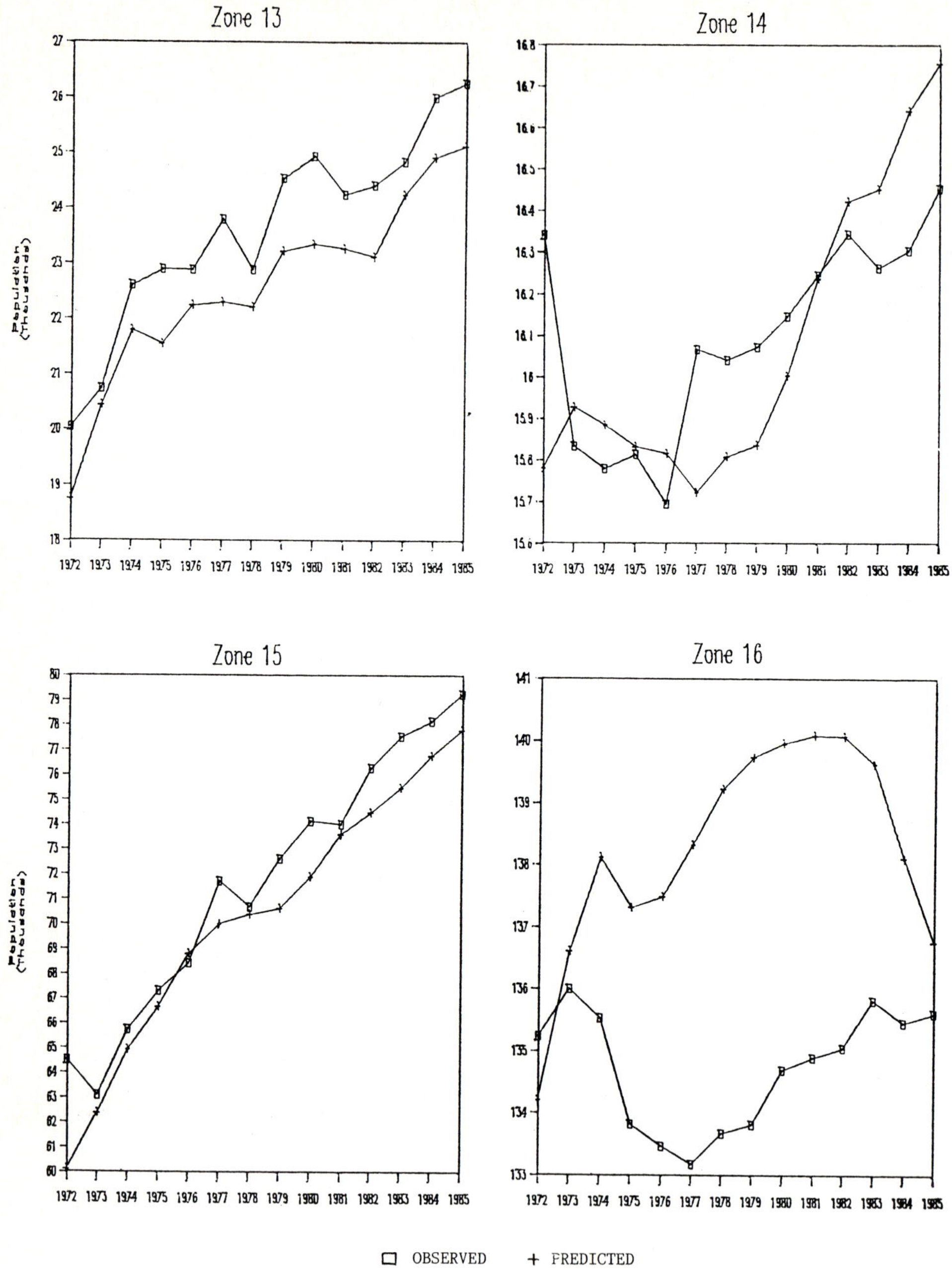

Figure 10.29. Observed and predicted population per zone, 1972 - 1984: zones 13 - 16 (continued)

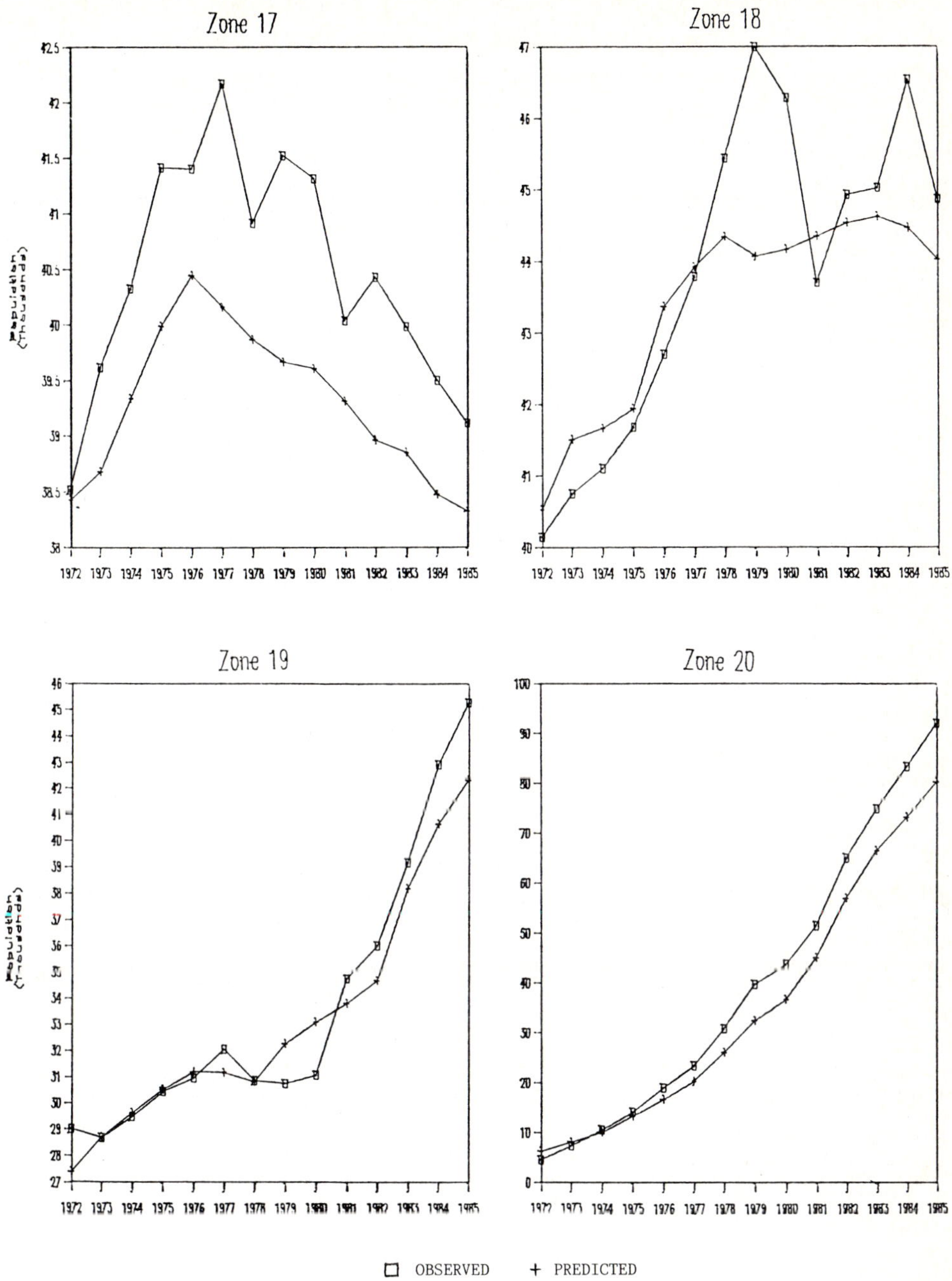

Figure 10.29. Observed and predicted population per zone, 1972 - 1984: zones 17 - 20

The development in the distribution of households according to age of the head is presented in figure 10.32. In Amsterdam the young categories (under the age of 25 and between 25 and 34 years) are increasing while the retired category decreases. In the Region the youngest age category grows until the second half of the seventies, next stabilizes and drops somewhat in the eighties. The share of senior citizens increased over the whole period. The middle-aged categories decrease first and show a tendency to grow again after 1980. However, the test of the model performance on this point as described before showed that the Regional results were not very accurate on this point.

10.11 Conclusions

In this chapter a model was tested for household relocation in the Amsterdam housing market area. It contains both a household demographic module and a housing market module. These submodels were developed and estimated in previous chapters. In this chapter they were linked in a consistent accounting framework and with the total model a simulation was performed for the period 1971 - 1984. The goal of this simulation was twofold. First a test was conducted on the overall performance of a basic model (model I) with the estimated sample coefficients in order to determine if the performance of the total model was within the acceptable range. Given the limitations of the basic coefficients (i.e. time and space independency) it was not expected that the outcomes would exactly tally with reality. Therefore the second goal of the simulation was to 'fine-tune' the model by making the coefficients of the household model time and zone dependent (model II). The results of model I were encouraging. The model was able to reproduce the observed suburban flows from the central city to the suburbs reasonably accurate resulting in a close approximation of the observed number of households in the Region in 1982. The Amsterdam results were less accurate showing a large decrease in the number of households instead of the observed moderate increase. Inspection of the results at the level of household distributions showed that the model coefficients can be regarded as 'averages' between urban and suburban household transition processes. In model II a number of coefficients were varied across time and across zones taking the estimated values as the point of reference. Rates of divorce and break-ups are different between Amsterdam and the Region and increase over time. Moreover, singles in Amsterdam are less inclined to double up than in the Region. These, and a number of other important transitions were adjusted in order to improve the model.

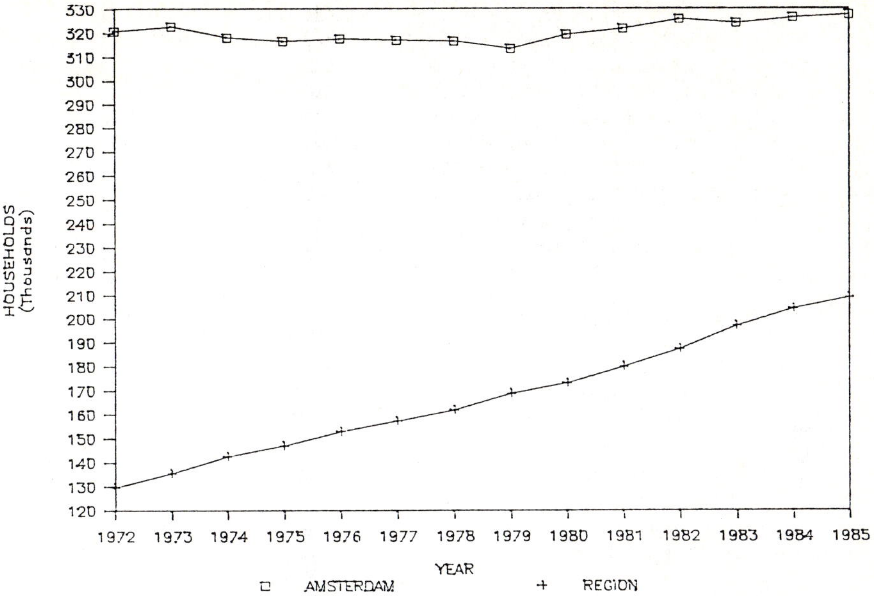

Figure 10.30. Total predicted household developments in Amsterdam and the Region, 1972 - 1984

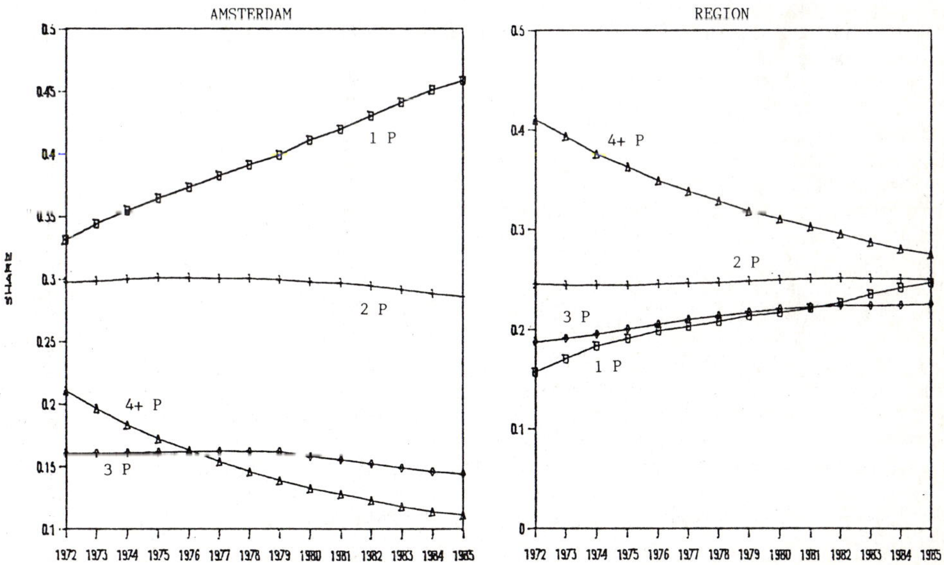

Figure 10.31. Developments in household size categories in Amsterdam and the Region, 1972 - 1984

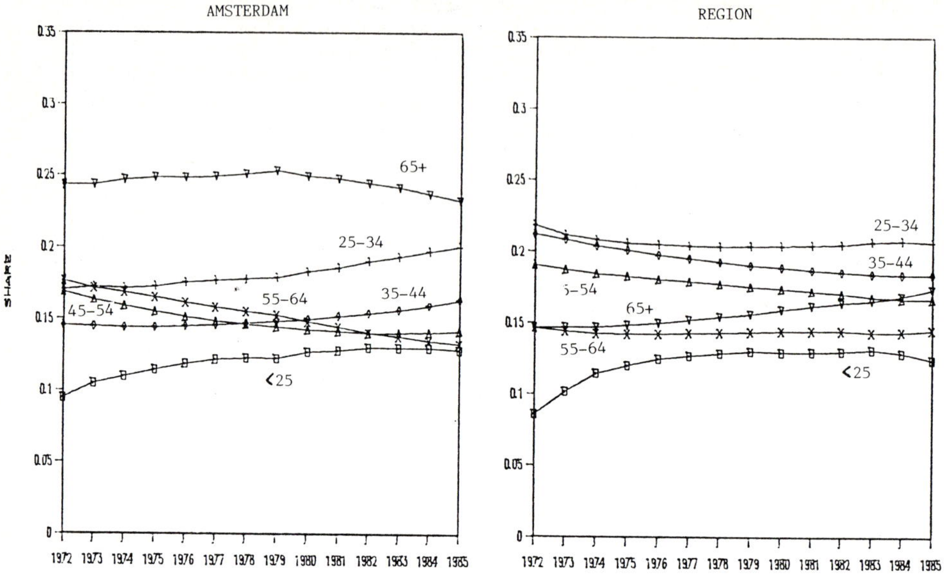

Figure 10.32. Developments in household age categories in Amsterdam and the Region, 1972 - 1984

The results for model II show that the observed trends in Amsterdam are fairly closely matched after these parameter adjustments. The total number of households in Amsterdam is reasonably well predicted by the model and the predicted distribution of households in Amsterdam according to size and age is close to the observed figures. However, the Regional results have not improved. The total predicted number of households is again close to the observed number but the distributions over size and age of the head are less accurate. Still, the total outcomes of model II are satisfying and give insights into the components of change in the household structure and the housing market in Amsterdam in the period 1971 -1984.

The first general conclusion to be drawn from this model exercise is that demographic and housing market factors are capable of explaining the general development in population and households at the regional level. The massive suburban migration in the seventies, followed by a period of stagnation at the end of the seventies and the start of re-urbanization in the eighties are reproduced to a large extent by the model.

A second general conclusion is that the dynamic treatment of household generation and dissolution in a housing market context is absolutely necessary in order to determine the components of change in the household structure (and thus: housing demand). The development in net household gains over the time period shows that the impact of this factor may vary considerably over time. It is interesting to note that the household transition parameters change over time in the direction of a higher rate of household formation. Paradoxically, the net rate of household reproduction is decreasing in the eighties in both Amsterdam and the Region. As the distribution of the population over household positions changes this rate of reproduction changes also. The results in Amsterdam indicate that in zones with a very high percentage of singles a net decrease in the number of households can occur due to internal household dynamics. This is indeed true for the inner city zones but also in other zones there is a clear tendency in that direction.

Thirdly, the disaggregated nature of the model makes a number of detailed observations possible. This was shown for the supply-demand ratio for specific dwelling types in zone 11 (Bijlmermeer). This zone has experienced high vacancy rates in certain parts of the housing stock since the seventies. The same phenomenon can be observed in the model outcomes. While the single family rented dwellings are still marketable in this zone, there is excess supply in the larger rental apartments and in the owner-occupier submarket. The model outcomes show that these vacancy rates can be explained wholly in terms of housing market conditions.

Fourthly, from the results on the migration component of the model it can be concluded that the concept of housing preferences can be used fruitfully in a modelling context. The goodness-of-fit tests on migration indicate that the structure of the preference functions for dwellings are quite stable over time and can be used in combination with supply to predict household relocations in an intra-urban housing market context.

Finally, it should be pointed out that the parameters of the household model estimated in Chapter 7 had to be modified in order to generate a realistic time path of household dynamics. The endogenisation of transition rates of demographic processes remains one of the future research topics in household modelling.

CHAPTER 11. HOUSING MARKET SCENARIOS FOR THE PERIOD 1985 - 2000

11.0 Introduction

In this chapter the model validated in the previous chapter will be used for the forecasting of population and dwelling stock developments in the period 1985-2000. In Chapter 10 it was concluded that the model results for the validation period 1971-1984 with respect to migration flows, population and households are in agreement with observed values both for the total figures as well as in more detail per age class and household class. This correspondence between the calculated and observed figures leads to the conclusion that the model developed in the previous chapters can be used for realistic scenario building with respect to the housing market developments in the Amsterdam region.

This chapter is organized as follows. The choice of two scenarios and the resulting input in the relocation model will be discussed in section 11.1. The results of the scenarios 1 and 2 are presented and compared with each other in section 11.2. and 11.3. The chapter is concluded with some remarks regarding the presented results and the policy implications related to them in section 11.4.

11.1 Choice of Scenarios

With a model as disaggregated as the relocation model described in the preceding chapters housing market projections can be made on a detailed level. This can be done by choosing specific zones in and outside Amsterdam where to build and specific dwelling types to build based on the planning and policy strategies developed by local and central governments. Regarding the choice of which input to use for the period 1985-2000 we judged it to be useful to concur with existing ideas with respect to future housing market developments for the Amsterdam region. Therefore the scenarios presented in this section are derived from the housing market projections made on the basis of policy goals of the municipality of Amsterdam, the province of North-Holland and the central government (Bosch, 1986), and figures of new houses to be built in the period 1985-1999 are adopted from the housing market input of these projections.

The projections for Amsterdam and surroundings start from three alternatives (Bestuursinformatie, 1984):

- the 'low' alternative
- the 'high' alternative
- the 'normative' alternative

The 'low' alternative is based on the expectation that the process of suburbanization (migration from Amsterdam to the so-called growth centres, see section 2.1, the period after 1965) will continue at the same rate as in the past while the policy goal of both the local and central government is to diminish suburbanization. In the period between 1984 and 1986 it became clear that this alternative is no longer realistic (and therefore will not be taken into account in the scenario building).

For the 'high' alternative it is assumed that the policy goal of decreasing suburbanization will be realized by building new dwellings in Amsterdam. The 'normative' alternative is based on the assumption that the construction quota (see again Chapter 2) in the growth centres are diminished in favour of building new dwellings in Amsterdam. The 'high' alternative agrees more or less with policy goals of the central government with respect to the development of Amsterdam, while the 'normative' alternative is more in agreement with the policy goals of the local government of Amsterdam (p. 21, Bestuursinformatie, 1984). The major goal of this last alternative is to increase the population of Amsterdam (whether this will be achieved, will be one of the subject of section 11.2).

On the basis of the two alternatives mentioned, i.e. taking into account their main assumptions with respect to demographic and housing market developments, two scenarios were built. The 'Yuppie' scenario, based on the 'high' alternative and the 'Family' scenario, based on the 'normative' alternative. Both these scenarios and the corresponding assumptions will be described below.

The central element in both scenarios is the governmental policy on the housing market. Attention is focussed on the building of new houses as a policy instrument to influence population development. Therefore the demographic components will be the same for both scenarios and will not change in time. This means that the rate of births and deaths and the coefficients for 'children leaving home', 'divorce', 'marriage', and 'number of elderly in non-households' are constant during the period 1985-2000 and equal to their values in 1984. Furthermore, for the period 1985-2000 the migration in and out of the study-area is fixed on the values in 1985, while the total number of migrants per year within the study-area has been set equal to 155,000 (the level attained in 1985). In the 'Yuppie' scenario every year of the period between 1986 and 2000 4,500 new dwellings are built in Amsterdam and 8,300 in the Region, 1,700 dwellings will be lost due to urban renewal. The distribution of new and dwellings no longer available over the zones (within Amsterdam and the Region) and the dwelling types is equal to the observed distributions in 1985. This means for instance that most of the new dwellings in Amsterdam will continue to be of dwelling type 1 and 6 and most of the demolitions will take place in the old city (zones 1 and 2). This will probably lead to an overrepresentation in Amsterdam of young persons living in small households. Compared to the 'Yuppie' scenario in the 'Family' scenario 2,000 more dwellings are built in Amsterdam during the period 1986-1995, (from 1996-2000 the number of new dwellings is equal to 4,500) and 1,100 less dwellings in the Region. The urban renewal process in Amsterdam results in a decrease of 300 extra dwellings per year. For the Region the distribution of new dwellings over the zones and dwelling types will be the same as in the first scenario, but for Amsterdam the distribution over the dwelling types is changed in favor of more single family units, aiming at a more 'balanced' age distribution in Amsterdam compared with the 'Yuppie' scenario. The distribution for the demolished dwellings remains the same as in the former scenario. These assumptions lead to the figures for the housing market scenarios as given in table 11.1.

Housing market figures	'Yuppie' scenario	'Family' scenario
- number of dwellings built in Amsterdam	4500	6500 (4500)
- number of dwellings built in the Region (excl. the ZIJP)	5300	4000
- number of dwellings build in ZIJP	3000	3200
- number of dwellings withdrawed in the study area	-1700	-2000
increase of dwellings in the study area per year	11100	11700 (9700)

Table 11.1. Housing market figures of the scenarios (in brackets figures after 1996)

The consideration of changing the distribution in the second scenario is to see whether the absolute population number and the age distribution in Amsterdam is influenced by the choice of which dwelling type to build. The distribution is changed through a doubling of the percentage of single family units within a specific dwelling size class and the increase in number of dwellings is subtracted from the corresponding class of flats (for instance, in the absolute increase in owner-occupied single family units with more than 4 rooms is subtracted from the owner-occupied flats with more than 4 rooms).

Starting point of the scenarios is 1985. In contrast to the base-year of the validation period (1971), for 1985 we do not need to estimate the occupancy matrix of households to dwellings in Amsterdam since reliable data are available from the '<u>koppelingsbestand</u>' of the municipality of Amsterdam (werkgroep Koppeling Bevolking-Vastgoed, 1985). This information was also used is setting up the test data for Amsterdam for the model I and II runs (see section 10.2). In this datasource the population of Amsterdam is linked with their housing situation and this source is therefore considered as very useful for constructing the occupancy matrix and the distribution of the population over the household types. For the Region the occupancy matrix is estimated in the same way as in 1971 with the computer program RIWILS, and using the WBO sample data as input.

Now the assumptions of the 'Yuppie' scenario and 'Family' scenario have been discussed we can turn to the analysis of the outcomes in section 11.2 to see whether the expectations with respect to the scenarios are realized.

11.2 Modelling Results of the Scenarios

In this section some modelling outcomes regarding population and housing market developments are presented. First some population figures for Amsterdam and the Region are given, secondly some housing market outcomes are discussed. In the figures 11.1 and 11.2 the results of the two scenarios for the number of households and persons are given respectively, the corresponding figures can be found in table 11.2 for Amsterdam and in table 11.4 for the Region.

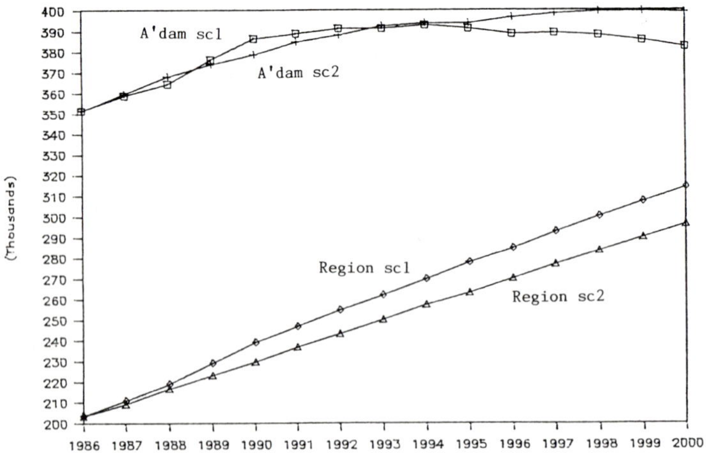

Figure 11.1. Predicted number of households in Amsterdam and the Region for the two scenarios, 1985 - 1999

year	Amsterdam the 'Yuppie' scenario number of households	 number of persons	Amsterdam the 'Family' scenario number of households	 number of persons
1985	351.5	679.4	351.5	679.4
1986	358.7	683.3	359.7	685.4
1987	364.3	685.4	368.2	688.9
1988	376.0	686.7	373.9	692.6
1989	386.3	687.2	378.7	695.8
1990	388.7	687.6	384.7	698.0
1991	391.2	687.3	387.9	700.5
1992	391.3	687.3	392.5	702.1
1993	392.8	686.2	393.8	703.0
1994	391.2	685.1	393.8	705.9
1995	388.5	686.1	396.6	706.7
1996	389.0	684.5	398.5	707.7
1997	387.9	684.1	399.4	708.8
1998	385.4	684.6	399.4	710.1
1999	382.1	686.2	398.8	711.7
	(numbers x 1000)		(numbers x 1000)	

Table 11.2. Number of households and persons in Amsterdam according to the scenarios, 1985-1999

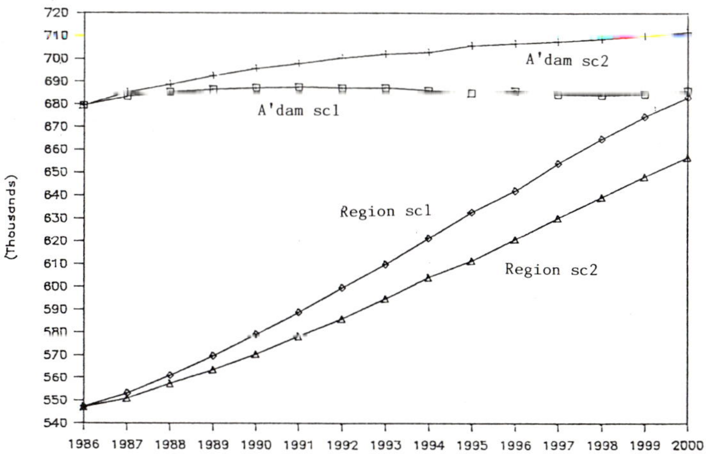

Figure 11.2. Predicted number of persons in Amsterdam and the Region for the two scenarios, 1985-1999

As can be seen both from the figures and the tables there are considerable differences in number of households and persons between the scenarios on the 1st of January 2000.

In the 'Yuppie' scenario the total population in Amsterdam increases in the period 1985-1999 with 30,600 households and only 6,800 persons. For the 'Family' scenario these figures are 47,300 households and 32,300 persons. In table 11.3 the results of the population figures for Amsterdam are compared with the outcomes of the alternatives mentioned above.

year	'high' alternative	'Yuppie scenario	'normative' alternative	'Family' scenario
1985	666.1 (675.6)	675.6 *	666.1 (675.6)	675.6 *
1986		679.4 *		679.4 *
1990	653.6 (663.1)	687.0	666.4 (675.9)	695.8
1995	670.1 (679.6)	685.1	696.4 (705.9)	705.9
2000	-	686.2	719.4 (728.9)	711.7
	numbers x 1000		*: observed	

Table 11.3. Comparison of alternatives and scenarios for Amsterdam (in brackets the corrected figures for the 1985 starting values)

From table 11.3 it can be noticed that the number of persons in the starting year 1985 of the Amsterdam alternatives is too low compared with the realized number. After correcting for the base-year (figures in brackets) a number of interesting phenomena can be observed. The decrease of population until 1990 in the 'high' alternative does not occur in the 'Yuppie' scenario. The reason for this is that the projections with the 'high' alternative were made in 1984 when it was not foreseen that the shift in trend from decrease to increase of population occurred in 1985 instead of 1990. As a result the population according to the 'high' alternative is lower than that of the 'Yuppie' scenario. For the same reason the results for 1990 of the corrected 'normative' alternative are much lower than those of the 'Family' scenario, while for 1995 they are the same for both projections. However, the Amsterdam alternative predicts far more population growth between 1995 and 2000 than the 'Family' scenario. This is caused by the fact that one of the main assumptions of the 'normative' alternative is that the population number is equal to 720,000 in 2000, so this is implicitly brought into the projection. But even when we compare the outcomes of the uncorrected 'normative' alternative and the 'Family' scenario it can be concluded that this policy goal is not met according to the 'Family' scenario.

The population results of the Region corresponding to the figures 11.1 and 11.2 are given in table 11.4. The differences between the two scenarios can clearly be seen. As the total population figures for the entire study area are the same in both scenarios (since total immigration and outmigration is the same), Amsterdam and the Region behave as 'communicating vessels'. Since the population in Amsterdam is growing in the 'Family' scenario due to the building of more dwellings, the population of the Region is growing slower than in the 'Yuppie' scenario. The total number of households in the study area is for the 'Yuppie' scenario in 2000 somewhat larger (696.4) than for the 'Family' scenario (695.4) due to the building of more small dwellings in the former scenario compared to the latter.

year	the Region the 'Yuppie' scenario number of households	 number of persons	the Region the 'Family' scenario number of households	 number of persons
1985	203.6	547.2	203.6	547.2
1986	211.0	553.1	209.5	551.0
1987	219.2	561.0	216.9	557.4
1988	229.2	569.7	223.5	563.7
1989	239.2	579.2	229.9	570.4
1990	246.8	588.9	236.9	578.4
1991	254.7	599.6	243.3	586.1
1992	262.0	609.9	250.2	594.9
1993	269.8	621.4	257.4	604.3
1994	277.9	632.9	263.3	611.7
1995	284.9	642.3	270.3	621.2
1996	292.8	654.2	277.1	630.5
1997	300.3	664.9	283.7	639.7
1998	307.4	674.6	290.2	648.5
1999	314.3	683.1	296.5	656.9
	(numbers x 1000)		(numbers x 1000)	

Table 11.4. Number of households and persons in the Region, according to the scenarios, 1985-1999

In the figures 11.3 and 11.4 for Amsterdam and the Region the difference between the distributions of the population over the four household categories is depicted. As expected the number of singles is rapidly increasing in time (mainly due to ageing of the population). In all household categories the number of households in Amsterdam is higher for the 'Family' scenario than for the 'Yuppie' scenario, and the distribution over the categories remains the same (see table 11.5). Since the population after 1995 is growing faster in the 'Family' scenario than in the 'Yuppie' scenario, despite the fact that

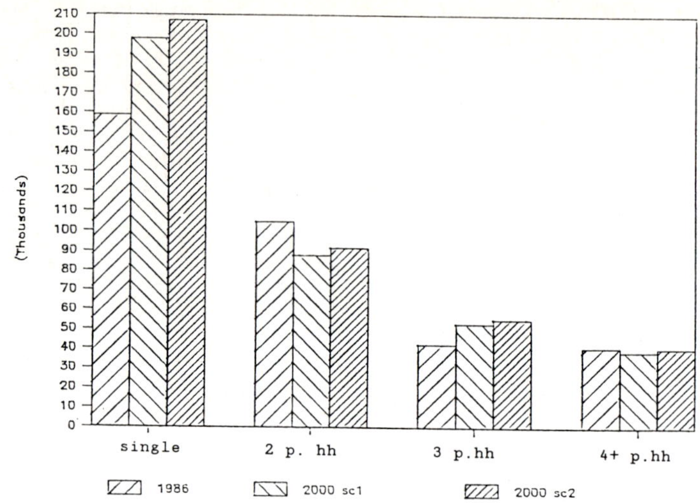

Figure 11.3. Predicted number of households per household category in Amsterdam for the two scenarios

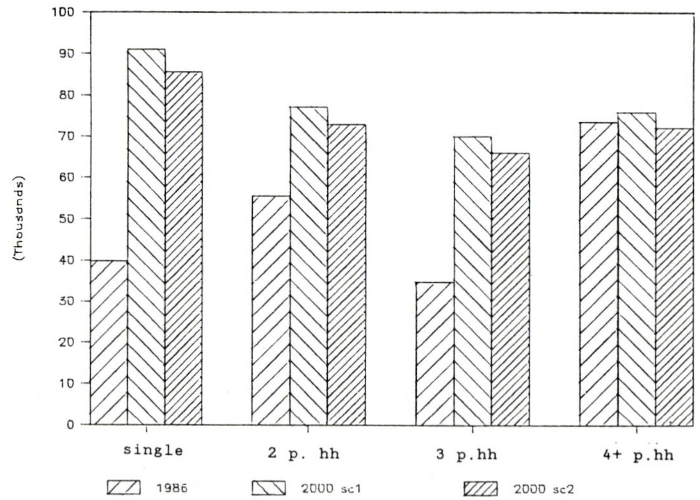

Figure 11.4. Predicted number of households per household category in the Region for the two scenarios

for that period the total number of dwellings built in Amsterdam is equal in both scenarios, we can conclude that both the building of more dwellings in scenario 2 as well as the shift toward the building of more single family units in

Amsterdam contributes to the growth of the population in Amsterdam. The distribution of household size and age of head is the same for both scenarios despite the differences in immigration into Amsterdam from the Region. This is due to the fact that the migrations to Amsterdam from the Region are only a small part of total immigration and probably the shift towards more single family units is not large enough.

The differences in population between the two scenarios are the result of differences in migration patterns between Amsterdam and the Region, since total migration in and out the study area is kept constant during the period 1985-1999. In general the population figures are higher in the 'Family' scenario compared to the 'Yuppie' scenario due to the fact that fewer people leave Amsterdam and more people migrate to Amsterdam. This is shown in the figures 11.5-11.8. The intrazonal migration within Amsterdam is higher in the second scenario (figure 11.5), while the outmigration to the Region is in general lower (figure 11.6). The immigration into Amsterdam from the Region is higher in the 'Family' scenario (figure 11.7), resulting in a lower number of intra-zonal migrations in the Region (figure 11.8).

Figure 11.9 and 11.10 show the effects of the differences in the supply of new dwellings between the scenarios. In the first scenario (the 'Yuppie' scenario) the outmigration of young persons (aged under 34) is higher than of the 'Family' scenario, whereas for older persons (aged over 34) outmigration is lower. For the immigration the process is reversed, i.e. in scenario 2 immigration of younger persons is lower and of older persons higher than in scenario 1.

Now the main population results of the scenarios have been discussed we will turn to the presentation of some outcomes regarding the demand and supply of dwellings. This is done by using the three ratios already presented in Chapter 10 in respectively figure 10.11, 10.14 and 10.15, i.e.:

- the supply/demand ratio,
- the notional/realized demand ratio, and
- the supply/realized demand ratio.

The supply/demand ratios for the two scenarios are given in the figures 11.11 and 11.12. As in the period 1971-1984 also during the scenario period the supply/demand ratio is higher for Amsterdam than for the Region indicating that in general the excess demand on the housing market is larger in the Region than in Amsterdam. The ratio for the Region is more or less equal in the two scenarios, but for Amsterdam the situation on the housing market until 1996 is slightly better in the 'Family' scenario than in the 'Yuppie' scenario, and vice versa from 1997 onwards (see table 11.7).

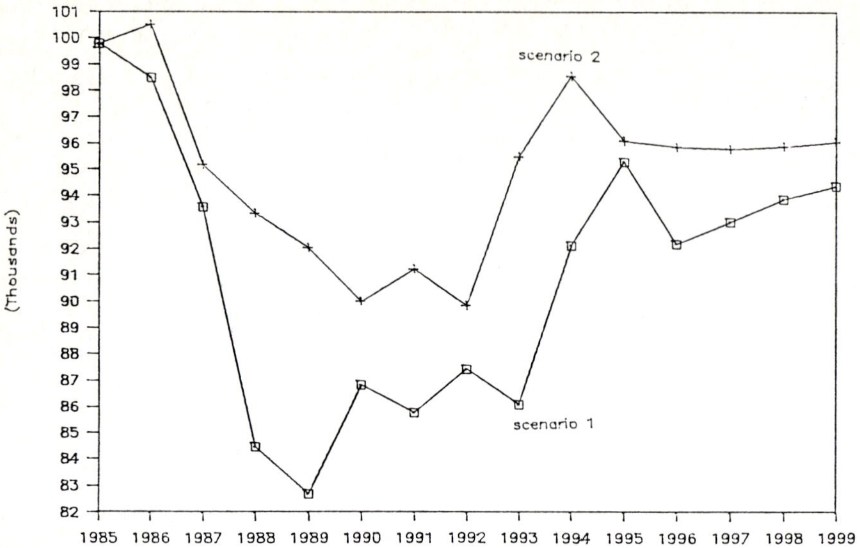

Figure 11.5. Intra-zonal migration in Amsterdam, 1985-1999

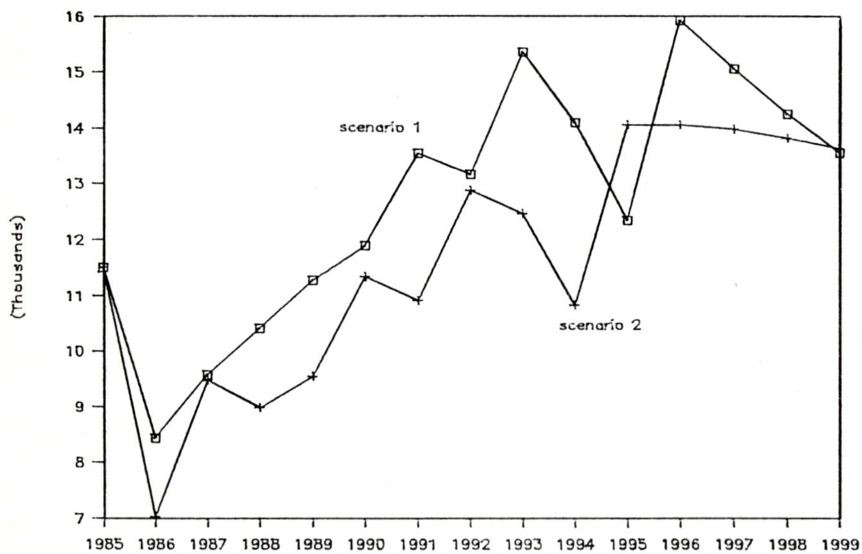

Figure 11.6. Migration from Amsterdam to the Region, 1985 - 1999

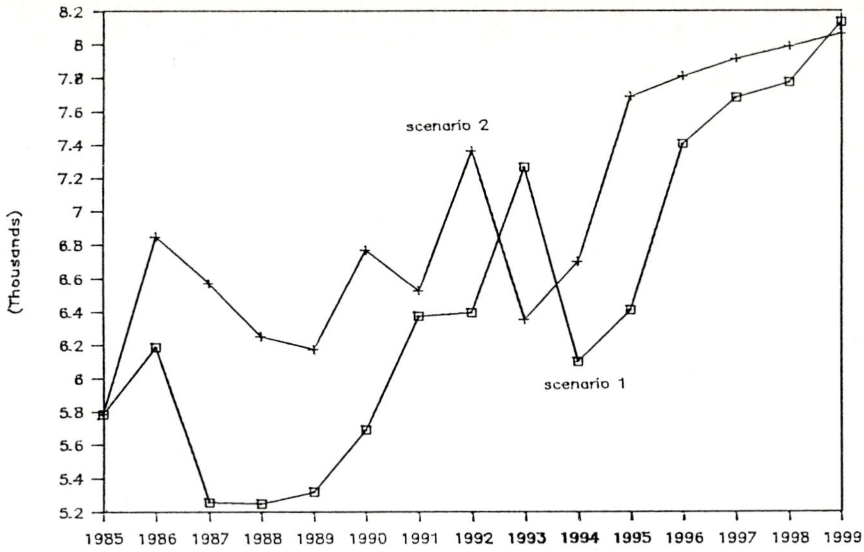

Figure 11.7. Migration from the Region to Amsterdam, 1985 - 1999

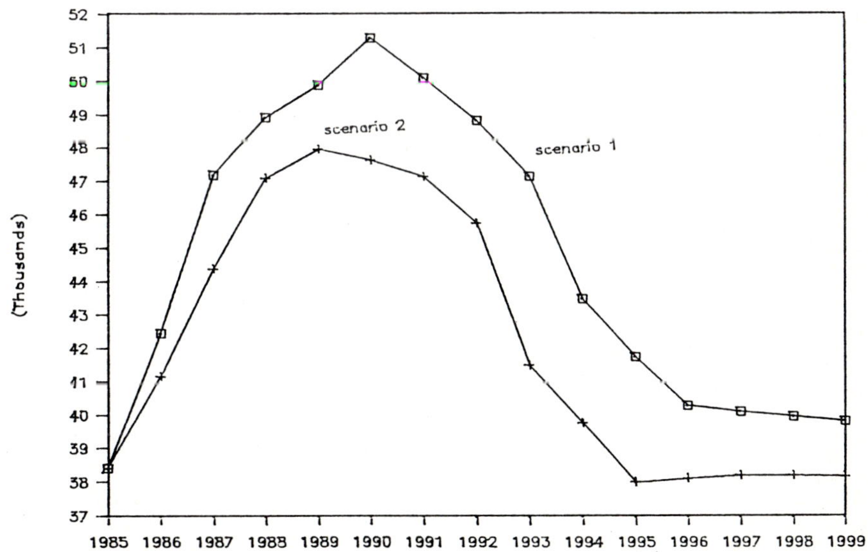

Figure 11.8. Intra-zonal migration in the Region, 1985-1999

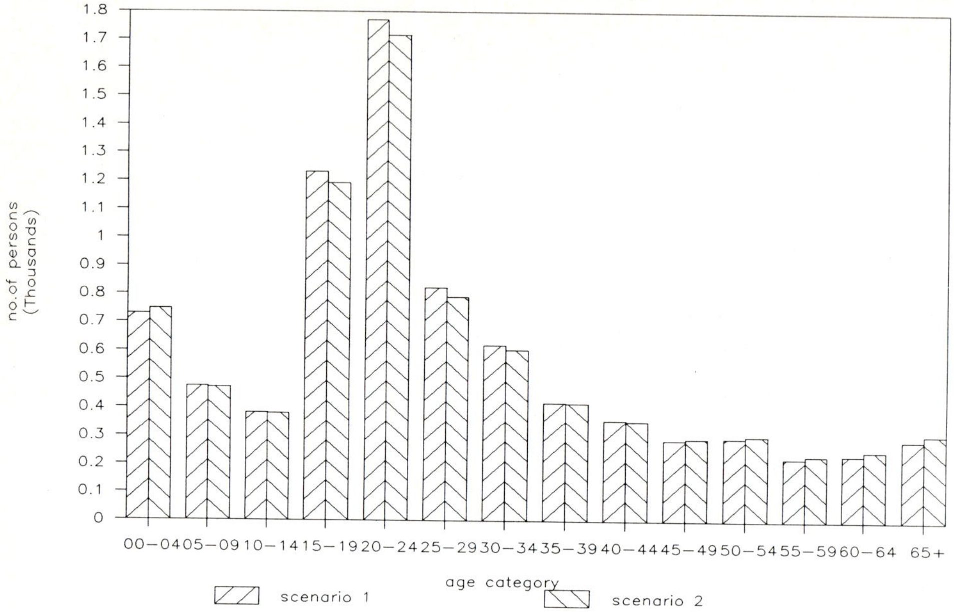

Figure 11.9. Age distribution of immigrants to Amsterdam, 1999

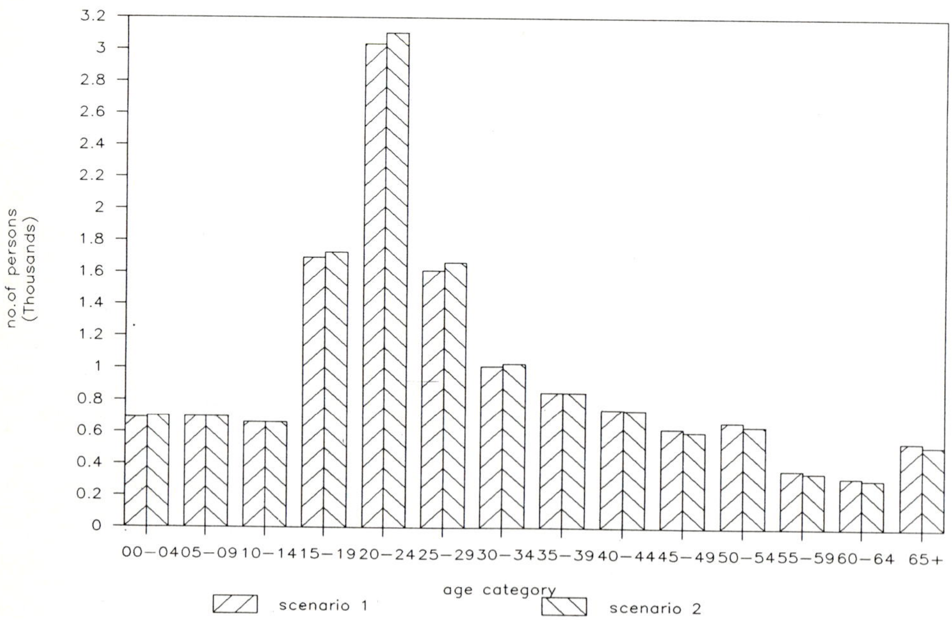

Figure 11.10. Age-distribution of migrants from Amsterdam, 1999

This turning point in the supply/demand ratio in 1996 is the result of the decrease in newly built dwellings in the 'Family' scenario to the same level as in the 'Yuppie' scenario after 1995. So it can be concluded that the distribution of the dwelling stock in the 'Yuppie' scenario is better than in the 'Family' scenario, i.e. the chance of realizing the notional demand for a household is higher. Thus more single family dwellings should only be built in addition to flats and not as substitutes for them.

year	Amsterdam scenario 1	scenario 2	the Region scenario 1	scenario 2
1985	0.35	0.35	0.21	0.21
1986	0.32	0.33	0.18	0.17
1987	0.28	0.30	0.18	0.18
1988	0.26	0.28	0.18	0.17
1989	0.24	0.27	0.17	0.17
1990	0.24	0.27	0.17	0.17
1991	0.25	0.27	0.17	0.17
1992	0.26	0.28	0.17	0.17
1993	0.27	0.29	0.17	0.17
1994	0.28	0.31	0.18	0.17
1995	0.31	0.33	0.17	0.17
1996	0.33	0.34	0.18	0.17
1997	0.35	0.34	0.18	0.17
1998	0.37	0.35	0.18	0.17
1999	0.40	0.36	0.18	0.18

Table 11.5. The supply/demand ratio for Amsterdam and the Region, 1985-1999

The differences between the scenarios regarding the ratio between notional and realized demand are not very large (see figure 11.13 for scenario 1), but compared with the validation period the ratio is higher, meaning that the change of a relocation for potential movers is decreasing during the period 1985-1999.

The last ratio given is the supply/realized demand ratio which shows the same pattern for the two scenarios (see figure 11.14 for scenario 2). Especially for Amsterdam the matching between supply and demand has improved considerably but is not yet as high as the ratio in the Region.

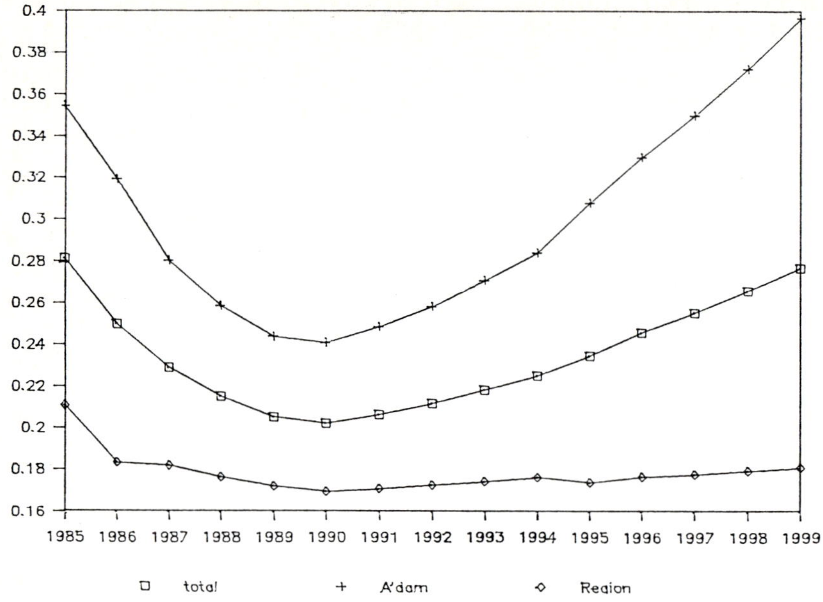

Figure 11.11. The supply/demand ratio in scenario 1, 1985 - 1999

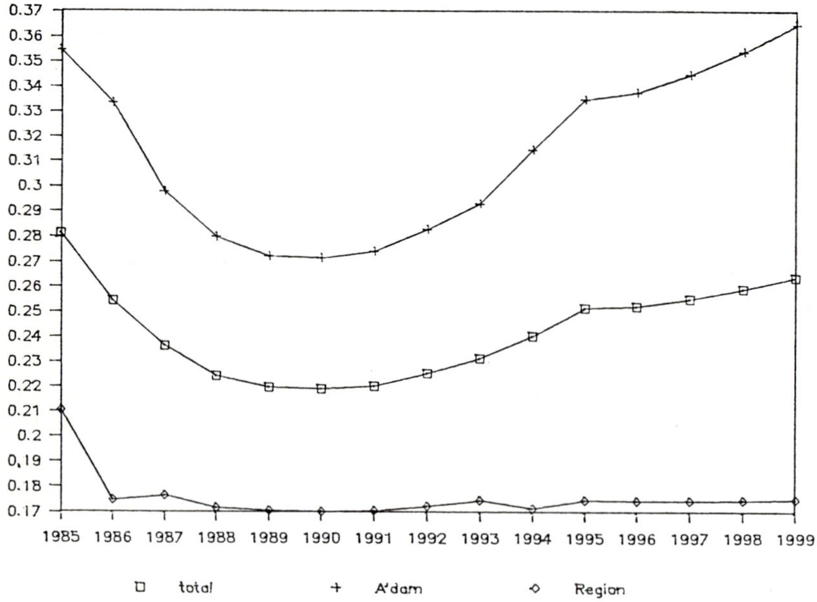

Figure 11.12. The supply/demand ratio in scenario 2, 1985 - 1999

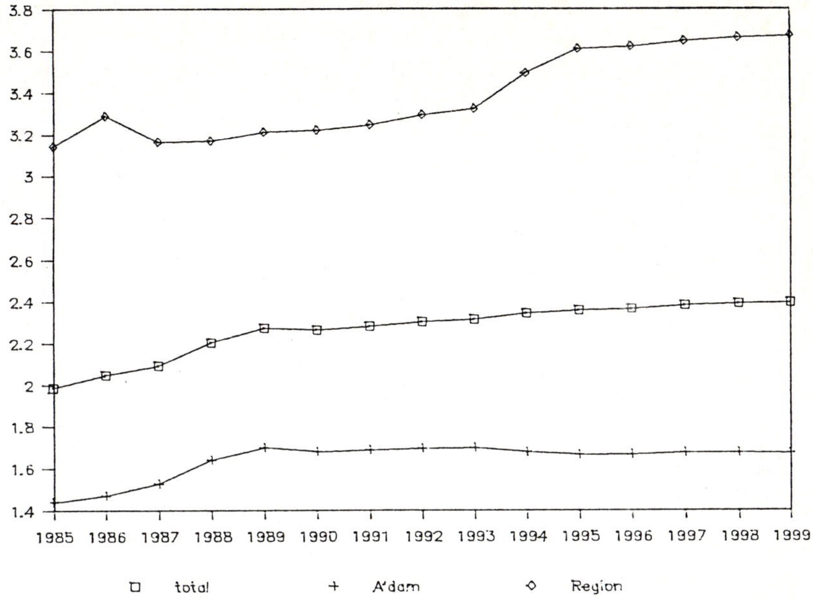

Figure 11.13. The notional/realized demand ratio for the 'Yuppie' scenario, 1985 - 1999

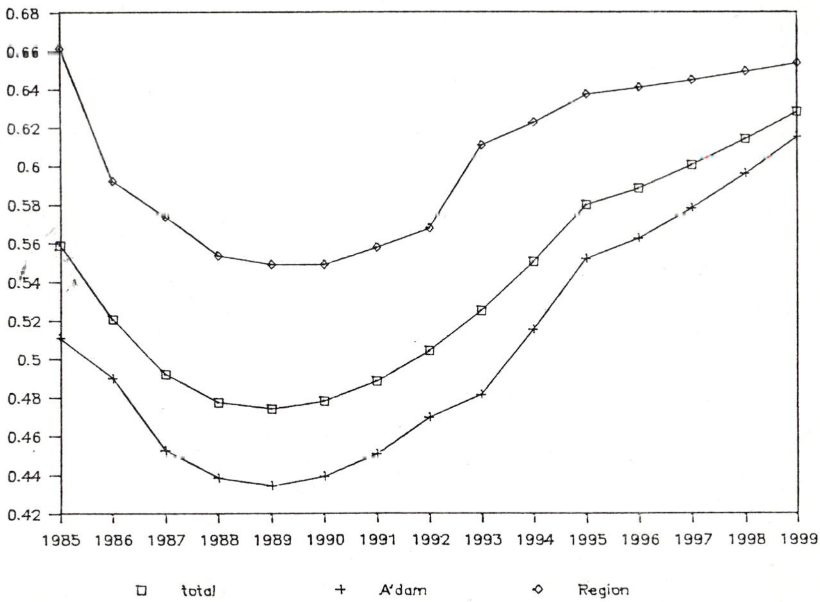

Figure 11.14. The supply/realized demand ratio for the 'Family' scenario, 1985-1999

11.3 Components of Household Change

The difference between the scenarios is solely in terms of housing construction quota. The main differences in model outcomes are in terms of the migration flows between city and suburb. A possible second order effect is a change in the internal household dynamics in the respective areas. Inspection of the demographic and migration component in the development of the total number of households in the scenarios shows that the curve of net household generation is highly similar for both scenarios. In Amsterdam (figure 11.15) net household generation drops fast until 1994 in both the 'Yuppie' and the 'Family' scenario.

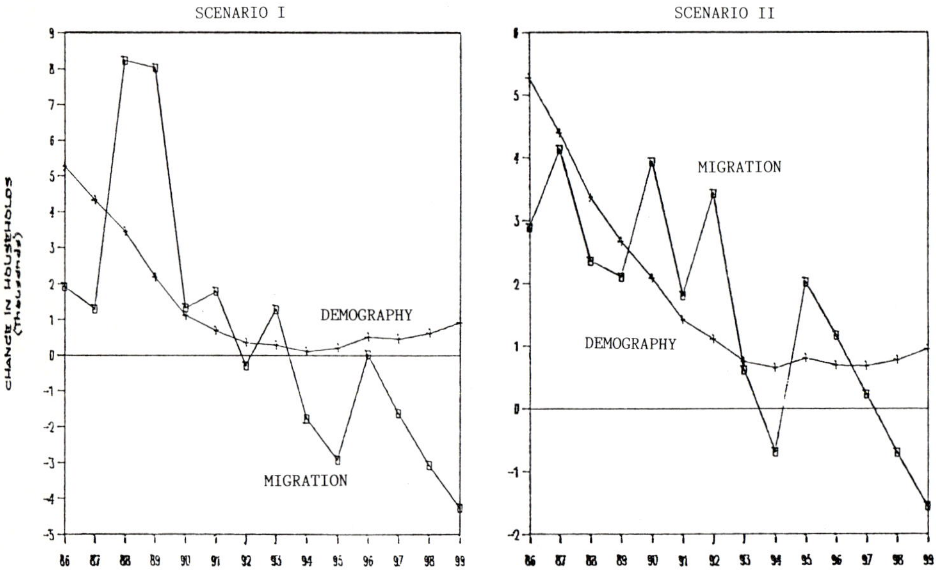

Figure 11.15. Components of household change in the two scenarios in Amsterdam

After 1994 there is a more or less stable situation with a slight trend upwards. The curve in the 'Family' scenario is on a somewhat higher level. Not surprizing, the net migration effect is higher for the 'Family' scenario, but even here it becomes negative again in the nineties. The total effect of demograpic and migration components on household generation has a tendency to become negative towards the end of the scenario period.

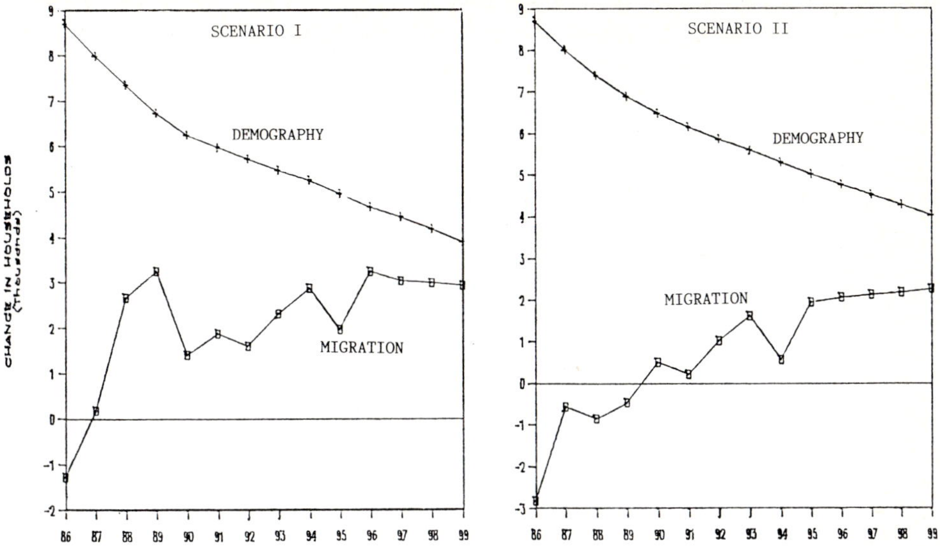

Figure 11.16. Components of household change in the two scenarios in the Region

Figure 11.16 gives the results for the Region. As foreseen in Chapter 10 the migration component is negative in 1986, but this is only a temporary situation. The trend is upwards again and results in positive migration components for both scenarios toward the end of the eighties. The demographic component is positive throughout the whole period, but declines steadily.

11.4 Conclusions

The most important results of the 'Yuppie' and 'Family' scenario have been presented in this section. The outcomes of the scenarios look very convincing and realistic compared with existing projections on the housing market in the Amsterdam region. In addition to the traditional population predictions we gained insight into population and household developments and into housing market dynamics. On the basis of the scenarios a number of conclusions can be drawn:

- The goal of the municipality of Amsterdam of having a population of 720,000 in the year 2000 will not be reached by building 6,500 dwellings (distributed over the dwelling types and zones according to the distribution in 1985) in Amsterdam in the period 1985-1995 and 4,500 dwellings in the period 1995-2000.

- To establish a 'balanced' distribution of households over households sizes, the building of single family units should not take place instead of building flats but additionally.

- The population growth in Amsterdam which started in 1985 will continue at least until the year 2000.

In this chapter we have chosen to elaborate on two already existing housing market scenarios. The input and the output of the two scenarios did not differ too much from each other, but even here already interesting differences between the two scenarios with respect to the development of the housing market in Amsterdam and the Region can be observed. For policy and/or planning purposes other alternative scenarios with respect to the housing market can now also be imagined and applied to the model developed in the previous chapters. One possible scenario, for instance, is to see how many dwellings (and in which zones) should be built in order to predict 720,000 persons in Amsterdam in the year 2000 using the relocation model. To establish this the number of dwellings built will be higher than in the 'Yuppie' and 'Family' scenarios (and probably even more single family units should be built).

An other possible scenario for which the results can be calculated with our housing market model is a more "free market" scenario. However, one must bear in mind that if for instance the price of one specific dwelling type changes relatively compared to the other dwelling types, then also the preference structure of households with respect to the dwelling type choice will change. The outcomes of the nested logit model (the coefficients and exogenous variables) are the result of the present situation on the housing market in Amsterdam and the Region. The restricted and institutionalized character of the housing market is embodied in the model results. When structural changes occur on the housing market the underlying preference structure must be estimated again before scenario building can take place in a reliable way. But when the necessary data are available from a individual or household survey the model can easily be adapted to this new situation.

In our view the housing market model can fruitfully be used for scenario building for the support of policy and planning decisions. Especially, a sensitivity analysis with small changes in building capacities and locations can offer to the decision-maker clear insight into the impact of potential policy decisions on the housing market.

CHAPTER 12. RETROSPECT AND PROSPECT

12.0 Introduction and Retrospect

The aim of this research was to develop a dynamic empirical model of household relocation for the housing market of Amsterdam. In Chapter 1 the basic theoretical issues relevant for model development and the objective and hypotheses are discussed.

Next, in Part I the necessary prerequisites for the model are treated. First, in Chapter 2 the historical development and population and housing market characteristics of the Amsterdam region are described. The next two chapters (Chapters 3 and 4) are devoted to the presentation of existing dynamic household and housing market models. On the basis of this discussion a choice is made for the use of multistate demography and random utility models within an overall accounting framework. So, in Part I the basic characteristics and features of the relocation model are established.

In relation to the data requirements these characteristics are discussed in Part II. Chapter 5 gives an introduction to the overall model framework and in the next chapters the various submodules are treated in detail. First, in Chapter 6, the problem of data requirements and missing data is discussed and an algorithm for missing data estimation is presented. In the next chapter the dynamic household model is developed and estimated from available longitudinal data. Chapter 8 presents the housing demand model and the coefficients are estimated from sample data. In the following chapter some results on the conditional probabilities of the housing demand model are given and the allocation model is developed.

In Part III the model is tested and various simulations are made. Chapter 10 gives results on simulations for the period 1971- 1984. These simulations establish the validity of the overall model, although some adjustments have to be made in demographic parameter values in order to make them time and zone specific. Finally, two model simulations are made for the period 1985-2000 and some general conclusions concerning housing and population policy of Amsterdam are drawn.

In this final chapter a number of general conclusions are drawn concerning both the model development and the empirical aspects of the project. First, in section 12.1, some general conclusions are drawn with respect to the basic hypotheses stated in section 1.3. Next, some more general comments are made covering both methodological and empirical issues. The final section gives a prospective view by discussing some of the possible further developments of the model and housing market models in a methodological and a planning context.

12.1 General Conclusions

Three basic hypotheses underlie the development of the household relocation model. They were presented in section 1.2: (a) life cycle developments related to housing circumstances are the main factors for intra-urban relocation decisions, (b) household relocations can be viewed as realizations of demand for new dwelling space in the presence of a vacancy, and (c) there is no short run equilibrium in the housing market, since price is fixed. These hypotheses resulted in a household relocation model which is driven by demographic and housing market factors alone. No variables related to the place of work, environmental conditions or other phenomena were included to predict household relocation decisions in the Amsterdam housing market.

A general conclusion from the modelling experience in relation to the first hypothesis has been that intra-urban relocation decisions can very well be predicted in terms of demographic and housing market factors. The word 'predicted' rather than 'explained' is used here since it can be questioned whether the observed strong relations between for instance age and the propensity to move really explain the process. In general it can be concluded that the life cycle concept as operationalized here in simple terms of age and household size transitions is a very fruitful concept for disaggregate household mobility prediction and that is perhaps one of the most important results of this modelling effort.

A second general conclusion to be drawn concerns the second hypothesis. Housing preferences can be used in conjunction with supply side constraints to predict actual household relocation behaviour. Moreover, the results of the estimation procedure have shown that households take into account supply side considerations in evaluating housing alternatives. An interpretation of this phenomenon in terms of individual housing market behaviour is that households are quite realistic in specifying their housing needs. They have an idea of what is available on the market and of their chances of getting a new dwelling. This element is included in the valuation of the various alternatives.This specification of individual demand functions introduces variations in the distribution of aggregate demand over the submarkets. In submarkets with a high supply level, demand tends to increase and vice versa. The results of the model simulations with this demand function were quite satisfactory and remained stable over time. So in our opinion these results have a reasonable value both from a theoretical and a modelling perspective.

With regard to the third hypothesis we believe that the allocation mechanism used in this model is only a simple approximation of the complex process of matching of demand and supply. Much effort was put in the estimation of housing demand using both household transition processes and housing preference functions. The allocation algorithm used is then simply to constrain these preferences by available supply. Although it has not been worked out in previous chapters the model could be defined in terms of optimization of consumer's utility under supply constraints. Some institutional elements were introduced but it is clear that this is only a first approximation. We will return to this topic in the final section.

12.2 Evaluation

Migration Theory

This model was built around the concepts of life cycle and changing housing preferences. These notions are well developed in migration and residential mobility theory, but operationalizations of these concepts are still scarce. Most theoretical contributions are more concerned with statistical testing than with parameter estimation. The main aim of the model was to use these concepts in an applied context. This implied both statistical tests and parameter estimation. In this phase of the project (part II) the importance of household changes for residential mobility was tested and the parameters were estimated. A second theoretical result was the introduction of macro level supply conditions in an individual utility function that proved to be highly significant. This specification which is consistent with the theory of random choice modelling, could be the link between housing preferences and observed allocation behaviour in an applied modelling framework. Finally, estimation of the housing preference functions has shown that in the decision structure the choice of the zone is influenced by unobserved attributes related to the available dwelling types. A model with a different nested structure was shown to be inconsistent with random utility theory.

Transferability of the Model

An important question to be addressed is the transferability of the model to other regions. Two aspects are relevant in this respect, i.e. the model structure and data needs. The model structure developed is quite general: housing demand, generated through dynamic household processes and related reevaluation of housing circumstances, is confronted with exogenous supply that results in household allocation. The results were shown to be quite stable over time in the period 1971 - 1984. So in principle the model structure could be applied in other regions as well. The specified intensities of demographic and housing preference functions are probably less transferable and should be estimated separately if used in other regions. The household processes in Amsterdam are to a certain extent unique. The need for estimation of region specific parameters is closely connected to data-requirements. For the estimation of the housing demand functions the national Housing Survey (WBO) could be used but problems arise when region specific household transition rates are necessary. For the model simulations use could be made of the large data sources of the municipality of Amsterdam for population and household distributions. However some flexibility can be introduced through the use of the data estimation technique developed in this project. So it can be concluded that the model is transferable if the problem of parameter estimation of the demographic model is solved.

The Accounting Framework: A Comprehensive Aggregation Scheme

The use of disaggregate models in a spatial interaction context has always been hampered by aggregation problems. In our opinion the use of an overall accounting framework has solved this problem. The accounting framework can be interpreted as a comprehensive weighting scheme for the utility functions. Missing information in this framework can very well be estimated by a suitable data estimation technique such as RIWILS. Another advantage of the accounting framework is the flexibility it introduces to combine different model techniques. In our case the dynamic household model was linked to the demand model. Other components can be introduced without problems. A disadvantage of the framework is the size. Introduction of more disaggregation would lead to an explosion of the number of cells in the system.

Empirical Results

The goal of this project was to develop an empirical model for household relocation in the Amsterdam housing market. The results of the model were presented and discussed in detail in chapters 10 and 11. Since the amount of information from the model is very large, due to the disaggregated nature of the model, the results were presented in a number of sections, each covering a part of the model, i.e. household demography, demand-supply ratios (disaggregated by zone and dwelling type), household allocation (migration) and the resulting overall development of households and population on a zonal basis. Not every outcome of the model could be tested, so the simulation remains at least partially speculative. Where possible a goodness-of-fit test was conducted on various levels of aggregation. At the most aggregate level the total population and total number of households could be compared with observed figures and other estimates. At the micro level migration flows could be compared even at the level of age distributions per year. In general the results on a lower level of aggregation remained quite satisfactory. Moreover, the differences in fit over the years are relatively small, indicating that the model is capable of reproducing intra-urban housing market behaviour under various exogenous circumstances. It should be noted, however, that in order to achieve these results the demographic parameters had to be made time-dependent. No statistical techniques could be used here since until now there are no satisfactory longitudinal data to estimate time paths for the coefficients. This area is the focus of current research in household demography and results in this area can fruitfully be incorporated in this model. To our judgement the results achieved so far show that the model is a valid instrument for empirical housing market analyses.

Two scenarios are developed on the basis of existing housing market policies of the local and central government. In the "Yuppie" scenario the number of dwellings built in Amsterdam is 4,500 and the main emphasis is to build small flats, while the number of houses built in Amsterdam in the "Family" scenario is 6,500 with a larger proportion of single family units. From the outcomes of the scenarios it is concluded that Amsterdam will go on growing but the policy goal of the municipality of Amsterdam of having a population of 720,000 inhabitants in the year 2000 will not be reached.

12.3 Prospects

Methodological Aspects

Multistate demographic models are relatively new tools in the analysis of dynamic processes. Current research in this field focusses on a number of topics that are relevant for the present model as well. The methodology is quite flexible. Central elements are the specification of the 'states' of the system and of the events (a transition from one state to another).

Demographic research so far has focussed on the age- and time dependency of the occurrence of these events. A further development would be to make the transition rates endogenous. So instead of a rate $\mu(x)$ (x is the age) a more general formulation could be $\mu(\underline{z})$ where $\underline{z}$ is a vector of relevant variables. If such a function could be specified and estimated the problems encountered in this model with the time-variance of the demographic intensities could in principle be solved. Estimation of these rate functions is possible with existing techniques, such as survival or hazard models. Another highly interesting development could be to extend the state space of the demographic model to include also housing market aspects. A simultaneous treatment of housing market decisions and life cycle decisions would be feasible in such a model. However, the micro-economic theory underlying the random utility models used in the housing demand model would have to be translated to this multistate form and much work still has to be done in that field.

A second area where large research efforts are necessary focusses on the concept of market equilibrium in institutionalized housing markets. Two concepts should be incorporated in a controlled housing market model: the concept of a dynamic equilibrium and the modelling of the impact of the complex institutions on housing market behaviour. Some recent developments in this area were discussed in Chapter 3, but the application of these micro-economic models in an empirical context is still very difficult. Related to this topic is the inclusion of models to generate choice sets for housing market behaviour.

Final Remarks: From a Prototype Model to an Operational Model

In our opinion a prototype of a planning model has been developed in this project. More work needs to be done to make it operational. Firstly, the data requirements of the model are high and a flexible data base is necessary to organize the data needed. It should also include the data estimation model so that it covers all the data needed for model performance. Secondly, the computer time needed to run the model is too high to allow many computer runs. Some modifications could be made, primarily in the allocation program, to reduce the computer overhead. Thirdly, in order for a planning model to be incorporated in the planning process, some effort has to be devoted to a model-user interface that allows flexible interactions between planners and the model.

References

- Akkerman, A., 1980, On the Relationship between Household Composition and Population Age Distribution, Population Studies, vol. 34, pp. 525-534.

- Akkerman, A., 1982, Demographic Input to Regional Planning, Demosystems, Edmonton.

- Akkerman, A., 1985, The Household Composition Matrix as a Notion in Multiregional Forecasting of Population and Households, Environment and Planning A, vol. 17, pp. 355-371.

- Allen, P.M., M. Sanglier, F. Boon, J.L. Deneubourg and A. De Palma, 1984, Models of Urban Settlement and Structure as Dynamic Self-Organizing Systems, DOT/RSPA/DPB-10/6, Washington.

- Alonso, W., 1964, Location and Land Use, Cambridge, Massachusetts, Harvard University Press.

- Amemiya, T., 1983, Nonlinear Regression Models, Handbook of Econometrics vol. I, Z. Chriliches and M.D. Intrihgator (eds.), pp. 333-389.

- Amsterdam in Cijfers, 1971-1986, Yearbooks of Amsterdam, Bestuursinformatie Gemeente Amsterdam, afdeling Statistiek.

- Anas, A., 1982, Residential Location Markets and Urban Transportation, New York, Academic Press.

- Anas, A., and L.S. Duann, 1983, Dynamic Forecasting of Travel Demand, Residential Location and Land Development: Policy Simulations with the Chicago Area Transportation/ Land Use Analysis System, paper presented at the International Symposium on New Directions in Urban Modelling, July 11-15, Waterloo, Ontario, Canada.

- Anas, A., and J.R. Cho, 1986, A Dynamic, Policy Oriented Model of the Regulated Housing Market: the Swedish Prototype, Northwestern University, Evanston, Illinois.

- Bacharach, M., 1970, Biproportional Matrices and Input-Output Change, Cambridge, Cambridge University Press.

- Baker, R.J. and J.A. Nelder, 1978, The GLIM System, Release 3, Numerical Algorithms Group, Oxford.

- Batten, D.F., 1983, Spatial Analysis of Interacting Economies, Boston, Massachusetts, Kluwer-Nijhoff Publishers.

- Berg, L. van der, R. Drewett, L.H. Klaassen, A. Rossi and C.H.T. Vijverberg, 1982, Urban Europe, a Study of Growth and Decline, Oxford, Pergamon Press.

· Bevolkingsprojecties voor Amsterdam tot 1995, Deel 1 gehele Stad, 1984, Projectgroep Bevolkingsprojecties, Gemeente Amsterdam.

- Bishop, Y.M., S.E. Fienberg, and P.W. Holland, 1975, Discrete Multivariate Analysis: Theory and Practice, Cambridge, Massachusetts, MIT Press.

- Blankenstein-Bouwmeesters, A.A.M. and P. Lukkes, 1984, Institutionele Beleggers op de Markt voor Onroerend Goed, Sociaal-geografische reeks, no. 29, Geografisch Instituut Groningen.

- Bongaarts, J., 1983a, The Formal Demography of Families and Households: an overview, Newsletter International Union for the Scientific Study of Population (IUSSP), no. 17, pp. 27-42.

- Bongaarts, J., 1983b, The Projection of Family Composition over the Life Course with Family Status Life Tables, paper presented at the IUSSP Workshop on Family Demography, December, New York.

- Bosch, K.W., 1986, Verkenning Woningmarkt Agglomeratie Amsterdam. Een onderzoek in opdracht van de Rijksdienst IJsselmeerpolders, unpublished manuscript, STOGO, Utrecht.

- Bovy, P., 1982, An Error Analysis of Traffic Assignment Preditions: a Statistical Model and Some Results, Colloquium Vervoersplanologisch Speurwerk 1982: Openbaar Vervoer, Kompacte Stad en Mobiliteit, Delft.

- Bras, W., 1983, The Formal Demography of the Family: an Overview of the Proximate Determinants, British Society for Population Studies; The Family. Occasional Paper no. 31, Office of Population Censuses and Surveys, chapter 3.

- Brouwer, F., P. Nijkamp and H.J. Scholten, 1983, Hybrid Loglinear Models for Spatial Interaction and Stability Analysis, Research Memorandum, Dept. of Economics, Free University, Amsterdam.

- Brown, A., and A.J. Fox, 1984, OPCS Longitudinal Study-10 years on, Population Trends, vol.37, London, pp.20-22.

- Brown, L.A. and D.B. Longbrake, 1970, Migration Flows in Intra-Urban Space, Annals of the Association of American Geographers, no. 60, pp.368-384.

- Brown, L.A. and E.G. Moore, 1970, The Intraurban Migration Process: a perspective, Geografiska Annaler, Series B, no. B52, pp. 1-13.

- Castro, L.J. and A. Rogers, 1981, A Simplified Formulation and an Alternative Parameter Estimation Method, WP81-63, IIASA, Laxenburg.

- CBS, 1959, Statistische en Econometrische Onderzoekingen, 's-Gravenhage, p. 130.

- CBS, 1971, Volkstelling, 's-Gravenhage.

- CBS, 1985, Statistiek van het Wetenschappelijk Onderwijs. De instroom in het studiejaar 1982/'83 regionaal bezien, 's-Gravenhage, Staatsuitgeverij.

- Clark, W.A.V., 1982, Recent Research on Migration and Mobility: A Review and Interpretation. Progress in Planning, vol. 18, New York, Pergamon Press, pp. 1-56.

- Clark, W.A.V., M.C. Deurloo and F.M. Dieleman, 1984, Housing Consumption and Residential Mobility, Annals of the Association of American Geographers, vol. 74, no. 1, pp. 29-43.

- Clark, W.A.V. and J.L. Onaka, 1985, An Empirical Test of a Joint Model of Residential Mobility and Housing Choice, Environment and Planning A, vol. 17, pp. 915-030.

- Clark, W.A.V. and W.F.J. Van Lierop, 1986, Residential Mobility and Household Location Modelling, Handbook of Regional and Urban Economics, vol. 1, P. Nijkamp (ed.), Elsevier Science Publishers.

- Clark, W.A.V., M.C. Deurloo and F.M. Dieleman, 1986, Residential Mobility in Dutch Housing Markets, Environment and Planning A, vol. 18, pp. 763-788.

- Daganzo, C.F. and L. Schoenfeld, 1978, CHOMP User's Manual, Research Report UCB-ITS-RR-78-7, Institute of Transportation Studies, University of California.

- Dam, J.A. van, and N.W. Keilman, 1987, LIPRO, een dynamisch model ter vooruitberekening van huishoudens, Intern Rapport NIDI, 's-Gravenhage.

- De HBO-student: Studiepatroon en achtergrondgegevens, 1983, Ministerie van Onderwijs en Wetenschappen, 's-Gravenhage, Staatsuitgeverij.

- De Jong, P.M., 1985, Prediction Intervals for Missing Figures in Migration Tables, dissertation University of Groningen.

- De Nederlandse Jeugd bij het Voortgezet Onderwijs. Landelijke en regionale gegevens. Analyse 1968 - 1976; Prognose 1977 - 1987, 1977, Publikatie 14, Commissie Planprocedure, Ministerie van Onderwijs en Wetenschappen, 's-Gravenhage.

- De Palma, A. and M. Ben-Akiva, 1984, Analysis of a Dynamic Residential Location Model with Transaction Costs, M.I.T., Cambridge, Massachusetts.

- Dekker F., P. Hooimeijer and M. Linde, 1985, Demographic Changes and the Housing Market: Nested Multinomial Logit Model of Residential Mobility and Housing Choice, paper presented at the 4th European Colloquium on Quantitative and Theoretical Geography, September 10, Veldhoven, The Netherlands.

- Ermisch, J., 1981, An Economic Perspective on Household Modelling, paper presented at the NIDI-workshop "Modelling of Household Formation and Dissolution", 12-14 December, Voorburg, The Netherlands.

- Espenshade, T.J., 1983, Marriage, Divorce and Remarriage Data: a Multiregional Approach, Environment and Planning A, vol. 15, pp. 1633-1652.

- Essen, P.G. van, 1977, Schattings- en Calibratie-programma's Vervoersmodellen, IWIS-TNO, Mededeling no. 14, Den Haag.

- Est, J.P.M. van, 1976, CADSS, Concentration and Deconcentration Simulation Study, A Spatial Model for Policy, Design and Research, Delft, PSC-TNO.

- Finney, D.J., 1952, Probit Analysis, 2nd ed., Cambridge University Press, Cambridge.

- Fischer, M.M. and E. Aufhauser, 1986, Housing Choice in a Regulated Market: a Nested Multinomial Logit Analysis, paper presented at the Thirty-Third North American Meeting of the Regional Science Association, Columbus, Ohio, November 14-16.

- Fischer, M.M. and P. Nijkamp, 1987, From Static towards Dynamic Discrete Choice Modelling, A State of the Art Review, Regional Science and Urban Economics, vol. 17, pp. 3-27.

- Floor, H. and T. de Jong, 1981, Ontwikkeling en Toetsing van een Woonallocatiemodel, proefschrift Rijksuniversiteit Utrecht, Elinkwijk B.V., Utrecht.

- Forrester, J.W., 1969, Urban Dynamics, Cambridge, Massachusetts, MIT press.

- Fratar, T., 1954, Vehicular Trip Generation by Successive Approximations, Traffic Quarterly, vol. 8, pp. 53-65.

- Fulpen, H. van, 1985, Volkshuisvesting in Demografisch en Economisch Perspectief, Sociale en Culturele Studies no. 8, Sociaal en Cultureel Planbureau, Staatsuitgeverij, s'-Gravenhage.

- Furness, K.P., 1962, Trip Forecasting, paper presented at a seminar on the use of computers in traffic planning, London.

Galler, 1984, Microsimulation of Household Formation and Dissolution, Department of Economics, University of Bielefeld.

Glass, R. and F.G. Davidson, 1951, Household Structure and Housing Needs, Population Studies, vol. IV, pp. 395-420.

Gleave, D. and M. Cordey-Hayes, 1977, Migration Dynamics and Labour Market Turnover.

Glick, P.C., 1977, Updating the Life Cycle of the Family, Journal of Marriage and the Family, vol. 39, no. 1, pp. 5-13.

Golob, Th.F., 1982, Continuous Urban Modeling: A Critical Review, White Paper on Research in New Methods of Urban and Regional Modeling, DOT.

Gordijn, H.E., and H.R. Heida, 1985, PRIMOS Huishoudenmodel, analyse en prognose van de huishoudensontwikkeling in Nederland, Ministerie van Volkshuisvesting, Ruimtelijke Ordening en Milieubeheer, Planologisch Studiecentrum TNO, Delft.

Haag, G. and W. Weidlich, 1984, A Stochastic Theory of Interregional Migration, Geographical Analysis, vol. 16, no. 4, pp. 331-357.

Hanemaayer, D., 1983, Kraken en Volkshuisvesting. Feiten en Implikaties, Stedebouw en Volkshuisvesting, pp. 362-370.

Hanushek, E.A. and J.M. Quigley, 1978, Housing Market Disequilibrium and Residential Mobility, Population Mobility and Residential Change, W.A.V. Clark and E.G. Moore (eds.), Studies in Geography, no. 25, Evanston, Illinois.

Hårsman, B., and B. Marksjo, 1977, Modeling Household Changes by "efficient information adding", Demographic, Economic and Social Interaction, Å.E. Andersson and I. Holmberg (eds.), Ballinger, Cambridge, Massachusetts.

Hårsman, B., and F. Snickars, 1983, A Method for disaggregate household forecasts, Tijdschrift voor Economische en Sociale Geografie, vol. 74, no. 4, pp. 282-290.

Hårsman, B., 1985, Applied Models of Household Formation and Housing Demand, Economic Faces of the Building Sector, F. Snickars, B. Johansson and T.R. Lakshmanan (eds.), Stockholm, Sweden.

Hensher, D.A. and L.W. Johnson, 1981, Applied Discrete-Choice Modelling, Croom Helm, London.

Herbert, J. and B. Stevens, 1960, A Model for the Distribution of Residential Activity in Urban Areas, Journal of Regional Science, vol. 2, pp. 21-36.

- Hickman, B.G., 1974, What became of the building cycle?, Nations and Essays in Honor of Moses Abramovitz, P. David and M. Reder (eds.), New York, Academic Press.

- Hoem, J.M. and U. Funck Jensen, 1982, Multistate Life Table Methodology: a probabilist critique, Multidimensional Mathematical Demography, K.C. Land and A. Rogers (eds.), New York, Academic Press, pp. 155-264.

- Huff, J.O. and W.A.V. Clark, 1978, Cumulative Stress and Cumulative Inertia: a Behavioral Model of the Decision to Move, Environment and Planning A, vol. 10, pp. 1101-1119.

- Ingram, G.K., J.F. Kain and J.R. Ginn, 1972, The Detroit Prototype of the NBER Urban Simulation Model, New York, Columbia University Press.

- Ireland, C.T. and S. Kullback, 1968, Contingency Tables with given Marginals, Biometrika, no. 55, pp. 179-188.

- Kain, J.F. and J.M. Quigley, 1975, Housing Markets and Racial Discrimination: a Micro Economic Analysis, National Bureau of Economic Research, New York.

- Kaufmann, F.X., A. Herlth, J Quitmann, R. Simm and K.P. Strohmeier, 1982, Familienenentwicklung - generatives Verhalten im familialen Kontext, Zeitschrift für Bevölkerungswissenschaft, vol. 8, no. 4, pp. 523-547.

- Keilman, N.W. and R. Gill, 1987, Kwantitatieve Methoden, vol. 23, pp. 85-115.

- Keilman, N.W., 1984, Dynamic Household Models, paper presented at the NIDI-workshop "Modelling of Household Formation and Dissolution", 12-14 December, Voorburg, The Netherlands.

- Kendig, H.L., 1984, Housing Careers, Life Cycle and Residential Mobility: Implications for the Housing Market, Urban Studies, vol. 21, pp. 272-283.

- Keyfitz, N., 1977, Introduction to the Mathematics of Population With Revisions, Reading, Massachusetts, Addison-Wesley.

- Klijzing, E., 1984, Household Data from Surveys Containing Information for Individuals, paper presented at the NIDI-workshop "Modelling of Household Formation and Dissolution", 12-14 December, Voorburg, The Netherlands.

- Kodde, D.A., and J.M.M. Ritzen, 1986, Vraag naar Hoger Onderwijs. Eindrapport, Beleidsgerichte Studies Hoger Onderwijs en wetenschappelijk Onderzoek, 's-Gravenhage, Staatsuitgeverij.

- Kruithof, J., 1937, Telefoonverkeersrekening, De Ingenieur, vol. 52, no. 8, pp. E15-E25.

- Kuysten, A.C., 1984, Application of Household Models in Studying the Family Life Cycle, paper presented at the NIDI-workshop "Modelling of Household Formation and Dissolution", 12-14 December, Voorburg, The Netherlands.

- Ledent, J., 1980, Multistate (increment-decrement) Life Tables: Movement versus Transition Perspectives, Environment and Planning A, vol. 12, pp. 533-562.

- Lierop, W.F.J. van, 1985, Spatial Interaction Modelling and Residential Choice Analysis, Hillegom, Van Lierop Ofsett, (also published by Gower, 1986).

- McCullagh, P. and J.A. Nelder, 1983, Generalized Linear Models, Chapman and Hall, London.

- McFadden, D., 1978, Modelling the Choice of Residential Location in Spatial Interaction Theory and Planning Models, Spatial Interaction Theory and Planning Models, A. Karlqvist, L. Lundqvist, F. Snickars and J.W. Weibull (eds.), Amsterdam, North-Holland, pp. 75-96.

- McMillan, D.B. and R. Herriot, 1985, Towards a Longitudinal Definition of Households, Journal of Economic and Social Measurement, vol. 13, no. 3/4, pp. 349-360.

- Medvedkov, Y.V., 1966, Concept of Entropy in Settlement Pattern Analysis, Papers of the Regional Science Association, pp. 165-168.

- Memorandum on Rent- and Subsidy-policy, 1974, Tweede Kamer der Staten-Generaal, 1974-1975, 13025, 's-Gravenhage.

- Michelson, W., 1977, Environmental Choice, Human Behavior and Residential Satisfaction, New York, Oxford University Press.

- Michelson, W., 1980, Residential Mobility and Urban Policy: Some Sociological Considerations, Residential Mobility and Urban Policy, W. Clark and E. Moore (eds.), Urban Affairs Annual Reviews, vol. 19.

- Ministerie van Volkhuisvesting, 1982, Basisgegevens voor de woningbouwprogrammering 1981-1986, afdeling Sociaal-Economisch Onderzoek, Zoetermeer.

- Mood, A.M., F.A. Graybill, and D.C. Boes, 1974, Introduction to the Theory of Statistics, Tokyo, McGraw-Hill.

- Muhsam, M., 1984, The Transition Probabilities in Demography of the Family, Demography of the Family, CICRED, Paris, pp. 37-43.

- Muth, R.F., 1969, Cities and Housing, Chicago, University Chicago Press.

- NEI, 1980, Verkeers- en locatiegedrag in het Noordelijke deel van de Randstad, deelrapport 1, Rotterdam.

- NEI, 1981, Woon- en Werkplaatsveranderingen in de Noordvleugel van de Randstad, deelrapport 2, Rotterdam.

- NEI, 1983a, Woon- en Werkplaatsveranderingen in de Noordvleugel van de Randstad, deelrapport 3, Rotterdam.

- NEI, 1983b, Woon- en Werkplaatsveranderingen in de Noordvleugel van de Randstad, deelrapport 4, Rotterdam.

- Nelder, J.A., and R.W.M. Wedderburn, 1972, Generalised Linear Models, Journal of Royal Statistical Society A, no. 135, pp. 370-334.

- Nelder, J.A., 1974, Log Linear Models for Contingency Tables; a generalization of classical least squares, Applied Statistics, vol. 23, pp. 323-329.

- Nijkamp, P., 1975, Reflections on Gravity and Entropy Models, Regional Science and Urban Economics, no. 5, pp. 203-225.

- Nijkamp, P., 1978, Gravity and Entropy Models: the State of the Art, Researchmemorandum no. 1977-2, Free University, Amsterdam.

- Nijkamp, P., A. Rima and L.J.G. van Wissen, 1985, Spatial Mobility in Models for Structural Urban Dynamics, Transportation and Mobility in an Era of Transition, G.R.M. Jansen, P. Nijkamp and C.J. Ruijgrok (eds.), Studies in Regional Science and Urban Economics, vol. 13, North-Holland, Amsterdam.

- Orcutt, G.H., M. Greenberger, A. Ruslin and J. Korbell, 1961, Micro-Analysis of Socio-Economic Systems: A Simulation Study, New York, Harper and Row.
- Payne, C., 1977, The Log-linear Model of Contingency Tables, Analysis of Survey Data, C. O'Muircheartaigh and C. Payne (eds.), New York, Wiley, pp. 105-144.

- Porell, F.W., 1982, Models of Intra-Urban Residential Relocation, Boston, Kluwer-Nijhoff publishers.

- Projektgroep Bevolkingsprojekties, Bevolkingsprojekties voor Amsterdam van 1 januari 1985-2000, Gemeente Amsterdam, 1984.

- Quigley, J.M., 1978, Housing Markets and Housing Demand, Analytic Approaches, Urban Housing Markets, Recent Directions in Research and Policy, L.S. Bourne and J.R. Hitchcock (eds.), Toronto, University of Toronto Press, pp. 23-44.

- Quigley, J.M., 1984, Consumer Choice of Dwelling, Neighborhood and Public Services, Regional Science and Urban Economics, vol. 15, pp. 41-63.

- Relou, W. and H. Heida, 1986, Woonvoorkeuren, Werkgelegenheidssspreiding en Woningbehoefte in de Toekomst, W3T, Planologisch Instituut TNO, Delft.

- Roest, W., 1973, Bouw en Economische Groei, Deventer, Kluwer.

- Rogers, A., 1973a, The Mathematics of Multiregional Demographic Growth, Environment and Planning A, vol. 5, pp. 3-29.

- Rogers, A., 1973b, The Multi-Regional Life Table, Journal of Mathematical Sociology, vol 3, pp. 127-137.

- Rogers, A., 1975, Introduction to Multiregional Mathematical Demography, New York, Wiley.

- Rogers, A., and J. Ledent, 1975, Multiregional Population Projection, DP-128, Center for Mathematical Studies in Economics and Management Science, Northwestern University, Evanston, Illinois.

- Rogers, A., and J. Ledent, 1976, Increment-Decrement Life Tables: a Comment, Demography vol. 13, pp. 287-290.

- Rossi, 1955, Why Families Move, The Free Press, Glencoe.

- Ryder, N.B., 1977, Models for Family Demography, Population Bulletin of the United Nations, pp. 43-46.

- Schmid, J., 1984, Principles Emerging from Sociology for Definitions and Typologies of Household Structures, paper presented at the NIDI-workshop "Modelling of Household Formation and Dissolution", 12-14 December, Voorburg, The Netherlands.

- Schoen R., and V. Nelson, 1974, Marriage, Divorce and Mortality: A Life Table Analysis, Demography, vol. 11, pp. 267-290.

- Schoen, R., 1975, Constructing Increment-Decrement Life Tables, Demography, vol. 12, pp. 313-324.

- Scholten, H.J., 1984, Residential Mobility and Loglinear Modelling, Recent Developments in Spatial Analysis: Methodology, Measurement and Models, G. Bahrenberg, M.M.Fischer and P. Nijkamp (eds.), Aldershot, Gower, pp. 271-287.

- Scholten H.J. and L.J.G. Van Wissen, 1985, A Comparison of the Loglinear Interaction Model with Other Spatial Interaction Models, Measuring the Unmeasurable, P. Nijkamp, H. Leitner and N. Wrigley (eds.), Dordrecht, The Netherlands, Martinus Nijhoff Publishers.

- Second Memorandum on Physical Planning, 1966, (Tweede Nota Ruimtelijke Ordening), Tweede Kamer der Staten-Generaal, Zitting 1977-1978, 15118, no's. 1-2, 's-Gravenhage, Staatsuitgeverij.

- Simmons, J., 1968, Changing Residence in the City, a Review of Intraurban Mobility, Geographical Review, vol. 58, pp. 621-651.

- Snickars, F. and J.W. Weibull, 1977, A Minimum Information Principle: Theory and Practice, Regional Science and Urban Economics, vol. 7, pp. 137-168.

- Speare, A. Jr., S. Goldstein and W. Frey, 1975, Residential Mobility, Migration and Metropolitan Change, Ballinger, Cambridge, Massachusetts.

- Stephan, F.F., 1942, An Iterative Method of Adjusting Sample Frequency Tables when expected marginal totals are known, Annals of Mathematical Statistics, no. 13, pp. 166-178.

- Stone, R., 1962, Multiple Classifications in Social Accounting, Bulletin de l'Institut International de Statistique, vol. 39, pp. 215-233.

- Stone, R., 1971, Demographic Accounting and Modelling, OECD, Paris.

- Third Memorandum on Physical Planning, 1973, (Derde Nota Ruimtelijke Ordening), Tweede Kamer der Staten-Generaal, Zitting, 's-Gravenhage, Staatsuitgeverij.

- Timmermans, H.J.P., 1984, Decision Models for Predicting Preferences among Multiattribute Choice Alternatives, Recent Developments in Spatial Data Analysis: Methodology, Measurement and Models, G. Bahrenberg, M.M. Fischer and P. Nijkamp (eds.), Gower, Aldershot, pp. 337-354.

- Timmermans, H.J.P., 1985, Spatial Choice Models, Research Paper University of Technology, Eindhoven.

- Turner, J., 1980, Non-equilibrium Thermodynamics, Dissipative Structures and Self-Organization, Studies in Biomedical Research, G. Scott and J. MacMillan (eds.), Iowa, Iowa State University Press, pp. 13-52.

- U.N., 1973, Methods of Projecting Households and Families, Population Studies, no. 54, United Nations, New York, (3).

- Veldhuisen, K.J. and L.L. Kapoen, 1977, Een Regionaal Locatiemodel, proefschrift Rijksuniversiteit Utrecht, Utrecht.

- Veldhuisen, K.J., 1985, Een Woningvraag-model, Planning no. 26, pp. 20-31.

- Verster, A.C.P., 1986, Lokatiegedrag van Beroepsbeoefenaars, de Invloed van Afstandsgebonden Kosten, Dissertation, NEI, Rotterdam.

- VH-plan, 1983, Gemeente Amsterdam, afd. Volkhuisvesting.

- WBO, 1983, Woningbehoefte-onderzoek 1981, Central Bureau of Statistics, 's-Gravenhage.

- Webber, M.J., 1983, Life-cycle Stages, Mobility, and Metropolitan Change: 2. a model of migration, Environment and Planning A, vol. 15, pp. 307-317.

- Weesep, J. van, 1982, Production and Allocation of Housing, The Case of the Netherlands, Geografische en Planologische Notities, no. 11, GPIVU, Amsterdam.

- Wegener, M., 1982, Modeling Urban Decline: a Multilevel Economic-Demographic Model for the Dortmund Region, International Regional Science Review, vol.7, no.2, pp. 21-41.

- Wegener, M., 1983, A Simulation Study of Movement in the Dortmund Housing Market, Tijdschrift voor Economische en Sociale Geografie, vol. 74, no. 4, pp. 267-281.

- Weibull, J.W., 1983, A Dynamic Model of Trade Frictions and Disequilibrium in the Housing Market, Scandinavian Journal of Economics, vol. 3, pp. 373-392.

- Weidlich, W. and G. Haag, 1983, Concepts of Models of a Quantitative Sociology, Berlin, Springer.

- Werkgroep koppeling Vastgoed-Bevolking, 1982, BI, DRO, GDH, GDV, Gemeente Amsterdam.

- Werkgroep koppeling Vastgoed-Bevolking, 1985, BI, DRO, GDH, GDV, Gemeente Amsterdam.

- Willekens, F., I. Shah, J. Shah and P. Ramachandran, 1980, Multistate Analysis of Marital Status Life Tables, Theory and Application, NIDI, Working Paper no. 17, Voorburg.

- Willekens, F., 1980, Entropy, Multiproportional Adjustment and Analysis of Contingency Tables, Sistemi Urbani, no. 2/3, pp. 171-201.

- Willekens, F., 1980, Multistate Analysis: Tables of Working Life, Environment and Planning A, vol. 12, pp. 563-588.

- Willekens, F., 1983, Specification and Calibration of Spatial Interaction Models. A Contingency-Table Perspective and an Application to Intra-Urban Migration in Rotterdam, Tijdschrift voor Economische en Sociale Geografie, vol. 74, pp. 239-252.

- Willekens, F., 1984, The Marital Status Life Table, <u>Family Demography, Models and Applications</u>, J. Bongaarts et al (eds.), London, Oxford University Press.

- Willekens, F.J. and P. Drewe, 1984, A Multiregional Model for Regional Demographic Projection, <u>Demographic Research and Spatial Policy</u>, H. ter Heide and F.J. Willekens (eds.), London, Academic Press, pp. 309-334.

- Willekens, F.J. and N. Baydar, 1985, Hybrid Loglinear Models, <u>Measuring the Unmeasurable</u>, P. Nijkamp, H. Leitner and N. Wrigley (eds.), Dordrecht, Martinus Nijhoff Publishers, pp. 141-176.

- Wilson, A.G., 1970, <u>Entropy in Urban and Regional Modelling</u>, Pion, London.

- Wilson, A.G., 1981, <u>Geography and the Environment, Systems Analytical Methods</u>, Chichester, John Wiley & Sons.

- Wilson, A.G., 1981, <u>Catastrophe Theory and Bifurcation: Applications to Urban and Regional Systems</u>, Croom Helm, London.

- Wilson, A.G., 1983, Making Urban Models More Realistic: Some Strategies for Future Research, Working Paper no. 358, University of Leeds, Leeds, pp. 8.

- Wissen, L.J.G. van, A. Rima and P. Nijkamp, 1986, Urban Household Dynamics: Methodology and Application, <u>Sistemi Urbani</u>, 2/3, pp. 179-195.

- Wolfbein, S., 1949, The Length of Working Life, <u>Population Studies</u>, vol. 3, pp. 286-294.

Index

age class \ hh. size	1	2	3	4+
1) <25	1	2	3	4
2) 25-34	5	6	7	8
3) 35-44	9	10	11	12
4) 45-54	13	14	15	16
5) 55-64	17	18	19	20
6) 65+	21	22	23	24

The definition of the 24 household types

dwelling characteristics \ number of rooms	1 or 2	3	4	5+
rented flats	1	5	6	9
owner occupied flats	2	2	2	2
rented single family units	3	3	7	10
owner occupied single family units	4	4	8	11

The definition of the 11 dwelling types

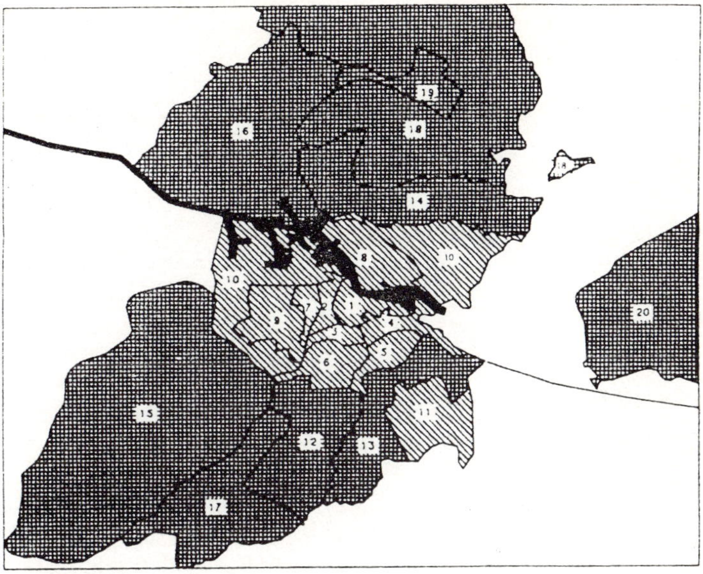

Amsterdam
1 Old City
2 Old West
3 Old South
4 East
5 Watergraafsmeer
6 New South
7 Bos en Lommer
8 North
9 Gardencities
10 Urban fringe (industrial and rural areas)
11 South-East (Bijlmermeer)

Region
12 Amstelveen
13 Amstelland
14 Waterland-Zuid
15 Haarlemmermeer
16 Zaanstad
17 Meerlanden
18 Waterland-Noord
19 Purmerend
20 ZIJP

Y-river and North Sea Canal

The study area divided into 20 zones